CRIME, HUMAN RIGHTS AND NATIONAL SECURITY

Crime, Human Rights and National Security

Dr. Krishna Mohan Mathur

GYAN

GYAN PUBLISHING HOUSE

NEW DELHI-110 002

Crime Human Rights and National Security

ISBN: 81-212-0516-6

Reprinted in 2011 in India by
Gyan Publishing House
23, Main Ansari Road, Daryaganj,
New Delhi - 110002
Phone : 23282060, 23261060
Fax : (011) 23285914
E-mail : books@gyanbooks.com
website: gyanbooks.com

Printed at: G. Print Process, Delhi

Respectfully Dedicated to

SWAMI ISWARANANDA GIRIJI MAHARAJ
OF SAMVIT SADHANAYANA, SANT SAROVER,
MOUNT ABU

उद्वयं तमसस्परि
ज्योतिष्पश्यन्त उत्तरम् ।
देवं देवत्रा सूर्यम्
अगन्म ज्योतिरुत्तमम् ॥ ऋग्वेद १-५०-१०

Seeking the exalted Light
of the rising Sun,
We were led beyond Darkness
to the greater Light,
the source of all divine inspirations
indeed we have arrived
in the end at the greatest,
the Light of Lights.

Rig Veda -1-50-10.

Contents

List of Tables

Preface

Thomas Jefferson said: "The trouble seems to be that too many people think the law should be enforced and not enough think it should be observed". This has resulted in increasing crime and violations of Human Rights and at times even the survival of nations is threatened. The present work titled *Crime, Human Rights and National Security* stems from my inner urge as a social scientist for expressing my various findings and perceptions on current issues. It is a very modest attempt by the author to explore some new themes in an objective manner. Some new areas of Indian Criminology have been explored by the author by analysing recent criminological trends. The efforts aim at providing a close scrutiny and an objective Indian perspective of the issues as are perceived by a social scientist and practicising criminologist. The first chapter covers Domestic Crimes in India: its Various Ramifications and Needed Responses. Although domestic crimes are a global phenomenon, but domestic crimes in India have increased manifold during the last two decades due to erosion of social and moral values. Dowry deaths, wife beating, child abuse, molestation of girls are domestic crimes which have become an inextricable part of the fabric of violence that shrouds Indian society. There is a requirement of comprehensive legislation by the Parliament on domestic crime and child abuse. Social control agencies like education system, religion, societal pressure and family system should explore ways and means of controlling and preventing domestic crimes. Indian criminology needs to develop its own culture based analysis of the crimes which are being committed in contemporary Indian society. The second chapter on "Economic Crimes in the Context of Liberal Economy" broadly covers white collar crimes and all offences which are calculated to obstruct the economic development of the country or endanger its económic growth. Some case studies have been incorporated to highlight the magnitude of economic offences. Corruption in various forms is an increasing economic crime. The Vohra Committee findings about organised crime syndicates and nexus between criminals, bureaucrats and politicians has been adequately covered. Role of various enforcement agencies in controlling economic crimes has been analysed in this chapter. An Action-Plan to deal with economic offences has been suggested. The third chapter titled "Crimes of Subversion by Explosives in India" broadly covers the problems and issues related to the crime of subversion in India which are on the increase particularly since the last decade. The series of twelve bomb blasts in Bombay on March 12, 1993 have opened the eyes of the people about the various ramifications of the crime of subversion by explosives. A bird's eye view of various bomb blasts in India has been attempted in this chapter. The media and books can play an educative role in bringing awareness in the people about the bombs and to make people aware of the precautions required to be taken. Legal aspects of the crime of explosion have also been briefly enumerated. Combating crime of subversion by explosives is a fire fighting exercise by police and para-military force, requiring preventive, confrontational and remedial measures.

The fourth chapter deals with "Accountability in the Management of Law & Order". Accountability in the management of law and order in a federal democratic system becomes complex and at times untenable. The scheme of police accountability as outlined in the Police Act has not yet incorporated the ingredients of the constitutional obligations of the police. A variety of factors have, over a period of time, diluted the accountability of the managers of law and order in India. In recent judgements Supreme Court has held that the defence of sovereign immunity is not applicable in a democratic society, every policemen needs to be taught what democracy means, he must understand how sacred human rights are, he must learn to respect the dignity of human beings, he must understand his ultimate accountability to the public and final answerability to the people and Rule of Law. The fifth chapter discusses various perceptions and perspectives of the human rights in India. These rights are contained in the concept of dharma which has been all pervading and regulating conduct of human beings in ancient India. The Preamble to the Constitution and the chapter on Fundamental

Rights contained in the Constitution show our firm commitments to human rights. In spite of constitutional provisions, there have been reports of violations of human rights not only by terrorists, and insurgents but also by the police and security forces. Custodial deaths are examples of human rights violations by the police and security forces. Notwithstanding the presence of a free media and independent judiciary there has been growing criticism, both nationally and internationally, of widespread abuse of human rights in India. The National Human Rights Commission has launched a campaign to increase human rights awareness in the country. In dealing with internal security challenges created by terrorists and insurgents, police and security forces face an uphill task in protecting human rights. Rights of women and children also need our concern and awareness.

Role of Public Participation in Internal Security has been analysed in the sixth chapter. Role of public participation in internal security depends in great measure upon peoples' awareness of their fundamental duties and their willingness to participate in nation building activities. Voluntary organisations can play a very constructive and positive role in internal security duties particularly during natural calamities and disasters. In crime prevention and criminal justice system, people have very important roles as informers and witnesses. One of the objectives of the police-public relations can be the direct involvement of the people in the prevention and detection of crime and in the maintenance of order. Chapter seven on "Training for Excellence for Internal Security" covers problems and issues related to training for excellence in organisations, which are assigned the task of maintaining internal security of the country. An Action-Plan for training in excellence for internal security has been suggested.

National security issues are highly complex and involve political, social, psychological, economic and military judgements with both short-term and long-term interdisciplinary perceptions. In the eighth chapter national security doctrines have been analysed and discussed. Internal and external threats to national security have been identified. National security planning requires institutionalised arrangements for indepth analysis of economic, political, social and international issues and their macro-level complexities. The security environment of the nation needs constant monitoring. The unity and integrity of the country can be best preserved by educating our people in the spirit of genuine nationalism, healthy patriotism and international humanism. Regarding India's defence expenditure in terms of its GNP, it constituted 3 per cent for 1993-94. In 1994-95, it was 2.8 per cent and for 1995-96 the Defence Budget is put up 2.5 per cent of the GNP. For 1995-96, para-military forces like CRPF, BSF, ITBP and Assam Rifles have claimed an amount of Rs. 3450 crores. There is a need for modernisation, expansion and better training for security forces to safeguard our national interests. A most dynamic long-term national defence strategy needs to be worked out and implemented effectively. The book identifies and analyses the various key issues confronting the national security today. An Indian citizen's perspective has been attempted by the author with a view to understand their complexity and multi-dimensionality of national defence and security. This book discusses the new realities as the author could perceive them. Appendix 'A' contains the text of Universal Declaration of Human Rights and Appendix 'B' contains the Protection of Human Rights Act, 1993 (No. 10 of 1994).

In the body of the book, I have deliberately tried to focus on the concrete concepts and prevalent practices rather than giving statistical details which go on changing from time to time. I have only attempted to initiate a dialogue and offer my comments and view points on various subjects covered in the book. I sincerely hope that my book will initiate some thinking and progressively serious research by social scientists and police researchers. I would consider my labour well rewarded if this study is found to be helpful in furthering the understanding of the various subjects covered by the book. I have great pleasure in expressing my deep felt and profound gratitude to Director General, CRPF and Director, Internal Security Academy, Mount Abu, who have been helpful to me in various ways in completion of this book. My special thanks are due to Sarvashri K.F. Rustomji, K.P.S. Gill, N.S. Saksena, J.F. Ribeiro, Dr. R.C. Jha, Dr. B. Varma, G.C. Singhvi, S. Venugopal Rao, Padmashree Dr. Subramanian and many other police officers of India, who have deeply influenced my thinking about the crime, human rights and national security. Dr. P.D. Sharma, Prof. Ramesh K. Arora, Prof. Ram Ahuja, Prof. S.R. Maheshwari, Dr. R.N. Singh, Prof. K.L. Kamal, Dr. J. Guha Roy, Dr. R.B. Jain, Prof. K.V. Kaliappan, Dr. S.L. Doshi, Dr. L.S. Rathore, Dr. Pradip Sohani and many others also deserve my special thanks. Conventional acknowledgements are really inadequate to express how much this book owes to all those who gave me their support. I record my sincere thanks to a number of trainee officers of Internal Security Academy, Mt. Abu who interacted with me and benefited me by their field experiences. In every chapter of this book, there are references to several authors and their books. It is with great pleasure that I acknowledge my gratitude to the authors whose books have served as sources of reference to me. I fully recognize my responsibility for recording my debt to them for their valuable ideas and views. This book can be useful to the criminologists, public administrators and citizens in general as well as serving police officers. Feedback will be most welcome. Suggestions for improvement will be gratefully acknowledged and considered for incorporation in the next edition.

I feel beholden to Swami Iswaranand Giriji of Mount Abu for his kind blessings and constant spiritual inspiration to me. My wife Prabha Mathur, my children Shikha, Pragya and Shiv Shubhang, gave me the moral support and encouraged me by sparing from all domestic liabilities for devoting full attention to complete the work. My thanks are due to Shri Niraj Kumar and Vishal Mathur who helped me in revising the typied script. I am thankful to my friends and colleagues with whom I have interacted to crystalise my nebulous ideas. My thanks are due to Shri T. Velayudhan, Shri K. Santosh Kumar, Shri J.C. Tanwar, Shri K. Narayanan and Shri G.R. Venugopalan, who have meticulously deciphered the manuscript and typed it out in a presentable form for the use of the publishers. I have a debt of gratitude to them. Shri V.S. Anandan, Librarian, Internal Security Academy, Mount Abu deserves special mention for making available all references and books which are used by me for references. Thanks are due to the publishers and printers, who brought out the book within a short period. This book is an oblation of Lord Shiva whose grace and blessings remained the divine force behind my academic endeavours.

KRISHNA MOHAN MATHUR

Ram Navmi — March 28, 1996
'Anugrah' Shri Ambica Colony,
for Sagar Boraj Link Road, Rawat Nagar,
Ajmer. (Rajasthan) Ph. No. 305001.

1

Domestic Crimes in India: Ramifications and Response

Broadly defined domestic crimes relate to wide range of non-accidental crimes committed by members of a family on other members of the same family. The low-visibility and the closed-door character of the domestic crime has hindered scientific investigations. The quality and quantity of reliable hard informations on the disturbing ramifications of the domestic crimes is so inadequate and insufficient that no scientific generalisations are possible with the result that lot many questions clearly await any precise answers. Erosion of spiritual and moral values, breakdown of strong-family ties along with psychopathological, psychological, psycho-social and socio-environmental factors contribute to a large measure for occurrence of domestic crimes in a plural society. The analysis of the problem of domestic crime and its important ramifications—domestic violence, wife battering, dowry deaths, child abuse and maltreatment of the elderly and the handicapped as discussed in this chapter, centres round the fact that while the problem is as old as is the institution of family, the perception of its criminality related aspects, is relatively recent. The victims of domestic crimes are unable to cry out and complain about their sufferings due to various social and psychological factors. The criminal justice system in India, due to absence of enough supporting evidence and defective procedures, quite often acts very slowly, ineffectively and inappropriately due to its various structural limitations and handicaps. Domestic crimes are global phenomenon and can be broadly classified into two categories :

1. Crimes identified under the Indian Penal Code under sections 375, 372, 373, 498-A, 376-A, 302/304B, 306, 398A, 307, 309 committed within a family.
2. Crimes identified under other local and special laws like offences under Dowry Prohibition Act, Immoral Traffic Act and other laws.

It is a paradox that the need to analyse and discuss crimes in domestic setting has arisen because domestic crimes occur within the family setting where people generally expect and should get warmth, affection, support, trust and love. "Family" or "household members" generally means spouses, parents, children, persons otherwise related by blood or marriage or persons living in the same household and include the aged, elderly person, handicapped and for some purposes even household servants, living and serving the family. There is so far lack of a clear definition of what constitutes domestic crimes.

The Patterns of Domestic Crimes

Domestic violence and family disputes are also very broadly covered in the term domestic crimes. These are part of the same process as far as police is concerned. Child marriage, dowry deaths, child abuse and violence over family property ownership are some of the main manifestations of domestic crime. The landscape of domestic crime has darkened over the years. According to a study conducted by the Department of Women and Child Development in 1991, a dowry death occurs every hour 42 minutes. It is shocking enough that women and children in families are vulnerable to crime in our violence—prone environment where moral and ethical values have been badly eroded and T.V. sub culture of violence has taken over the society in general. Dowry deaths, wife battering, child abuse, spouse assault and molestation of girls are domestic crimes which have become an inextricable part of the fabric of violence that shrouds Indian society.

Case Studies of Domestic Crimes in India

1. *Murder of children by their mother* : *The Hindustan Times*, dated 13th February 1990 published this tragic news.

"Mother ties kids to rails, four killed" at Madurai. According to the report a 30-year old woman Pettakokku who had a quarrel with her husband over his illicit relationship with several women, left her house at Thurumbuvanam in Madurai district and decided to commit suicide alongwith her four children. In the gruesome tragedy, three male children in the age group of 2 to 8 who were tied alongwith their six-month old sister to the rails by their mother, were chopped to pieces when the Madurai bound Rameshwaran passenger ran over them in the early hours of February 11, 1990 while her last child escaped with serious injuries and was later hospitalised.

2. *Murder of domestic servant*: A ten-year old domestic servant Nanku was ill-treated and killed by their employees. The decomposed body of the servant was found lying in the bedroom of his employer's house in Mayur Vihar, 268-B-Pocket-C, Phase II at New Delhi on January 23, 1990. The police reached the spot after reportedly informed about the alleged murder by some unidentified person over phone and found the decomposed body with head-injuries lying on a jute mat in one of the bedrooms of the first floor house. Both the legs of the deceased were reportedly burnt. The neighbours alleged that Mrs. Shivani Pandey used to frequently beat her servant and sometimes even did not give food to eat.[1]

Murder of employers by domestic servants: Incidents of domestic servants turning merciless killers have been increasing at an alarming rate in Delhi and other metropolitan cities. Domestic servants are involved in dacoity, murder, attempt to murder, robbery and theft. In 1992, there were 495 incidents of crime involving servants. Figures came down to 423 in 1993 and figures reported were 196 upto 31 July 1994 in New Delhi/Delhi city alone. A domestic servant who murdered his 77-year old master and two members of his family including a three-year-old mercilessly and in brutal and diabolical manner was sentenced to death by the Supreme Court on 11 August, 1994.[2]

3. *Murder of wife and children*: On the intervening night of October 10-11, 1983, Suresh Chandra Bahri, committed murder of his wife in an extremely brutal, gruesome, diabolical, revolting and distardly manner so as to arouse intense and extreme indignation of the society. Her body was truncated into two

parts in a devilish style evincing total depravity simply to gain control over the property. Later he took his two innocent children at Dhubli farm making them believe that they were being taken on a pleasure trip to the farm and then they were done to death by inflicting severe injuries on neck and other parts of the body and threw their bodies in the Varuna river having no consideration for the human life and that too for his own flesh and blood. The 40-year old Delhi businessman has been sentenced to death by the Supreme Court on July 8, 1994. In its 129-page verdict, a divisional bench consisting of Dr. Justice A.S. Anand and Mr. Justice Faizan Uddin has given life sentences to two conspirators of Suresh Bahri-Burbachan Singh and Rajpal, who had helped him in doing away the three innocent persons.[3]

4. *Bridegroom burnt to death in Tamil Nadu*: Press Trust of India, Coimbatore July 10, 1994 reported that the all-too commonly taken recourse to bride burning was given tragic twist in Tamil Nadu's Unumalpet town where a young man who married against his parents' wishes was done to death by his mother and aunt at their house on 9th July, 1994 night. The police said that the youth Ramalingam had been in love with a girl Sukanya. Ramalingam finally married Sukanya but as neither of their parents were willing to accept the couple, he insisted on his right to stay at his home. Enraged by this obstinate stand taken by Ramalingam, his mother and aunt allegedly poured kerosine on him and set him ablaze.[4]

5. *Man raped his daughter*: Om Pal, 41, father of eight children, has been arrested by the Gandhinagar police for allegedly raping his 12-year old daughter in his Chander Nagar Jhuggi on July 22, 1994. The arrest was made on a complaint lodged by Om Pal's wife. The police said Om Pal came home drunk on July 21, 1994 afternoon. He told his daughter to change her clothes which looked shabby. While she was in a state of undress Om Pal allegedly raped her. His other children were around and told their mother when she came back from work.[5]

6. *Girl strangled to death by grandmother*. A family row ended in tragedy when an old woman allegedly strangled her seven-year old granddaughter and dumped her body in the Yamuna river. Bhagwanti, 65, was arrested for killing Deepika whose body was found by the area police on November 10, 1994. The police said the accused had a strained relationship with her

daughter-in-law and wanted to avenge her humiliation at the hands of the latter. The girl's body was fished out by the fire brigade from the Yamuna near Nizamuddin bridge. The Trilokpuri police registered a case and launched a search to identify the girl. Some farmers living on the banks of the river told the police that they had seen an old woman with "grey hair" accompanying a young girl in the fields on November 7, 1994. The police team found an old woman hiding in a jhuggi along the banks. Her appearance matched the description given by the farmers. "She appeared to be scared. When we questioned her about the girl she disclosed her identity and conferred she had murdered Deepika", said Mr. Dharampal Singh, Station House Officer of Trilokpuri in East Delhi. "She appeared guilt-ridden and broke down while narrating the incident. She kept cursing herself for killing her granddaughter" Mr. Singh said. According to the police, Bhagwanti's relations with her daughter-in-law were strained for the past few months. Bhagwanti used to live with her son's (Shiv Prasad) family along with her two daughters in Mahavir Enclave, Dabri. "The daughter-in-law reportedly used to harass her and disturb Bhagwanti during prayers," Mr. Singh said. The police said Bhagwanti used to perform prayers for her daughter's marriage. According to the police Bhagwanti decided to kill her daughter-in-law to avenge humiliation. She picked up Deepika, a class II student, on her way back from a Government school on November 7, 1994 afternoon. "She wanted to kill her somewhere near but finding the place too crowded, took her on a bus across the Yamuna. They got down, strolled into the nearby fields and in a secluded spot strangled her before dumping off her body into the river", the police said. They said Shiv Prasad did not register a police complaint since he did not suspect his mother. Bhagwanti was arrested on 8th November, 1994 and remanded to a day's police custody.

7. *Man fatally stabbed by step-brothers*: A 30-year old man Suresh was stabbed allegedly by his three step-brothers and two others while his wife, Krishna was assaulted by her sister-in-law while the couple were on their way to a cousin's house at Kanjhawla in North-West Delhi on November 13, 1994. There was a dispute over property between the brothers. The police said Suresh died on the spot while Krishna is being treated in

a hospital. Suresh had been arrested on charges of murder two years ago and had come out on bail a few days ago. On November 13, 1994 the couple were going to a relative's house when they were accosted by Suresh's step-brothers, Praveen, Vijay and Sanjay and their two accomplices, Jagdish and Anand. The men attacked Suresh with an axe and even fired at him while Krishna was assaulted with bricks by Saroj and Rajbala, wives of Praveen and Vijay respectively.[6]

The Concept of Domestic Crime

Domestic crime can be broadly defined as any unethical, immoral or criminal act committed within the family by one of its members or the emotional abuse which seriously harms life, body, psychological integrity or liberty of another member of the family. Domestic crimes include dowry, murders, wife beating, widow-burning, sex determination test (Ammocentesis), female foeticide, female infanticide, witch-hunting, virginity test, Devdasi system, increasing desertions and child abuse. Exploitation of the girl child and sale of girls for sexual exploitation are also domestic crimes. Domestic crimes consist of: (a) physical aggression, minor and major blows (burns and damage to internal organs); (b) sexual abuse including molestation, rape and in extreme cases assassination or feminicide, and (c) emotional abuse which includes manifestations including psychological degradation, verbal humiliation, continual threats of abandonment, the threat of physical abuse, economic blackmail and imprisonment in the home. Domestic crimes like psychological cruelty, physical aggression, sexual harrassment or imprisoning in the home are the products of the patriarchal traits at the familial and social level which contradict the eternal values of equality, liberty and dignity. Domestic crimes are generally found in patriarchal model of social system which imposes relationships of hierarchy and domination. Domestic crime include homicide, spouse-assaults, woundings (hurt and grievous hurt), robbery, rape and certain other sexual offences committed by any person within the domestic four-walls. Foeticide, female infanticide, dowry deaths, child abuse and domestic violence are speedily increasing in our country. Unlawful, dangerous, unhygienic and unethical termination of pregnancy on grounds other than mentioned in law can be regarded as a domestic crime. Medical Termination of Pregnancy (MTP) Act 1971 lays down liberal grounds under which women have obtained the right to safe, scientific and legal abortions. However MTP does not cover a situation where gender of the unborn does not happen to be of the choice of woman/man who are parents of the unborn. According to one estimate, 78,000 foetus were aborted in the last decade. Child Marriage (Restraint) Act, 1978 raising the minimum age of marriage to 21 for boys and 18 years for girls, has made offence cognisable for purpose of investigation and imposed restrictions on marriage. In a modern society, violence can take a variety of characteristic: (a) quantitative, referring to the degree of violence which is exercised, (b) axiological, in relation to justice, (c) psychological and sociological for the invisible forms and structures of its production in a system of social relations, (d) cultural for the values and norms which define and regulate it. Domestic violence and domestic crimes are generally overlapping and inter-mixed. All over the world, women and children are generally the victims of domestic violence and crimes. Some recent statistical data of domestic crime related to dowry are as under:

Statewise Figures of Domestic Crime

I			*II*	
Incidents of cognizable crimes under local and special laws during the year 1992			*Murder for dowry and culpable homicide not amounting to murder during the year 1992*	
Sl. No.	*State / UT*	*Dowry prohibition act*	*Dowry Murder*	*CH*
1.	Andhra Pradesh	86	57	2
2.	Arunachal Pradesh	0	0	0
3.	Assam	60	26	1
4.	Bihar	693	139	10
5.	Goa	0	0	0
6.	Gujarat	2	25	0
7.	Haryana	0	8	16

8.	Himachal Pradesh	5	1	0
9.	Jammu & Kashmir	3	4	0
10.	Karnataka	344	38	2
11.	Madhya Pradesh	42	37	85
12.	Kerala	0	1	3
13.	Maharashtra	6	98	47
14.	Manipur	0	0	0
15.	Meghalaya	0	0	1
16.	Mizoram	0	0	0
17.	Nagaland	0	0	0
18.	Orissa	84	12	3
19.	Punjab	3	22	14
20.	Rajasthan	1	146	12
21.	Sikkim	0	0	0
22.	Tamil Nadu	310	2	0
23.	Tripura	0	2	0
24.	Uttar Pradesh	365	1499	13
25.	West Bengal	86	19	2
26.	A & N Islands	0	0	0
27.	Chandigarh	0	0	0
28.	D & N Haveli	0	0	0
29.	Daman & Diu	0	0	0
30.	Delhi	4	5	0
31.	Lakshadweep	0	0	0
32.	Pondicherry	4	0	0
	Total	2098	2141	211

As per 1993:

(i) Dowry death : 4366

(ii) Cruelty by husband : 15590

(iii) Rape incidents : 8153

Domestic Violence

Sati Prevention Act 1987 (Act 4 of 1988) provides legislative protection in matters relating to the practice of Sati. There is stringent punishment for abetment of Sati. To meet the challenge of increasing domestic violence, criminal acts were amended in 1983 and 1986 to create special categories of offences to deal with cruelty to wives, dowry harassment and dowry death. The first amendment introduced a new section cruelty to wives section 498 A-Indian Penal Code. It included physical and mental cruelty. Denial of food, insistence on perverse sexual conduct, turning a woman out of house or confining her in the house and denying access to minor children will generally constitute mental torture. The second amendment introduced new section 304 B in Indian Penal Code to counter the menace of dowry deaths. Dowry deaths and torture cases have high level of incidence in Maharashtra, U.P., West Bengal and Andhra Pradesh. There were 52 cases under Sati Prevention Act reported in 1990 and 18 cases in 1991. In 1991, 9 cases from Haryana, 6 cases from West Bengal and one each from Bihar and Pondicherry were reported under Commission of Sati (Prevention) Act 1987.

Domestic crime and domestic violence are closely interlinked. Domestic violence appears to be a crime in India that is largely unreported and even unnoticed by the society. Common reasons for not reporting domestic violence include: (1) It's a family or private matter; (2) Victims are ashamed or embarrassed to report it; (3) fear of reprisals; and (4) many victims do not view their victimization as crimes.[7] Until recently, most police officers and even social scientists were of the opinion that since it occurs in private residences inaccessible to the police, there was no way the police could prevent it. A research study has concluded that in domestic assault cases reported to the police, an arrest should be made unless there are good, clear reasons why arrest would be counter productive.[8] In about 90 per cent of all domestic violence cases, men are the offenders. A research study reveals that about 25 per cent of the victims of domestic violence reported that they had been the victims of at least three similar crimes in the previous six months.[9] Living in India, we have all known or at least heard of one such victim in the course of our lives.[10]

Domestic Crimes in India and Abroad

Domestic crimes include all offences and criminal acts committed within the domestic walls of a family and include sexual abuse, battering of members of the family, ill-treatment and harassment of newly married women for dowry and all other type of criminal offences. Sexual abuse includes all forms of sexual activity involving genital contact for either the offender or the victim, and would include genital folding and vaginal, anal or oral intercourse as well. Sexual abuse in broad terms also includes other forms of direct physical contact such as holding of breasts, buttocks or thighs or sexual kissing. It includes non-contact sexual activity like the deliberate exposure of the offender's or victim's private parts for the offender's sexual gratification, photographing the victim in the nude or in suggestive sexual postures or poses. Dowry deaths, family conflicts, cruelty by husbands and relatives all are manifestations of domestic crimes. Many of the offendes enumerated in Indian Penal Code against the body, if committed within a family, will constitute domestic crime. It is difficult to define domestic crimes in specific terms since it is a broad generalisation of criminal acts committed in a family setting and are committed within the four-walls of a domestic boundary. Domestic crimes connote all those crimes which are pertaining to the house or household or performed at home. In December 1988 there was a report of a suicide case in which a man had committed suicide due to oppression of his wife and mother-in-law. In the male dominated society mostly women commit suicide—many be due to dowry harassment or failure in love. Disharmony in family institution and domestic crimes are increasing in modern day life. Incidents of servants turning merciless killers have been increasing at an alarming rate sending panic waves across the city and the police officials are apprehensive.[11] Spouse assault has existed since the inception of the institution of marriage (Engale 53-58; Phesians 6 : 22-26; Davis 197 : 311). Recently certain laws have been passed in India against spouse assault because of many bride-burning cases.

A number of studies carried out by criminologists, social scientists and police officers indicate that domestic crimes are on the increase in Indian society. An increase in domestic crimes is inevitable for the following reasons :

1. The increase in population has a positive relationship with crime.
2. Social awareness and political awakening has led a feeling of relative deprivation amongst the backward classes, women, children, bonded labour and other weaker sections of society. They are now not ready to accept and suffer domestic crimes at the hands of their elderly persons of the family itself.
3. Breakdown of joint family system, family feuds over property, lack of satisfaction of lust for sex in poor families at times lead to domestic crimes.
4. Ineffective policing and costly criminal justice system are partly responsible for not bringing culprits of domestic crimes to the justice.

Cases of sexual acts against children below 10 years have increased alarmingly by over 178 per cent during 1991. As many as 1099 cases were recorded in 1991, compared to just 394 in 1990.[12] In fact the revelations by adults who had suffered sexual abuse in their childhood reveals that most sexual abuse takes place within the family itself; the offenders include uncles, elder cousins, step-fathers and step-brothers as well as close relatives, brothers, fathers and grandfathers.

Sale of Girl Child

On 8th September 1991 *The Times of India* wrote "At the centre of the storm over the 14-year old Ameena and her marriage to 60-year old Arab groom is the small but different mohalla of Barkas—in Hyderabad a bride bazar for the last 15 years". Most of the poor families sold their girl to stave off hunger. About 33 per cent of girls are sold to pimps by their parents, uncles, friends or local guardians. The Child Marriage Restraint (Amendment) Act 1978 and Immoral Traffic Prevention Act are unfortunately never effectively implemented or enforced by the police. Section 372 of Indian Penal Code has defined the offence of "selling minor for purposes of prostitution etc." Section 373 of IPC mentions the offence of "Buying minor for proposes of prostitution etc." Cases reported under Immoral Traffic Prevention Act were as under :

1990 — 16426

1991 — 14639

1992 — 12580

In matters of domestic crimes, crime statistics cannot convey the whole truth. Domestic crimes are generally not reported to the police for the following reasons :

1. Reluctance of the police to register cases.
2. Reluctance of the victim to report cases to the police in view of considerations of the honour of the family.
3. Domestic crimes can cause embarrassment to the family members when investigated by the police.
4. Victims of domestic crime have no confidence in the criminal justice system that quick and certain justice would be meted out to the criminal.
5. There are many invisible costs of securing justice in terms of tension, harrassment, repeated adjornments, inexpressible anguish, etc., which the victims want to avoid.

In India if a wife is beaten and humiliated, well, it is only a domestic matter and she is advised (usually by her parents and brothers) to keep her misery under wraps. The social pressures on the helpless victim of domestic violence are crippling.[13] There is a well known recent case of Prerna Katke whose attempts to file complaints of physical torture against her husband were met with hostility and indifference by the Maharashtra police. It was subsequently with the intervention of the Malula Sahayak Kaksha, Bombay, a women organisation that her complaint was recorded by the Matunga Police Station. She subsequently filed a writ petition in Bombay High Court against State Govt.

During the last two decades domestic crimes have increased both in magnitude and in dimensions. Dowry deaths, cruelty by husbands and their relatives particularly of young wives, child abuse and crime against women are increasing by India over the years. Some of the important amendments made in the Dowry Prohibition Act 1961 during the last two decades are stated below :

(i) Punishment will be given only to the taker of dowry.

(ii) Complaints about dowry can be made within 10 years of marriage.

(iii) The clause "as consideration for the marriage" is deleted from the definition of dowry under section 2 of the Act of 1961.

(iv) Setting up of family court and special court for trial of bride burning cases have been provided;

(v) Permissible wedding expenses is linked to the income of the bride's parents and

(vi) A minimum of 6 months of imprisonment with a maximum of 2 years of imprisonment and fine of Rs. 10,000 has been provided.

In the tragic case of Subedar Tewari, Veena was married to Dr. Narendra. The conduct of Dr. Narendra was licentious that he had extramarital relationship with his 22 years old niece. It was also alleged that he had illicit incestuous relationship with his sister Meera. Supreme Court held death of Veena to be homicidal and sentenced Dr. Narendra to life imprisonment.[14] Abuse of children and cruelty to children have existed in India since ages (Gokhale and Sohani 1979) child labour, child sacrifice, infanticide, child marriage and molestation of children by close relatives are certain domestic crimes which are not easily even noticed by the criminologists and the society in general. The dark figures of domestic crimes cannot be easily estimated because there is much more submerged domestic criminality than appears on the surface. Domestic crimes are increasing because family life is gradually getting more and more disturbed due to tensions, lack of understanding between couples, lack of tolerance in family and emotional incongruities of the broken homes. There are many domestic crimes in India against which there are even no remedies. The Immoral Traffic (Prevention) Act 1959 as amended upto 1986, Dowry Prohibition Act 1961 as amended upto 1986, Indecent Representation of Women (Prevention) Act 1986 and the Commission of Sati (Prevention) Act 1987 are important legislations relating to women which need close study to identify various domestic crimes. One can easily imagine the plight of battered women in our own country. Here this violence occurs without social remorse, legal redress or political protest.[15] There has been rise in domestic crimes as can be seen by the following figures:

Offences	*1987*	*1990*	*1991*	*1992*	*Percentage Increase from 1987 to 1991*
Dowry deaths	1912	4836	5157	4962	167.7
Cruelty by husbands and his relatives	11603	13450	15949	19750	37.5

The criminal law (Second Amendment) Act 1983 (Act 46 of 1983) has created a new offence of cruelty by husbands and relatives of husband (Section 498-A IPC) to tackle the over growing problem of wife baiting with a view to extracting dowry after marriage or goading her to commit suicide. According to IPC Section 498-A, "Husbands or relative of husband of a woman subjecting her to cruelty, whoever, being the husband or the relative of the husband of a woman, subjects such woman to cruelty, shall be punished with imprisonment for a term which may extend the three and shall be liable fine. (*Explanation* : For the purpose of this section cruelty means: (a) any wilful conduct which is of such a nature as is likely to drive the woman to commit suicide or to cause grave injury or danger to life, limb or health, (whether mental or physical) of the women; or (b) harassment is with a view to coercing her or any person related to her to meet any unlawful demand for any property or valuable security is on account of failure by her or any person related to her to meet such demand.")

Child Abuse: A Burning Question

Domestic crimes in the form of child abuse are rapidly increasing in India and an increasing number of adults are coming forward to narrate instances of sexual abuse when they were children.[16] A random sample conducted in 1985 by the Tata Institute of Social Sciences, with a majority of respondents being between 20 and 24 years old from the middle income group in Bombay found that one out of every three girls and one out of every 10 boys have been sexually abused in childhood.[17] A survey conducted in 1984 covering 2000 adults revealed that 10 per cent had been abused as children. The Red Crisis Centres in U.K. report that a majority of women clients come to disinter the trauma of unspoken abuse buried since they were children. Indian children are particularly vulnerable to sexual abuse because on the one hand we do not talk about sex and on the other hand girls are interacting very early with the adult world in a joint family system in rural areas. The girl child labour rose by 33 per cent last year. Driver and Droisen define childhood sexual abuse as "any sexual behaviour directed at a person under years of age without that person's informed consent. Sexual behaviour may involve touching parts of the child or requesting the child to touch oneself, itself or others; ogling the child in a sexual manner, taking pornographic photographs, or requiring the child to look at parts of the body, sexual acts or any material in a way which is arousing to oneself; and verbal comments or suggestions to the child which are intended to threaten the child sexually or otherwise to provide sexual gratification to oneself". The World Health Organisation (WHO) states that one in every 10 children is sexually abused. In Delhi, 54 per cent of the rape victims were found to be below 15 years and in 80 per cent of these cases the rapist was known to the child (according to the police records of 1992). A recent survey indicates that one in every six girls were being sexually abused. It is particularly disturbing because the victims have almost no support system.[18] Research studies of North America indicate that one in four girls and one in six boys are sexually abused before the age of 18 years. Apart from the preponderant effects of sadness, depression, anger, helplessness and distrust of men, sexually abused children have been found to be suffering from a variety of psychological and behavioural disturbances such as bed-wetting, sleep disorders, low self-esteem, etc. A survey carried out in 1965 of 1000 college going girls in the USA indicated that 25 per cent of them had sexual experience with an adult before age 13, and only 6 per cent of the offences were reported. Another study carried out by Florence Ruah of the USA indicated that one of every four females were sexually abused before reaching the age of 18.[19] Incest has been defined as sexual relationships between members of the immediate family other than husband and wife. Some of the characteristics of incest include :

(1) Brother-sister incest is the most common in many families.

(2) Incest usually develops in multi-problem families where often members are isolated from each other.

(3) Father, uncles or elder brothers are often the offenders and such incestuous elders are often chronic alcoholic.

(4) The incestuous father is often confused regarding family roles and attempts to escape from adult realities. About 70 per cent of the father-daughter incest situations last longer than one year.

(5) The typical incestuous family is character disordered and within a situation that fosters narcissistic and self-centred individuals.

(6) The incestuous father is often authoritarian, domineering and inspires fear in the family. Often he was sexually abuse as a child. Usually he has strong unmet needs for personal warmth.

There are no research studies on victim offender relationships in domestic violence cases so far carried out in India. In USA Deptt. of Justice has prepared a special report in which victim-offender relationships in domestic violence cases existed as under : [20]

Victim-Offender Relationships in Domestic Violence

Offender is	*Percentage of Incidents*
1. Spouse	40
2. Ex-spouse	19
3. Parent of child	1
4. Sibling	2
5. Other relative	3
6. Boy friend or ex-boy friend	10
7. Live in friend	9
8. Other non-relatives	1—6

Generally when police is called to the scene of a domestic crime, police officers usually adopt one of the three responses :

1. Give advice and compromise between parties.
2. Order the offender to leave the residence for at least eight hours.
3. Arrest the offender.

The child sex offenders in 75 to 85 per cent cases are someone the child knows, loves or trusts. Some 45 per cent are relatives, father's brothers, uncles or grown up cousins.[21]

In New Delhi, the data collected by the city crime branch suggests a staggering rise in incestuous rapes. The cases reported to the police jumped from three in 1990 to 17 in 1994 and nine had taken place upto April 1995. In Delhi in the last four years 46 cases were reported. On April 23, 1995 a 16-year old girl from Mongolpuri in north-west Delhi alleged, she has been raped by her father and brother for over a week. The same day an auto-rickshaw driver was held for raping his eight-year old step-daughter in the contonment area of South Delhi. What is ominous, the statistics reveal that six of the nine rapes were committed by fathers on minor daughters. Uncles come next, being involved in 13 rapes since 1990. According to Sunil Mittal of Delhi Psychiatry Centre, "Incest is a combination of psychological and biological disorder found generally among persons who fail to grow out of their adolescent fantasies." In India, society has to travel a long way before those guilty of incest can be prosecuted by the law.

Sociologist Richard Gelles emphasised that the causes of child abuse are complex. He concluded that if we are to treat and prevent the abuse of children, we must stop thinking of the abuse as a "Sick" person who can be "cured" and "begun working on social-structural variables such as unemployment."[22] Stress, unemployment and underemployment, helplessness of children and social isolation are some of the social structural variables responsible for child abuse. In the past few years, an increasing number of husband abuse cases have been reported.[23] Another child abusers 30 to 40 per cent are close or well-known acquaitances, baby sitters, teachers, doctors and neighbourhood friends. A study conduct by the Family Planning Association of India disclosed that 68 per cent of the women surveyed had been victims of sexual molestation by an uncle or another male relative when they were children.[24]

Some of the common dimensions of child abuse are as under :

1. Maltreatment and physical abuse of child including excessive beating, cruel, unusual and hard physical punishment resulting in physical damage, hurt, injury to body or limbs.
2. Neglect or non-fulfillment of the child's basic and development needs like food, shelter, clothes, recreation, education and health care.
3. Emotional neglect or denial of normal emotional attachment or concern that compels a child to feel insecure, unwanted, unworthy or not cared by the family.
4. Sexual abuse of children by adults like pedophilia, incest, child rape, child prostitution.
5. Abuse or maltreatment of children in formal child care settings/juvenile correctional institution, like juvenile remand homes.
6. Child exploitation by engaging them to beg or child labour in hazardous occupations or overwork beyond normal permissible working hours.
7. Exposure to immoral, anti-social or anti-legal environment or work for unconscionable gains and maiming of children for purpose of begging.
8. Female infanticide.

"The incidence of child sexual abuse at the hands of male relatives or neighbour, according to Dr. Pritam Bhatnani, is more prevalent in India than one was willing to concede earlier". The rape of a child is one of the most serious domestic crimes. Rape of a child is absolutely shattering for her at a tender age. The traumatic experience invariably causes irrepairable physical and psychological damage. There are many serious problems of rehabilitating a child who has been sexually abused. The cases of paedophilia (rape of children below 10 years) have been increasing alarmingly over the last two decades. Nearly one-fourth of the reported rape victims are minors. Exploitation of child labour is most common child abuse. The girl children are sold to pimps by their parents due to their utter poverty, ignorance and economic compulsions, and forced into prostitution. Girl infants are let to die, sometimes drowned or given poison by their parents who perceive a daughter as an economic liability and burden.

Dowry Deaths and Harassment to Women

To plug some of the loopholes in the Dowry Prohibition Act 1961, amendments have been made in 1984 and 1986 whereby dowry was made a cognizable offence, there was an increase in punishment to five years and a fine upto Rs. 10,000. The girl, parents, relatives and social organisation could file a complaint and the prior sanction of government for prosecuting husband has been dropped. It has been made non-bailable offence. In spite of all these amendments, the problem of dowry continues. Bihar, Tamil Nadu, Uttar Pradesh and Karnataka reported the bulk of cases under Dowry Prohibition Act in that order constituting 81.6 per cent of the cases. In India, there were 2155 cases in 1990, 1841 cases in 1991 and 2102 cases in 1992.

The harassment and psychological torture of married women by their husbands and the members of the husband's family has of late caused much concern to the nation.[25] As many as 1319 cases of dowry deaths were registered during 1986 and 1418 during 1987. In 1988, there were 518 cases of dowry deaths and in 1990, there were 6823 cases of dowry deaths.[26] Dowry related domestic violence figures in Maharashtra for three years are as under :

Harassment and Dowry Related Domestic Violence

Domestic crimes	*1991*	*1992*	*1993*
Suicides over dowry	344	285	349
Attempted suicide over dowry	30	62	48
Murder over dowry	74	75	81
Attempted murders over dowry	41	27	15
Cruelty by husbands and in-law	5396	6168	6746

(*Source* : Maharashtra State Police Records)

According to India's admission in Lok Sabha more than 922 women were burnt to death in1988. In 1987, dowry deaths claimed 1572 victims in various states. Uttar Pradesh accounted for 533 deaths in 1987. In 1992, 70 per cent cases (1499 out of

2141 of murder for dowry) were reported from Uttar Pradesh alone. Foeticide is violence on an unborn baby if it is identified as a girl because to be born as a girl itself is ghastly social crime in India. Can't we prevent this domestic crime? These crimes cannot be prevented nor can it be proved easily unless the victims bring it to the notice of other members of the family and even to the pclice if so required. In India harassment and ill-treatment of women by middle class and lower class families for not bringing enough dowry is well known although no figures are available. Figures of dowry death do not indicate the correct state of affairs. Incidents of crimes reported under Dowry Prohibition Act for three years are reported as under :

1990 — 16426

1991 — 14639

1992 — 12580

Family Disputes

Section 376-A punishes sexual intercourse with wife without her consent by a judicially separated husband under Criminal Law Amendment Act 1983 new provisions provide for the camera trial and non-disclosure of the identity of the victim.

From 1971 to 1984, approximately 25293 males and 29536 females have committed suicide in India due to the quarrel with their parent-in-laws. During the last 14 years (1971-1984), 15918 males committed suicide in India due to quarrels with their spouses when 22434 females died for the same reason. The husband-wife relationship at times creates family disputes.

Wife-Beating : A Domestic Crime

Physical violence against wife and child are the commonly occurring happenings in many societies. Martin (1976), Walker (1979), Strausetal (1980) and Bowker (1978, 1983) have done considerable research work upon the problem of wife-beating.[27] Greenblat (1985) has analysed the normative aspects of wife-beating by analysing how various socio-demographic factors like age, sex, beliefs about violence and moral values can effect the individuals approval-disapproval and tolerance of wife-beating in different situations.[28] In India, Ram Ahuja (1987) in his study has referred to wife beating as such crime and studied its frequency, methods, severity, motives of beating and the cause.[29] Noor Mohammed (1984) in his study found that wife beating is more common among socially and economically backward people.[30] In most cases wives are reluctant to report to police. In a case dealt in the Supreme Court, an educated woman after establishing her husband's culpability regarding cruelty to her, petitioned the court to forgive her husband.[31] The degree and frequency of the wife battering varies from home to home. In the poverty-striken homes it is a common feature but rich families are not free from the episode. Marital violence is a part of the normative structure in patriarchal societies. According to Ram Ahuja, there is no woman who has not suffered at one time or another, the harassment, humiliation, exploitation or domestic violence which always shadows her sex.[32]

During the first European conference on violence against women in Marseilles in southern France, the minister of state for health, social and urban affairs Ms. Simone Veil promised to expand existing structures to receive women and give them a greater say in society.

According to Ms. Gallard, more cases of conjugal violence are being reported than in the past years. In the conference these points were discussed :

(*i*) Buttered women belong to all categories and of all age groups.

(*ii*) A large part of the battered women have either none or little income of their own, i.e., they depends on their husbands.

(*iii*) Most of the Victims had no formal education.

(*iv*) Spouse's drinking or psychological problems, jealousy, unemployment are some reasons which provoke violence against women.

Ms. Gallard, Ms. Monnier, lawyer Philippe Chaudount and other prominent personalities expressed their views.[33]

Spouse Swapping: An Evil Practice

India Today, June 15, 1994 issue has brought out a report on spouse swapping which denotes another kind of prostitution being forced on reluctant wives and can be included in domestic crimes. Spouse swapping is irresponsible, group sex and is done by a negligible percentage of the baser elements of society who only prove that they are sick and dominated by animal instinct, notwithstanding our education and social status. The husband cannot be absolved of the guilt of extramarital relationships just because the wife is doing the same thing or vice versa. It can simply be termed as prostitution by consent and the so-called husbands and wives are nothing but dignified pimps. Those couples are immoral and should be punished under Immoral Traffic Act. Women should seek advice or get a divorce or report to police if their husbands are forcing them to indulge in this evil practice. This self-destructive behaviour has destroyed families in the West with children being the main victims. The aggressive advertising compaigns for condoms, the availability of pornographic magazines and the explicit sex in blue movies have resulted in the evil practices of spouse-swapping which is simply immorality and degeneration of the highest order. Generally it turned out that men had problems persuading their wives to swap and in many cases it is done out of compulsion, harassment, torture or threat of divorce. By all standards it should be labelled as a crime.

Factors Behind these Crimes

It is not easy to answer why people commit domestic crimes. Psychologists assert that domestic crimes are results of frustration-aggression typothesis combined with deviant personality trait-concept. Certain domestic crimes are done with financial/property motives and psychopathic personality traits are generally found in domestic crime. Alcoholism is directly responsible for many domestic crimes such as incest, battering women, assault on child and other members of the family. Narcotic drugs and alcoholism are factors responsible for many domestic crimes. The explanation of criminal behaviour, apparently must be found in social interaction in which both the behaviour of the person and the overt or prospective behaviour of other persons play their parts.[34] For beating of women and many other domestic violence in society "a sub-culture of violence" is responsible to a large extend. Wolfgang and Ferracuti have shown that "a sub-culture of violence" existed in the urban lower class and this sub-culture is carried by families as well as other groups.[35] An important and noticeable feature of these crimes is that they are committed within the safe precincts of home and the culprits are mostly close relations. Generally the family ties are so strong and effective that the truth does not come out and there are no eye-witnesses to testify the guilt in a court of law. This is why guilty persons of domestic crimes go scot free and are seldom brought to book and punished in India.

Abuse of Elderly Parents

There are also cases of abuse of elderly persons "granny bashing" and parental abuse. It is sometimes referred as the king hear syndrome after the aging character in Shakespeare's play who was mistreated by his two daughters. Abuse of the elderly includes not only violent attacks but also such acts as withholding food, stealing savings, verbal abuse and threats of being sent to old age homes.

Child Sex Offenders

Regarding sex offences involving children, Finkelhor has formulated a model, which seeks to integrate the diverse views and empirical date. Finkelhor has expressed his views in this way :

Model of Child Molesting[36]

1. Emotional congruence	Children attractive because of their low dominance and male socialization to dominance; offender immature, low self- esteem, aggressive.
2. Sexual Arousal	Children sexually arousing due to offencive's socialisation through personal experience, models or child pornography; possibility of psychological explanation, e.g., hormonal levels.
3. Blockage	Problems in formimg adult relationships with women; related to sexual anxiety, poor heterosocial skills, attitudes towards sex.
4. Disinhibition	Offender able to overcome inhibitions through drugs, alcohol, cognitive distortions or situational stress disrupts inhibitors.

Child sex abusers appear to be a distructive group from a psychological view-point; research has elucidated a number of distinguishing cognitive and behavioural features of old offender populations.[37] The weight of evidence with child offenders suggests that there are individuals who are sexually aroused by children (Freund 1967; Freund and Langevin 1976).[38] Many domestic crimes are committed by the persons due to emotional imbalances, poor self-esteem, and circumstantial factors. There is need for research regarding domestic crime offenders in India. The psychological profile of a child abuser points to a sad and inept personality with poor impulse control, low self-esteem, average or below average I.Q., lack of awareness about his own negative feelings, suppressed hostility and negative feelings towards children and a low frustration tolerance, contributory sociological background includes social isolation, bad housing, lack of training in parenthood and alcoholism or drug abuse. The close proximity to one another due to cramped family quarters, lack of privacy, indiscreet sexual behaviour by adults in front of children and the possibility of discipleasing a fond close relative often makes the child involve herself in sexual activity without understanding the seriousness or gravity of such behaviour. At a workshop in Bangalore held by voluntary organisations and psychatrists, many shameful secrets were disclosed. "Only 61 per cent of the girls have ever been able to disclose their experiences to anyone. Fifteen per cent of the 348 girls who put down their experience in the workshop said that they had in fact been seriously abused or raped and 31 per cent before their 10th birthday. Fifty-five per cent of the abusers were male family members".[39]

Reasons for Increase in Domestic Crimes

Sociologists, political scientists, criminologists, economists, psychologists analyse causes of domestic crimes through their own tunnel visions. These crimes are increasing due to following main causes :

(1) Geographical isolation and urbanisation.

(2) Household density leading to physical child abuse, bedroom sharing and sexual molestations.

(3) Breakdown of family ties leaving negative physiological and psychological impact of stress.

(4) Unmanageable family composition in joint family systems.

(5) Role disturbances in families leading to sibling quarrels, and absence of an affectionate mother-child relationship.

(6) Unequal distribution of power in the marital dyad and strained father-mother relationship.

(7) Poverty, materialism and greed for money and material comforts leading to dowry deaths, harassment of women by husband and in-laws.

(8) Ineffective social control systems including religion, and state authority.

(9) Ineffective laws and their ineffective enforcement and collapse of criminal justice administration.

(10) State of social anomie and normlessness due to erosion of moral and spiritual values.

(11) Growing sub-culture of violence in the society.

(12) Lack of community awareness about the problem and their indifference to the problems.

Is Child Labour a Domestic Crime ?

Poor parents, out of economic compulsions, send their children to earn for their daily bread. The bulk of the child labour is in unorganised sector of which 90 per cent is in rural areas. Child labour is mainly a problem of the poorer sections where parents are hard put up to provide food, clothing, shelter, education and recreation of reasonable standard for their children. According to a study by Indian Council of Child Welfare in Delhi, 70 per cent of children work for more than 12 hours a day and the wages paid to them are less than those prescribed under the Minimum Wages Act Article 39(c) of the Constitution which lays down that no one would be forced by economic necessity to enter into a vacation unsuited to his age or strength. Article 24 of the Constitution provides that children below the age of 14 years shall not be employed at work in any factory, mine or any other hazardous employment. Is it not a domestic crime to deprive a child opportunities for education by their parents? Under the National Child Labour Programme only 126 special schools have been opened to cater to the needs of 7000 children in nine districts.[40]

Need for Protection and Better Deal

The perspective plan for Indian women for 2000 AD prepared by the department of women in the Ministry of Human Resource Development envisages mass-media to emphasise women's identity and sensitisation of administrative machinery to the needs, urges and problems of women. The perspective plan report suggests measures to rehabilitate victims of crimes like dowry, rape and Sati.[41] The victimological perceptions of offences against domestic crimes open a new vista for the criminologists and social scientists to probe into and make concrete recommendations. What can be done for prevention of domestic crimes? How can victims of domestic crimes get relief and justice in our democratic society? These are important issues which need our close scrutiny and examination. Some agencies need to be built up to provide psychological counselling and relief to the victims of domestic crimes. There is an urgent need for conducting workshops on "Child Abuse Awareness and Prevention Programme". Awareness raising and preventing programme against child abuse, need to be launched all over the country. There is need for legal literacy for women. *Our Laws* is a series of 10 illustrated manuals presented in a most simple language so that one can understand and absorb the information relevant to him. The major objective of this project is to create awareness about the existing laws that concern women, viz., working women, contract labourer, bonded labourer, Hindu Adoption and Maintenance Act, Marriage and divorce, property, dowry, rape, kidnapping and abduction.[42]

Awareness of Sex Offenders and Abusers

The sex abuse of children is a social time bomb with the potential for destroying many futures. To stop victimisation of children we must educate them. We have to educate our children about sex offenders and child abusers.[43] Some of the important basic lessons for children are as follows :[44]

1. Children should be told the importance of telling parents about the improper advances made by others even by the family members especially over night.
2. Children rarely lie about sexual molestation and parents should encourage them to confine all their problems and mutual trust should be built up.

3. Children should be told about bad and psychologically sick people who are harmful and dangerous and have to be kept away.
4. Children should be taught and urged to think about escaping and surviving if abducted by unknown persons by screaming for help particularly when in crowded place or near police stations.
5. Safety in numerous should be stressed.
6. Children should be told not to get allowed by fame, lure or a modelling job or the chance to compete in a beauty contest and parents should generally accompany children in talent pursuits.
7. Children should be made conscious to recognise when there is "a bad touch" by someone.
8. The child lures prevention programmes need to be given to the children.

It is necessary to educate parents about child abuse problems. Parents to address the problem of childhood sexual abuse is likely to be a tough job in India.

How to Control and Contain these Crimes ?

Some of the basic issues relating to domestic crimes are as under :

1. What measures of intervention are we prepared to tolerate to prevent domestic crimes ?
2. Should we adopt the traditional liberal view of the family as an essential social institution and keep the agents of the State at an arms length ?
3. What measures of state intervention are we prepared to tolerate in cases of perceived child abuse ?
4. How much avoidable child abuse (particularly sexual abuse), are we ready to tolerate in the interest of family harmony and perceived greater good of the individual rights ?
5. What role can be assigned to the non-governmental voluntary organisations in prevention, detection and reporting of domestic crimes ?

6. Should we identify and statutorily define what constitutes gross child abuse which calls for State intervention?

There is an urgent need to control domestic crime with a view to prevent the emotional destabilisation of children and to correct the emotional deprivation of broken homes. There should be a nationwide movement for the protection of battered women and crisis management for battered women. In England, a shelter for battered women in Chiswick, called refuge has been functioning for the last 23 years providing compassionate care to women and children under its roof. It runs Britain's only domestic crisis hotline which receives 10000 calls a year from abused women.[45] In USA, social service wing of the police in many cities provide family counselling, drug information and referral services to the community. Intervention in family disputes has always been a necessary function of the police since these incidents often result in a disturbance of the peace and many even had to a serious assault or homicide.[46] Domestic crimes can be prevented by bringing awareness about them in the community by aggressive police-public education programmes and personal contacts with the people. Percentage of convictions in India under Dowry Prohibitions Act is very unsatisfactory and low. Out of cases tried in court under Dowry Prohibition Act convictions were secured in 32.7 per cent in 1990, 35.4 per cent in 1991 and 37.8 per cent in 1992.[47]

Theoretical Explanations of Wife-Battering

Hierarchy structure of patriarchial family has legitimized wife-battering for subordination, domination and control of women.[48] According to the theory of patriarchal control, husbands develop standards of gratification for completely dominating their wives and children. When this domination is threatened they feel deprived, suffer psychic distress and in their uncontrollable rage they beat their wives for domestic domination. Adler has linked marital violence to marital power struggle. The thesis is that a major use of marital violence is to increase one's power over a mate. Battering is done for getting total control over every aspect of women's lives.[49] The theory of "learned helplessness", advanced by Walker, averts that repeated beatings produce passivity in abused wives and their helplessness permeates every aspect of their life.[50] The cyclical theory of Walker maintains that the interaction between husband and wife tends to follow a cyclical pattern: (a) tension-building phase, (b) the explosion or accute battering incident, and (c) the calm loving respite. According to Professor Ram Ahuja, the social bond theory explains violence against women in terms of structural conditions, i.e., family crises, role frustrations, inappropriate upbringing and unfortunate incident of life which create anxieties and stresses that affect the adjustment, attachment and commitment of husband to his wife. Ahuja's social bond theory is based on a conjunctive approach that takes into account social factors like stressful situations, personality traits of aggressors and victims and cultural millieu in which the individuals are socialized.[51] Goode advanced coercion theory to explain wife-battering. According to him, use of physical force is an integral part of the institution of the family and is one of the means to maintain control in the family.[52] Empirical data proves that wife-battering is a complex phenomenon that can only be explained by a multi-causative theory that takes into consideration the following main causes :

1. Hierarchial structure of family with a power struggle for subordination and control of women in a patriarchial setting;
2. Economic, social and psychological pressures on families and frustration by the heads;
3. Structural conditions of families and role frustrations;
4. Learned helplessness of the women and cultural acceptability;
5. Gender bias in society;
6. Cultural domination of males over females and their periodical reassertion;
7. Social upbringing and sub-culture millieu in which individuals are socialised;
8. Passive defence by women;
9. Lack of social awakening about their rights in women;
10. Psychological factors, personality traits of aggressors, etc.

Need for Comprehensive Law

The National Commission for women has stirred a hornet's nest by initiating the first even countrywide debate on the menace of child rape in all its socio-medico-legal complexity. In Delhi alone, 400 cases involving girls below the age of 10 years and the number of victims of rape cases in the age group of 10 to 16 years was 2105 in 1990. As per police record, 70 per cent of the child rapes take place in the victims domestic area. In 1990, out of 79 named cases, 48 were either family friends or relatives and in 1989 out of 132 named cases 68 were neighbour and 64 were close friends or relatives. According to Dr. K.K. Singhal, a medico-legal expert, the adverse effects on the victims mind may manifest at any stage and under any circumstances. These effects include feeling of insecurity, stunted personality, neorosis, hysteria, inferiority complex, suicidal instincts, insanity and a strong feeling of revenge. There is an urgent need for a comprehensive law for dealing with offenders of child rape and sexual child abusers in India. There is a requirement of comprehensive legislation by the parliament on domestic crimes and child abuse. The age of the child for this purpose should be 18 years as in the juvenile justice Act. The general invisibility of the domestic crime within and outside the homes coupled with poverty, unemployment, inhuman living conditions has a direct link between violence on the screen and domestic crime rate. Awareness about domestic crimes among the parents and children is also needed. Supreme Court in V.N. Pawar *vs* State of Maharashtra has observed "wife burning tragedies are becoming too frequent for the country to be complacent. Police sensitization mechanism which will prevent the commission of such crime must be set up if these horrendous crimes are to be avoided-like-wise, special provisions facilitating easier proof of such special class of murders on establishing certain basic facts must be provided for by appropriate legislation" (AIR 1980 SC 1271).

Domestic Crime and the Role of Police

In domestic crime intervention, police help is invited by the victims, otherwise it is interference in the domestic life of the people. In a service oriented functions of police work, timely help and assistance to the victims of domestic crime by the family intervention police team as a community mental health resource can build up cordial police-public relations in a community. For dealing with domestic crimes separate special social police wing on the type of social police of Sweden or the Juveinte police of Japan should be constituted and they should be given further training in handling such domestic crime. According to one research paper "22 per cent of police deaths and 40 per cent of police injuries sustained nation-wide are incurred as a result of calls to intervene in family disputes."[53] In India, there has been many successful detection and punishments in domestic crime cases. Some successful leading detection cases, referred by Trilok Nath, are murderous servant, the faithless husband, and husband murders wife, in his book *Crime and Detection in India.* Domestic crimes in India are becoming much more complex all over the country and therefore what is demanded of our police officers is something much more difficult than even before—far greater imagination and resourcefulness, the ability to look ahead and anticipate situations. To intervene in situations of domestic crime, police is only one of the control system within society and the extend and nature of its effectiveness will depend on other systems, e.g., medical, educational, economic, religious and social welfare control systems as well as civil law.

Again the process of labelling various acts as domestic crime involves the appreciation of the circumstances of the parties involved, their socio-economic milieu and social class as well as the attitude to the aggressive conduct adopted by the on-looker. While handling domestic crime, police officers must remember the following the ethical basic techniques :

(i) Understand and respect the ethnic and cultural backgrounds;

(ii) Phrase questions with respect to self-dignity and pride;

(iii) Request, do not demand information.

(iv) Use proper titles in addressing individuals;

(v) Probe personal type questions only upon willingness to respond;

(vi) Be a good listener and show impartiality;

(vii) Develop good rapport with members of the family and use safety valve technique;

(viii) Use visual observation;

(ix) Try conflict resolution techniques; and

(x) Exhibit professional image.

Supreme Court, in Lachhama Devi *vs* State of Rajasthan AIR 1988 SC 1985 and in Joint Women Programme *vs* State of Rajasthan AIR 1987 SC 2060 noted that in many cases of dowry death, investigations made by the police were totally inadequate. About the role of judiciary, the Supreme Court (in Kundubala Subrahmanayam *vs* State of Andhra Pradesh (1993) 2 SC 684-700-702 has observed : "The role of courts assumes greater importance and it is expected that the courts would deal with dowry death cases in a more realistic manner and not allow the criminals to escape on account of procedural technicalities or insignificant lacunae in the evidence, as otherwise the criminals would receive encouragement and victims of crime would be totally discouraged by the crime going unpunished. The courts are expected to be sensitive to cases involving crime against women". Realising the need for a collective social action against domestic crimes, the Supreme Court observed : "Awakening of the collective conscience is the need of the day Change of hearts and attitude is what is needed .... Laws are not enough to combat the evil. A wider social movement of educating women of their rights to conquer menace is what is needed." Kundubala *vs* State of Andhra Pradesh (1993) 2 SCC 684, 700-702.

Concluding Remarks

There is a need for a well-planned and clear policy regarding devising ways to control domestic crimes. Social control agencies like education system, religion, societal pressure and family system should explore ways and means of controlling and preventing domestic crimes. For dealing with these crimes, a small element of police women should form part of each police station, including those situated in rural areas. Policemen and women dealing with these crimes need to be given special attitudinal training to equip themselves well for the effective policing against domestic crimes. The protracted criminal trial, lack of public cooperation and defective police investigations are serious impediments is securing justice in these cases. Mere laws cannot achieve the objective and deliver justice to the victims of domestic crime unless a proper and effective machinery is devised for enforcements of laws.

Counselling services should be given to the victims of domestic crime. Special court should be set up for speedy trial. Publicity campaigns to educate women and children are necessary. Mass media and electronic media can play a very crucial role. It may be useful to establish women guidance bureau, juvenile cells, family dispute mediation centres, victim witness programmes and abused spouse shelters. Academicians, social workers and voluntary organisations must conduct comprehensive statewise surveys of domestic crime in India to disseminate an awareness of the nature and magnitude of domestic crimes in India. Legal literacy and awareness programmes should be conducted in schools and colleges to bring about a change in the attitudes of victims of domestic crimes. Present legal system has failed to provide proper protection to the victims of these crimes on account of (a) victim's reluctance to report against the offenders, (b) victim's acceptance of the superiority of the offender, and (c) inadequate attention given to the nature and gravity of the these crimes by the courts and the police. Special reporting centres other than police stations should be established where victims can be given proper emotional support and guidance. The investigation should be made by specially trained police officers preferably by women police officers who understand the psychological, social, economic and situational factors which result in commission of such types of offenders. Facts relating to the psychological background and socio-economic condition of the offender need to be taken into consideration. Special family courts should be created to try offenders of domestic crimes and the procedures adopted for examination of the offenders, witness and victims should be more informal and even sometimes in camera to ensure secrecy. Courts while passing orders, on domestic crimes, should protect the economic interests of the victims. Research should be encouraged and conducted to find out causes, extent and magnitude of these crimes in India. Psychological studies on offenders of domestic crimes should also be carried out. Sexual child abuse instances that call for state intervention need to be identified. Involvement of the community or the neighbourhood in the prevention of child abuse can yield very good results. Greater awareness regarding child abuse and other domestic crimes needs to be created through mass-media and academic programmes. The evil effects of sub-culture of violence propogated by electronic media like TV and cinema need to be curbed by effective censorship and public opinion. Public cooperation need to be sought for reducing domestic crimes.

REFERENCES

1. Dr. K.M. Mathur, *Police in India—Problems & Perspectives,* Gyan Publishing House, New Delhi, 1991, pp. 244-45.
2. *The Hindustan Times,* 13th August, 1994, Servant Sentenced to Death—H.T. Legal Correspondent.
3. Murder of Wife, Children, Businessman to be Handed—*The Hindustan Times,* New Delhi 19 July 1994. Death for killing wife, children—Also, *The Times of India,* New Delhi, 19 July, 1994.
4. *The Times of India,* New Delhi, July 12, 1994, p. 9.
5. *The Times of India,* New Delhi, 23 July, 1994.
6. *The Hindu,* November 15, 1994.
7. Masters, Ruth and Roberson, Cliff, *Inside Criminology,* Prentice Hall, Englewood Cliffs, New Jersey, 1990, p. 380.
8. Lawrence W. Sherman and Richard A. Berk, *The Specific Deterrent Effects of Arrest for Domestic Assault,* American Sociological Review, Vol. 49, 1984, pp. 261-72.
9. Ruth Masters and Cliff Roberson, *Inside Criminology,* 1990, p. 381.
10. Dina Mehta, In Violation of the Vows, *The Times of India,* June 24, 1994.
11. *The Hindustan Times,* August 13, 1994, Fatal Neglect on Verification.
12. Crime in India 1991, National Crime Racords Bureau.
13. Dina Mehta, Family & Home Column, In Violation of the Vows, *The Times of India*, New Delhi, June 24, 1994.
14. Subedar Tewari *vs* State of U.P. AIR 1989-SC 733.
15. Dina Mehta, In Violation of the Vows, *The Times of India*, New Delhi, 24 June, 1994.
16. *Police Research and Development*, Quarterly—Oct-Dec. 1993, p. 22.
17. Abused children turn into adult abusers, *The Pioneer,* Sept. 15, 1993.

18. Somra Jha Nambiar, It can't Happen to My daughter, *The Sunday Times of India Review*, July 24, 1994.

19. Florence Rush, *The Best kept Secret: Sexual Abuse of Children,* Englewood Cliff, N.J. Prentice Hall, 1980.

20. U.S. Department of Justice, BJS Special Report : Preventing Domestic Violence Against Women, Washington D.C., U.S. Govt. Printing Office, 1986.

21. Dr. K.M. Mathur, *Police in India—Problems and Perspectives,* Gyan Publishing House, New Delhi, 1991, p. 252.

22. Gelles, Family Violence, 1979, pp. 32-37, 42-53 (Beverly Hills. Calif Sage Publications, 1979).

23. Sue Titus Reid, *Crime and Criminology,* Fifth edition, Hold, Rinchart and Winston in New York, 1988, p. 253.

24. Parag Trivedi, A Molestor in the Family, *Sunday Review—The Times of India,* 8 April 1990.

25. K.M. Mathur, *Police in India—Problems and Perspectives,* Gyan Publishing House, New Delhi, 1991, p. 235.

26. Figures presented before the Parliament, *Indian Express*, July 31, 1991.

27. D. Martin (1976), *Battered Wives,* Glide Publication Sanfranciso. L.E.F. Walker (1979). *The Battered Women,* Harper & Row, New York; Straus M.A. Gellis R.J. and Steinnetz S.K. (1980) "Behind closed doors violence in American family, Ancher New York; Bowker L.H. (1978) *Women Crime and Criminal Justice System,* Lexington Mass, Bowker L.H. (1983) *Beating Wife,* Lexington Mass.

28. Green Blat C.S. (1985) Don't hit your unless ...... Preliminary findings on normative support for use of physical force by husbands victimology 10(1-4) 221-41.

29. Ram Ahuja, *Crime Against Women,* (1978), Rawat Publications, Jaipur, India.

30. Noor Homanned (1984), Battered wives—A study of socially and economically backward people of slum areas, *Indian Journal of Criminology* 12(2)-102-7.

31. *Indian Express* (1985)—Wife forgives an unworthy husband—May 8, 1985.
32. Ram Ahuja, *Crime Against Women*, 1987, p. 8.
33. *The Times of India* (Ahmedabad).
34. (a)—Edwin-H-Sulherland and Donald R. Cressey, *Criminology* J.B. Lippin Cott Company, Phila-dilphia,Tenth Edition, 1978, p. 174.
35. Marwin E. Wolfgang and Franco Ferracuti, The Sub-culture of violence—Towards an Integrated Theory in Criminology, London, Social Science Paperbacks, 1967, pp. 153-63.
36. D. Finkelhor (1986), A source book on child sexual abuse; Beverly Hills, Calif Sage.
37. Clife R. Hollin, Psychology and Crime—An introduction to criminological psychology, Routledge, London, 1989, p. 97.
38. For details and further study refer Freund, K (1967), Diagnosing homo or heterosexuality and erotic age preference by means of a psychological test, Behaviour Research and Theraphy 5-209-28; Freund D and Langevin R (1976) B/Sexuality in homosexual pedophilia—Archives of Sexual Behaviour 5-415-23.
39. Samora Jha Nambiar, It can't happen to my daughter, *The Sunday Times of India Review,* July 24, 1994.
40. H.C. Baveja, Removing the Stigma of child labour, *Times of India,* 20 July 1994.
41. Promilla Kalha, Behind the Scene—Better Deal for Women, *The Hindustan Times*, New Delhi, March 7, 1988.
42. GOI Ministry of Human Resource Development (Deptt. of Women and Child Development), Development of Women in India—A status paper.
43. Kennith Wooden, How Sex offenders lure our children,Adopted by *Readers Digest* 1988, Vol. 133, No. 798 from Child Lures—Family Guide.
44. For details consult, K.M. Mathur, *Police in India*—Problems and Perspectives, pp. 253-54.

45. Dina Mehta, Family & Home Column—In Violation of the VOWS, *Times of India,* New Delhi, June 24, 1994.

46. Patrick V. Murphy, Police Response to Family Disputes in Police Programmes for Preventing Crime and Delinquency, Edited by Dan G. Pursuit, J.D. Gerelitti, Brown and Ward, Charlie, C. Thomas 1972, p. 227.

47. Crime in India, 1991, National Crime Records Bureau, 1994, p. 236.

48. Dobash, R. Emerson and Russel P. Dobash (1979), Violence Against Women—A Case Against Patriarchy, Free Press, New York.

49. Adler, Emily S (1981), The Underside of Married Life : Power, Influence and Violence, in Lee H. Bowker "Women and Crime in America" MacMillan, New York. ..

50. Walker, Lenore E. (1979): *The Battered Women*, Harper and Row, New York.

51. Ahuja, Ram (1987), *Crime Aginst Women,* Rawat Publishers, Jaipur.

52. Goode, William J. (1971), Force and violence in the family; *Journal of Marriage and Family* 33, 624-636.

53. Lawrence E. Newman and J. Leonard Slinberg, Consultations with Police on Human Relations, *American Journal of Psychiatry* 126, April 1970, p. 1421.

2

Economic Crimes in the Context of Liberal Economy

The economic model, evolved in India after independence, with its diverse elements, avoiding extremes and charting the famed middle path, represented a broad national consensus for mixed economy. The major elements of this economic model were:

(i) Acceptance of mixed economy;

(ii) Public sector for some key industries;

(iii) Agricultural restructuring with liberal support for rural development programmes;

(iv) National development planning for attaining accelerated economic development;

(v) Overriding goal of growth of national income;

(vi) Commitment to socialistic pattern of society as a social goal;

(vii) Increased social consumption and extension services for the rural poor and backward classes; and

(viii) State's direct economic role.

The Indian Economy has undergone dramatic changes during the last five years due to new economic policy. In the beginning of the 1990s, India was in the midst of an unprecedented economic crisis. Its main components were a critical balance of payment situation and large budget deficits with low per capita income. The economy's full potential was not being used and the economy was afflicted with deep seated structural weaknesses which stemmed from overregulation of economic activity, pervasive governmental interference and a development strategy which was inward looking.[1] As a result, the capital output ratio was high and domestic investment had low rates of return. Liberalisation and globalisation are the two hallmarks of our recent economic reforms. The 1990-91 BOP crisis forced the authorities to adopt a far-reaching economic adjustment programme to correct the serious distortions and reduce State intervention. Since 1991, when the economic reforms began, the former Government managed to tide over the crisis it had inherited but in its place, new problems have cropped up today.[2] It is not clear whether at the time, we decided to liberalise and integrate with the global economy, our policy makers carried out an overall assessment of the global economic and strategic situation towards formulating the most optimum strategy for maximising our economic benefits and security interests.[3] Adoption of new structural adjustment programme in India, with its emphasis on liberalisation, derugulation and state withdrawal and the inclination towards privatisation and globalisation, is bound to give rise to more economic crimes. Though India had earmarked upon a liberalisation process in full earnest, the country of more than 900 million people was faced with immense diversities and problems.[4] The move had released the suppressed energies of the country's economy. It is necessary to build a safety net for millions of workers and poor people so that the process spells not ruination or an intolerable lowering of living standards for them but a progressive advancement. Liberalisation should not mean only the opening up of India's vast markets also adequate inflow of capital investment and technologies. Liberalisation process is likely to increase the scope for more economic offences and white collar crimes. The economic liberalisation policy has yielded fantastic results in the past four and half years.[5] There has been 12 per cent industrial growth rate and a low inflation rate of 6.1 per cent and these trends are indicative of a healthy state of affairs. The 6.5 per cent rise in Gross Domestic Product (GDP) and sizeable foreign exchange reserves indicate an overall encouraging economic situation. Economic crimes or white collar crimes are also bound to increase with the expansion of the economy. A few white collar crimes can have far greater effect on the economic fabric of the society than all thefts, burglaries, robberies and dacoities put together could do. Since the mid-1980s, a new ethics has accompanied the neo-liberal shift in the agenda of the state in India. This new ethics endorses the virtues of individualisation, greed and unabashed consumerism as opposed to the common good, selfless services and austerity in living. In India, crores of public money has been spent on the rural development programmes yet no remarkable change is visible at the grassroots. The liberalisation and globalisation of the world system has brought a structural transformation where transnational corporations have emerged as the single most powerful actors in the world affairs. Atul Kohli affirms that new challenges forced on India reflect a crisis of governability and powerful leaders in India often have proved to be enemies of institutions such as political parties.[6] Liberal economy is going to benefit the dominant pressure groups. This group consists of the industrialists, capitalists, large traders, rich farmers, white collar workers and professionals.[7] Raja J. Challiah Committee on the circulation of the so-called black money in the Indian economy estimated its quantum about Rs. 40,000 crore in the early 1980s. It is estimated that now this amount has crossed to Rs. 80000 crores.[8] The stock exchange market scam of Harshad Mehta dramatised the commanding position of speculators in the 1990s and it led the Finance Minister to admit that it revealed "systemic crisis and failure to detect a scam of such a magnitude."[9] The Ram Nivas Mirdha Committee on the stock market exchange scam of the 1990s indicated many foreign banks for undertaking speculative activities in India. A close look at the new economic policy characterising the present regime indicates that claim for corruption reduction through liberalisation, derugulation, privatisation State withdrawal and globalisation are not only exaggerated, these are also misleading.[10] Tax evasion, manipulation, loan defaults, excessive pricing, etc. are clear manifestations of high degree of corruption in the private sector. The recent report regarding the Reserve Bank of India (RBI) sending a list of 5775 defaulters with amounts of more than Rs. one crore to all banks is quite revealing and disturbing. The total default of Rs. 35000 crores, including those under one crore, defaults of above Rs. one crore account for around 60 per cent of the total amount and that the list includes India's top corporate entities.[11] The recent exposure of Value Based Advance Licencing

(VABL) scam which involved large-scale malpractices around the duty-free import licenses issued to exporters for meeting their input needs, is another example of economic crimes and corruption. The amount of black money in circulation in 1994-95 as revealed by a member of the Parliamentary Standing Committee on Finance, recently amounted to Rs. 300000 crore at 1980-81 prices this figure is more than the advance estimate of GDP figure of 250000 crore put up by the Central Statistical Organisation.[12]

Liberation Spawns White Collar Crime

"The economic liberalisation programme is not without its side-effects, warns a secret Home Ministry Report. The study has pointed to an emerging form of criminal behaviour—white collar crime. The report indicates such crimes have registered an increase in a period which corresponds with the liberalisation process initiated at the beginning of the current decade."[13] Cases of white-collar crime went up from 4942 in 1961 to 26891 in 1991 marking a rise of over 600 per cent. Crimes like criminal breach of trust, cheating and counterfeiting showed an increase during the period 1988-92. The upward trend of white collar crimes is significant in the sense that this is the period when the government started liberalising its economic policies. Among the states, Gujarat was the home to the maximum increase in the incidence of white collar crime during the period 1988-92. Gujarat with 2317 reported cases of white, collar crime in 1988 accounted for less than 5.6 per cent of the total cases registered in the country. In 1992 Gujarat saw 7022 cases of white collar crime registered under this category. The CBI is probably the most important agency that has a special wing to deal with economic crimes. The incidence of white collar crime is more significant in states known for rapid industrialisation. Gujarat, Rajasthan and Karnataka are favourites with industrialists and investors and these states accounted for 73.2 per cent of the increase in the incidence of white collar crime during the period 1988-92. Defrauding nationalised banks has become a fine art in India with 27317 cases involving Rs. 707.14 crores being registered between 1976 and 1993.[14] The following table indicates the number of bank frauds which were noted during the period of 1991 to March 1993.

Bank Frauds

Year	*No. of frauds*	*Amount involved (Rs. in Lakhs)*
1991	996	4960.14
1992	1063	13425.38
1993 (Upto March)	340	1129.00

According to RBI officials, frauds are generally committed in the areas of misappropriation of cash/remittances, fraudulent encashment of negotiable instruments, withdrawal through forgery, misutilization of discretionary limits, non-observance of prescribed norms in granting credit facilities, opening/issue of letters of credit, bank guarantees and foreign exchange dealings. With more liberalisation and opening of the economy the following economic offences increase in the society.

(i) Hoarding, smuggling and black marketing in essential commodities.

(ii) Contravention of controls and regulatory measures regarding industry and agricultural sector.

(iii) Crimes dealing with spurious drugs and drug addiction.

(iv) Defalcation and misappropriation of amounts of subsidies in cooperative societies and in banks.

(v) Evasion of taxes, foreign exchange regulations, cases under the Customs Act, the Central Excise Act, Income Tax Act, Gold Control Rules and similar other economic offences.

(vi) Corruption, misuse of Govt. authority, manipulation of stocks and shares, profiteering.[15]

Types and Categories of Economic Crimes

The concept of economic crime can be traced in The Bhagavadgita:

"लोभः प्रवृत्तिरारम्भः कर्मणामशमः स्पृहा ।
रजस्येतानि जायन्ते विवृद्धे भरतर्षभ ॥"
अध्याय १४, श्लोक १२

(With the preponderance of Rajas (passion) O Best of the Bharatas (Arjuna), greed, inactivity, undertaking of action with an interested motive, restlessness and a thirst for enjoyment make their appearance.)

Generally criminologists have termed economic crime as white collar crime. Criminologists Johnson and Donglas in their famous work *Crime at the Top* have given the following definition :

"White collar crime is an illegal act or series of illegal acts committed by non-physical means and by concealment or guile, to obtain money or property, to avoid the payment or loss of money or property or to obtain business or personal advantage." Money laundering can occur in various guises and can be conducted through any form of business enterprise that has the potential to receive significant quantities of currency legitimately as part of its normal operations. Money laundering techniques vary in sophistication depending upon the criminal's ultimate objective. Money laundering is an economic crime related to foreign currency manipulations. Economic crimes have a much wider canvas and have tremendous varieties. Economic crimes can, however, for purpose of this study, be broadly categorised as under :

(1) Abuse of official authority for granting favours and taking pecuniary benefits; corruption, bribery and other connected activities;

(2) Banking, commercial and insurance frauds;

(3) Tax and duty evasions and smuggling;

(4) Counterfeiting currency notes and coins;

(5) Forgery of documents, criminal misappropriation and criminal breach of trust;

(6) Hoarding and black marketing of statutorily controlled items;

(7) Cheating and chit fund frauds;

(8) Smuggling and foreign exchange violations including import-export violations; under invoicing of exports and under/over invoicing of imports;

(9) Illegal antique deals;

(10) Trafficking in drugs and money laundering of the proceeds.

(11) Hawala transactions racket (compensatory payment) in violation of foreign exchange regulations.

(12) Violations of industrial labour and environmental regulations for economic gains;

(13) Tax and duty evasions including evasion of excise duty, income tax, etc;

(14) Concealment of assets in insolvency proceedings;

(15) Any other illegal act to obtain money or property or economic gains wrongfully or to avoid the payment of legal dues or to retain money or property wrongfully.

(16) Obtaining unaccounted cash and donations for so called election expenses;

(17) Manipulation of accounts, including extinguishing of capital reserves before liquidation of companies or setting of *benami* sole-selling agents;

(18) Theft of power and water, particularly organised cases involving large scale and continued pilferage.

(19) Misappropriation of agricultural and industrial subsidies.

(20) "Any other offences calculated to prevent or obstruct the economic development of the country or endanger its economic growth."[16]

The Present Scenario of Economic Offences

If we analyse economic crimes in India we find that cases of corruption are rapidly increasing in Indian society. In 1993, 1282 cases were registered by the CBI and 1387 cases were investigated during the year. During 1993, 302 persons were arrested in cognizable offences under the prevention of corruption act. In 1993, there were 9478 cases under the various offences relating to foreign exchange regulation act 1973 pending for investigation and 852 cases were sent for trial during the year 1993 on completion of investigation. As regards offences under Income Tax Act during 1993-94 financial year 5026 searches were conducted and assets worth Rs. 396.46 crores were seized by the Ministry of Finance, Central Board of Direct Taxes. During the year 1993-94, 933 number of prosecutions were decided and there were 50 number of convictions under direct taxes enactments. Under the Customs Act, 1962, 1234 peoples were arrested and 679 people were prosecuted under Customs Act 1962 by the Directorate of Revenue Intelligence. Under COFEPOSA Act 1974, 555 detention orders were issued and 372 persons were actually detained. Similarly under PIT (NDPS) Act 1988, 124 detention orders were issued and 96 persons were actually detained during the year 1993. During 1993, 350 persons were convicted under Customs Act 1962 while 274 people were acquitted. In the year 1993, 13723 persons were arrested under Narcotic Drugs Act.

In economic crimes, individuals or persons are generally not the victims; it is generally against the society at large. In many economic crimes there is no specific victim who would complain. Import of goods by over invoicing and underinvoicing, tax and duty evasions, foreign exchange violations including Hawala transactions, bank frauds, smuggling of goods, narcotics and gold, etc., are examples of such economic crimes. Economic offenders are mafia gangs who select crimes which involve high stakes but the smallest danger of detection and identification and against which the ultimate victims are least likely to fight. Economic crimes transcend barriers of sex, status and nationality and are democratic in nature. These crimes are generally white collar crimes which are a class apart because the administrative, investigative, legal and judicial procedures for many of them, have been different from the procedures for other rapidly violations of criminal law. Edwin H. Sutherland, in December 1939 in the presidential address before the American Sociological Society, said : "White collar crime is committed by persons of respectability and social status in the course of their occupation." However during the last four decades, powerful mafia groups and criminal syndicates have emerged all over the world who commit economic crimes. In economic offences, the violations of laws by the offenders are complex and their effect diffused. Many business companies commit economic crimes by various modus operandi. The following modus operandi have come to notice in respect of economic offences committed by directors of companies in India :

(a) Manipulation of accounts, including by transfer of funds among group companies *inter se*, forgery of vouchers.

(b) Extinguishing capital reserves and other funds before liquidating companies.

(c) Showing false purchase of raw material and other items. Another variation of this is excess payment to suppliers and sharing the diverted funds with such suppliers.

(d) Setting be-naming sole selling agents with a view to showing reduced profit for the company and diverting the excess profit to such benami agents, who are generally relatives or close friends of the active directors.

(e) Use of company funds to seize control of other companies.

(f) Obtaining loans from banks and the public either without security or on the basis of false/inflated security.

(g) Evasion of excise duty, income tax and so on.

(h) Illegal sale of import licence or import material in the black market."[17]

In 1988, the Bofors gun deal was alleged to have received kickbacks in the award of 1600 crore defence contract. This marks an important landmark in the history of economic crimes in India.

Economic Crimes Reported by National Press :

Some case studies

There are increasing instances of "changing contours of crimination"[18] in the contemporary Indian society. The effects of corruption in a developing nation[19] can be noticed in various security scandals.[20] Black money has entered Indian economy in a big way and all over India crime syndicates have become a law into themselves.[21] The author has selected just a few newspaper reports to bring out how economic offences are increasing in our society. There have been complaints of Ministry of Urban Development extorting bribe amounting to Rs. 40000 each for allotment of 10 government quarters. (*The Times of India*, July 21, 1995). Life Insurance Corporation of India, is riddles with a racket involving fraud to the extent of billions of rupees every year as a result of which development officers, medical officers, banks and LIC bureaucracy fatten their wallets year after year while LIC incurs heavy losses. (*Asian Age*, June

22, 1995). Voluntary Organisations connected with Council for Advancement of People's Action on Rural Technology (CAPART) take bribes to clear application for funds and recently 700 have been black-listed for economic crimes. (*The Telegraph*, July 1, 1995).

(1) The Jain Hawala Case and Involvcment of the Politicians

The Jain Hawala Case is concerned with illegal transfer of nearly 48 crores to S.K. Jain in his multi-crore pay-offs to politicians and bureaucrats. Directorate of Enforcement and CBI are dealing with the case. When this case first surfaced four years ago it appeared that the sheaf of rough papers and diaries listing payments to 115 politicians and bureaucrats was a big success for investigators. So far CBI has chargesheeted only eleven retired bureaucrats from public sector undertakings apart from the Jains.[22] This was part of a larger, international chain involving illegal transfer of money, stands established beyond doubt by both the CBI and Directorate of Enforcement. The CBI's flow chart of money-transactions totalling Rs. 65 crore is given on the next page in a tabular form.

Doordarshan News on 16th January, 1996 reported that three Cabinet Ministers namely Shri Vidhyacharan Shukla, Shri Balram Jakhar and Shri Madhav Rao Scindia were involved in Hawala racket. There were names of seven other politicians including Parliament Opposition Leader for BJP Shri L.K. Advani. CBI approached Supreme Court to permit them to proceed against these politicians and Cabinet Ministers. Shri L.K. Advani, BJP Supremo tendered his resignation from Opposition (Parliament) leadership. These reports indicates that there is criminalisation of politics and very high politicians of various political parties are involved in economic crimes.[23]

(2) 30 Held in Multi-crore Land Scam

Thane unit of the Anti-Corruption Bureau (ACB) on January 5, 1995 unearthed a multi-crore land scam in the city (Maharashtra State) and registered cases of criminal offences against 30 persons including the former Thane District Collector and Konkan Divisional Commissioner G.B. Pingulkar. In the present case, the money involved is said to be running into several crores and huge housing complex of about thirteen buildings housing 368 flats.[24]

CBI's Flow Chart of Money Transactions (Totalling Rs. 65 Crore)

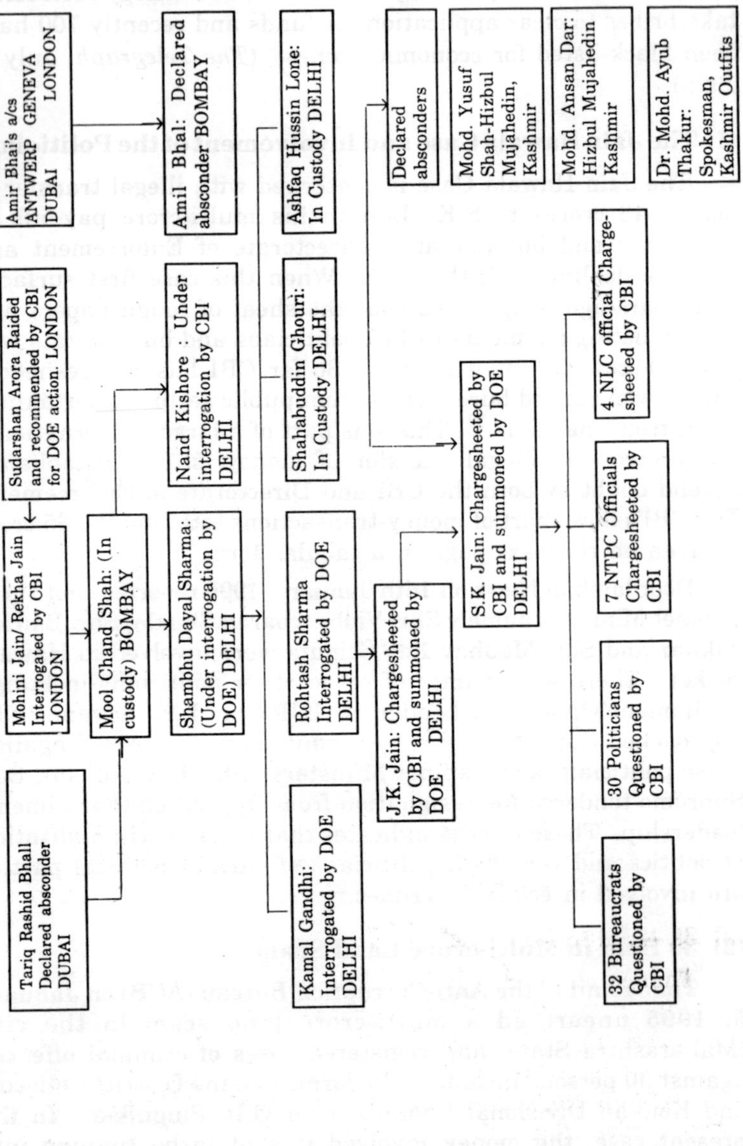

(3) CAG Indicts Bihar Welfare Deptt. for Fund's Abuse

The Comptroller and Auditor General of India has indicted Bihar's Health and Family Welfare Department for gross abuse of central funds and indulging in financial profligacy. As a result of misuse and non-use of funds, 253 out of 827 persons were taken ill between 1990 and 1992 and died of Japanese Encephalitis. Despite the fact that IDPL had quoted Rs. 2.25 for every packet of the ORS containing 27.5 gm, the department purchased three lakhs packets of ORS at the rate of Rs. 3.25 per packet from the KAPL. Medicines worth Rs. 12.20 lakh were purchased between 1988-89 and 1990-91 by the hospital from the local market which according to the rates quoted by the medical stores depot should have cost only Rs. 6.81 lakh.[25]

(4) Currency Smuggling

The sharp rise in currency smuggling into the country is the direct fall out of an increase in Hawala rackets, in the past few years. Delhi Enforcement Directorate has made following currency seizures.[26]

Year	*Total (in Rs.)*	*Persons arrested*
1992	1.5 crores	8
1993	1.3 crores	26
1994	4.87 crores	41
1995 (Upto Nov. 30)	5.26 crores	34

Most of the foreign currency finds its way into the booming black market and is later picked by the hawala operators at a premium. Indians abroad are often lured by hawala operators or their agents with the offer of a premium on the foreign exchange.[27]

(5) Rs. 4.15 Crores Foreign Exchange Racket Busted

The Enforcement Directorate at Madras has broken a Rs. 4.15 crore racket in foreign exchange and arrested two persons following searches made in the premises of a money changer-cum-travel agent at Madras and Tiruchirapalli. All currency found its way to black market dealers and in order to cover up the illegal transaction the money changer had created bogus records to show that the amount had been released to various passengers proceeding abroad.[28]

(6) Customs seize forex worth Rs. 7 lakh

Foreign currency worth over Rs. 7 lakh (13045 Pounds and 5000 Dollars) was seized by the Preventive Unit of the Air Customs from Jagjit Singh Sawhney at New Delhi on his way to London while boarding a Kazhakhastan Airlines flight on Jan. 13, 1996. Jagjit according to Mr. R.K. Chakravarthy, Customs Commissioner is engaged in garment trade at London for the past 25 years and is on a business trip to India.[29]

A Survey of Economic Crimes in India

Enforcement of laws relating to Narcotic Drugs and Psychotropic Substance Act and the related offences are dealt with, by various agencies such as Narcotic Control Bureau, the Directorate of Revenue Intelligence, the Customs and Central Excise, the Central Bureau of Narcotics and other Central and State agencies. The incidence of white collar crimes in India from 1961 to 1993 has been given below in a tabular form.

White Collar Crimes in India

Year	*Incidence*	*Percentage to total*
1961	26391	4.3
1971	32323	3.4
1981	39347	2.8
1986	43287	3.1
1987	41615	3.0
1988	41594	2.9
1989	43307	2.8
1990	43594	2.7
1991	49428	2.9
1992	52455	3.1

1993	50846	3.0
Percentage change in 1991 over 1971	83.8	
Percentage change in 1993 over 1992	3.1	

At the end of this chapter, we have provided 15 tables which throw the fresh light on this topic and give more relevant figures. Table 1 gives Narcotics drugs statistics related to Drug seizures, Drug trafficking and related items. 1488 persons were convicted in 1993 for Drug trafficking as against 761 persons in 1992. Table 2 gives details of Statewise cognizable crimes under Prevention of Corruption Act. Table 3 gives details of persons arrested in various States under Prevention of Corruption Act. Table 4 gives data related to cases under Prevention of Corruption Act dealt by the CBI. Table 5, 6 and 7 give the statistics of offences under Foreign Exchange Regulations Act, 1973. Table 8 gives details of searches and seizures conducted by the Income Tax Department during 1993-94. Table 9 gives details of prosecutions under the Direct Taxes. Table 10 gives details of seizures under Customs Act 1962 for 1993. Table 11 indicates the value of principal commodities seized under Customs Act. Table 12 gives details of persons arrested, prosecuted and convicted under Customs Act and COFEPOSA Act during 1993. Table 13 gives statistics of persons arrested and prosecuted by Narcotic Control Bureau. Table 14 gives details regarding enforcement of import and export Control Act 1947 for the year 1993. Table 15 shows details of persons prosecuted for tax evasions and other offences. How far these tables give the correct picture of economic crimes is left for the readers to judge. Incidence and rate of cognizable crimes under Narcotic Drugs and Psychotropic Act for last six years has been as under.

Incidence and Rate of Cognizable Crimes

Year	*Incidence*	*Rate*
1988	13357	1.7
1989	12831	1.6
1990	14176	1.7
1991	20944	2.5
1992	22478	2.6
1993	21887	2.4

The menace of Narcotics and Drug dependence is a very serious challenge to the Indian society.[30]

Economic Offences and their Manifestations in Hawala Transactions

All over the world economic offences are manifested in Hawala transactions. Figure given in the next page shows the Matrix of economic offences related to Hawala transactions. In many cases when the Government of India imports some foreign goods such as arms, defence equipment, or other valuable goods, the seller abroad is instructed to pay the agreed bribe/pay off money into the bank account in a tax haven country of a politicians/ senior bureaucrats generally through a commission agent. Smugglers generally use the Hawala route for drug trafficking or arms sale/purchase. Another important variation of economic offences is an export oriented racket in which totally false or over-invoiced export are shown so as to get into India purported export earnings in foreign earnings in foreign exchange to justify (or account for) duty free imports of raw material made by the same exporter earlier. In this system the advance licences facility is abused. In this racket the importer abroad has necessarily to collude with the exporter in India. Hawala transactions are done by doctors, engineers, computer professionals, industrialists, tourists and non-resident Indians with a view to either get more foreign currency or transmit money into India unauthorised with criminal intentions of violating the Foreign Exchange Regulations.

Matrix of Economic Offences Related to HAWALA Transactions

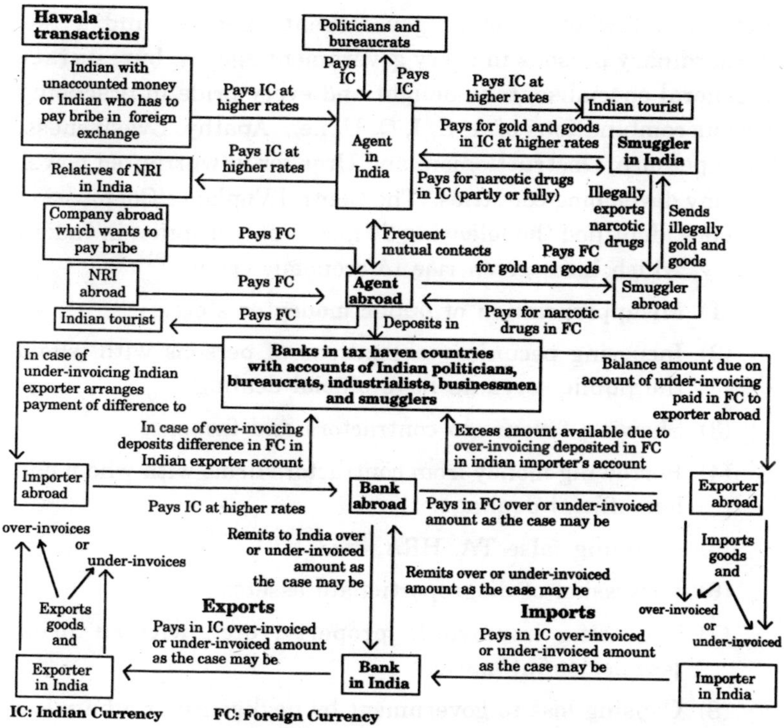

Some Tax Haven countries:

The Bahamas, Bahrain, Bermyda, British Islands (Anguilla, Antigua, British Antilles, **British Virgin Islands**, Cayman Island, Monleserrat, Nevis, St. Lucia, St. Vincent), Channel Islands, Costa Rica, **Liberia**, **Antilles**, Liechtenstein, Luxembourg, Netherlands, Panama and Switzerland.

Violations of sections 8 and/or 9 of the Foreign Regulation Act 1973	Violations of Indian Penal Code Sections 120 B (criminal conspiracy) 420 (cheating) 409 (criminal Breach of trust) 467 (forgery of valuable security)	Violations of preven-tion of corruption Act 1988
Section 624 of the Companies Act 1956		Violations under Income Tax Act 1961

Corruption : An Increasing Economic Crime

"Speed Money", or "Greasing the palm" or "kickback" or "pay-off" or "scaming" are more fashionable terms today. Adultering life-saving drugs, selling state secrets, using sub-standard material in building dams, flyovers, high rise complexes, etc., to the detriment of the society are instances which can be multiplied. Barring a few exceptional government agencies and a few extraordinary persons in every government agency, bureaucracy in general specialise, take delight and every pride in practising various combinations of A, E, I, O, U, i.e., Apathy, Evasiveness, Incompetence, Obstructionism and Urge for unwarranted power in many developing countries. The Central Vigilance Commission has once identified the following 27 modes of corruption in Indian society, which have given rise to economic crimes:[31]

(1) Misappropriation of public money or stores;

(2) Incurring pecuniary obligations of persons with whom the public servants have official dealings;

(3) Showing favours to contractors and firms;

(4) Borrowing money from contractors/firms with whom one has official dealings;

(5) Claiming false TA, HRA, etc.;

(6) Possession of disproportionate assets;

(7) Acquiring immovable property, etc., without prior permission/intimation;

(8) Causing loss to government by negligence or otherwise;

(9) Abuse of official position/powers;

(10) Acceptance of illegal gratification in recruitments, postings, transfers, promotions, etc.;

(11) Misuse of government employees for personal work;

(12) Production of forged certificates of age of birth, of community (caste/tribe certificates);

(13) Irregularities in the reservation of seats in Railways/ Air;

(14) Non-delivery of money orders, insured covers, value payable parcels;
(15) Replacement of new postage stamp by old ones;
(16) Irregularity in the grant of import/export licences;
(17) Misuse of imported and allotted quotas by various firms with the connivance of public servants;
(18) Irregularity in the grant of telephone connections;
(19) Moral turpitude;
(20) Acceptance of gifts;
(21) Underassessment of income tax, estate duty etc., for pecuniary gain;
(22) Misuse of advances sanctioned for purchase of scooters, cars or other advances;
(23) Abnormal delay in settlement of claims for compensation;
(24) Wrong assessment of claims of displaced persons;
(25) Cheating in connection with the purchase/sale of plots for residential purpose;
(26) Unauthorised occupation/sub-letting of government quarters; and
(27) Acceptance of sub-standard stores/works.

During 1993, there were 2483 cases registered under the Prevention of Corruption Act and related sections of IPC. Out of which 1387 cases were investigated during the year. A total of 316 persons were convicted for corruption during 1993 and 1179 persons were reported for regular departmental action.[32] Due to defective and almost non-functional criminal justice system and an all round "Culture of Corruption", there has been a rapid spread and growth of criminal gangs and economic offenders. "It is apparent that crime syndicates and mafia organisations have established themselves in various parts of the country. The nexus between the criminal gangs, police, bureaucracy and politicians has come out clearly in various parts of the country."[33]

India is rated among the five most corrupt countries of the world. Conducted by Transparency International, the international survey on corruption has identified 45 most corrupt countries of the world. Topping the list are India, Venezuela and Brazil. India is in the second category and the countries bracketed with it in the matter of corruption are Pakistan and China.[34] There are various modes of corrupt practices and there is no social space in India uncontaminated. There are many government reports indicating corruption by men holding high public offices in the government.[35] Even when there are natural disasters, funds sent for relief and rescue operations are misutilised and misappropriated. It is very unfortunate that during such calamities and disasters, there are complaints of misappropriation of funds and resources.[36]

Why Economic Crimes are Increasing ?

With liberalism and new economic policy, a new trait of administrative culture is discernable, the existence of a parallel "black administration where influence, favours, money, privileges, misuse of public funds, falsifying records and bending of rules/ regulations play crucial roles".[37] India is today facing a five-point crisis : (i) Crisis of leadership, (ii) Crisis of mobility, (iii) Crisis of focusing, (iv) Crisis of bureaucracy, and (v) Crisis of vision with the result that the Indian economic scenario is full of conondrums—bereft of ethics—full of squandering games by the politician, businessperson, bureaucrat, landlord nexus, no accountability at any level and the commandos and terrorists are ruling the roost.[38] The Vohra Committee Findings made public in August 1995, in a nutshell has made the following major conclusions[39] :

(1) Organised crime syndicates/Mafia have overtime acquired astronomical monetary resources, invariably packed in suitcases and gunny bags, which are used to develop an extensive net-work of contacts with bureaucrats, and politicians, media persons and strategically located individuals in the non-state sector, which mount pressure not to take action against the offenders or go slow in the cases against them.

(2) Such crime syndicates have become a law unto themselves with considerable political clout, seriously jeopardising the smooth functioning of the administration and the safety of life and

property of the common man, so much so that the network of the mafia is virtually running a parallel government, pushing the state apparatus into irrelevance and even the members of the judicial system have not escaped the embrace of the Mafia."[40]

(3) The Mafias, too big to be tackled, have graduated to big business and their muscle power is sustained by their enormous financial power, which in turn is secured by the Mafia elements committing economic offences with impunity. 'The Mafia giants', 'the economic lobbies', 'the big smuggling syndicates' with international linkages, have spread into and infected various economic and financial activities, including Hawala transactions, circulation of black money and operation of a vicious parallel economy causing serious damage to the economic fibre of the country.

(4) Though there is a plethora of public agencies designed to deal with these nefarious activities, they are reduced to ineffectiveness, verging on irrelevance, by means of corruption and kickbacks, as the financial stakes are astronomically high and pressures are brought to bear through postings, transfer, and sharing of the loot.

The economic crimes are flourishing in India and other countries due to the social economic and political environment where organised crime syndicates have acquired tremendous powers and influence. A number of informal methods have been adopted by the resourceful economic entities to curry favour with the political leadership and the bureaucracy at various stages of the power structures. The use of money power to indulge in sabotaging economic laws/regulations, tax evasion, obtaining industrial licences, finances, permission to import etc., smuggling, shoddy construction, illicit brewing etc., led to a marriage of convenience between the wielders of political and economic power in all the developing countries. Emergence of power-brokers, neglect of democratic ethos, absence of mass-based politics, and evaporation of public ethics have all contributed to the crisis in economic crimes. "There has been a rapid spread and growth of criminal gangs, armed *senas*, drug mafias, smuggling gangs, drug peddlers and economic lobbies in the country which have over the years developed an extensive network of contacts with the bureaucrats/government functionaries at the local levels, politicians, media persons, and strategically located individuals in the non-state sector. Some of these syndicates also have international linkages."[41] Unfortunately the moneyocracy has infiltrated into the political system through crypto-criminal methodology and a new dependencia syndrome has come to stay, the result of which is criminalisation of politics and politicisation of criminals.[42]

Economic Criminals Tend to Infiltrate the Political Structure

Out of the top experts on economic crime, Dr. Berry A.K. Rider has stated that once organised criminals cells are established in a country, there is a strong incentive for them to seek to infiltrate the political structure. Indeed in the long run for organised crime to survive and proper, it must do so. Apart from protecting its investment, it will enable greater opportunities for economic exploration on to be realised. Accordingly to the Rider's thesis on economic crime, once the infiltration of criminals and bad money has begun, it is very difficult to remove this cancer. Corruption breeds corruption. Rider asserts that this head of these criminal organisation, through money power, try to build up lobbies in law enforcement agencies, fudicary and bureaucracy in their attempt to rule out the political system. It is the economic crime syndicates who sake in huge profits through either gold or arms smuggling drug trafficking or through commissions from foreign contracts who finance misguided and frustrated politicians and the purchase of arms and ammunition for carrying out terrorist and subversive activities for disturbing governments established through constitutional process.

Role of Enforcement Agencies

Indian policemen are unfortunately trapped between the outdated laws and instructions of the past and the fast changing socio-economic and political environment where increasing violence, economic offences, disregard for law and open defiance to the social norms are the grim realities of the time.[43] State police, due to its various other duties, is ill-equipped to deal with economic crimes. State police and particularly the economic wing of the State police have an important role to play in controlling economic crimes. CBI with its specialised wing dealing with economic offences is the most crucial agency for investigation of cases relating to economic crimes. The Department of Revenue functions through the following main agencies :

(i) Central Board of Excise and Customs (CBEC)—It is responsible for the prevention of smuggling and is assisted by the Director General of Revenue Intelligence (DGRI) and the Directorate General of Anti-Evasion (DGAE). The D.G.R.I. deals with the evasion of customs duties, the DGAE with Excise duty evasion.

(ii) Central Board of Direct Taxes (CBDT) administers Income Tax Act, Wealth Tax Act, etc.

(iii) Central Economic Intelligence Bureau (CEIB) is responsible for coordination and strengthening the intelligence gathering activities and the investigative and enforcement actions of the various agencies for investigation into economic offences and the enforcement of economic laws. The CEIB is expected, *inter alia* to attend to the following tasks[44] :

   (a) Identification of major sources generating black money; directing and developing intelligence about such sources; planning and coordinating action and operations against such sources.

   (b) Assisting the various enforcement agencies in strengthening the intelligence gathering infrastructure and building up their capability for storage and retrieval of intelligence.

   (c) Conducting investigative and analytical studies in difficult areas of black money operations and monitoring indicators thereof."

(iv) Enforcement Directorate is concerned with the enforcement of the investigation and penal provision of the Foreign Exchange Regulation Act; Collection of intelligence relating to foreign exchange offences; enquiries into suspected violations of the FERA, etc.

(v) Narcotic Control Bureau (NCB) is responsible for the administration of the Narcotics Drugs and Psychotropic Act.

Intelligence Bureau as the premier intelligence agency has been recommended the following tasks:

(a) Identification of the nexus between the criminals/ mafias and the anti-national elements;

(b) Identification of the nature and dimensions of these linkages and the modus operandi of their operation;

(c) Assessment of the impact of these linkages on the various institutions, viz., the electoral, political, economical, law & order and the administrative apparatus;

(d) Nexus, if any, between the domestic linkages with foreign intelligence;

(e) Necessary action to show effective action to counteract/neutralize the mafia activities; and

(f) Political and legal constraints in dealing with the cover/illegal functioning of the linkages.

Research and Analysis Wing (RAW) monitors the activities of certain organisations abroad only in so far as they relate to their involvement with Narco-terrorist elements and smuggling arms, ammunition, explosives, etc., into the country. Economic laws in India are enforced by various agencies and the role of the state police is rather limited. Almost all the economic offences created by special statutes are non-cognisable, that is, the state police cannot investigate such cases without the permission of the magistrate. Notable exceptions are criminal breach of trust, and cheating under the Indian Penal Code, offences under the Narcotic Drugs and Psychotropic substances Act 1985 and the Import and Export (Control) Act 1947, which are cognisable. The following offences under various statutes are made non-cognisable :

(i) Section 624 of the Companies Act 1956,

(ii) Section 62 of the Foreign Exchange Regulation Act 1973,

(iii) Section 104 of the Customs Act 1962,

(iv) Section 279-A of the Income Tax Act 1961.

The major conclusions of the Vohra Committee report indicate that though there is a plethora of public agencies to deal with these nefarious activities, they are reduced to ineffectiveness, verging on irrelevance, by means of corruption and kickbacks as the financial stakes are astronomically high and pressures are brought to bear through postings, transfers and sharing of the loot. There is hardly any purposive coordination, sharing of information and its worthwhile use, common command and accountability.[45] Police have a very important role to play in dealing with economic offences but they have to build up an infrastructure which could be able to cope up with the problems of crime, socio-economic offences, smuggling, corruption, drug-trafficking which are increasing everyday.[46]

An Action Plan to Deal with Economic Crimes

The Eighth United Nations Congress on the Prevention of Crime and the Treatment of Offenders, held at Havana from 27th August to 7th September 1990 adopted many resolutions for consideration of the General Assembly. It recognised that the growing threat of organised crime, with its highly destabilizing and corrupting influence on fundamental social, economic, and political institutions, represents a challenge demanding accrued and more effective international cooperation. It was imperative to launch a major effect to control and eventually eradicate the destructive phenomena of illicit drug traffic and abuse and of organised crime. Raising public awareness and mobilizing public support are important elements of any preventive action for dealing with economic crimes. Improvement in the efficiency of law-enforcement and criminal justice are important preventive strategies based on more efficient and fair processes that act as a deterrent to economic crimes.

In order to deal with the menace of economic crime, a multi-pronged action plan is suggested below :

(i) The Vohra Committee has recommended that a nodal agency should be established for the collection, collation and operationalisation of all information relating to the activities of crime syndicates. It would have to be ensured that the information available with the nodal set-up is used strictly and entirely for stringent action against the crime syndicates, without allowing any scope whatever of its being exploited for political gain. It would be logical if the nodal set-up is under MHA, directly handled by the Home Secretary who can be assisted by one or more selected officers of the Ministry for collation and compilation of all information received from the IB, CBI, RAW and the various agencies under the department of Revenue.

(ii) The Vohra Committee has also recommended to set up a system under which the heads of the various intelligence and revenue agencies shall meet on a regular basis and exchange vital information, without there being any leakage.

(iii) Since the main mode of communication/contacts of the mafias operating at the international level is through telephonic communications, the effective monitoring of the telephone calls made from India/received from abroad can yield useful information and for doing so, the Government should grant sanction to certain telephone connections.

(iv) Since banks have an important role to play in economic crimes, the bank managers should be placed under legal obligation to render reports on all heavy transactions and suspicious accounts to the enforcement agencies. Such a practice also exists in the United Kingdom.

(v) For controlling economic crimes and the activities of the criminal syndicates, the following suggestions have been made by the Director, CBI :

(a) Identification of offences and award of deterrent punishments including preventive detention.

(b) Trial procedures should be simplified and hastened.

(c) Surveillance should be carried out through finger prints, photographs and dossiers.

(d) Monitoring mechanisms should be established at the state and central levels.

(e) Establishment of special cells in the State CIDs and CBI.

(f) Suitable amendments should be introduced in the existing laws to more effectively deal with the activities of mafia organisations etc. A comprehensive review of the existing laws pertaining to economic crimes should be carried out.

(g) CBI should carry out a detailed study of 10-15 cases which would provide useful information regarding the administrative/legal measures which would be required to be taken to effectively tackle the functioning of the mafia organisations and economic offenders.

(h) Legislation should be enacted that defines new economic offences with respect to money laundering and organised fraud and the offence of opening and operating accounts under a false name of individual or company.

(i) For effective control of economic offences, viable remedies should be developed for forfeiture of the proceeds of the crime including provision for the freezing or withholding and the confiscation or forfeiture, of property used in, or derived from, the commission of economic offences.

(j) The transnational dimensions of organised economic crime require the urgent development of new and effective cooperative arrangements on a more comprehensive and permanent basis.

It is generally felt that the criminal justice system as existing at present in India is utterly inadequate. Cases are not heard timely, functioning of the Government lawyers is grossly inadequate; all this results in a low percentage of convictions and mild punishment. Unless the criminal justice system is thorough revamped and geared up, the work of the enforcement agencies cannot be effective. It is a general feeling that field officers of the various enforcement agencies are often pressurized by senior government functionaries or political leaders, apparently at the behest of the crime syndicates and economic offenders. Unless the field level officers are offered effective protection, they cannot be expected to maintain interest in vigorously pursuing action against the activities of such elements. Ways and means need to be found out for providing motivation and encouragement to field level functionaries who are committed to fight economic offenders. Besides nodal agency at the MHA level, at State and district levels there should be a forum for exchanging notes between various agencies engaged in the task of prevention, detection and prosecution of economic offences such as the Police, the CBI, DIR, Customs, Central Excise, etc. This forum would promote free flow of intelligence and information and facilitate better understanding and cooperation between various agencies.

At times delay or refusal of the government to give prosecution sanction frustrates the efforts of the investigating and enforcement agencies. Laws related to economic laws need to be amended since there is no need for Government sanction for prosecuting any economic offenders. Even in cases of corruption cases against Government servants, sanction should be presumed if a *prima facie* case is established. This would require amendment in the relevant provisions of laws. Special courts should be set up for trial of economic offences and the onus of proving the innocence should be on the persons charged with the commission of economic offences. Economic offences should be made cognizable and non-compoundable. Greater vigilance is needed on the country's borders and sea coasts so that smuggling, Narco-terrorism and other economic offences do not get patronage from foreign powers and anti-nation forces operating outside the country. Law enforcing agencies, which are entrusted with the task of dealing with economic crimes, must be adequately trained, motivated and provided required organisational support—special economic wings with special training are required in the police to deal with investigation of economic offences.[47]

Concluding Remarks

On March 8, 1996, the former Finance Minister Dr. Man Mohan Singh said in Lok Sabha that the level of economic offences in the country was not "at all alarming" considering the rapid expansion of economic activity. "Such offences would continue as long as high duties existed". To reduce offences relating to excise duties, the government was extending the modified value-added tax (MODVAT) system to all production sectors. "The government has directed enforcement agencies to maintain a strict vigil and set up their preventive operations in view of "some increase" in the incidence of economic offences during the last three years."[47(a)]

The citizens have an important role to play in preventing, controlling and detection of economic crimes. The citizen is not merely a passive recipient of rights and entitlements but rather a responsible member of a closely bound up citizen body inspired by shared purposes and common ends.[48] There is a need to kindle passionate patriotism and trigger the activism of national reconstruction. There is need to ignite women and youth power in India. Let us begin this operation transformation with our women and youth power whose latent power and potential for struggle have not been unified and geared to clench public life. Centuries ago Plato wrote, "The punishment that the wise and the good men of a country, who decline to take interest in the affairs of their country, must suffer is to be ruled by fools and knaves." The wise, honest and good citizens of India must learn to shed their apathy from participating in the political, economic and social process of our democratic society. Positive panacea for fighting economic crimes is moral education. A climate of character, a culture of honesty and integrity must be created in our society. One useful practical method of putting some curb on economic crimes would be to have citizens vigilance groups at the district, state and central levels. Resurrection efforts are needed through character building by way of rejuvenation of ethical teachings in educational curriculae, control of visual media to arrest spread of consumerism and vulgar obscenity, raising an army of moral managers, curbs on culture of permissiveness, transparency of government functioning and its accountability at different levels and finally the will to act in keeping with the democratic ideals of social justice, equality and fraternity. All possible measures must be taken for fighting corruption under a well-planned strategy.[49] In federal parliamentary democracy, people have a very important role to play in combating corruption and economic crimes. In order to effectively deal with political corruption, India must establish Lokpal and Lok Ayuktas to deal with complaints against ministers and other political representatives who are involved in economic crimes. It is high time that criminalisation of political representatives at all levels be prevented immediately and suitable statutory and constitutional provisions be made well in advance of the Lok Sabha elections in 1996. It is high time that we must call a halt to influx of criminals into the ruling classes at various levels and citizens can play an important role by proper electing their representatives. "We have a difficult task but beyond the difficult task I do see the glow of a bright future."[50]

REFERENCES

1. K.C. Roy chowdhury, On the Fallow Middle Ground, *The Telegraph* 5 January, 1996.
2. Jay Shree Gupta, Mixed Outlook, *Sunday,* 7-13 January 1996, pp. 44-45.
3. K. Subrahmanyam, India and the World—Stability, Security and Development, *The Times of India*, New Delhi, 27th Dec. 1995.

4. Dr. K.R. Narayanan, Inaugural Address at the convention on "Liberal Values". *The Hindustan Times*, 7 January, 1996.
5. Mr. Deepak Banker, Banker Links Industrial Success to Land Reforms, *The Telegraph*, 4 January, 1996.
6. Atul Kohli, *Democracy and Discontent : India's growing crisis of governability*, Cambridge, Cambridge University Press, 1991, p. 402.
7. See Parnab Bardhan, *The Political Economy of Development in India*, Oxford, Basil Blackwell, 1984.
8. See Chugh, R.L. and I.S. Uppal, *Black Economy in India*, Tata Macgraw Hills, 1986. Bagai SS *Black Money in India*: Bombay Bagai Tax Law Service 1991: Ray S.K., *Economics of the Black Market*. Boulder West View Press, 1981.
9. C.P. Bhambhri, Legitimacy and Accountability of State Systems—New Challenges *Indian Journal of Public Administration*, July-Sept., 1995, Vol. XLI No. 3, p. 327.
10. Dolly Arora On the Tragedy of Public domain. Corruption, Victimisation and the New Policy Regime, *Indian Journal of Public Administration*, July-Sept., 1995, Vol. XLI No. 3, p. 384.
11. See *Business Standard*, New Delhi, Dec. 26, 1994.
12. See *Economic Times*, New Delhi, July 7, 1995.
13. Ashwini Sarin, Liberalisation spawns white collar crime, warns report, *Indian Express*, 18 August 1995.
14. Krishna Murthy Andavolu, Alarm Bell over bank frauds, *The Times of India*, New Delhi, March 14, 1994.
15. Dr. K.M. Mathur, *Internal Security Challenges and Police in a Developing Society*, RBSA Publishers, Jaipur, 1989, p. 388.
16. Govt. of India, Third Report of the National Police Commission, 1980, pp. 37-38.
17. K. Madhavan,The white collar crime—The most devastating of them all, *Frontline*, July 30, 1993, p. 130.
18. See Kothari, Rajni, Changing Contours of Criminalisation, *Radical Humanist* 48(12) March 1985, pp. 9-12.
19. Bayley D.H., The effects of corruption in a developing nation, *Western Political Quarterly* 19, 1966, pp. 719-32.

20. Ramachandran K.S., *Scanning Scam how and why of the Securities Scandal*, New Delhi, Neo Pub., 1993.

21. For further study see Kabra K.N., *The Black Economy in India : Problems and Policies*, Delhi, Chanakya, 1982, also Kabra K.N. *India's Black Economy and Mal Development*, New Delhi, *Patriot,* 1986.

22. For further details see Charu Lata Joshi, Jain Hawala case—Gang that can't shoot straight, *India Today,* Dec. 31, 1995, pp. 26-29.

23. Doordarshan News on 16 Jan., 1996.

24. *The Hindustan Times*, 6 Jan. 1996.

25. *Indian Express*, 5 Jan. 1996.

26. *Indian Express*, Jan. 8, 1996.

27. Sanjiv Sinha NRE Accounts being misused for currency smuggling, *Indian Express*, January 8, 1996.

28. *The Assam Tribune*, 11 Jan., 1996.

29. *The Hindustan Times*, 14 Jan., 1996.

30. See K.M. Mathur *Indian Police Role & Challenges*, Gyan Publishing House, New Delhi, 1994, pp. 116-44.

31. Govt. of India, Committee on Prevention of Corruption Report, New Delhi, Ministry of Home Affairs, 1964, Chairman K. Santhanam.

32. National Crime Records Bureau, Crime in India, 1993, New Delhi, Dec. 1994.

33. Govt. of India, Vohra Committee Report, MHA (Chairman N.N. Vohra).

34. *The Times of India*, May 6, 1995.

35. See further details K.M. Mathur—*Police, Law and Internal Security*, Gyan Publishing House, New Delhi, 1994, pp. 128-31.

36. K.M. Mathur, *Management of Internal Security and Related Issues*, Gyan Publishing House, New Delhi 1995, pp. 165-66.

37. O.P. Dwivedi, Administrative Heritage, Morality and Challenges in the Sub-Continent since the British Raj,

Public Administration and Development, Vol. 9, July 1989, p. 249.

38. Anand Das Gupta, Economic Management and Ethics—The Vedantic Answer, *The Indian Journal of Public Administration*, July-Sept. 1995, Vol. XII, No. 3, pp. 309-10.
39. Vohra Committee Report MHA GOI, in July 1993, Report made Public in Aug. 1995.
40. GOI, Report of the Vohra Committee (Chairman N.N. Vohra) Para 6.2(II).
41. Report of Vohra Committee (Chairman N.N. Vohra) Para 6.2.
42. Justice V.R. Krishna Iyer, Ethical Entropy in Public Life, *Indian Journal of Public Administration,* July-Sept. 1995, Vol. XLI, No. 3, p. 346.
43. K.M. Mathur, *Indian Police—Role & Challenges*—Gyan Publishing House, New Delhi, 1994, p. 55.
44. GOI,Vohra Committee Report—MHA Para (iii).
45. GOI, Vohra Committee Report—Aug. 1995.
46. See K.M. Mathur, *Internal Security Challenges & Police in a Developing Society*—RBSA Publishers, Jaipur, 1989, pp. 238-39.
47. K.M. Mathur, *Problems of Police in a Democratic Society*. RBSA Publishers, Jaipur, 1987, p. 240.

47a. *The Times of India,* Parliament Questions—No Need for Alarm on Economic Offences: Man Mohan, March 9, 1996, p. 9.

48. Michael Walzer—in Terence Ball, James Farr and Russell L. Hanson (eds.) Political Innovation and Conceptual Change, Cambridge, Cambridge University Press, 1989, p. 216.
49. For further details see K.M. Mathur, *Police, Law & Internal Security*, Gyan Publishing House, New Delhi, 1994, pp. 147-50.
50. The former Prime Minister Shri P.V. Narasimha Rao addressed to civil servants on Jan. 30, 1993.

TABLE 1

Economic Crimes Related to Narcotics Drugs (1990-93)

Events / Persons involvement	*1990*	*1991*	*1992*	*1993*
Drug Seizures				
1. Persons arrested (including foreigners)	4302	5300	12850	13723
2. Foreigners arrested	234	93	116	144
Destruction of Manufacturing Facilities : Persons arrested	NA	NA	7	NA
Drug Trafficking				
1. No. of persons prosecuted	4299	5546	7172	9964
2. No. of persons convicted	551	855	761	1488
3. No. of persons acquitted	1160	1940	1762	1633
Under COFEPOSA/ PIT (NDPS) Act				
1. No. of detention orders issued	211	109	97	116
2. No. of persons detained	190	80	80	92
Forfeiture of Property				
1. Cases	—	2	5	—
2. Value (in Rs.)	—	603000	888337	—
Frozen Property of Drug Traffickers				
1. Cases	18	8	4	7
2. Value (in Rs.)	17985040	7023158	37026070	904044

Source: Directorate General, Narcotics Control Bureau.
Notes: 1. NA stands for not available.
2. Figures are provisional.

TABLE 2

Cognizable Economic Crimes Registered and their Disposal by Anti-Corruption and Vigilance Departments of States and UTs under Prevention of Corruption Act and Related Sections of IPC During 1993

State / UT	*Pending investigation from previous year*	*Cases regd. during the year*	*Total cases for investigation*	*Cases chargesheeted*	*Cases pending for Dept. sanction for prosecution*
Andhra Pradesh	82	164	246	105	23
Arunachal Pradesh	0	0	0	0	0
Assam	49	19	68	0	0
Bihar	133	40	173	20	35
Goa	0	0	0	0	0
Gujarat	106	205	311	214	140
Haryana	119	54	173	47	9
Himachal Pradesh	174	20	194	34	1
Jammu & Kashmir	347	142	489	35	34
Karnataka	114	179	293	57	33
Kerala	144	29	173	30	9
Madhya Pradesh	547	101	648	206	49
Maharashtra	433	316	749	216	137
Manipur	32	2	34	2	0

(Contd ...)

State/UT	*Pending investigation from previous year*	*Cases regd. during the year*	*Total cases for investigation*	*Cases chargesheeted*	*Cases pending for Dept. sanction for prosecution*
Meghalaya	1	0	1	0	0
Mizoram	2	0	2	0	0
Nagaland	0	0	0	0	0
Orissa	267	145	412	96	78
Punjab	147	154	301	125	40
Rajasthan	382	176	538	120	117
Sikkim	5	6	11	3	0
Tamil Nadu	288	66	354	3	11
Tripura	0	0	0	0	0
Uttar Pradesh	52	13	65	6	4
West Bengal	4	3	7	1	0
A&N Islands	0	0	0	0	0
Chandigarh	0	0	0	0	0
D&N Hav.	0	0	0	0	0
Daman & Diu	0	0	0	0	0
Delhi	71	56	127	14	8
Lakshadweep	0	0	0	0	0
Pondicherry	7	5	12	0	0

TABLE 3

Persons Arrested in Cognizable Economic Crime Cases Under the Prevention of Corruption Act and Related Sections of IPC in States & UTs During 1993

State / UT	*Persons in custody for investigation at the beginning of year*	*Persons arrested during the year*	*Persons in whose cases chargesheets were laid*
Andhra Pradesh	164	156	131
Arunachal Pradesh	0	0	0
Assam	0	0	0
Bihar	86	5	56
Goa	0	0	0
Gujarat	628	283	310
Haryana	408	89	46
Himachal Pradesh	65	25	0
Jammu & Kashmir	672	0	29
Karnataka	NA	NA	NA
Kerala	81	6	2
Madhya Pradesh	210	31	210
Maharashtra	262	4	258
Manipur	4	2	2
Meghalaya	97	0	0
Mizoram	0	0	0
Nagaland	164	159	137
Orissa	413	159	47
Punjab	330	183	260
Rajasthan	0	93	0
Sikkim	6	3	0
Tamil Nadu	97	54	8
Tripura	0	0	0
Uttar Pradesh	38	1	11
West Bengal	14	6	0
A&N Islands	0	0	0
Chandigarh	3	0	0
D&N Hav.	0	0	0
Daman & Diu	0	0	0
Delhi	56	63	16
Lakshadweep	0	0	0
Pondicherry	1	4	0

TABLE 4

Cognizable Economic Crime (Cases) Registered Under the Prevention of Corruption Act and Related Sections of IPC During 1993

1. No. of cases pending investigation from the year 1992	:	1201
2. No. of cases registered during the year 1993	:	1282
3. No. (Total) of cases for investigation during the year 1993	:	2483
4. No. of cases investigated during the year 1993	:	1387
5. No. of cases in which chargesheets were laid during the year 1993	:	595
6. No. of cases reported for regular departmental action during the year 1993	:	596

(*Source* : CBI)

TABLE 5

Economic Offences Regarding Foreign Exchange Regulation Act 1973 for the year 1993

1. No. of searches/inspections/raids conducted during the year	:	1234
2. No. of searches/inspections/raids resulted in recoveries or seizures	:	843
3. Value of property seized or recovered other than the currency	:	Not maintained
4. Indian currency seized and taken over for investigation	:	672.23 lakhs
5. Value of foreign currency seized (in Indian rupee) and taken over for investigation	:	451.93 lakhs
6. No. of cases pending investigation from the year 1992	:	4438
7. No. of cases registered for investigation during the year 1993	:	5040
8. Total cases for investigation during the year 1993	:	9478

(Action taken by Enforcement Directorate, New Delhi)

TABLE 6

Economic Offences Regarding Foreign Exchange Regulation Act, 1973 for the year, 1993

1.	No. of cases pending for trial from the year 1992 (U/s 56 + 57 of FERA, 73)	:	1555
2.	No. of cases sent up for trial during the year 1993	:	852
3.	Total cases for trial during the year 1993	:	2407
4.	No. of cases ended in conviction	:	78
5.	No. of cases ended in acquittal	:	18
6.	No. of cases otherwise disposed of	:	233
7.	No. of cases pending trial at the end of year 1993	:	2078

(Action taken by Enforcement Directorate, New Delhi)

TABLE 7

Economic Offences Regarding Foreign Exchange Regulation Act 1973 for the year 1993

1.	No. of persons arrested during the year 1993	:	184
2.	No. of persons discharged from custody or on bail on closure of the case against them or otherwise and without adjudication or trial	:	184
3.	No. of persons convicted on trial	:	78
4.	No. of persons acquitted on trial	:	18
5.	No. of persons discharged or whose cases were withdrawn or were otherwise disposed of after trial	:	233

TABLE 8

Searches and Seizures Conducted by Income Tax Department During year 1993-94 against Economic Offenders

1.	No. of searches conducted	:	5026
2.	Value of assets seized (in crores)	:	396.46
3.	Unaccounted income disclosed in the statements recorded U/s 132(4) in the course of searches (in crores)	:	448.83

(Action taken by Central Board of Direct Taxes, Ministry of Finance, New Delhi)

TABLE 9

Prosecutions Under the Direct Taxes Enactments During the Financial year 1993-94

1.	No. of prosecutions launched	:	491
2.	No. of prosecutions decided	:	933
3.	No. of convictions	:	50
4.	No. of compoundings	:	413
5.	No. of acquittals	:	470

(Action taken by Central Board of Direct Taxes, Ministry of Finance, New Delhi)

TABLE 10

Value of Seizures Under Customs Act 1962 for the year 1993 from the Economic Offenders

1.	Total No. of seizures (All India)	:	52963
2.	Total value of seizures (in Lakhs)	:	38896

(Action taken by Directorate of Revenue Intelligence, New Delhi)

TABLE 11

Value of Principal Commodities Seized Under Customs Act 1962 for the year 1993

Articles seized	*Qty.*	*Value (in Lakhs)*
Gold	1372 Kgs	5913
Silver	42237 Kgs	2565
Watches	—	139
Synthetic fabrics	—	311
Electronic goods	—	3581
Drugs	—	1581
Others	—	24806
Total	—	38896

TABLE 12

No. of Economic Offenders Arrested, Prosecuted, Convicted and Detained Under Customs Act, COFEPOSA/PIT NDPS Act During 1993

Action taken under Customs Act 1962

1. Arrested : 1234
2. Prosecuted : 679
3. Convicted : 274

Action taken under COFEPOSA Act 1974

1. Detention orders issued : 555
2. Persons actually detained : 372

Action taken under PIT NDPS Act 1988

1. Detention orders issued : 124
2. Persons actually detained : 96

(Action by Directorate of Revenue Intelligence, New Delhi)

TABLE 13

Action Against Economic Offenders Dealing with Narcotics and Drug Trafficking

1. No. of persons arrested including foreigners	:	13723
2. No. of foreigners arrested	:	144
3. Action taken against persons involved in drug trafficking :		
(a) No. of persons prosecuted	:	9964
(b) No. of persons convicted	:	1488
(c) No. of persons acquitted	:	1633
4. Action taken under COFEPOSA/PIT NDPS Act 1988	:	
No. of detention order issued under PIT (NDPS) Act 1988 with No. of persons detained in bracket	:	116 (92)

TABLE 14

Action Against Economic Offenders Regarding Import and Export (Control) Act 1947 for the year 1993

1. No. of inspections conducted during the year 1993	:	334
2. No. of cases pending investigation from the year 1992	:	3406
3. No. of cases registered for investigation during the year 1993	:	983
4. Total cases for investigation during the year 1993	:	4389
5. No. of cases pending investigation at the end of the year 1992 or 1993	:	3564
6. Amount of penalty or fine realised (in Rs.)	:	2827000

(Action taken by Directorate General of Foreign Trade, Ministry of Commerce, New Delhi)

TABLE 15

No. of Proceedings of Prosecutions Launched Against the Delinquent Assessees for Economic Offences

1. Tax Evasion	:	224 (552)
2. Other offences	:	127 (389)
3. Total No. of penalties U/s 271 (1) (C)	:	351 (941)

(Action taken by Central Board of Direct Taxes, New Delhi)

3

Crimes of Subversion by Explosives in India

On July 7, 1994 the Prime Minister of India warned that the nation's integrity was under threat from subversive forces, unleashed in the name of religion and ethnicity, by agencies both within and outside the country with a view to create anarchy and chaos. Calling for utmost vigilance against the threats to destablise the country, the Prime Minister said, forces inimical to India had forced a nexus between Narco-terrorism and the mafia.[1] Even an open society needs to defend itself against those who seek to subvert it through violence—not taking precautions against such individuals would be akin to allowing cancer cells to spread.[2] The crimes of subversion are all those covert activities and methods which aim at undermining the integrity and internal security of a country by encouraging the growth of disgruntled and disloyal groups and elements. Subversive activities are essentially covert operations and often long range and therefore difficult to detect and still more difficult to prove in a court of law. The "Master-agent-Provocator" operates through local fifth columnists provocators, disgruntled elements, political parties, hired criminals, unconscious agents and media people. Subversive activities act like slow poisoning in the body-politic and encourage strife and fissiparous tendencies, foment regional, ethnic communal or caste tensions and violence, infiltrate into armed forces and para-military organisations to subvert their loyalty. Money, arms, training, dissemination of misinformation and sabotage are the common weapons in the arsenal of subversive organisations who want to weaken the economic and socio-political bases fomenting discontent. Subversion is any rebellious activity carried out in a country, organised, supported or directed by a foreign power, using for its own purposes the dissatisfied elements in a society. Open display of propaganda by a foreign power, related to a systematic campaign to help an indigenous rebel group seize power, also constitutes subversion. The modern technique of subversion can be illustrated by the Nazi subversion of Czechoslovakia in 1938-39, its communist subversion in 1948, the American subversion in Chile in 1970-73, Nicaragua in 1983-86 and India in 1984-86 (assassination of Mrs. Gandhi and Khalistan movement). Subversive organisation is often called "Fifth Column". If the opinion influencing activities seek to impair, or have the effect of impairing, relations of loyalty within the target state, they fall into the category of psychological attack or "subversive activities". Subversion is designed to undermine the military, economic, psychological or political strength of a nation. All elements of the resistance organisation contribute to the subversive effort but the clandestine nature of subversion dictates that the underground perform the bulk of the activities.

Historical Background

Subversion, according to the Webster's *New Collegiate Dictionary*, means the act of subverting; the state of being subverted; overthrow especially : a systematic attempt to overthrow or undermine a government or political system by persons working secretly within the country involved. According to the *Oxford English Dictionary*, subversion means overthrow, demolition (of a city, stronghold etc.); the turning (of a thing) upside down or uprooting it from its position. Political crimes such as subversion, espionage, treason find mention in ancient Hindu Scriptures.[2a] Kautilya's *Artha Shastra* lays down in various details ways and means to suppress and control the revolt. Conspiring against the King (state) has been mentioned as a serious crime. *Vishnu Smriti* (VII-18-19) extends capital punishment for subversion and for attacking kings, forts, army, kingdoms and allies. *Kamandaka* (IX-9-10, XIV, 16) makes reference for treason as a political crime. *Mudraraksasa* (Act VII) finds reference of political crimes. Kautilya's *Artha Shastra* has mentioned punishments for setting fire (explosives), *Vishnu Smriti* (V-9-11) prescribes corporal punishment for incondiaries. Katyayana mentions subversion as a political crime, creating dissatisfaction among the constituent elements of the state

(919-52, 955-56) *Kamandaka* emphasised that for the offence of subverting the state there was no other punishment than death. (XIV-6). In *Mudraraksasa* there is an instance of Sresthi Candanadasa being taken to the execution ground for doing what was politically unwholesome. (Rajapathyakarimam) (Mudra VII) Subversion has been considered a political crime in ancient India. There are references in *Valmiki's Ramayan* of Hanuman doing subversion by explosion in Ashok Vatika.

Conceptual Background

The term "subversion" is commonly used to imply "the working from within a nation to overthrow the established government, particularly by weakening it through secret means. Subversion may be promoted by either revolutionaries or agents of an outside power".[2b] Generally in a plural, federal, multireligious and multiethnic nation state, sabotage and other subversive terrorist acts are used to promote the breakdown of law and order as well as to discredit the government's ability to maintain it. During wartime, a subversive group allied to the enemy is often called a "fifth column", but in peace time they are called criminals resorting to subversion. In the United States, FBI is responsible for most investigative work involving subversion and Internal Security Act (MC CARRAN Act) of 1950 is the principal anti-subversion law. The presence of totalitarian political groups (having firm belief in violence) in a democracy poses a particularly stubborn theoretical and practical problem when subversion is resorted through explosives and bombs. A democracy is under no obligation to commit suicide by permitting a small minority to destroy the system by use of subversion by explosives. Subversion in politics means action designed to destroy or overthrow an existing government or its constitution.[3] Most governments are empowered, usually by statute, to prevent their subversion. In the USA, for example, the subversive Activities Control Act of 1950 provides for legislative and executive control of communist movements that are suspected of subversion. In India, the Explosives Substance Act 1908, the Explosive Act 1884 and the Terrorist and Disruptive Activities (Prevention) Act 1987 (No. 28 of 1987) and the National Security Act 1980 (Act No. 65 of 1980) as amended from time to time are statutes under which crimes of subversion by explosion are punishable. The Explosives Rules 1983 made by the Central Government in exercise of powers conferred by the Explosives Act 1884 (4 of 1888) are most relevant.

The National Security scenario is quite disturbing as various special groups are actively involved in their efforts to subvert and sabotage the nation-state by resorting to achieve their undesirable objectives outside the political system. Well organised groups have dared to challenge the authority of the state and have intensified their secessionist and subvertive activities in India. The discovery of ULFA Campus in Tamil Nadu, coordinated activities of Nexalities in Andhra Pradesh and Orissa, extensive use of land mines to ambush police vehicles by Karnataka's Veerapan group, the subversive activities of the criminal mafia gangs in Maharashtra and Gujarat and the connection of Pakistan's Inter Service Intelligence and Jamaate Islami with the J & K militants are all examples of subversive activities at the behest of the foreign powers and their agents. In the present circumstances, terrorism and insurgency are being employed by a "syndicate" of "outside forces" to create chaotic conditions in India with a view to destabilise and subvert the established order.[4] Armed extremism, insurgency and terrorism are warlike activities which are being employed by a group of anti-national people and foreign mercenaries inducted from across the borders to destablise the democratic political system by subverting the loyalties of its people, by sowing the seeds of ethnic and religious divisions and by encouraging sub-national separatist movements. The classic examples of secessionist movements are J & K, Punjab and Nagaland where various subversive groups are trying to "disrupt key elements in an established society" by creating panic and fear through use of bombs and explosives. According to Barry Buzan, these subversive groups target the following basic components of the nation-state :

(a) Physical components—The people and the territory of the nation-state subject to its authority.

(b) Institutional components. The institutions of law, criminal justice system, state legislature and the government which governs the state.

(c) Metaphysical components—The support and loyalty of the people, morale of the people, loyalty of the government servants and the general feeling of security and safety of the populace.[5]

"India felt the full impact of Terrorism in Europe in August 1979 when it learnt with sorrow and shock about the blast which killed Mountbatten along with three others. The same afternoon 18 British soldiers were killed in another blast".[6] In Assam, 34 explosions occurred in 1980 and about 50 between January and April 6, 1981. In early 1975, a hand grenade was used to kill Mr. L.N. Mishra, the then Railway Minister of India in Bihar. In August 1984, there was a serious bomb blast at Meenamabakkam (Madras) Airport which killed 30 persons and injured more than 30 others. The crimes of subversion can be categorised broadly into three distinct groups, namely (i) subversion by espionage (ii) subversion by lethal weapons, and (iii) subversion by explosives. The principal task of crimes of subversion by explosives is to destroy the wealth and property of the target country and to create terror and panic in the minds of the government, police and security forces and the public. Generally criminals of subversion are referred as terrorists who with intent to overawe the government or to strike terror in the people, carry out acts by using bombs, dynamite or other explosives in such a manner as to cause death or injuries to any person or persons or damage to or destruction to property or disruption of any supplies or services essential to the life of the community.

Bombs and Explosives : A Threat to Internal Security

The invention of gunpowder, TNT and other variations of modern explosives has added another weapon in the armoury of the terrorists, insurgents and criminals for subversive activities. As early as in 1605 Guy Fawkes made the historic, though unsuccessful attempt to blow up the British Parliament. It was the fatal bombing of Tsar Alexander II which triggered the Russian revolution, Explosive devices have been increasingly employed for the purpose of sabotage and subversion. Destruction of road and railway bridges and culverts and planting of mines to hinder the movement of troops were common occurrences faced by the Nazis in the occupied territories of Europe and Russia. In Bangladesh the Mukti Bahini brought into use a variety of explosive devices for use against the Pakistani troops. News of explosions in the north-eastern region of India have been on the increase. In Assam alone 34 bombs exploded in the year 1980. In 1981, their number rose to approximately 130 and the powerful bomb which exploded in the town of Hojai in Assam killed 10 people on the spot and wounded 15 seriously. In 1982, the number rose to approximately 200 by June. In October 1983, a time bomb in a city bus in Gauhati injured 14 commuters. On

November 7, 1987, 17 persons were killed and 60 injured by explosion of powerful bomb at Gauhati Railway Station. Around 200 bomb explosions were recorded in Punjab during the last ten months of the Akali Dal aggressive agitation ending May 1983. In May 1982, the PLA of Manipur placed powerful dynamite sticks in the airconditioning plant of Palika Bazar in Delhi but it was discovered in time and defused without causing any damage. In West Bengal during Naxalite days of 1969-72, thousands of bombs were exploded by the extremists causing death or injuries to the people and disrupting normal life of the community.

The making of bombs is one craft which has greatly advanced since the beginning of the twentieth century and terrorists have made full use of improved methods to employ bombs for political purposes.[7] Bombs are well established terrorist arms for subversion openly used by terrorists, criminals and psychopaths. During the last two decades criminals, terrorists, insurgents and foreign-trained mercenaries have been increasingly using explosives, explosive devices and various types of bombs in furtherance of their nefarious subversive activities all over the world. Somehow or the other bomb blasts, as part of a conspiracy to exert extreme pressure for acceptance of wild demands or to spread terror, have become the most natural modus operandi of those involved in separatist or terrorist activities.[8] Forces of destabilisation have been operating in India during the last five decades in a set pattern. On 15th January, 1994, the Minister of State for Internal Security Mr. Rajesh Pilot said, "A well knit gang operating at the behest of Pakistan to destablise the country by fomenting trouble has been busted through simultaneous raids in Andhra Pradesh, Karnataka, Maharashtra and Uttar Pradesh, leading to the arrest of 30 persons alongwith a huge cache of arms, ammunition, equipment, explosives and foreign currency".[9] The serial twelve blasts in Bombay on March 12, 1993 were part of a larger conspiracy to "wage an unconventional war against the government of India to destablise the economy and destroy its secular character by whipping up feelings of the affected community to facilitate the destruction of the country. According to Mr. L.K. Advani, "criminalisation of politics in the last two decades, besides Pakistan's attempt to destablise India, was a major factor behind the Bombay and Calcutta bomb carnages."[10] Subversive sabotage through explosion not only undermine the country's production, economy and morale but also inhibit the general helplessness of the masses.[11] The Air India's Boeing 747, Kanishka plunged into the Atlantic Ocean, as a result of subversion by terrorists who implanted explosives on June 23, 1985 resulting in death of 329 persons.[12] India has witnessed crimes of subversion by explosives during the last four decades in many parts of the country. Naga Insurgency disrupted rail traffic by planting explosive devices killing numerous passengers and injuring many other innocent people.[13] In Assam alone 34 bombs exploded in the year 1980. About 200 bomb explosions were reported in the first half year of June 1982 in Assam. Around 200 bomb explosions were reported in Punjab during the first ten months of Punjab agitation ending May 1983. The bomb planted near the dias erected for the then Central Minister Shri L.N. Mishra, caused death of the minister due to bomb explosion in Bihar. In an unfortunate incident on April 9, 1993 twenty-two members of the Tamil Nadu-Karnataka Police force were killed when a land mine planted by the sandalwood smuggler Veerappan's gang went off at Plar bridge on the Karnataka side of the border.[14] One jeep carrying the commandos was blown to bits and twenty-eight others, including Tamil Nadu S.P., P.K. Gopalkrishnan were injured in the blast. In Punjab and Kashmir, the use of land mines and other explosive devices by the terrorists is quite popular. On 2 February 1991, there was a bomb blast attack on the then Director General at Ludhiana in which approximately 3 kg unexploded explosive was found later at the spot and 2 kg explosive had exploded. The explosive material consisted of RDX, Carbon and Bunder in ratio 80 : 10 : 10 alongwith PE TW and binder in ratio 85 : 15 with white putty type material. It caused damage to the car of D.G. and both the doors and windows bore splinter marks and holes and another vehicle was damaged, injuring one officer of the rank of S.P. On 7 June 1991, Hon'ble the then Minister of State for Home Affairs was attacked with the explosive device near village Cill district Ludhiana and the explosive material was RDX of approximately 1.25 kg quantity. The author has personally visited both the places to inspect the site of incident. Over the years terrorists have been improving their techniques, equipment and know-how of explosives and have been acquiring more and more sophisticated and hi-tech explosive devices. In Punjab, 1991 was the year of major explosives when a large number of police and VIP vehicles were targetted and damaged through both cordless and remote control devices used for detonation of explosives.[15] In Punjab, Kasmir and north-eastern states there is the special problem of smuggling of sophisticated weapons and explosives of the most modern type including RDX from Pakistan and other foreign countries.[16] The security of any nation is largely conditioned by its geo-political and geo-strategic environment, by its domestic milieu, by the dynamics of international system, economic and social conditions of the state and the value system of its people.[17] At a critical time when Pakistan is waging a low-intensity war by proxy, India cannot afford to neglect the internal security challenges posed by crimes of subversion by explosion. The growing sophistication in use of explosive devices by the terrorists and other subversive agents confirms that the successful investigation of crimes committed by subversive terrorists and other foreign agents demands a very high degree of professionalism. A look at the terrorism in the northern Ireland and other parts of the world will be useful in gearing the investigation machinery to meet the challenge.[18] There is need for a close cooperation between the investigating agencies, forensic experts, bomb disposal squads and the para-military forces operating in the area. As the police and security forces are the first to arrive at the place of explosion, their training in forensic awareness has to be given high priority. The covert action is an inseparable part of the espionage activity.[19] Usually covert actions practised by the foreign intelligence agencies include sabotage, subversion, financial and technical support to terrorists. The sabotages of internal security of a country often operate in more than one way.[20] Subversion, sabotage, espionage and intelligence gathering are all covert efforts to destablise the security of a country.

Subversion : A Part of Game Plan

In modern age subversion is used as a very effective tool for the subversion of the following systems of the enemy state or hostile state :

(i) Subversion of the political system ;

(ii) Subversion of the social system ;

(iii) Subversion of the economic system ;

(iv) Subversion of international relations of other countries and their foreign policies.

(v) Subversion of morale and loyalty of the citizens of another country.

(vi) Subversion through sabotage, espionage and counter intelligence.

(vii) Subversion of the value systems and cultural norms of hostile country.

(viii) Subversion of the law and order situation through labour unrest, communal riots, linguistic agitations, political agitations and ethnic unrest.

(ix) Subversion through demoralisation of police, para-military forces and army through infilteration and other espionage activities.

(x) Subversion through Narco-terrorism and assistance to insurgents and other militant groups. These subversive activities are generally carried out by intelligence agencies through their agents operating in the target country. In India LTTE, Naxalites, North East insurgents groups like NSCN, PLA, and terrorist organisations are being used by Pakistan for carrying out subversive activities.

Covert Operations

The term "covert action" is an euphemism for subversive violence perpetrated by one state against another. In the present time all super powers carryout "Covert Operations" through their intelligence agencies. Covert actions can comprise of the following covert operations—

(i) Psychological operation.

(ii) Political warfare.

(iii) Economic warfare.

(iv) Preventive direct action such as support for rebel gangs and organisations engaged in sabotage, anti-sabotage, subversion against hostile states including assistance to refugee liberal groups.[20a]

Legal Perspective of Crimes of Subversion

All crimes of subversion by explosives are legally offences against the state. It comprises of ten sections of Indian Penal Code sections 121 to 130. Sections 121, 121A, 122 and 123 of I.P.C. deal with waging or attempting or conspiring to wage or collecting men and ammunition to wage war against the Government of India. The subject of explosives has been dealt in Indian Explosives Act 1884, the Explosives Rules 1940, the Explosives Substance Act 1908, Indian Penal Code Section 286, Indian Post Office Act 1898 (Sections 19 and 61), Railways Act (Section 59), Merchant Shipping Act (Section 143A), Explosives (Temporary Provisions) Act 1949 and Damage to Public Property Act 1984. In case explosives are smuggled from outside the country, the conservation of foreign exchange and Prevention of Smuggling Activities Act 1974 will also apply to the criminals of subversion by explosives. The Explosives Substance Act 1908 deals with the explosives substance and there are three penal sections.

Section —3. Punishment for causing explosion likely to endanger life or property.

Section — 4. Punishment for attempt to cause explosion or for keeping explosives with intent to endanger life and property.

Section — 5. Punishment for making or possessing explosives under suspicious circumstances.

Section — 6. Deals with abettors.

Section 286 IPC deals with those persons who show negligent conduct with respect to explosive substance and the punishment is upto 6 months or with fine which may extend to 1000 rupees or with both.

Section 19 of the Indian Post Office Act 1898 deals with transmission by post of any thing injurious, which is strictly prohibited.

The Indian Explosives Act 1884 deals with the manufacture, possession, use, sale, transport and import of explosives. Section 4 defines the word "Explosives" as gun powder, dynamite, gun cotton, blasting powders, coloured fires and other substances including signals, fuzes, rockets, detonators and ammunition, etc.

Section 5 (3) is a penal section which reads like this :

"Any person contravening the rules made under this section shall be punishable:

(a) If he/she imports or manufactures any explosives in such contravention, with imprisonment of a term which may extend to three years, or with fine which may extend to 5,000 rupees, or with both.

(b) If he/she possesses, uses, or transports any explosives in such contravention, with imprisonment for a term which may extend to 2 years or with fine which may extend to 3000 rupees or with both, and

(c) In any other case, with fine which may extend to 1000 rupees.

To establish a charge under this section the prosecution has to approve the contravention of the rules and that the breach of these rules by the accused person. The omission of the words "knowingly" or "intentionally" shows the intention of the legislature in enacting these provisions. The mere possession of explosives and breach of rules by the accused is sufficient to convict him.

Sections 8, 9 and 9A deal with enquiry into accidents. Whenever there occurs any explosion or any accident, by explosion with loss of human life or serious injury to personal property, the occupier of the place or the person in charge of the carriage or vehicle or vessel shall immediately give notice thereof to the Chief Inspector of Explosives and to the Officer-in-charge of the nearest Police Station. Any person who fails to give such notice shall be punished under section 8(2) of this Act. An inquiry into such accident shall immediately be conducted by the concerned person.

According to National Crime Records Bureau 392 persons died during 1989 in India by explosions and 556 persons died during 1990 by explosions. (Source—Accidental deaths and suicides in India 1989 and 1990 NCRB, New Delhi). In 1992, a total of 358 bomb incidents have taken place in Punjab and Jammu & Kashmir as against 262 in 1991. In 1992, 694 persons were killed and 1868 were injured in various bomb explosions.

Major Bomb Blasts in Delhi

A survey of major bomb blasts (1985-91) in different parts of the capital has given below:

1985 : More than 35 persons were killed and about 50 injured in a series of eight bomb blasts in different parts of Delhi on the evening of 10th May, 1985. The explosions which started around 6.30 p.m. continued till midnight. The areas affected by the incidents included the Inter-State Bus Terminal, Sarojini Nagar, Gandhi Nagar, Vasant Vihar, Ashram Chowk and Mangolpuri. There were more explosions on May 11. These blasts were part of a larger series of bomb blasts in different Indian cities that day and were in retaliation of the anti-Sikh riots of 1984. The bombs planted by Punjab militants took a toll of about 80 lives.

The years 1985 and 1986 saw a proliferation of "Transistor bombs" in the capital. This consisted of a cheap transistor, fitted with a crude bomb, that was left in a public place.

1987 : There was an explosion inside Palika Bazar, Connaught Place, and explosives were also discovered outside Palika Bazar.

1988 : There were three blasts. The most sensational was the May 11 blast at an office of Citi Bank in which two people died and 15 were injured.

1988 : There were four blasts. The most shocking was a powerful blast at the New Delhi railway station, which killed more than a dozen people. It was engineered by Punjab militants.

1990 : An explosion in a Delhi-Panipat bus took a toll of 10 lives. The bomb was planted by Punjab terrorists in the capital, but it exploded near Panipat.

1991 : This was the year of bomb blasts, at least in Delhi. There were 12 explosions in the capital in the first six months alone. At least four people were killed and 40 injured (10 of them seriously) when a bomb exploded in the market area behind Red Fort on December, 22. A bomb was detected on Air India's Boeing Emperor Akbar and a packet-bomb went off in a pavement market in Karol Bagh without injuring anyone. A bomb also exploded in the Indira Gandhi International Airport on June 24, injured 13 people, most of them slightly.

Bomb Blast in Delhi

Place & date of incident	*Persons killed*	*Persons injured*
American Airlines (17.1.91)	—	—
Behind PHQ building (22.2.91)	—	5
Tis Hazari Court (22.1.91)	1	53
Opp. LNJP Hospital (25.1.91)	—	1
Jubilee Cinema (27.1.91)	1	6
Nirula Restaurant (18.3.91)	1	3
Mohan Singh Place (22.3.91)	—	4
Shani Bazar, Khyala (23.3.91)	15	58
Palika Parking (26.4.91)	3	9
Attempt on the life of Sh. Jagdish Tytler (18.5.91)	2	35

(Contd....)

Place & date of incident	*Persons killed*	*Persons injured*
Trilok Puri (6.6.91)	—	3
I.G.I. Airport (25.6.91)	—	13
Railway Track, Patparganj (15.7.91)	—	—
Behind Red Fort (22.12.91)	4	44
Arya Samaj Road (30.12.91)	1	1
Mall Road (26.1.92)	1	32
Kamla Nagar in Police Vehicle (8.2.92)	—	1

According to Police Research and Development BPR & D Journal April-June 1992, there were seventeen bomb-blasts in the capital in the 14 months, leading to 40 odd arrests but not a single conviction till date. The only conviction secured so far by the cops is in one bomb blast case of 1989. The frequency of bomb blasts in the capital reached a new high from January 17, 1991, when an explosion shook the American Airlines office in Connaught Place. No one was injured, but five days later two blasts occurred simultaneously behind the Police Headquarters premises and in Tis Hazari premises, claiming four lives and causing injuries to 58 more. On May 25, terrorists lobbed Chinese stick grenades at an election meeting of Congress candidate Jagdish Tytler, killing two persons and injuring 35. The three other explosions, at Khayala (March 23), Red Fort Sunday Bazar (December 12) and Mall Road (January 29, 1992), accounted for 20 deaths and 134 injuries. The explosives used by terrorists ranged from Chinese stick grenades and fuse bombs to improvised devices.

Bomb Blasts in Other Parts of the Country

Although crimes of subversion by explosion are on the increase, some of the major incidents of bomb blasts during the last four years of the country were as under :

On 24 January 1992, Shri J.N. Saxena has called four senior officers to a meeting at 12.30 p.m. in his office to discuss the security arrangements for the Ekta Yatra to be lead by Dr. M.M. Joshi, senior leader of the BJP, on 26 January 1992. At 1300 hours a powerful bomb tore the roof apart, seriously injuring the police officers and setting the timber debris ablaze. There are many theories speculated about the nature of the incident :

(a) Flower-pot theory.

(b) Rocket attack theory.

(c) Table drawer theory.

(d) Roof and ceiling theory.

(e) Time bomb theory.

(f) Remote device explosion theory.

From the study of the fragments and the remnants of the event, no specific conclusion has been so far arrived. This incident highlights the destructive potency of the modern explosives and capability of the terrorists to smuggle such explosive devices "Adlib".

1993

(1) March 12 — Multiple blasts in Bombay-300 killed, 1000 injured.

(2) March 16 — Stored bombs and other explosives went off in a second floor apartment of Central Calcutta in Bowbazar area in which 70 persons died, and more than 100 were injured. Police found another 24 bombs inside a plastic bag in the rubble.

(3) March 19 — Bomb exploded in a Sealdah-Calcutta rail platform. One person died.

(4) April 6—10 crude bombs found outside an East Delhi House, apparently 'planted' by a vengeful neighbour and police has arrested the culprit.

(5) April 9 — Bomb explodes in the compound of the court of District Judge, Motihari (North Bihar) injuring three persons.

(6) April 17 — 13 bombs seized from two widely separate places in Bombay.

(7) May 6 — Bombs exploded in the parking plot of Ahmedabad city police headquarters damaging one jeep.

(8) May 11 — Police in Guwahati defuse a powerful bomb planted near the city police headquarters.

(9) July 1 — Three crude bombs thrown at the Mathura crowd injuring four persons.

(10) July 13 — Blast in a lavatory of the All India Institute of Medical Sciences, New Delhi injuring one person.

(11) August 8 — 10 killed in explosion at Madras in State headquarters of the Rashtriya Swayamsevak Sangh (RSS).

(12) August 30 — Blast in a lavatory of the Delhi High Court.

(13) September 11 — Explosion near covoy of Youth Congress Chief in Delhi killing eight persons and injuring 31 persons. Two top Punjab militants Keepa and Professor consumed cynide pills.

(14) September, 11 — Two railway employees were killed and another injured when a bomb exploded inside the Secunderabad Railway Reservation Complex.

(15) September 27— One person was injured in a powerful bomb blast near Manipur Agricultural College at Iroisemba Hill near Imphal. The bomb was planted by underground Metai militants.

(16) September 29 — 56 kilograms of RDX were seized from a house in Sahibabad by police where two Punjab militants Kuldeep and Deepak were residing.

(17) December 6—One person was killed and 30 other injured in a series of explosions in five trains and a bus. It was the first time of its kind in which a series of blasts in trains, seemingly in a planned manner, had taken place in different parts of the country within a span of a few hours. The trains were : Secunderabad-New Delhi Andhra Pradesh Express, Delhi bound Rajdhani Express from Hawrah, Delhi bound Rajdhani Express from Bombay, Howrah bound Rajdhani Express from Delhi and Flying Mail from Surat to Bombay.

1994

February 7— Blast opposite the Ambala side octroi post on G.T. Road 10 kilometres from Ludhiana left 10 persons dead and five others seriously injured.

April 22 — 12 persons were injured when a bomb went off in a cinema hall in Madhubani town in Bihar. Two bombs were planted by the criminals and the second bomb was defused by the police.

December 19—A powerful explosion destroyed eight buildings including four residential houses in Srinagar. The explosion is by far biggest ever experienced in Kashmir in its five-year period. A ten feet wide and five feet deep crater was created.

December 24—ten army persons were killed and 12 injured when remote controlled explosives, planted by the suspected militants, exploded on the road, blowing off two army vehicles at Bhatakhas three kms from Mendhar town of Poonch district in the Jammu region.

1995

On 26th January 1995 on Republic Day parade at Jammu, eight persons were killed and 54 injured in a series of 3 bomb blasts at 10.20 morning. Hizbul Mujahidden was behind Republic Day blast in Jammu. Two constables of the Jammu & Kasmir Police, Mohammed Amin and Gujjar Ahmed, had planted the three explosive devices which went off. The first bomb blast took place at about 10.20 a.m. followed by two other explosions in quick succession. The bombs were planted at least seven to ten days before the event. There are more than 200 government employees in the Jammu region alone which were identified as having links with militants. The bomb blasts were probably set off by remote control device. The terrorists have used I.E.D. in several incidents in U.P. Some of which resulted in heavy casualties. The most notable such explosion took place in Rudrapur in October 1991 in which 44 people were killed and a large number of persons sustained serious injuries. Timer devices have been used in some incidents. Intelligence reports indicate that terrorist groups are in possession of a large quantity of high explosives and sufficient expertise for assembling indigenous explosive devices.[21] The involvement of Pakistan's Inter-services Intelligence in the conspiracy to blow up trains at the Jammu Tawi Railway Station on 7th January 1995 was fully established by the Intelligence agencies of the State Police and the Central Govt., according to DGP Shri M.N. Sabherwal.[22]

1996

1. January 3, six persons were killed and 34 injured in a blast in Sadar Bazar near the Tonga Stand on Qutaub Road.

2. In April at least 17 persons killed including 8 foreigners and 29 injured when the Arjun Guest House in Paharganj gave

way on April 20, in Central Delhi Police rules out a bob, and insisted it was a building collapse possible trigerred off by a cylinder blast.

3. On May 21, 15 persons were killed in Lajpat Nagar blast, in which 40 persons were injured and five building catch fire. The bomb is suspected to have been placed in a Maruti Car which was parked at the fountain square. The explosion ripped the car and is suspected to have sparked flames. The fire raged for more than two hours engulfed the area in smoke. The NSG bomb experts said it was likely the blast was caused by research developed explosives (RDX) and supposed to be done by J & K out-fits.

4. On May 22, a major bomb blast killed 22 persons and 30 passengers were injured when a powerful bomb ripped through a Rajasthan Roadways bus near Mahuawa in Dausa district about 150 kms. from Jaipur. The bus was badly damaged due to explosion and caught fire.

Need for Professional Police Response

Police response to a bomb threat may require the deployment of officers for searching, evacuation and crowd control, traffic control, suspect device inspection, removal and neutralisation of bomb or explosion after identification, plus followup investigations. Intelligence has to gather relevant information about potential criminals, type of explosive used, type of detonation device used, quantity and quality of explosive, political and foreign links of the criminals and the modus operandi of the criminals. Police must contact bomb disposal squads and seek cooperation of the people to come forward to give evidence in courts as witnesses. There are four phases to a police bomb threat response; information, evaluation, action and analysis.[23] There are in all police organisations bomb search procedures and bomb disposal procedures including search and disposal of bombs in motor vehicles.[24] For reasons of security, details cannot be given here. Under no circumstances should the police officer arriving at the scene should touch a suspected bomb or explosive and at least 300 feet area around should be cleared from all people. Bob Huntley has given a very interested autobiography titled *Bomb Squad — My War Against the Terrorists.*[25]

A state can deal with any threat so long as its security

apparatus including the police and the intelligence agencies are well prepared and unfethered in taking action against subversive elements.[26]

Against crimes of subversion by explosion, preventive security falls into three main areas. These are Perimeter Protection, Internal Security and Vital Area and Personnel Security.[27] The internal security systems provide initial perimeter defence, entry control, vital area protection, use of close circuit, T.V. and other anti explosive devices and education in bombing security. Bomb threat procedures are to be adopted and responses can be any or any combination of the following :

(i) Full evaluation.

(ii) Localized evaluation.

(iii) Personal work area search.

(iv) Security personnel search.

(v) Police search.

Role of Science and Technology

Criminals of subversion by explosion have been using a large variety of explosive devices including very sophisticated devices. The first problem is the safe disposal of bombs of explosive devices to protect the personal and the property around the bomb. In India Investigating officers get the services of the Army, trained N.S.G. personnel or officers from forensic science laboratories to destroy the bombs and to collect required evidence to get required information about the perpetrators. The second problem is the study of the site after the bomb explosion has occurred in order to collect clues which may help the investigating officers to reach the perpetrator and to identify the nature and quality of explosive used by the criminals. A very close study of the explosive device and the examination of the site of explosion can give some clues about the perpetrators provided the scene of crime has been carefully protected till arrival of forensic experts. It is, therefore, necessary that the investigating officers should be fully conversant with the nature of various kinds of explosives, the mechanism of the explosive devices and the phenomenon attending the explosion. Many a times criminals of subversion use mixtures of arsenic disulphite, potassium chlorate, potassium nitrate, sulpher, picric acid, aluminium, RDX and other modern devices. For safe handling of the bombs and for its dismantling, it is necessary for the experts to thoroughly understand the construction of the bombs, its body, type of fragments, their effective range, the types of explosives and their effectiveness, the type of detonation devices used etc. A very large number of detonating devices have been used by the terrorists, insurgents and criminals including use of remote control systems and micro switches. Bomb disposal squads need to be called to assist the investigating officers. However, some knowledge and expertise in handling various bomb explosives need to be given to the investigating officers. Forensic science laboratories in the states and at the centre have been providing assistance to the investigating agencies. The field experience of the author indicates that many times forensic science laboratories are not able to provide desired technical assistance in the field due to the following reasons.[28]

(a) Non-availability of information/know-how from one source.

(b) Lack of facilities for experimentation to clarify doubts.

(c) Lack of authorisation to F.S.L. staff to handle high explosive.

(d) Lack of suitable qualified and dedicated staff.

Explosive division of Forensic science laboratories need to be provided government authorisation to handle live explosives and each explosive division should build up know-how and create facilities for chemical analysis of debris to identify the types of explosives used in the explosion and the type of detonation technology used.[29]

Role of Transnational Agencies

Terrorist organisations emerges for a variety of reasons; they flourish like laboratory cultures of radical chic and international publicity but each group needs its own special cause, ideology, philosophy and modus operandi to initiate its life cycle. In each case the origin seems simple. The combination of a grievance and a vision can make a man throw a bomb.[30] Almost the majority of the underworld characters involved in the bomb blasts in Bombay and Calcutta were Muslims and the involvement of the odd Hindu like Mangesh Pawar shows that Hindus too figure in smuggling fraternity.[31] Ibrahim Dawood in Dubai, the Memons of Bombay, Rashid Khan of Calcutta, Rusi Pathan of Bhopal,

Mangesh Pawar of Bombay, are all belonging to criminal-smuggling gangs and are the underworld characters linked with bomb blasts. In controvertible evidences of Pakistan involvement in the Bombay bomb blasts have come to light following intensive interrogation of arrested persons like Memon family members. Abdul Razak Suleman, Hanifa Abdul Razak, Rahim Yakub, Yakub Abdul Razak Memon and subsequent investigations by C.B.I. Sleuths in Bombay indicate Pakistan's Inter-Services Intelligence (ISI) Agency as the master-mind behind the bomb blasts on March 13, 1993. The sabotagers were trained at a camp near Islamabad and the underground mafia was used to smuggle explosives to perpetrate the crime. Huge consignments of high powered explosives were smuggled on the coastline of Gujarat and Maharashtra with the logistic support from the smugglers.[32]

What really makes a criminal of subversion by explosives ? "Some come to it by chance, some by design," for "wide is the gate and broad is the way" that leads to this particular form of destruction. The ranks of such criminals/terrorists include many types, idealists as well as criminals and psychopaths.[33] In Andhra Pradesh, Nexalites of the People's War Group (PWG) owned responsibility for the bomb blast in November 1993 near the A.P. State Electricity Board at Hyderabad. According to reliable sources a close nexus among LTTE, ULFA, PWG, Punjab & J & K militants has been well underway. The planned links between the LTTE, Pakistan's ISI and support elements in Myanmar and Bangladesh has now been fully established.[34] The main aim of these criminal groups of subversion is to encourage selected disruptive organisations in India, create regional, ethnic and religious cleavages with a view to spreading disorder and turmoil; undermine the administrative authority of the government and subvert the loyalty of the executive arms of the government and the police force. With the rise of fundamentalist groups in Kashmir, terrorists have intensified crimes of subversion with the aim to balkanise and weaken India. Indoctrination and training of selected leaders has been organised in POK to create militant cadres and loyalties of local police and government servants were subverted systematically and specially trained groups organised anti-government and anti-Indian agitations. Pakistan had now gained considerable expertise in launching covert operations and sponsored terrorism, planned and supported and inspired from across the border by Pakistan. This phase opened with bomb blasts, kidnappings, assassination and arson punctuated by violent demonstrations.[35] The world has to be told — and told effectively of the heinous crimes. Pakistan and its mercenaries in Kashmir have been committing against human rights through murder, arson, extortions and molestation directed against innocent people—Hindus, Muslims and Sikhs.[36] It is scarcely surprising that Dawood Ibrahim's name should come to occupy a central role in the investigation of the horrific serial bombing in Bombay. But pointing the needle of suspicion towards the Dawood ISI—Pakistan axes is one thing, using this to tar the entire Muslim community with the criminal brush is quite another.[37]

It would have been easier to deal with criminals, terrorism insurgents and extremists who are involved in subversion by explosions, if they were all merely pure criminals, motivated by personal gains unfortunately many of them are ideologically motivated and enjoy the sympathies of large sections of people on grounds of nationality, race, religion or political ideology.[38] They seek publicity, "the propoganda of the deed"[39] and attempt to undermine public confidence in government, and expose apparent weakness of the administration, criminalisation of politics in the last two decades besides Pakistan's attempt to destablise India, was a major factor behind various bomb blasts in India.[40] The network of terrorist organisations operating in the name of Islam has proliferated in the recent years and there are powerful forces behind it.[41] There is little doubt that several international terrorist groups inimical to Indian interests have joined hands to smuggle weapons and explosives into India. The similarity of tactics and other methods among ULFA, the Nexalite groups, Bodo and Manipur insurgents and the Punjab and Jammu & Kashmir terrorists points towards a single training and co-ordinating agency.[42]

Terrorism, subversion, insurgency and armed struggle require large flow of funds. International connections encompass various aspects, doctrinal, financial and technical being the main ones for carrying out crimes of subversion by explosion. Money comes through foreign aids, contributions, gifts, ransoms, taxes in liberated areas but mainly from the treasuries of the governments who are their main sponsors. The Khalistani/Punjab terrorists were getting training and finances from the foreign governments besides liberal contributions from Sikhs abroad. In 1983, over

25 lakhs of rupees were looted by the terrorists from various banks at Delhi and other towns of Punjab. The latest presumed source of funding for terrorists is through involvement in drugs.[43] On 12 March 1993 serial bomb blasts in Bombay were a part of the Pakistan's Inter-Services Intelligence (ISI) conspiracy to start a civil war in India.[44] However in the wake of globalisation of terrorism, even the technique of explosion or the type of explosives do not give definite indications because there are no longer group specific. During the last three years in the world LTTE has emerged as the most formidable group which has the planning ability and availability of explosives on which it relies and can produce a suicide bomber whenever required.[45] The former Minister of State for Home, Mr. Rajesh Pilot informed Lok Sabha on 14th June 1994, that Kashmiri militants have been carrying out sabotage activities even outside Jammu & Kashmir and there are reports that Inter-Services Intelligence of Pakistan has plans to create violence and subversion in vulnerable areas in various parts of the country.[46] Various terrorist and insurgent groups get explosives and technical know-how from foreign powers like Pakistan. "When the terrorists are supported by countries with diplomatic representation cutting the terrorist's supply of explosives becomes almost impossible, because these countries which actively encourage terrorism have no compunction, about using the diplomatic bag to smuggle weapons and explosives to their surrogate worries.[47] The second source of supply is the theft of commercial explosives from mines and quarries. Another way of explosives is by raiding military establishments. Most of the militant groups of Punjab and Kashmir are getting training, funds and support from Pakistan. The bomb explosion in Gauhati in November 1992 which claimed more than two dozen lives appears to be the handiwork of Bodo Security Forces. In October 1992, suspected Bodo militants had blown up two coaches of a passenger train on the north bank of Brahmaputra killing 25 persons.[48] Large scale training, supply of arms, ammunition, explosives funds as well as tactical planning by the ISI have resulted in Low Intensity Conflicts (LIC) which have been contained by the security forces.[49] The more than superficial wounds caused by ISI's endeavours in Punjab and J & K are not easy to bind.[50] Insurgencies in the North-East draw their sustenance from a hostile China, the present-day Bangladesh and from like minded rebel groups across the Myanmar border.[51] Internal unrest in India has attained unduly exaggerated

proportions bringing the fabric of the nation with serious security implications. In Punjab, Babbar Khalsa group, Khalistan Commando Force (KCF), Khalistan Liberation Front (KLF), All Sikh Student Federation and Bhindranwala Tiger Force of Khalistan were all terrorist groups having training, finance and support from Pakistan. All these terrorist groups have close links with Pakistan-ISI and have been committing crimes of subversion by explosions.

Offences under explosives and explosive substances Act for the period from 1980-92 are given below :[52]

Offences Under Explosives and Explosive Substances Act

Year	*Total crimes*
1980	2399
1981	2818
1982	3071
1985	3373
1986	3205
1987	3304
1988	3712
1989	4322
1990	5600
1991	5447
1992	8899

According to National Crimes Records Bureau as shown in Table 1 given in the annexure, there were 8899 incidents of cognisable crimes under explosives and explosive substance Act during the year 1992 as reported in Crimes in India 1992. As given in Table 2 of the appendix, during 1992, out of total 12504 cases for investigation pending, in 7291 cases investigations were completed and 4460 cases remained pending for investigation. During 1992, out of 17185 cases pending trial in courts, trials were completed in 4773 cases and 12402 cases remained pending for trial as shown in Table 3. Thus trials were completed in 27.77 per cent cases. During 1991, 6442 persons were arrested under offences whereas in 1992, 6942 persons were arrested. Table 4 shows number of men and women arrested during 1992 under explosives and explosive substances Act in various states and union territories. Table 5 indicates disposal of persons arrested under explosives Acts. A total number of 1745 persons were convicted for offences under the explosives Acts during 1992.

Equipments for Detecting Explosives

Today terrorists all over the world use highly explosive items to fulfil their mission. To deal with the present day situation, it is necessary that the police personnel should be in a position to inspect any item for the presence of explosive. Since the policemen who have to tackle such problems are not necessarily explosive experts, some device/equipment which can detect the presence of explosive substances is of paramount importance. Detecting any explosive device as quickly as possible can save both life and property. Various explosive detectors based on the vapour pressure and Ion mobility theory are known and are being used by the police. However, Forex Search Instrument is a device which can be utilized in detecting mines and other explosives in remote conditions.[50] The equipment is also useful for searching and detecting explosives concealed under water upto a depth of 30 meters. This device assisted by a differential field measuring arrangement measures the degree of interference caused by ferromagnetic object which are components of mines and other underwater explosive devices. This instrument can be utilized by the police, paramilitary forces and army as well so that maximum vigilance could be paid against explosive threat. The introduction of this equipment into police service would be a boon to the law enforcing agencies.

Abas Security Products have introduced the new DEMON detector, which is claimed to work equally well in the detection of explosives and narcotics and makes a valuable contribution in the fight against both terrorism and drug smuggling.[54] The self-contained unit includes a battery powered, hand held search tool, capable of detecting all types of commercial and military explosives, including Semtex H. The range of detectable narcotics is similarly comprehensive, including cannabis, cocaine, heroin and amphetamines. The design satisfies the practical requirements in carrying out speedy searches of hidden areas found in cars, trucks, aircraft freight containers, luggage and so on. These include high sensitivity and instant response, in a compact, portable, simple-to-use unit. The operational principles of the DEMON employ gamma ray backscatter technology.

Graseby Security have released a new explosives detector, the GVD6, which is intended to complement airport X-ray systems. The detector has been designed to utilise the advanced Ion Mobility Spectrometry (IMS) technology.[55] This system provides for a greater selectivity and an enhanced sensitivity. With the introduction of a needle probe the unit can also be used with greater accuracy for searching packages and baggage. The equipment, which is simple to handle, does not require a carrier gas, thus providing an advantage in weight. All the operational controls are touch sensitive and a 40 character LCD readout provides the operator with general information including comprehensive fault diagnosis.

As a part of a policy switching its product range from military to civil applications, Westinghouse has launched a new device called the Illegal Substance Detector (ISD).[56] This is a hand-hold electronic/biochemical device designed to detect the presence of drugs or explosives in less than 45 seconds. The subject of a recent field test at a major European airport as well as by the US Customs Service at several border crossings, the ISD consists of disposable collectors or probes, about the size of a credit card. These collect residual particles when swept across any surface, the probe then being inserted into a small, reusable electronic unit which analyses the chemical reaction that takes place in the presence of minute quantity of an illegal substance. Westinghouse claims the ISD to offer many advantages over test products currently available, the device being designed to help law enforcement agencies and airport authorities cope with the huge problem of illegal drugs and explosives. Weighing less than three pounds, the ISD is powered by a conventional nine-volt battery, is easy to use and requires less than one hour of training. The electronic analyser gives a digital readout of the test result and requires no subjective interpretation. The initial capacity of the sensor is for the detection of cocaine but cards are being developed to detect such explosives as nitro-glycerine and pentaery thritoltetranitrate (PETN). Another card under development will detect heroin.

Training of Police and Security Forces

President Kennedy once in a message to U.S. Congress said in May 1961 :

> "We need a greater ability to deal with guerrilla forces, insurrection and subversion, and we must help train local forces to be equally effective. This is another type of war, new in its intensity, ancient in its origin-war by guerrillas, subversives, insurgents, assassins; war by ambush instead of by combat; by infiltration instead of aggression, seeking victory by eroding and exhausting the enemy instead of engaging him ...... It requires in those situations where we must encounter it and these are the kind of challenges that will be before us in the next decade if freedom is to be saved—a whole new kind of strategy, a wholly different kind of force, and therefore, a new and wholly different kind of military training.[57]

The recent deaths of 15 members of police by land mine show deficiency in training and failure of intelligence. Training of police and security forces in handling explosives is important because death or permanent injury can be the cost of poor judgement or unexperience. Training and experience can generate capability of diffusing an explosive. While the experienced handler employing all of the accepted precautionary methods may minimize the risk of an untoward incident, it must be remembered that bombs and explosives are engineered, planned and ultimately designed to explode, and there is no absolute safe method of handling many times. All police officers need to be given adequate theoretical and practical training about bombs, management of bomb threats, letter bomb security, bomb threat security responses and police responses to various critical situations. Many foreign training institutions have developed bomb-threat response guides to assist police organisations in contingency planning for bomb threats and incidents. A bomb security emergency scheme can be formulated by each state police organisation and should be immediately implemented at the time of a bomb threat or explosion.[58]

The Bureau of Police Research and Development MHA New Delhi has recently published a 'Manual on Explosives' (in Hindi) by Shri T.N. Mishra, former Director, Special Protection Group.[59] It provides detailed and systematic information about various types of explosives used by the criminals. It also explains different triggering and fusing devices for the detection and disposal of bombs. The Manual would prove useful as training material for the police personnel in equipping them to face the growing menace of bombs and explosives. Intelligence and counter-intelligence apparatus of the state and central governments must be fully geared and equipped with modern equipments to identify and neutralise the subversive elements of the society. There should be specially trained, equipped and motivated police bomb squads in cities and various states to handle bomb related problems of internal security. Our intelligence system needs revamping and restructuring so that it may effectively neutralise the subversive activities of the fifth columnists by timely warning and preventive measures.

People's Cooperation

One of the most practical way to reduce the risk involved in a bomb blast is to educate people about the bombs and to make people aware of the precautions to be taken in the event of a bomb suspected situations. The mass and electronic media can play an effective and educative role. Media can warn and educate the people not to touch or pick up unclaimed baggage or other suspected objects in public places like bus stands, railway stations, cinema houses, shopping complexes, parks, etc. They can also help the police by informing them about any suspicious object. The national convention on India's fight against destabilisation and subversion, held on May 2, 1987 at New Delhi has called upon all secular, anti-imperialist forces to raise their united voice against all forces of subversion and destabilisation.[60]

How to Deal with Crimes of Subversion

According to Rustamji, India is a very deceptive country. It seems to be weak, distracted, politically divided and split by rioting. Suddenly the terrorists find they have been detected and defeated by the sheer might and size of the country and its enormous security apparatus. The truth is that we have defeated them all from 1947 to till today.[61] The best defence against terrorism, insurgency, espionage and subversive activities can be provided by the people who should never be allowed to be alienated from the government. A unified joint zonal command and control structure is required to facilitate intelligence gathering and implementation of various counter-measures. The current situation requires well considered long-term and short-term solutions to combat crimes of subversion by explosives and other foreign-sponsored anti-national activities. In this modern age of organised crime where syndicates operate nationally, crime enforcement and investigation can no longer be a localised issue. Indeed to control crimes of subversion by explosion and other such organised syndicated crimes, a centralised approach that transcends state boundaries is imperative. It may be politically expedient but strategically unwise to allow local police alone to handle subversive activities manifesting themselves in different parts of the country.[62] We should hasten and come to grips with the subversive activities in different parts of the country in a centrally directed and coordinated manner. In a democratic country having a federal system with 25 states and seven union territories, where subversive activities have national ramifications, their handling should evoke a national and not merely a local or even a state-wide response, in the overall national interest. The present trend of crimes of subversion by explosion may soon need the intervention of robots to handle such bombs and explosives. Modernisation of the police force, improved communications and transport, computerisation of crimes and criminal records, development of human resources and continuous on-the-job training for effective performance are the most urgent needs of the police force if they have to effectively control syndicated crimes of subversion and terrorism.

Behind the crimes of subversion, the international game of destabilisation should be thoroughly analysed and handled the way diplomacy demands. Combating crimes of subversion is a fire-fighting exercise for police and para-military forces, requiring preventive, confrontational and remedial measures. For central police organisations directly dealing with subversion by explosives, equipment and weaponry have to be constantly updated. Obviously crimes of subversion by explosives demand a multipronged attack but the strategies have to be long range as well as short range. To accomplish this, the state, the media and the intelligentsia should create an ethos wherein subversive criminal activities get due condemnation from all segments of the society.

TABLE 1

Crimes of Subversion

Incidence of Cognizable Crimes (LSL) Under Explosives and Explosive Substances Act in States and UTs

	1990	*1991*	*1992*
States :			
1. Andhra Pradesh	276	436	385
2. Arunachal Pradesh	3	6	12
3. Assam	81	75	23
4. Bihar	694	582	677
5. Goa	9	3	6
6. Gujarat	46	59	86
7. Haryana	33	24	32
8. Himachal Pradesh	8	7	9
9. Jammu & Kashmir	945	235	192
10. Karnataka	65	52	58
11. Kerala	92	171	314
12. Madhya Pradesh	496	450	429
13. Maharashtra	212	173	3193
14. Manipur	5	4	9
15. Meghalaya	5	5	2
16. Mizoram	8	6	3
17. Nagaland	3	9	8
18. Orissa	70	102	70
19. Punjab	102	151	96
20. Rajasthan	198	204	234
21. Sikkim	0	4	4
22. Tamil Nadu	437	517	316
23. Tripura	27	24	10
24. Uttar Pradesh	1584	1835	2421
25. West Bengal	171	282	281
	5570	5406	8870

Union Territories :			
26. A & N Islands	5	0	3
27. Chandigarh	0	0	0
28. D & N Haveli	0	0	1
29. Daman & Diu	0	0	0
30. Delhi	23	38	23
31. Lakshadweep	0	0	0
32. Pondicherry	2	3	2
Total (UTs)	30	41	29
Total (All-India)	5600	5447	8899

TABLE 2

Disposal of LSL Crime Cases by Police during 1992 Under Crime Head Explosives and Explosive Substances Act.

Total No. of cases for investigation including pending cases	*No. of cases in which*					*No. of cases pending investigation*
	Investigation was refused	*Investigation was completed*				
		Charge found false/ mistake of law etc.	*Final report true submitted.*	*Charge sheets were laid*	*Total (3+4+5)*	
(1)	(2)	(3)	(4)	(5)	(6)	(7)
12504	123	178	1030	6713	7921	4460

TABLE 3

Disposal of OSL Crime Cases by Courts during 1992 Under Crime and Explosives and Explosive Substances Act.

Total No. of cases for trial including pending cases.	*No. of cases*				*Pending trial.*
	Compounded or withdrawn.	*In which trials were completed*			
		Convicted	*Acquitted or discharged*	*Total (3 + 4)*	
(1)	(2)	(3)	(4)	(5)	(6)
17185	10	2342	2431	4773	12402

TABLE 4

Persons Arrested Under Explosives and Explosive Substances Act in States, UTs and Cities during 1992.

	Male	*Female*	*Total*
States :			
1. Andhra Pradesh	553	1	544
2. Arunachal Pradesh	18	1	19
3. Assam	48	0	48
4. Bihar	1000	22	1022
5. Goa	14	3	17
6. Gujarat	83	2	85
7. Haryana	38	0	38
8. Himachal Pradesh	11	0	11
9. Jammu & Kashmir	26	0	26
10. Karnataka	89	0	89
11. Kerala	420	0	420
12. Madhya Pradesh	491	0	491
13. Maharashtra	142	0	142
14. Manipur	11	0	11
15. Meghalaya	2	1	3
16. Mizoram	5	0	5
17. Nagaland	10	0	10
18. Orissa	110	0	110
19. Punjab	81	0	81
20. Rajasthan	256	0	256
21. Sikkim	9	0	9
22. Tamil Nadu	432	9	441
23. Tripura	18	0	18
24. Uttar Pradesh	2463	1	2464
25. West Bengal	545	0	545
Total (States)	6875	40	6915

Union Territories :			
26. A & N Islands	3	0	3
27. Chandigarh	0	0	0
28. D & N Haveli	1	0	1
29. Daman & Diu	0	0	0
30. Delhi	21	0	21
31. Lakshadweep	0	0	0
32. Pondicherry	2	0	2
Total (UTs)	27	0	27
Total (All-India)	6902	40	6942

TABLE 5

Disposal of Persons Arrested Under Explosives and Explosive Substances Act by Courts during 1982

Total No. of persons under trial including those from previous year	*No. of persons whose*			*No. of persons convicted.*	*Percentage of persons*	
	Cases compounded or withdrawn	*Trial completed*	*Trial remained pending*		*whose trials remained pending Col.*	*convicted to trials completed Col.*
(1)	(2)	(3)	(4)	(5)	(6)	(7)
19994	27	3264	16703	1745	83.5	53.5

REFERENCES

1. The Prime Minister P.V. Narasimha Rao, National integrity threatened, *The Times of India,* 9 July 1994, addressed to the conference of Director General and Inspector General of Police in Delhi.

2. M.D. Nalpot, The Ostrich Option, Ignoring Jobs at Indian Security, *The Times of India* 8 January, 1995.

2(a). For further details consult Kautilya's *Arthasastra* translated in English by R. Shamshastri, Mysore, 1960, Vishnusmriti—

SBE Series, Delhi 1965, Kamandakiya Nitesaren Ed. J.P. Vidyasagar, Calcutta 1875 *Mudraraksasa* (Visakhadatta) KT Telang, Bombay, 1900; *Katyayana Smrti,* Sangraha NC Pandopadhaya, Calcutta 1947; Sukladas *Crime and Punishment in Ancient India*, N/Dly 1977, Ram Mohan Das, *Crime and Punishment in Ancient India*, Bodh-Gaya, 1982; K.M. Agarwal, *Kautilya on Crime and Punishment*, Almora, 1990.

2(b). *New Standard Encyclopaedia*. Standard Educational Corporation Chicago, Volume Fourteen (Sma to SZO) P S —863.

3. *Encyclopaedia Britannica*. Micropaedia Vol. IX, p. 637.
4. Major General Afsir Karim, AVSM (Retd.) *Transnational Terrorism — The danger in the South-Lancer Papers*, New Delhi, 1993, p. 1.
5. For further details consult Barry Buzan *People, State and Fear—The National Security Problem in International Relations,* University of North Carolina, 1983.
6. The Growing Roots of Terrorism, By N.S. Saksena, *The Hindustan Times,* Dec. 14, 1979.
7. Christopher Dobson and Ronald Payne, *The Weapons of Terror—International Terrorism at Work,* The Mac Millan Press, London, 1977, p. 14.
8. *The Free Press Journal,* Editorial—Bomb Culture, 2 Oct. 1993-94, p. 4.
9. *Hindu*—16 January 1994—Destablisation bid at Pak's instance-Staff Reporter, Hyderabad.
10. *Indian Express*, Ahmedabad, March 19, 1993—Advani Blames Blasts on Criminalisation.
11. Dr. K.M. Mathur, *Police in India—Problems and Perspectives*, Gyan Publishing House, New Delhi, 1991, p. 82.
12. See K.M. Mathur, *Internal Security Challenges and Police in a Developing Society*, RBSA Publishers, Jaipur, 1989, pp. 187-88.
13. K.M. Mathur, *Problems of Police in a Democratic Society*, RBSA Publishers, Jaipur, India, 1987, p. 161.
14. For details see K.M. Mathur, *Indian Police—Role and Challenges*, Gyan Publishing House, New Delhi, 1994, p. 306.
15. For a very comprehensive and educative description consult

Decade of Explosive threat in Punjab, written by Dr. S.N. Sharma pp. 75-89.

16. K. M. Mathur, *Management of Internal Security and Related Issues*, Gyan Publishing House, New Delhi, 1995, p. 27.
17. K.M. Mathur, *Police, Law and Internal Security*, Gyan Publishing House, New Delhi, 1994, p. 7.
18. For details consult Dr. B.B. Arora, Forensic Aspects of Current Trends in Terrorist Crimes in Northern Ireland — A paper presented at XXIV All India Police Sciences Congress, March 1991, p. 135.
19. In search of enemies; CIA Story, Norton N.Y., 1978.
20. Dr. P.D. Sharma, *Policy—Internal Security and Developmental disorder in India*—Uppal Publishing House, New Delhi, 1988, p. 7.

20a. Final report of the select committee to study government operations with reference to intelligence activities —VS— Senate Book 1— Washington, 1976, pp. 131-32.

*21. S.V.M. Tripathi, *Terrorism in Terai of Uttar Pradesh*. S.V.P. N.P.A. Magazine, Jan-June, 1992, p. 25.

*22. *Hindu,* January 9, 1995—ISI behind bid to blow up trains.

23. Graham Knoles, *Bomb Security Guide*, Security World Publishing Co. Inc., Los Angeles, 1975, p. 144.
24. For further details consult Thomas G. Brodie and Albert W. Gleason, Bombs and Bombing, Charles C. Thomas—Springfield, 1973, pp. 54-100.
25. For interesting details consult Bob Huntley — Bomb squad. W.H. Allen, London, 1977.
26. Prakash Singh, The Crumbling edifice of law enforcement *Indian Express,* Ahmedabad Edition, January 9, 1995, p. 6.
27. For further details see Graham *Knowles, Bomb Security Guide*, Security World Publishing Co. Inc., Los Angeles, 1976, pp. 15-32.
28. Dr. O.P. Chugh, Role of Science and Technology in the Investigation of Terrorist Activities, XXII All India Police Science Congress Papers, November, 1988, pp. 118-22.
29. Consult V.J. Clancy — (1972) Diagnostic Feature of Explosion Damage, 6th International Meeting of Forensic Science Edenbury.
30. Christopher Dobson and Ronald Payne, *The Weapon of Terror*, 1979, p. 151.

31. Swaminathan, S. Anklesaria Aiyer—Muslims and Bombs. *The Times of India*, Ahmedabad.
32. RDX landed in the first week of Feb.—*Indian Express*, 6 April, 1993.
33. Christopher Dobson and Ronald Payne, *The weapons of terror — International Terrorism at work*. The Mac Millan Press, 1979, p. 17.
34. Major General Afsir Karim, Transactional Terrorism: The Danger in the South, Lancer Papers, New Delhi, 1993, p. 16.
35. Major General (Retd.) Afsir Karim, *Kashmir—The Troubled Frontiers*, Lancer Publishers, New Delhi, 1994, p. 95.
36. O.N. Dhar, The Proxy War, *The Hindustan Times*, November 29, 1992, p. 5.
37. Rajdeep Sardesai, Muslims and the Blasts, *The Times of India*, 10 April 1993.
38. N.S. Saksena, The growing roots of terrorism, *The Hindustan Times*, December 14, 1979.
39. Ernest Evans, *Calling a Truce to Terror*, Westpost, 1979, p. 40.
40. Advani blames blasts on criminalisation of politics, *Indian Express*, March 19, 1993.
41. Islamic links possible. *The Times of India*, 15 March 1993.
42. Major General Afsir Karim, *Transnational Terrorism—The danger in the South Lancer* papers, New Delhi, 1993, p. 78.
43. Stephens Segeltar, *Invisible Armies—Terrorism in the 1990*, Michael Joseph—London, 1986, p. 279.
44. Prabhat Sharan, I.S.I. had plans to start civil war, *Indian Express*, March 16, 1993.
45. K.F. Rustomjee, *International Terrorism: The Radical Humanist*, August 1993, p. 10.
46. *The Hindustan Times*, 17th December, 1994—questions in Lok Sabha.
47. Christopher Dobson and Ronald Payne, *The weapons of terror*, International Terrorism at work. The Mac Millan Press, London, 1979, p. 113.
48. Bodo Challenges, *The Hindustan Times*, 23 November 1992. Also Portents in Assam—*The Times of India*, 25 November, 1992.

49. Lt. Gen. K.M. Vohra (Retd.), Kashmir Ending the Impasse, *The Hindustan Times*, 17 March 1993.
50. S.K. Singh, India and Pakistan. The unchanging reality, *The Hindustan Times*, 1992.
51. Lt. Gen. V.K. Sood (Retd.), The North East—Roots of Alienation, *The Hindustan Times*, 2 Oct. 1992.
52. National Crimes Record Bureau-Crime in India 1992 and previous year issues of crime in India.
53. Weapons and equipment of counter Terrorism by Micheal Dewar and BPR & D, Jan-March 1994, New Delhi.
54. Intersec.

    Issue. Volume issue 3 July/August 1991.

    BPR & D, Oct.-Dec., 1991, New Delhi.
55. Security and Protection Equipment.

    Issue : July-1990.
56. Intersec. Vol. 12 Issue : 3 July-Aug., 1992.
    BPR & D, Oct.-Dec., 1992, New Delhi.
57. Roger Hiloman, two American counter-strategies to guerrilla warfare. The case of Vietnam-in Tsang Tsou (ed) China in crisis, Vol. 2, University of Chicago, Chicago, 1965, pp. 289-309. See Charles M. Simpson III-Inside the Green Berets-Berkeling Book, New York, 1984.
58. For further details consult.

    P.N. Rachhoya, *Bomb and Explosives-Operation, Investigation and Security Guide*, Kirti Publication, Jaipur, 1988, p. 183.
59. BPR & D, New Delhi Quarterly Journal. July/Sept., 1993.
60. For further details consult Daraba Singh (Ed). *Destabilisation and Subversion, New Challenges*, Patriot Publishers, New Delhi, 1987, p. 72.
61. K.F. Rustamji—*International Terrorism—The Radical Humanist*, August, 1993, p. 11.
62. P.R. Raj Gopal, *Not in Isolation, The Illustrated Weekly of India,* August 25, 1985, p. 13.

4

Accountability in the Management of Law and Order

"It is time now to raise more specifically the question of who is accountable to whom and for that?"[1] The problem of accountability in the management of law and order has remained unresolved during the last five decades in India. Effective management of law and order is the basic function of a State. In a federal democratic system, the question of accountability for the law and order becomes complex and at times untenable when some state governments play truant and some petty political conspirators abot and aid organised lawlessness. It is in this context that "the scheme of accountability should be given a fresh look". Historically the managers of law and order have concentrated more on the confrontational aspects of the problem and have failed to pay due attention to preventive, curative and accountability aspects of law and order problems. Administration of law and order in any country developes its characteristics generally in accordance with the values and attitudes prevalent not only in the special milieu which has to be protected but also those of the policemen themselves.[2] The frequency with which questions relating to the administration of law and order are raised in the Parliament reveals its anxiety to establish the position that it is in overall charge of India's administration, free to invade at will, the legislative and executive domains of the state. Law and order constitutionally falls under the list II in which states have full jurisdiction but centre has a duty to protect a state against internal disturbances under Article 355 of the Constitution.

Some of the important cases indicating the law and order situation in the country are as under :

(i) On February 7, 1994 the police allegedly resorted to a lathi charge on a funeral procession and dragged away the corpse in Jabalpur (M.P.).

(ii) On March 7-8, 1994 twenty-five houses belonging to tribals were set on fire and two persons were killed in a village of Jhabua district of M.P.

(iii) On November 23, 1994 at least 120 persons were killed including 75 women, 30 children and 400 persons were injured in a stampedo following a lathi charge at Nagpur.

Even after 49 years of Independence, Constitutional democracy in India is facing the "crisis of governability". The democracy in India can be considered stable and successful when the Governments headed by political parties of different ideologies in different States and the Centre are able to manage law and order effectively and without fear of any serious violations of rule of law.

Meaning of Accountability

Accountability means responsibility for the proper performance of an assigned task. Accountability is an obligation to reveal, explain and to justify one's actions. It refers to the way in which responsibilities, financial or other, the origin of which may be political, constitutional or hierarchical, are discharged.[3] Accountability in the customary sense refers to financial accountability and it means (i) justification of estimates, (ii) the superintendence of the use of appropriate funds, (iii) the device for timing the rate of expenditure, and (iv) the audit and settlement of accounts.[4] However as a general term accountability is identical to responsibility and implied responsibility for acts in the realm of administration. This means that Government servants and bureaucrats are required to do their work in such a way that actually or contingently, their every move or act may be open to public scrutiny. A civil servant is required to perform his duties in such a manner that these can be defended and justified even if brought under the most minute and critical review. In the realm of public administration a recognized aspect of accountability is for substantive achievement. Accountability for substantive achievements is recorded in the annual agency reports and in special statements and analysis from time to time. A more subtle type of accountability is the maintenance in full vigour of the organisation itself. Another aspect of accountability, diffused throughout an organisation, is the maintenance of wholesome public relations, public acceptability of the agency and its programme.[5] "Accountability is that quality of a system that obliges the participants to pay attention to their respective assigned and accepted responsibilities, to understand that it does matter. Thus, the likelihood that agreed goals and objectives will be attained in enhanced". (Report of the Goyal Commission on Financial Management and Accountability Ottawa 1978). Accountability seems to have amendment of ambivalence and it is not always easy to define it in operational terms. Accountability is partly legal, partly administrative concept—a matter of answering for the act or performance to an appropriate authority in an organisation by those who are entrusted with the duty of carrying on its activities. Accountability, it is often said, of the Government servants tempers administrative efficiency either by subjecting it to a detailed parliamentary supervision or to legalistic interpretation in courts. In democratic societies public accountability of the executive is the essence of political modernisation in institutional terms[6]. In a democratic society spheres of accountability are broadly as under :

(1) Accountability to the laws of the land and the constitution.
(2) Accountability to the organisation to which one belongs.
(3) Accountability to the political masters and executives.
(4) Accountability to the people and the nation.
(5) Accountability to the individual's conscience and moral ethical value system.
(6) Accountability to the International Community and humanity at large.

Dimensions of Management of Law and Order

Shri R. Venkataraman, Former President of India on October 29, 1987 said: "Law and order is a state subject but the Centre has overall responsibility and provides the necessary and appropriate help in the matter. Therefore greater mutuality is clearly needed".[7] The concept of management of law and order situation in broad terms can consist of the following functions :

1. *Planning*: Anticipating events like riots, agitations and preparing in advance to deal with events. Planning of manpower, weapon and tactics.
2. *Organising*: Pooling resources and organising pattern of deployment of state police and other CPOs for various law and order situations like riots, agitations, bandhs.
3. *Staffing*: Selecting people for various assignments and tasks, particularly selecting district superintendent of police, District Magistrate or Deputy Commissioner and SHOs, at Police Station level.
4. *Directing and Motivation*: Providing guidelines and policy decisions regarding various bandhs through Internal Security Schemes and VIP Security orders.
5. *Coordinating*: Administrative and operational co-ordination of various agencies like CRP, BSF and State armed Units. How Central and State force should co-exist, work together and be accountable is one of the major problems of today.[8]
6. *Reporting and Monitoring*: Events and incidents are to be reported to the control room and to district, State and Central level agencies.
7. *Budgeting and Financial Management*: For use of CRP State Government have to make payments for each day.
8. *Leadership Functions*: At various levels leadership becomes important.
9. *Decision-Making*: At Central and State levels decisions on policy matters have to be taken.
10. *Training*: Training of the Civil police, state armed police and all Central Police Organisations must prepare them for their responsibilities and tasks assigned to them. Training to all the agencies connected with management of law and order is a gigantic task.

Management of law and order is generally the task of "plural executives". It is basically the responsibility of the State Governments. But in disturbed areas like Jammu & Kasmir and North Eastern States of India, Central Government has a vital role to play.

The Government of India has the Constitutional responsibility to uphold the laws of the land and the Constitution and can even dismiss state governments subverting the laws of the land. According to N.S. Saksena, "the record of the Govt. of India in this respect is poor simply because it cannot get over its own political motivations".[9] At the State level, the Home Minister and Home Department constitute the civil wing which is responsible for management of law and order in the States. According to the National Police Commission, accountability in the management of law and order can be assessed or determined by the following criteria :

(i) Sense of security prevailing in the community and police reputation of integrity and courtesy.

(ii) People's willing co-operation and participation in maintenance of law and order.

(iii) Extent to which law and order is maintained, taking into account the forces which promote lawlessness.

(iv) The manner in which law and order is maintained through (a) use of force; (b) through people's co-operations.

(v) Quality of service rendered in a distress situations like cyclone-havoc, flood damage, famine, earthquakes.[10]

All disorders and protests in developing societies are neither unhealthy nor do they need loyalist resistance by a status-quist administration. Managers of law and order must know when to intervene and how to intervene to preserve law and order in democratic societies. When the conditions of social anomie become wide-spread and deep-rooted, the organisations entrusted with law and order tend to lose their legitimacy and public credibility.[11]

The System of Accountability

Ministerial accountability to the legislative assemblies and parliament is political. Ministerial accountability for the actions of their officials is managerial accountability. Constitutional responsibility includes responsibility for actions done by their subordinates in pursuance of his policy. Ministers have to be accountable for the actions of their officials, whether the orders emanated from him or whether he connived at them or whether he did not take action after having come to know that certain things have been done.[12] In parliamentary form of Government this is a healthy British convention. The Constitution of India has clearly amplified that Police, law and order and administration of Justice are State subjects. The Union Government is indirectly involved since Central Police Organisations, administration of arms and ammunition and training of Police are in the Union list. Police are not exclusively managers responsible for law and order because law and order agencies at the district level include: (a) the magistracy, (b) the police, (c) Courts of Law, (d) the armed forces, and (e) the citizens. Seen from a wider perspective there are many other agencies/organisations which have a vital role to play in management of law and order at the national level, namely, (i) The Govt. of India, (ii) The State Government, (iii) The district magistrate, (iv) Intelligence agencies, (v) Armed Forces including Central Police Organisations, (vi) The Jails Political Executives, and (vii) Public opinion. India has a federal system of government in which management of law and order is entrusted to the State Government. At the State level State Government with Home Minister at the accountability level is responsible for law and order management although Chief Minister has also indirect responsibility. While the Minister-incharge of the police will always be responsible to answer for the police in the legislature, he is not expected to interfere in its day to day management and law enforcement functions. He should exercise his directive power through the head of the State Police, who is appointed by the Government on the advice of the Minister. How to fix accountability for various security, lapses in law and order situations is a difficult question. For example, on 26th January 1995, eight persons were killed and more than 54 persons were hurt when three bomb blasts at the Maulana Azad Stadium in Jammu during Republic Day Parade. Two Superintendents of Police Mr. P.N. Ganjoo S.P. (Security) and Mr. G.H. Kinnah S.P. (Security Civil Secretariat) have been placed under suspension. Besides the Government has transferred Deputy Commissioner and Senior Superintendent of Police of Jammu district. According to primary investigation RDX is believed to have been used in the series of bomb explosions which were set off by remote control devices. Who is to be held collusion of responsible for the grave security lapses? Can someone rule out some security personnel with the militants? Planting of the bombs could have been possible only with some amount of connivance and collusion of local police with the militants. How and what can be ways and measures to fix direct responsibility and also vicarious liability?

During the last four decades the issues of accountability has cropped up many times during riots, and other disturbances. A minister who cannot ensure accountability surely deserves to be censured but that cannot be the end of the matter. The fact is that checks and balances as envisaged by the Constitution have ceased to deliver.[13] The accountability of the police in India is still governed by Sections 3 and 4 of the Police Act, 1861. The 'Superintendence' of the State Police vests in the State Government and its 'administration' in the Inspector General of Police. In a district, it vests in the District Superintendent of Police subject to "the general control and direction of "the District Magistrate". The degree of superintendence or directional control intended to be exercised by the State government or the District Magistrate has not been specified. In accordance with the present scheme, the state police is accountable to the political executive at the level of the government; its administrative accountability is to be Inspector General of Police at the State level, and in a district, to the Superintendents of Police, subject to the general oversight of the District Magistrate. The Central Police Organisations are accountable to the Central Government through the Ministry of Home Affairs. In Metropolitan cities like Delhi, Bombay, Madras and Calcutta where there is Commissionerate system, police officers are having adequate magisterial powers to deal with various law and order problems. In the district system District Magistrate is the overall incharge to oversee the management of law and order situations. A variety of factors have, over a period of time, diluted the accountability of the managers of law and order in India.

The scheme of police accountability as outlined in the Police Act has not yet incorporated the ingredients of these constitutional obligations of the police. The presumption is that the police should discharge its obligations under Articles 21 and 22 of the Constitution within the broad framework of the Criminal Procedure Code and the Indian Evidence Act, London Metropolitan Police Commissioner has rightly said: "The public has every right to expect and we have a duty to provide a cost-effective non-discriminatory service that works well at all levels."

On January 2, 1995 an incident took place in Akuluto in Nagaland culminating in some casualties, arson and damage to civilian properties. In another case on December 27, 1994, security forces had exchanged firing at Mokokchung resulting in some casualties, damage to the property and arson. In February 1995, men of 16 Rashtriya Rifles comprising 5 officers, 15 JCOS and 400 jawans were moving in a convoy to Nagaland to assist the State Government in its anti-insurgency operations while passing through Kohima, the convoy was fired at and in its defence, para-military force exchanged fire for 20 minutes. Constitution of India bars any State Government from taking action against the Central forces deployed in aid of civil power. Sections 2(a) (i) and (ii) of the Commissions of Inquiry Act specify that an appropriate Government under the circumstances is the Central Government. The Seventh Schedule of the Constitution (entries I and II) takes away Central forces (including Army, Navy and Airforce and other para-military Central Police Organisations like CRPF) from the State Government's authority for the purpose of ordering a probe for omissions and commissions in discharge of their functions in aid of the civil power. An Inquiry Commission can be appointed by the Union Government under section 3 of the Act to look into a matter of public importance. On March 29, 1996, Chief Justice A.M. Ahmadi ordered the status quo be maintained.

Doctrine of Sovereign Immunity and Accountability

Supreme Court in Nilabati Bahera *vs* State of Orissa (1993) has held "given the extensive abuse of power by the State and its officials, particularly the police, it is important that the guilty are made accountable".[14] Police officers are often accused for violating the following human rights in India :

1. Arbitrary and unlawful arrests—violation of Article 22.
2. Arbitrary and unlawful searches.
3. Arbitrary and illegal detention in custody.
4. Custodial deaths—tortures and use of third degree during interrogation.
5. Disappearances from custody and "encounters".
6. Partial, and at times communal bias during handling riots.

Supreme Court has held that the defence of sovereign immunity is not applicable in a democratic society. The doctrine of sovereign immunity is alien to the concept of human rights: "A claim in public law for compensation for contravention of human rights and the fundamental freedoms is an acknowledged remedy for enforcement and protection of such rights." (Supreme Court-division bench judgement on March 30, 1993). In PUDR *vs* Police Commissioner Delhi the Supreme Court awarded Rs. 50000 as compensation to the family of Ram Swaroop who was beaten to death by the Police (AIR 1989-4 Sec 730). The doctrine of sovereign immunity is opposed to our constitutional ethos. Sovereign immunity and acts of State are related concepts in modern age. A state under the constitutional jurisprudence does not plead "Act of State" defence against a citizen. The doctrine of sovereign immunity has become 'archaic' and anachronistic and has been discarded in most of the democratic countries in the wake of the intensified world-wide movement for the protection of human rights. In M.C. Mehta *vs* Union of India, the Supreme Court held that it would award compensation only in "appropriate cases" and "not in every case where there is breach of fundamental rights".

On January 23, 1995 the Supreme Court directed the Uttar Pradesh Government to pay compensation of Rs. 50000 to two brothers, wrongfully confined in a police station in Noida for seven days without any criminal case registered against them whatsoever. On a habeas corpus petition, a division bench comprising Mr. Justice Kuldip Singh and Mr. Justice N. Venkatachallia made it clear that the government can recover the compensation amount from Sub-Inspector S.K. Sharma of the concerned police station in Noida, who has been held responsible for the illegal confinement. In recent years Supreme Court has assumed the role of a "Sentinel on the QUI VIVE" (State of Madras *vs* V.G. Row AIR 1952 SC 196) and has awarded compensation to citizens for the violations of their fundamental rights in appropriate cases. In one case Supreme Court awarded a sum of Rs. 30000 as compensation as an interim measure for violation of his fundamental right resulting in his illegal detention (Rudul Sah *vs* State of Bihar AIR 1983 Sc 1086; Indira Singh *vs* Union of India Writ Petition (Criminal) No. 118 of 1990 decided on 23 March 1990).

Since police and para-military forces are accountable to the law and the people, they need to take adequate care for protecting human rights.[15] In PUDR *vs* Police Commissioner Delhi the Supreme Court awarded Rs. 50000 as compensation to the family of Ram Swarup who was beaten to death by Police (AIR 1989-4 Sec. 730). Indian Police must develop a culture of respect for human dignity and reorient its attitude towards the public.[16]

Some Basic Issues

National Police Commission has spelt out three spheres of police accountability; the police are accountable to the people, police have an accountability to law and the police functionaries are accountable to the organisations (VII Report of May 1981) Police accountability concerns how police work is to be controlled (rendered impartial, efficient and consensual), whether through the very limited means of retrospective explanation or through the much more direct system of prospective control.[17]

In all democratic societies, problem of accountability is of paramount importance. The National Police Commission has observed that "In a democratic society, each department of the Government including the police is ultimately accountable for its performance to the people. However, direct accountability to the people in a society like ours may prove difficult. It has, therefore, been constitutionally laid that the public service is accountable to the elected representatives of the people at the forums of Parliament and State Legislatures through the Minister/ Ministers concerned". During the last four decades, the question of accountability in the management of law and order has assumed a very serious dimension because management is generally carried out by the "Plural Executives" and it is difficult to fix up individual's responsibilities and accountability. In various forums, people generally discuss the following issues of accountability :

1. Why there was breakdown of law and order immediately after the assassination of former Prime Minister Smt. Indira Gandhi on 31st October 1984 and why at places like Delhi and Kanpur so many people were killed in riots and who should be held responsible?
2. Why the disputed 'Ram Janam Bhoomi-Babri Masjid structure' could not be saved from destruction on 6th December, 1992 and why there were serious communal riots in almost 15 States of India?
3. Why insurgency situations continue in various States of North East and who is responsible for violent crimes and ethnic conflicts there?
4. Why the law and order situation in Kashmir valley has not been properly handled so far and who are responsible for deteriorating law and order situation in Kashmir?

5. Why the Bombay bomb blast series of Jan. 1993 could not be detected in time and why there was serious law and order situation in Bombay following the bomb blasts which resulted in exodus of people from Bombay and serious problems of communal nature arose there?
6. Why there is so much of lawlessness in States like Bihar and U.P.?

One can go on adding questions of similar nature. People generally ask who is to be blamed? Who are the people who should be made accountable for not being able to manage the law and order situation in various parts of the country? In words of Shri N.S. Saksena, "after every serious failure of law and order there are loud declarations from the Prime Minister and Chief Ministers that the guilty will be severly punished. However, it has not happened even in one per cent of tens of thousands of riots which have taken place from 1960s to 1991".[18] The frequent communal riots and other law and order problems in Uttar Pradesh, Maharashtra, Gujarat amd many other States and cities during 1992 and early 1993 have shocked the people of India and they are keen to know who are accountable for mismanagement of law and order.

Technically and theoretically district administration and the police are only accountable to the law, Constitution and the people and they could have defied the directives of the State Governments of Uttar Pradesh. But the pragmatic down to earth approach demands that district administration and police have to follow the broad directives and policies which were laid down by the Government of Uttar Pradesh and not to use force particularly not to resort to firing to disperse the Kar Sevaks from the disputed structure area.[19] How can Police and district officials disregard the instructions of the Chief Executive of the State? In a federal system like India, State Governments are entirely responsible for law and order maintenance. But law and order is so complex a problem that ultimately the District and district along cannot be held accountable because policy decisions are taken at the level of State Government. Chief Minister, Home Minister and Director General of Police are ultimately policy framers. "On reason why even relatively minor problems blow up into major law and order situations is that the inter-service rivalry between the IAS and the IPS has totally vitiated the atmosphere in districts and there is no coordination". Indian politicians, according to David H. Bayley, are ready to condemn the police at the drop of a hat and do so loudly and fairly regular. Politicians express the attitude that people must be continually defended from injustices, exactions and stupidities of the police".[20]

An experienced retired Police Officer has stated: "It is common place to say that the Home Ministry has a crucial role in dealing with internal security—laying down policies, working out strategies to be implemented both through the political system and the official machinery, provide governmental direction and support for the agencies directly responsible for ensuring internal security, etc. Issues with overriding political considerations are also dealt with by the Home Ministry and sometimes short-term and narrow interests, which subserve partisan political considerations, may clash with overall and long-term interests of the country itself.[21] According to the working group set up by the Administrative Reforms Commission on Police Administration (1967) on the whole, the legal position emerges that the police have complete functional independence in the investigation of cases and enjoy considerable independence of action in matters of dispersal of unlawful assemblies and maintenance of public order. But during the last many years, police have been getting pressures from political masters, eroding their functional independence. However one cannot defend the rationale of police independence from control of instructions simply on the ground that in enforcing the law, there should be responsibility only to the law.[22]

Operational Failures and Lapses by Police

Police have to be held responsible and accountable for the following types of administrative and operational lapses and failures :

1. Partisan approach.
2. Use of Excessive Force—Excessive firing during agitations.
3. Abuse of discretionary powers.
4. Failure of Intelligence.
5. Delayed response to deteriorating law and order situations.
6. Poor Police Community Relations due to rough handling of public.

7. Corruption.
8. Illegal arrests detentions and marches.
9. Custodial tortures and deaths.
10. Encounters and involuntary disappearances.
11. Massive concealment of crime and minimisation of offences.
12. Non-action at times indifference.
13. Violations of Human Rights.
14. Undemocratic and arrogant behaviour use of abusive language.
15. Police indiscipline and increasing criminality in Police organisations.
16. Unhelpful and at times inhuman approach during curfews, raids and encounters.

Differing Political Perceptions

Shri K.F. Rustamji has observed: "The sad fact is that in our democracy we seldom think in a democratic way".[23] Accountability for the management of law and order lies with the Central and State establishment who are constitutional responsible for the task. "What is immediately relevant is the erosion of the very concept of ministerial accountability to the Parliament and the people".[24] For management of law and order, the responsibility of the ministers is both individual and collective. Many of us may not agree with Dr. Hardwari Lal, a political thinker when he writes: "In some States and even at the Centre, power has passed into the hands of unscrupulous politicians...... This has happened because the doctrine of ministerial accountability as buttressed by the prescribed oath of office has been given the go-by. In Britain, whence we have borrowed the parliamentary system of government, the accountability of ministers is both individual and collective. After the December 6, 1992 demolition at Ayodhya, Prime Minister Shri P.V. Narasimha Rao dismissed the U.P. Government and three other BJP led Governments. Almost with one voice the National Integra tion Council had urged the Prime Minister to dismiss the U.P. Government and take control of the disputed site; and the legal and Constitutional ways of doing so were clearly spelled out." But the Prime Minister had decided to be irresolute. A similar irresolution on the government's part was again evident during the riots and the frenzy that followed the demolition.[26] Article 352 is clear and categorical that imminent danger is enough to activate the power for declaring emergency. Whenever the security of any part of the territory is threatened by an armed rebel (grave internal violent upheaval), emergency proclamation can be made by the President (i.e. Central Cabinet). Article 353 vests executive power in the union is a plenary manner to control the situation.[27] Article 355, incongruously placed with emergency provisions is apparently the foundation of the powers granted by Articles 352 and 356. The first part of the Article 355 spells out the Union's duty to protect every state against external aggression and internal disturbances. Indecision and passivity of the Centre "cannot absolve the Centre of its responsibility and the failure in discharge of that responsibility".[28] Political observers, according to Arvind N. Das, were intrigued by the Prime Minister's statement in the Lok Sabha during the no-confidence motion asking for strengthening of Article 356 of the Constitution to enable the Centre to take pre-emptive action against state governments.[29] Article 356 has been misused many times generally to suit the political interests of the party in power at the Centre.[30]

According to many political thinkers, the law and order scenario has become a cause for serious concern since political will is totally lacking when it comes to making the police an effective agency for dealing with the situation today and tomorrow when a meaga-situation could in all probability be expected to develop because of increasing population, unemployment and criminalination with anti-social elements continuing to upgrade the techniques and resources.[31] There is a proper record of all past law and order incidents of serious violence maintained in the Ministry of Home Affairs and the State Home Departments, the Intelligent Bureau. We often blame Intelligence Bureau which may not be at fault. However what is invariably at fault is its proper and contextual assessment. Many past incidents indicate that police officers again and again fall in the trap at the instance of politicians and senior bureaucrats who want blood and tough measures when violence commences and retreat at once when the violence declines and become earnest votaries of law, justice and non-violence. K.F. Rustamji has observed: "They say the police are good shock-absorbers of the chariot of State. But can they stand reckless joy-riding".[32] How long will police leadership allow these things to happen. It is not that the senior police leadership lacks proper perception of the relatives. What they lack is unity in resisting wrong and illegal orders.

If we want police and para-military personnel to behave in an impartial, unpartisan fashion when dealing with riots in Bombay or Ahmedabad, we have to insist that those responsible for massacres of the kind that occurred in Sopore be punished severely, publicly and soon.[33] Police must seek help from known sociologists and psychologists to have a closer interaction with the police and security forces to weed out mentally sick people who can resort to inhuman acts. For ensuring accountability monitoring of the performance managers of law and order can be done by the following ways :

(i) Internal monitoring (Training) and organisational.

(ii) Public monitoring.

(iii) Partnership monitoring by Courts and voluntary citizen committies.

(iv) Monitoring by crime surveys and analysis of various other law and order situations including riots.

(v) Independent monitoring groups like Amnesty International.

Action Against Officials

The Government of India has decided to initiate action against a number of top officials named in the Verma Commission report on the assassination of Rajiv Gandhi. The officials named in the Verma Commission report are the then Cabinet Secretary V.C. Pandey and Home Secretaries Shiromani Sharma and R.K. Bhargawa, Intelligence Bureau Director M.K. Narayanan and Secretary (Security) G.S. Bajpai. While the bureaucrats may be proceeded against the withdrawal of the elite S.P.G. cover, the top intelligence and security officials might be called upon to explain their failure to assess properly the perception of threat to Mr. Rajiv Gandhi from LTTE. BJP President L.K. Advani has sharply criticised the Government for its reported decision and has said "such a move would be prima-facie malafide". Verma Commission report was submitted to the Government way back in June 1992 and why such decision has been taken now. How long political considerations will determine accountability concept in Indian democracy.

Evaluation of Management of Law and Order

According to K.F. Rustamji, "Our planning of manpower, weapons and tactics has certainly been defective. I would say we have no long-term plans at all. We have not tried to forecast, what type and quantum of forces we will need, what type of training, what weapons and methods of coordination". It is difficult to evaluate the performance of managers of law and order as they are "plural managers" and responsibility on individuals is difficult to be fixed. There are also constitutional and legal constraints in pinpointing extent of accountability. Secrecy in the government at various levels is another factor hindering individual accountability. Accountability cannot be ensured in a system which has become as apaque as ours. The government's functioning has to be subjected to norms which guarantee transparency.[34] According to Sunanda K. Dutta Ray, "There is lack of perspective at the central decision making level...vote banks play a major role in Congress (I) calculations".[35] According to experienced retired Police Officers, "Political considerations and caste loyalties are taking primacy over improving the efficiency or performance of the Police".[36] According to a senior retired police officer, "while the State leaders are playing havoc with the police system almost all over the country in varying degrees, the original sin was tragically committed by the Centre".[37] Some of the main mistakes in our policies pertaining to the management of law and order are as under :

(1) Panicky and thoughtless decisions.

(2) Defective planning of manpower, weapons, and tactics without any long-term plans.

(3) Frequent deployment of army over long periods.

(4) Barbarity and banditry by the police forces and reckless searches and insults to citizens.

(5) Improper use of Central forces.[38]

Delhi riots of 1984 and Bombay riots of 1993 indicate that the attitude of State Police towards minorities is prejudicial, biased and at times partial.[39] Kerala High Court in the ISRO espionage case on 16th January 1995 has observed, "when the security of the nation is at stake, the investigating agency should act in a more and vigilant manner without any pre-conceived notions". By implications, the High Court held that C.B.I. investigation was biased and "not carried out on proper lines".

Dilemma of Accountability

On many occasions there is dilemma in pointing out accountability due to the following main reasons :

1. Lack of clarity of goals and organisation mission in federal set up in plural societies.
2. Differing political perceptions of Centre and States.
3. Corrupt politicians and their interference.
4. Lack of effective police leadership and system of passing the brick.
5. Proliferation of higher posts in police organisations and dilemma for the subordinates.
6. Ineffectiveness of Criminal Justice System.
7. Lack of professionalism in Police at various levels.
8. Lack of Institutional safeguards for straight forward police officers.

According to K.F. Rustamji, "There is improper way of using Central forces by putting CRP and BSF under the operational command of the state forces who see no need for correct policing." Central Police Organisations must have an independent operational role and functional autonomy. K.F. Rustomji has rightly observed, "There is bungling and fumbling and a lot of blame throwing. We set out to do a lot of senseless things, raise the wrong hopes, apply the wrong tests, spread panic in the administration and refuse to face it with the calm confidence which a mature democracy, which has perfected its operational plans ought to be able to achieve". Generally every one talks of strong-arm methods, toughness, firmness, teaching them-a-lesson tactics. They say, "Do what you like, we want results". We have not been able to learn lessons from the past experience. We are never quick to see a movement developing, never quick to take preventive action.

Suggestions and Recommendations

1. As the custodian of the Constitution Governor of a State should assume direct responsibility for maintenance of law and order when he is convinced that the conditions in the State are leading towards large scale violence and lawlessness.
2. All laws dealing with law and order, public peace and tranquity need to be amended suitably to empower officers of Central Police Organisations to exercise reasonable powers for preserving law and order in the States where these forces are deployed. This would enable them to act independently to discharge their functions pertaining to law and order without waiting for the orders of the State Governments.
3. If Constitutional and legal changes are made to take the political motivation and petty party interests out of law and order management, India can within a few years, become a peaceful and law-abiding society.[40] Four things need to be done without further delay. The Police and the Central Police Organisations must be completely insulated from political pressures and considerations. Law and order administration should be brought on the concurrent list of the Centre by a Constitutional amendment so that Centre is not a mute spectator to the demolition of the law enforcement machinery and the destruction of its ethos. The recommendations of the National Police Commissions for reform and reorganisation of the police must be implemented in a time bound programme and fourthly training of police organisations must be effectively restructured to mould police into a truly democratic police, which should be accountable to the law, Constitution and the people.
4. Problems of growing communal tension, terrorism, kidnapping, hijacking, insurgency, election violence and agrarian unrest warrant that "the security arrangements be overhauled and it needs a drastic face-lift. The monitoring review and analysis of intelligence information gathered by various agencies could be strengthened and a system for accountability by various intelligence agencies emphasised upon for better and effective coordination

amongst the agencies".[41] The need of today is modernisation, good communication, quick response, reform of State police, better arms, ammunition and equipment. There is need for better training, dynamic leadership and strong political will to manage the law and order. The ultimate sanction for the accountability of police administration to the people lies in the democratic moves and healthy public opinion.[42]

5. All over the world it is now recognised that whichever political party or organisation that puts up a demonstration or a large political function must bear the responsibility of orderly behaviour of the participants. A Central legislation for fixing the responsibility on the organisers and leaders of political agitations, demonstrations, processions, rallies, etc., for the repayment of the assessed damage caused by acts of the participants and an autonomous board for uniformed implementation of the proposed law in all States.[43] The full cost of public and private property damaged during various riots and agitations needs to recovered from the agitationists and protesters and the party organising these agitations. Tamil Nadu has already enacted a law in 1994 to claim compensation from the political parties for damages to Government property done during political agitations. Regarding departmental accountability National Police Commission has recommended a guiding principle that "a functionary in the department at a particular level should be held accountable only with respect to functions and duties assigned to him" and conversely "the accountability should not extend to duties over which he has no direct control". DGP-cum-IGP may be responsible for generally maintaining law and order throughout the State but he cannot be held responsible for each isolated incident in a particular district. In a similar manner it would be wrong to hold the S.P. or the SHO accountable for each isolated incident in their respective jurisdiction. The District Magistrate has a very limited role in the matter of administrative control, but he has a very important role to play in terms of police accountability. "A focal point of accountability must continue to exist in order to ensure

that police behaves liked a civilised force and not like the TON TON MOSCOUTE OF PAPA DOC DUVALIER".[44]

What is needed is a clear, consistent and comprehensive policy in matters of management of law and order. In a democratic society intensive basic training in management of law and order needs to be imparted. People's cooperation to the managers of law and order is most essential requirement. A democratic ethos has to be built laboriously for educating the masses and the common man about their obligations and responsibilities for orderly behaviour while in crowd or carrying out political demonstrations. "In a democratic set-up, where police authority rests upon the consent of the governed and where indeed a special front is made of securing public cooperation, police are called upon to constrain the very people they are responsible to. How much political wisdom, acumen and sobriety is required for the policeman to realise that though he speaks with society's authoritative voice, he is at the same time, responsible to that society and is accountable to the same people".[45] For firmly establishing a real democratic society, every policeman needs to be taught what democracy means, he must understand how sacred human rights are, he must learn to respect the dignity of the human beings, he must understand his ultimate accountability to the public and final answerability to the people and Rule of Law.[46]

REFERENCES

1. Fritz Morstein Marx (Editor), *Elements of Public Administration*, p. 529 quoted by Dr. K.M. Mathur, in *Problems of Police in a Democratic Society*, RBSA Publishers SMS Highways, Jaipur, 1987, p. 1.
2. K.M. Mathur, Law and Order Administration with Special Reference to Terrorism, *Indian Journal of Public Administration*, Vol. XXXVI, No. 2, April-June 1989.
3. D.C. Hane and B.L.R. Smith (eds), The Dilemma of Accountability in Modern Governments: Independence Versus Control, Bondan, 1971, p. 311.

4. *Elements of Public Administration,* edited by Fritz Morstein Marx, p. 529.
5. Leonard D. White, *Introduction to the study of public administration,* 1955, p. 222.
6. For detailed analysis regarding the Problems of Police Accountability in a Democratic Society refer K.M. Mathur, *The Problems of Police in a Democratic Society*, particularly Chapter III, p. 15, RBSA Publishers, SMS Highways, Jaipur, 1987.
7. R. Venkataraman, Law & Order Mutual Responsibility, *The Hindu*, 30 October 1987.
8. See K.F. Rustamji, *Bureaucracy, Police Administration and Insurgency in India—Where we Defaulted.*
9. N.S. Saksena, *Law & Order in India*, Abhinav, Publications New Delhi, 1987, p. 47.
10. National Police Commission Report (Dharam Vira Commission) Sixth Volume, Para 61.42.
11. Surinder Suri, Social values under stress, *The Times of India*, 30 June 1987.
12. For further details see S.C. Vajpayi, Question of Accountability, Political and Managerial Aspects, *Indian Express*, 19th September 1993.
13. Vivek Bharati, An Area of Darkness—Governance without Accountability, *The Times of India*, 28 March 1993.
14. For details see the *Hindu*—16 January 1994. Making the Police accountable.
15. K.M. Mathur, *Indian Police—Role and Challenges*, Gyan Publishing House, New Delhi, 1994, p. 305.
16. K.M. Mathur, *Police in India—Problems and Perspective*, Gyan Publishing House, New Delhi, 1991, p. 287.
17. Mike Brogden—*Tony Jefferson, and Sandra Walklate—Introducing Police Work*, p. 172.
18. N.S. Saksena, *India towards down in law and order 1985-1994*, Rohil Khand Publications, 1994, p. 57.
19. K.M. Mathur, *Police, Law and Internal Security* Gyan Publishing House, New Delhi, 1994, pp. 357-58.
20. David H. Baylay, *Police & Political Development in India* 1968, p. 367.

21. Shri T. Ananthachari, Revamping Home Ministry—Complexity of Internal Security Problems calls for reform, *Indian Express,* 19th January 1994.
22. Geoffrey Marshall, *Police and Government,* p. 117.
23. K.F. Rustamji, Need for new security attitude, *Indian Express,* 13 October 1986.
24. Hardwari Lal, Accountability—Erosion of Concept, *The Hindustan Times*, 19th January 1995.
25. *Ibid.*
26. Raj Mohan Gandhi, Religion and Politics—To ban or not,*The Hindustan Times*, 10th August 1993.
27. For similar views see Justice V.R. Krishna Iyer-A Barbarity and an Otiosity (A critical complication of Ayodhya aftermath) *The Hindu*, 10th Dec. 1992.
28. V.P. Dutt, Ayodhya—The real issues—*The HindustanTimes*, 9 Jan. 1993.
29. Arvind N. Das, Centre failed to use Article 355 on December 1992, *The Times of India*, 24th December 1992.
30. S.R. Maheshwari, Abuse of Article 356, *Indian Express,* 22nd Dec. 1992.
31. Lalit Shastri, Law and Order in M.P., *The Hindu,* 3 June 1994.
32. K.F. Rustamji, Shock Absorbers—Role of the Police, *The Hindustan Times*, 26 June 1994.
33. Tavleen Singh, In the Valley of Fear, *Indian Express,* 28 Feb. 1993.
34. Vivek Bharati, An Area of Darkness-Governance without Accountability, *The Times of India,* 28 March 1993.
35. See Simanda K. Dutta Ray, North East, in Turmoil—Lack of Perspective at the decision making level.
36. Shri Prakash Singh, The Crumbling Edifice of Law Enforcement. *Indian Express,* Jan. 9, 1995, Ahmedabad. Edition.
37. Prakash Singh, The Crumbling Edifice of Law Enforcement, *Indian Express*, Ahmedabad Edition, 9th January 1995, p. 6.
38. K.F. Rustamji, Police Administration and Insurgency in India Tour Notes, p. 171. Quoted by Dr. K.M. Mathur in *Management of Internal Security & Related Issues*, Gyan Publishing House, New Delhi, 1995, p. 41.

39. For similar views, see Kalpana Sharma, A story of two Riots, *The Hindu,* 20 August 1993.
40. For similar views, see N.S. Saksena, *Law & Order in India,* 1987, part VI.
41. Parliamentary Committee on Home Affairs—Tabled in Parliament on April 28, 1993—See, *The Hindu*, 29th April 1993.
42. K.M. Mathur, The Problem of Police Accountability in a Democratic Society, *The Indian Police Journal*, April-June 1979, p. 42.
43. K. M. Mathur, *Internal Security Challenges and Police in a Developing Society*, RBSA Publishers, S.M.S. Highways, Jaipur, 1989, p. 106.
44. M.N. Buch, Needed A New Police Act, *The HindustanTimes*, 8th March 1996.
45. K.M. Mathur, Police Accountability to the Law and the People, *Police Research & Development Journal*, Jan-March 1980, p. 5.
46. K.M. Mathur, *The Problems of Police in a Democratic Society*, RBSA Publishers, Jaipur, 1987, p. 14.

5

Human Rights : Perceptions and Perspectives

The term "human rights" is a dynamic concept and it endeavours to adapt itself to the needs of the countries and their people. These rights are sometimes known as basic rights, fundamental rights, natural rights or inherent rights. The protection of human personality and of its fundamental rights is the ultimate purpose of all the national and international laws.[1] Although human rights are necessary for sustaining human life and promoting development of man yet the internal political structure, levels of social, technological and economic development, the resource bases and the religio-cultural background of the countries, do have a profound bearing on the policies and priorities of various countries towards human rights.

Human rights like fundamental rights, are paramount, sacrosanct, eternal and transcendental in nature and ought to be treated as inalienable and inviolable for preserving the dignity of the people. These rights, however, cannot be imagined without the security and existence of a well-regulated society. Society and the State can alone guarantee the human rights to the individual but also demand observance of social norms from the citizens. "The imperfections and frailty of human nature is the justification for the laws of social control. They do not reject liberty but only regulate it to keep it on the trail of social justice".[2] Human rights are those minimal rights which every individual must have against the state or other public authority by virtue of being a "member of the human family" irrespective of any other consideration.[3] There are rights which are inherent in all citizens, because of their being human. These are the rights which are inalienable because the enlightened conscience of the community would not permit the surrender of those rights by any citizen even of his own volition. These are the rights which are invoilable because they are not only vital for the development and efflorescence of human personality and for ensuring its dignity, but also because without them men would be reduced to the level of animals.[4]

Definition of Human Rights

Little effort has been made to create a comprehensive map of the totality of human rights, and there has been little discussion on the detailed content of particular rights. Often even the very concept of human rights is left obscure.[5] The United Nations Charter refers to human rights in its preamble and six other articles. Learning about one's own rights builds respect for the right of others and points the way to more tolerant, peaceful societies.[6] The Universal Declaration of Human Rights adopted and proclaimed by the General Assembly resolution of 10th December 1948 forms one of the main milestones in the history of Human rights. Indian Constitution contains a variety of human rights termed as fundamental rights. In India, human rights have been defined under "the protection of Human Rights 1993 (No. 10 of 1994)" as under:

2(I) (d) "Human rights" means the rights relating to life, liberty, equality and dignity of the individual guaranteed by the Constitution or embodied in the International Covenants and enforceable by Courts in India.

It is a matter of great national pride for all Indians that human rights concept prevailed in its hightest form in our Indian scriptures and religious books.[7] One Vedic Sloka enunciating the tenets of human rights is as under :

सर्वे भवन्तु सुखिनः
सर्वे सन्तु निरामय ।
सर्वे भद्राणि पश्चन्तु
मा कश्चिद् दुःख भाग्यवेत ॥

Human rights were known in ancient India. For example, in 1367 B.C. Bahmani and Vijayanagar kings entered into an agreement for the humane treatment of prisoners of war and the sparing of lives of the enemy's unarmed subjects.[8]

Human rights as a concept is very ancient and some references pertaining to human rights can be found even in ancient Indian Scriptures.

> "Man is not an individual. He is a social organism. God loves him only who serves other beings: men, cattle and other creatures. His glory lies in being a member of a big family. On the one hand, man is bound by blood-kinship—his parents, his wife, his children and on the other, he is linked with every individual of society whether near or far from his. It is given to man to link himself with those who constitute his ancestry, and also think of those who could be his posterity. Man thus lives, works and dies for society possessed of certain inalienable rights. Man is expected to develop his craft, sciences and technology and lead society from poverty to prosperity, with a happy today and a happier tomorrow". (from the *Atharva Veda*)

This work contains a systematic body of political ideas and embodies a comprehensive theory of kingship, Government and preservation of war. In ancient age there was a rule that after dusk upto morning don there will be no firing by the troops and there used to cease-fire with setting of the sun. The *Yajnavalkya Smriti* and the *Narada Smriti*, both are still authoritive source books of Hindu law, specifying *inter alia,* rules of drafting, pleading, procedure and judicial conduct. Both authoritive sources of human law specifically various rules pertaining to protection of human rights. The concept of Dharma has been eternal spring of Hindus' ethic and has been all-pervading, governing and regulating conduct of human beings. The five *Yamas*—ahimsa (non-violence), truth, non-theft, total abstinence and non-possession and five *Niyamas*—purity, contentment, penance, study of scriptures and surrender to God were enunciated by great saint Patanjali to attain self-discipline and to establish equilibrium in society. The creation of perfect man, son of eternity, was aimed at establishing an egalitarian, non-exploitive and humane social order.

Chapters 39 to 108 of the celebrated Tamil book on Philosophy, Tirukkural, speak almost all the civil, political, economic, social and cultural rights. Ideas of freedom of criticism, curriculum of education, freedom from corruption, seeking advice from foreign experts, duty of a country to sustain the burden of the influx of refugees and socialist pattern of society could be found in this text of Tiruvalluvar who authored it almost two thousand years ago. In Valmik's *Ramayana* also there are certain fundamental human rights enumerated. In *Ramayana,* Lord Rama advised Lakshman not to use a weapon of war which could destroy the entire humanity including those who did not bear arms because such destruction in mass was forbidden in ancient laws of war. In the *Mahabharata*, Arjun observing the laws of war refrained from using Pashupatastra—a hyper-destruction weapon because human rights of civilians have to be kept in mind.

India has enacted the protection of Human Rights Act 1993 (No. 10 of 1994) with a view to provide for the constitution of a National Human Rights Commission, State Human Rights Commissions in States and Human Rights Courts for better protection of human rights and for matters connected therein or incidental thereto. The Act received the assent of the President of India on January 8, 1994 and published in the Gazette of India Extra Part II, Section 1 dated 10 January, 1994. The Protection of Human Rights Act 1993 (Act No. 10 of 1994) contains 43 sections and is divided into the following eight chapters. Chapter I: Preliminary—Sections 1 and 2 National Human Rights Commission. Chapter II: National Human Rights Commission Sections I and II. Chapter III: Functions and Powers of the Commission—Sections 12 to 16. Chapter IV: Procedure Sections—17 to 20. Chapter V: State Human Rights Commissions—Sections 21 to 29. Chapter VI: Human Rights Courts—Sections 30 and 31. Chapter VII: Finance, Account and Audit—Sections 32 to 35. Chapter VIII: Miscellaneous—Sections 36 to 43.

This Protection of Human Rights Act 1993 is a very important landmark in the history of human rights jurisprudence.

Changing Perspectives and Expanding Dimensions

Despite the apparently fixed positions, few shifts within each perspective on human rights have been visible during past few years. Violations of human rights in India are now seen as violations of the democratic principles enshrined in the Indian Constitution as well as violation of India's international commitment of humanitarian international law and international covenants. Another perspective on human rights has national unity, integrity and stability as the focal point as it defensively justifies the use of repressive measures in the context of abnormal situations of disturbed areas like Jammu & Kashmir for maintaining national security. The shift in the perspectives of the Amnesty International is reflected in 1992 when this well-known international body took notice of the fact that "armed opposition groups in Jammu and Kashmir have been responsible for numerous and grave human rights abuses including hostage-taking, assassination of politicians and their families, deliberate killings of civilians including journalists and torture and rape."[9] Condemning such abuses, the Amnesty International urged such groups to release all hostages and respect human rights and humanitarian standards. At international level, the resolution co-sponsored by India on gross violation of human rights perpetrated by terrorists groups and expressing of solidarity with the victims of terrorism was adopted by the United Nations Human Rights Commission. "The marked shift," according to Balraj Puri, "interestingly enunciated by Shri Atal Bihari Vajpayee at U.N. Conference on human rights at Geneva, asserted India's determination to maintain highest standards of human rights. He quoted at length relevant provisions of the Indian Constitution, cited the role of independent judiciary, Human Rights Commission, Free Press and NGOs in the field of Human Rights. Far from denying the fact of excesses, he quoted figures of punishments to erring officials of the security forces."[10] Ever since early 1994, the issue of human rights was not an internal affair of a sovereign State. The appointment of the National Human Rights Commission on October 12, 1993 is another landmark in the approach towards upholding the human rights and in checking the State in its abuses of civil liberty. Allowing TADA to die a natural death is another important milestone in the history of human rights. Judicial activism amd public litigation cases are also various stages in the evolution of the human right issues.

Human rights can be analysed from three perspectives: (1) Socio-economic dimensions, (2) Legal dimensions, (3) Role of international organisations and NGOs in promotion of human rights. Karel Vasak, has categorised human rights into the three generation of rights. His thesis is as following:

The first generation rights were those rights which emerged from the American and French revolutions. They were aimed at securing the citizen's liberty from arbitrary action by the State. They correspond by and large to the civil and political rights in the International Bill of Rights. They are said to be negative rights in that they call for restraint from the State.

The second generation rights emerged with the Russian revolution and were echoed in the welfare state concepts which developed in the West. They correspond largely to the economic, social and cultural rights and they require positive action by the State.

The third generation rights, as Vasak sees them are a response to the phenomenon of global interdependence. Individual States acting alone can no longer satisfy their human rights obligations. The problems that are now being faced require international co-operation for their resolution. These problems include the maintenance of peace, the protection of the environment and the encouragement of development. The third generation rights necessarily benefit individuals and peoples.[11]

From a sociological perspective, for proper realisation of human rights, it is essential that the society as a whole accepts the basic norms of human rights. According to Sir Hersch Lauterpacht, "the protection of human personality and of its fundamental rights is the ultimate purpose of all law, national and international." The International Bill of Human Rights is normally defined as consisting of the U.N. Declaration of Human Rights 1948, the International Covenant on Economic, Social and Cultural Rights 1966, the International covenant on civil and political rights and the optional Protocols thereto. Office of the U.N. High Commissioner for Human Rights was created in December 1993, following the recommendations of the Vienna Conference. Alston and many others have identified the following important phases of human rights activities :

1. 1945-55 was the standard setting or normative phase. The Universal Declaration on Human Rights was drafted, the bulk of the work on drafting the two Covenants was completed. Other Conventions including those on Genocide

and Refugees were drafted. This lofty work, however, stood in stark contrast to the UN's inability to react to specific human rights violations.

2. 1955-65 phase was an attempt to correct this by the promotion of human rights. It was a period of attempting to influence the situation by working with governments through the procedure of periodic governmental reports and the provision of advisory services. The achievements in this phase were modest.
3. Within the next decade, 1965-75, came the phase of protection of human rights and an attempt to do something more directly about violations of human rights. New techniques were developed for appointing special rapporteurs to investigate situations. The problem of what to do with the thousands of communications received by the UN on the human rights issues was tackled, and in 1970 ECOSOC adopted the procedures under resolution 1503. The idea of a High Commissioner for Human Rights was launched.[12]
4. After 1976 human rights have become an international concern and demand enforcement with international pressures on defaulting states. Ahmad Yamani feels that the western liberal democratic tradition is so overzealous in its defence of the individual's freedom, liberty, rights and dignity that it overlooks the acts of some individuals in exercising such rights in a way that jeopardizes the community.[13] "Presenting another perspective, Legesse argues." If Africans were the sole authors of the universal declaration of Human Rights, they might have ranked the rights of communities above those of the individuals.[14]

Human rights have three basic premises which are as under:

(1) The individual necessarily remains the primary subject of international human rights law.

(2) International human rights law recognises the existence of groups.

(3) The full enjoyment of individual human rights requires certain human rights to devolve, wholly or in part, upon groups.

Human Rights have following important propositions:

(1) There is a hierarchy among the subjects of human rights law.

(2) There can be no human rights which detract from the individual's human rights.

(3) Human rights law does recognise certain rights of groups.

(4) The diversity of the cultures and civilizations, beliefs and traditions, history and aspirations reflected in polico-legal system, give rise to ever changing meaning to "human rights".

It is necessary to understand the distinction between human rights and humanitarian laws. Humanitarian law refers to those rules of International law which aim to protect persons suffering from the evils of armed international conflict, directly serving military purposes. The Status of Guerrilla in an international conflict was uncertain and people fighting wars of liberation were denied minimum humanitarian treatment by their adversaries. The Diplomatic Conference in 1977 adopted two Protocols additional to the Geneva Conventions of 1949. Article I(4) of the Protocol I, 1977 covers the wars of national liberations while Protocol II relates to non-international armed conflict. Protocol II, 1977 develops and supplements to Article 3 common to the Geneva Convention 1949. It covers non-internal armed conflicts in which hostilities reach a certain degree of intensity. States can easily evade their obligations to observe human rights in conflict situations by denying the armed character of the conflicts or claiming that the low level of violence does not reach the threashold required for the applicability of the Protocols.

In India, all citizens are entitled to human rights but besides women and children, there are certain groups which need greater priorities. The following groups deserve special study in the context of human rights:

(1) *Protection of minorities*. An extensive system of provisions protecting minorities was built into the network of treaties concluded at the end of the World War I. For many newly created States of Europe, a price for nationhood had to be paid in the form of a guarantee to respect the cultural, religious, and even linguistic freedom of minorities within their borders, and a promise that there would be no institutionalised discrimination.

(2) *Prescribing racial and other forms of discrimination*: Various conventions, including the International Convention on the Elimination of All Forms of Racial Discrimination, the ILO's Discrimination Convention (No. III) and UNESCO's Convention against Discrimination in education, extend their protection to members of groups defined by reference to race, colour, descent, sex, national or ethnic origin, political or other opinion, economic conditions, or birth.

(3) *Protection of indigenous populations*: ILO convention No. 107 concerning indegenous and tribal populations sanctions affirmative action in favour of the populations concerned. ECOSOC in its Decision 1982-84 established a Working Group to review developments relating to the promotion and protection of the human rights and fundamental freedoms of indigenous populations, with special attention to the evolution of standards concerning the rights of indigenous populations.[15]

Human Rights and Indian Constitution

The founding fathers of Indian Constitution envisioned a comprehensive concept of human rights. Most of the articles of the United Nations General Assembly Resolution of 10 December 1948, Universal Declaration of Human Rights and the two International Covenants of 1966 are the building blocks of India's Constitutional Rights. The Constitution of India, in its Preamble, resolves to secure to all its citizens:

(i) Justice — social, economic and political.

(ii) Liberty — of thought, expression, belief, faith and worship.

(iii) Equality — of status and of opportunity and to promote among all.

(iv) Fraternity — assuring the dignity of the individual and the unity and integrity of the nation.

Our Constitution provides and guarantees the fundamental rights to all the citizens and these rights are the human rights.

Human rights as enumerated in the Constitution as fundamental rights are as under:—

1. *Right to Equality*
   - (i) Equality before Law (Article 14)
   - (ii) Equality of opportunity in matters of public employment: (Article 14)
   - (iii) Prohibition of discrimination on grounds of religion, race, caste, sex or place of birth (Article 15)
   - (iv) Abolition of untouchability (Article 17)
   - (v) Abolition of titles (Article 18).
2. *Right to Freedom*
   - (i) Freedom of speech etc. (Article 19)
   - (ii) Protection in respect of conviction for offences (Article 20)
   - (iii) Protection of life and personal liberty (Article 21)
   - (iv) Protection against detention in certain cases (Article 22).
3. *Right Against Exploitation*
   - (i) Prohibition of traffic in human beings and forced labour (Article 23)
   - (ii) Prohibition of employment of children in factories etc. (Article 24).
4. *Right to Freedom of Religion*
   - (i) Freedom of conscience and free pursuit of profession, practice and propagation of religion (Article 25)
   - (ii) Freedom to manage religious affairs (Article 16)
   - (iii) Freedom as to payment of taxes for promotion of any particular religion (Article 27)
   - (iv) Freedom as to attendance at religious places or religious worship in certain educational institutions (Article 28).
5. *Cultural and Educational Rights*
   - (i) Protection of interest of minorities (Article 29)
   - (ii) Right of minorities to establish and administer educational institutions (Article 30).

6. *Right to Constitutional Remedies:*
   (i) Right to Constitutional remedies (Article 32).

India has ratified and acceded to the following international covenants which came into force from the dates mentioned below:

(i) International Covenant on Economic, Social and Cultural Rights of 1966 (3rd January 1976). Adopted and opened for ratification and adopted by U.N. General Assembly.

(ii) International Covenant on Civil and Political Rights (Adopted by U.N. General Assembly on 16th Dec. 1966) (Entry into Force on 23 March 1976).

All public servants including members of the State and Central Police Organisations are duty bound to uphold the Constitution of India and to adhere to the human rights enunciated to International Covenants referred above. Rights in India are only those fundamental rights and international covenants which are enforceable by courts in India and therefore a thorough analysis of all laws and acts has to be carried out to find the broad dimensions of human rights. State and Central Police Organisations are protectors of human rights and it is therefore necessary that they should understand the challenges which are before them in the field of human rights violations. Human rights can be restricted and limited by the sovereign States in the interest of the general welfare of the people of the nation-State during public emergencies which threaten the life of the nation. Limitations can be determined by law but only for the purpose of securing recognition of the rights of others and for meeting the just requirements of morality, public order and the general welfare in a democratic society. Rights cannot be exercised contrary to the purposes and principles of the United Nations.

Human Rights of Women

The World Congress on Human Rights having met and deliberated in New Delhi from 10 to 15 December, 1990 has urged governments to satisfy the convention on elimination of all forms of discrimination against women and to establish commissions to monitor compliance with it. The World Congress has called upon governments and the media to disseminate freely information dealing with human rights especially those of women and to take action at every level of society with a view to changing attitudes which may result in discrimination against women and girls. The World Congress has condemned all forms of gender discrimination, including discrimination in respect of the right to be born. The World Congress has suggested legislative and other measures to ensure that no person who tends or medically examines any pregnant women shall reveal any information, either to the woman herself or to any other person, which might indicate the sex of the unborn child. It is imperative to eliminate gender discrimination in respect of education so that education should be free and compulsory for both female and male children atleast upto the age of 16 years. The World Congress has recommended that national laws be examined and revised in order to remove discrimination in the areas by (a) marriage, (b) inheritance, (c) matrimonial property, (d) matrimonial relations, and (e) adoption and guardianship. It has recommended the establishment of family Courts based on the following principles: (a) simplified laws and procedures, (b) privacy of hearing, (c) policy of appointing family court judges in equal gender proportions and (d) providing counselling and mediation services as part of the court process. The World Congress has called upon all the governments to take immediate steps to ensure that all discriminatory laws, regulations and regulatory procedures which restrict the movement of women within a country and which restrict the rights of women to travel outside the country should be repealed. Though the UN Convention on Elimination of All Forms of Discrimination against Women (CEDAW) was adopted by the General Assembly in 1979, India ratified it in June, 1993. In India, there has been a sharp increase in the incidence of violation of human rights of women. According to a government publication, there is one rape every 54 minutes, there is one molestation every 26 minutes, one abduction every 42 minutes and one criminal offence against women every seven minutes. Rape victims in India come mostly from the lower rings of the society. The Criminal Law Amendment Act 1983 has brought some important changes in the existing laws of rape. It amends of Section 376 of the IPC and extends the minimum period of punishment in rape cases to seven years. Section 114A states where sexual intercourse by the accused has been proved and the victim states before the court that she did not consent, the court will presume that there was absence of consent. The Act provides for trial in camera. The new Section 228(a) of the IPC also makes disclosure of the identity of the victim an offence punishable with imprisonment for two years. By the amendment of the Child Marriage Restraint Act 1978, the age of marriage was raised to 18 years. Section 357 of the Cr. P.C. provides for the compensation to rape victims and the offender, not the State is ordered to pay compensation to the victims. In India, in 1990 a total number of 68317 crimes were committed against women and in 1993 the figure rose to 83,954, an increase of about 23 per cent. In India everyday 32 women are raped, 16 killed for dowry and 57 are molested.

Human Rights of Children

Article 25(2) of the Universal Declaration of Human Rights (1948) provides that "Motherhood and childhood are entitled to special care and assistance. All children, whether born in or out of wedlock, shall enjoy the same social protection. Article 10 of the International Covenant on Economic, Social and Cultural Rights asserts that "Special measures of protection and assistance should be taken on behalf of all citizens and young persons without any discrimination for reasons of percentage and other conditions. Children and young persons should be protected from economic and social exploitation." The UN General Assembly adopted the convention on the rights of the children on November 20, 1989. The provisions of the convention apply for four areas of children rights, namely, survival, development, protection and participation. The Vienna Declaration of Human Rights (1993) insists that all states should, with international co-operation—(a) combat "exploitation and abuse of children by addressing their root causes"; (b) device effective measures against female infanticide, harmful child labour, sale of children, child prostitution, child pornography, as well as the other forms of sexual abuse; (c) organise "means of improving the protection of children in armed conflicts and programmes of "after care and rehabilitation of children in war zones" as well as those in especially difficult circumstances."

The 1989 UN Convention on the Rights of the child apply for four main areas of children's rights, namely, survival, development, protection and participation. The Rights to Survival include provisions of adequate food, shelter, clean water and primary health care. There are the basic rights to ensure the survival of a child. The Rights to Develop include access to information, education, cultural activities, opportunities for rest, play and leisure and the right to freedom of thought, conscience and religion. The Rights to Protection include assurance of protection not only from violation of rights but also from all kinds of exploitation and cruelty, arbitrary separation from the family and abuses in the justice and penal system. Protection is vital for especially vulnerable groups among children like abandoned children, street children, displaced children, etc. The Rights to Participation include the right to express opinions and the right to play an active role in the community and society through freedom of associations, etc. Since children by virtue of the fact that they are human beings and entitled to the rights enjoyed by adults, the UN Declaration on the rights of the child affirmed by the Convention provides for States to ensure mental, physical and moral development of the children. India has ratified the Convention on Rights of child of 1989.

Human Rights to Safe Environment

The Articles 3 and 25 can form the basis of a safe and healthy environment. The rights were reiterated in the 1992 Stockhold Declaration at the UN Conference on Environment. The recent resolution of 6 March 1990 adopted at 52nd Meeting of the Commission of Human rights of UN Economic and Social Councils. Over the last two decades, the concept of a human right to a safe and clean environment has emerged as one of the basic rights in a number of states. Article 12 of the International Covenant on Economic, Social and Cultural Rights recognize the rights of everyone to the highest attainable standard of physical and mental health, and agree to take steps to activate the full realization of this right, including the improvement of all aspects of environmental and industrial hygiene."

Human Rights and the International Instruments Relating to Human Rights

The status of International Instruments related to human rights as on 31st Dec. 1993 is shown in the table below:

International Instruments (date of entry into force)	*Total No. of States Parties*	*Total No. of Asian States*	*Ratification accession notification of succession acceptance etc. by Asian States.*
(1)	(2)	(3)	(4)
1. International Covenant on Economic, Social and Cultural Rights (3 January 1976)	122	18	Afghanistan, Democratic (North) Korea, Democratic Yemen, India, Iran, Iraq, Japan, Jordan, Lebanon, Mangolia, Nepal, Sri Lanka, The Philippines, Syria, Vietnam, Cambodia, Israel, Republic of Korea.
2. International Covenant on Civil and Political Rights (23 March 1976)*	122	18	Afghanistan, Cambodia, Democratic (North) Korea, Democratic Yemen, India, Iran, Iraq, Japan, Jordan, Lebanon, Mangolia, The Philippines, Republic of Korea, Sri Lanka, Syria, Vietnam, Israel, Nepal. *(Contd.)*

*Following 39 State parties have so far made declarations recognising the competence of Human Rights Committee under Article 41 of the Covenant: Algeria, Argentina, Austria, Australia, Belarus, Belgium, Canada, Chile, Congo, Denmark, Ecuador, Finland, Gambia, Germany, Guyana, Hungary, Iceland, Ireland, Italy, Luxemburg, Malta, The Netherlands, New Zealand, Norway, Peru, The Philippines, Poland, Republic of Korea, Senegal, Silvenia, Spain, Sri Lanka, Sweden, Switzerland, Tunisia, Ukraine, USA, UK and Zambia.

(1)	(2)	(3)	(4)
3. Optional Protocol to the International Covenant on Civil and Political Rights (23 Mar. 1976).	74	4	Republic of Korea, Mangolia, Nepal, The Philippines.
4. Second Optional Protocol to the International Covenant on Civil and Political Rights aiming at the abolition of the death penalty (2 March 1976)	19	Nil	
5. Convention on the Prevention and Punishment of the Crime of Genocide (12 Jan. 1961)	111	27	Afghanistan, China, Cambodia, Democratic Yemen, Fiji, India, Iran, Iraq, Israel, Jordan, Laos, Lebanon, Maldives, Mangolia, Myanmar, Nepal, Pakistan, Papua, New Guinea, Republic of Korea, South Vietnam, The Philippines, Saudi Arabia, Sri Lanka, Syria, Vietnam, Democratic Republic of Korea.
6. Convention on the non-applicability of Statutory Limitations to War Crimes and Crime against Humanity (11 Nov. 1970)	38	8	Afghanistan, Democratic Yemen, India, Laos, Mangolia, The Philippines, Vietnam, Democratic Republic of Korea.

(Contd.)

(1)	(2)	(3)	(4)
7. International Convention on the Elimination of All Forms of Racial Discriminations (4 Jan. 1969).*	137	27	Afghanistan, Bangladesh, China, Cambodia, Democratic Yemen, Fiji, India, Iran, Iraq, Israel, Jordan, Kuwait, Laos, Lebanon, Maldives, Mangolia, Nepal, Pakistan, Papua, New Guinea, The Philippines, Quatar, Republic of Korea, Sri Lanka, Syria, United Arab Emirates, Vietnam.
8. Convention relating to the Status of Refugees (22 April 1954)	117	11	China, Cambodia, Fiji, Iran, Israel, Japan, The Philippines, Yemen, Papua, New Guinea, Republic of Korea.
9. Protocol relating to the Status of Refugees (4 Oct. 1967)	118	11	China, Cambodia, Fiji, Iran, Israel, Japan, Papua, New Guinea, The Philippines, Yemen, Republic of Korea.
10. Convention relating to the status of Stateless persons (6 June 1960)	37	3	Fiji, Israel, Republic of (South) Korea.
11. Convention on the reduction of the Statelessness (13 Dec. 1975)	17	Nil	Nil

(Contd.)

*Following 18 States parties have so far made declarations recognising the competence of the Committee on the Elimination of Racial Discrimination under Article 14 of the Convention: Algeria, Australia, Bulgaria, Costa Rica, Denmark, Equador, France, Hungary, Iceland, Italy, Netherlands, Norway, Peru, Russian Federation, Senegal, Sweden, Ukraine and Uruguay.

(1)	(2)	(3)	(4)
12. Convention on the political rights of Women (7 July 1954)	103	18	Afghanistan, Democratic Yemen, Indonesia, Israel, Japan, Jordan, Laos, Lebanon, Mangolia, Fiji, Nepal, Pakistan, India, The Philippines, Papua, New Guinea, Republic of Korea, Thailand.
13. Convention on the nationality of Married Women (11 August 1958).	60	6	Fiji, Israel, Malaysis, Singapore, Sri Lanka, Jordan.
14. Convention on the Consent to Marriage, Minimum Age for Marriage and Registration of Marriages (9 Dec. 1954).	40	4	Democratic Yemen, Fiji, the Philippines, Jordan.
15. Slavery Convention of 1926	73	11	Afghanistan, Bangladesh, Fiji, India, Iraq, Israel, Lebanon, Myanmar, Nepal, Syria, Yemen.
16. Protocol Amending the Slavery Convention (7 Dec. 1953).	55	8	Afghanistan, Bangladesh, Fiji, India, Iraq, Israel, Myanmar, Syria.
17. Slavery Convention of 1926 as amended in 1953 (7 July 1955)	88	18	Afghanistan, Bangladesh, Fiji, India, Iraq, Israel, Jordan, Kuwait, Mangolia, Myanmar, Nepal, The Philippines, Papua, New Guinea, Pakistan, Saudi Arabia, Sri Lanka, Syria, Yemen.
18. Supplementary Convention on the Abolition of Slavery the Slave	106	20	Afghanistan, Bangladesh, Cambodia, Fiji, India, Iran, Iraq, Israel, Jordan,

(Contd.)

(1)	(2)	(3)	(4)
Trade and Institutions and practices Similar to Slavery (30 April 1957).			Kuwait, Laos, Malaysia, Mangolia, Nepal, Pakistan, The Philippines, Saudi Arabia, Singapore, Sri Lanka, Syria.
19. Convention tor the suppression of the Traffic in persons and the Exploitation of the Prostitution of others (25 July 1951)	65	16	Afghanistan, Bangladesh, India, Iraq, Israel, Japan, Jordan, Kuwait, Laos, Pakistan, Republic of Korea, the Philippines, Singapore, Sri Lanka, Syria, Yemen.
20. International Convention on the Suppression and punishment of the Crime of Apart held (19 July 1976)	98	21	Afghanistan, Bangladesh, Cambodia, China, India, Iran, Iraq, Kuwait, Laos, UAE, Maldives, Mangolia, Pakistan, Nepal, The Philippines, Quatar, Sri Lanka, Syria, Vietnam, Jordan, Yemen.
21. Convention on the Elimination of all forms of Discrimination against Women (3 Sept. 1981)	125	20	Bangladesh, Bhutan, China, Cambodia, Democratic Yemen, Indonesia, Iraq, Japan, Jordan, India, Israel, Laos, Maldives, Mangolia, The Philippines, Republic of (South) Korea, Sri Lanka, Thailand, Vietnam, Nepal.

(Contd.)

(1)	(2)	(3)	(4)
22. Convention against Torture and other Cruel, Inhuman or Degrading Treatment or Punishment (26 June 1987).*	76	8	Afghanistan, Cambodia, China, Israel, Jordan, Nepal, Yemen, The Philippines.
23. International Convention against Apartheid in Sports (3 April 1988).	56	10	India, Iran, Iraq, Israel, Jordan, Nepal, Mangolia, The Philippines, Quatar, Syria.
24. Convention of the Rights of the Child (2 September 1990).	149	76	Bangladesh, Bhutan, Cambodia, China, Fiji, India, Israel, Jordan, Kuwait, Lebanon, Myanmar, Laos, Republic of Korea, Indonesia, Maldives, Mangolia, Nepal, Pakistan, Papua, New Guinea, The Philippines, Vietnam, Sri Lanka, Syria, Thailand, Yemen.

*Following 36 State parties have so far made declarations recognising the competence of the Committee against Torture under Articles 21 and 22 of the Convention:
Algeria, Argentina, Austria, Australia, Bulgaria, Canada, Crotia, Cyprus, Denmark, Equador, Finland, France, Germany, Greece, Hungary, Italy, Liechtenstein, Luxemburg, Malta, Morocco, Netherlands, New Zealand, Norway, Portugal, Poland, Russian Federation, Spain, Sweden, Switzerland, Silvenia, Togo, Tunisia, Turkey, UK, Uruguay and Yugoslavia.

India has so far ratified the following International Instruments:

(1) International Covenant on Economic, Social and Cultural Rights.

(2) International Covenant on Civil and Political Rights.

(3) International Convention on the Elimination of all Forms of Racial Discriminations.

(4) International Convention on the Suppression and Punishment of the Crime of Apartheid.

(5) International Convention against Apartheid in Sports.

(6) Convention on the Prevention and Punishment of the Crime of Genocide.

(7) Convention on the Non-application of statutory limitations to war crimes and crimes against humanity.

(8) Convention on the right of the child.

(9) Convention on the Elimination of All Forms of Discrimination against Women.

(10) Convention on the Political Rights of Women.

(11) Slavery Convention of 1926.

(12) 1953, Protocol amending the 1926 Convention.

(13) Slavery Convention of 1926 as amended.

(14) Supplementary convention on the abolition of slavery, the above trade and institutions and practices similar to slavery.

(15) Convention for the suppression of the traffic in persons and the exploitation of the prostitution of others.

Indian Constitution has incorporated various provisions pertaining to human rights in its Constitution and other laws of the land. The Universal Declaration of Human Rights is the Magna Carta of human rights although the Declaration was not a treaty and was adopted by the General Assembly as a resolution having no force of law. It was adopted to provide a common understanding of the human rights and "a common standard of achievement for all peoples and all nations." India's legal provisions about human rights are indicated in the Table below:

Human Rights Provisions in U.N. Documents and in Our Constitution and Laws

S. No.	*Provision in U.N. Documents*	*Provision in the Constitution of India and/or Central Act, if any*
(1)	(2)	(3)
1.	All human beings are born free and equal in dignity and rights and should act in a spirit of brotherhood, (Universal Declaration of Human Rights 1948, Art. 1)	Preamble and Article 51A(e)
2.	Prohibition of discrimination on grounds of race, colour, sex, language, religion, political or other opinion : national or social origin, property, birth or other status, special measures taken for purpose of securing advancement of certain social or technic groups requiring such protection not to be deemed social discrimination. (Universal Declaration of Human Rights, Article 2 : Declaration of the rights of the child, 1959, principle 1 ; International Convention on the Elimination of All Forms of Racial Discrimination, 1966, Articles 1 (4), 2 and 5 : International Covenant on Civil and Political Rights, 1966, articles 24 and 26 ; and International Covenant on Economic, Social and Cultural Rights, 1966 Article 2(2).	Articles 15, 16 and 17 : Protection of Civil Rights Act, 1955 : Untouchability (Offences) Act, 1955.

3. Right to life, liberty and security of person; deprivation of liberty to be only on such grounds and in accordance with such procedure as may be established by law; right to seek pardon or commutation of sentence of death; sentence of death not to be imposed for crimes committed by persons below 18 years of age and not to be carried out on a pregnant woman (Universal Declaration of Human Rights, Article 3; International Convenant on Civil and Political Rights, Articles 6 and 9).	Article 21; Indian Penal Code, 1860, Section 54; Code of Criminal Procedure 1973, Sections 416, 432-434.
4. Freedom from slavery or servitude, and cruel, inhuman or degrading treatment; prohibition of slave trade, of traffic in women and children, and of forced or compulsory labour. (Universal Declaration of Human Rights, Articles 4 and 5; Declaration of the Rights of the Child, principle 9 ; International covenant on Civil and Political Rights, Articles 7 and 8; Declaration on Elimination of Discrimination against Women, 1967, Article 8 ; Supplementary Convention on the Abolition of Slavery, the Slave Trade, and Institutions and Practices similar to Slavery, 1956 ; Convention concerning the Abolition of Forced Labour, 1957).	Articles 17, 23 and 51 A(e); Indian Penal Code, Section 370 ; Untouchability (Offences) Act, 1955; Suppression of Immoral Traffic in Women and Girls Act 1956; Bonded Labour System (Abolition) Act, 1976.

5. Equality before the law and equal protection of law; equality before the law in the enjoyment of the right of access to any place or service intended for use by general public, such as transport, hotels, restaurant, cafes, theatres and parks, equality of opportunity and treatment in respect of employment and occupation. (Universal Declaration of Human Rights, Articles 6 and 7; Discrimination (Employment and Occupation) Convention, 1958, Articles 2; International Convention on Elimination of all Forms of Racial Discrimination, Article 5; and International Covenant on Civil and Political Rights, Article 26).	Articles 14, 15, 16 and 39 A : Protection of Civil Rights Act, 1955 as amended up-to-date.
6. Rights to an effective remedy to protect fundamental rights granted by Constitution or law (Universal Declaration of Human Rights, Article 8; Internation Covenant on Civil and Political Rights, Article 2 (3)).	Articles 31 D, 21, 39A, 226 and 227.
7. Protection against arbitrary arrest, detention or exile (Universal Declaration of Human Rights, Article 9; and International Covenant on Civil and Political Rights, Articles 6(1) and 9).	Article 22, Code of Criminal Procedure, 1973, Sections 49, 50, 56, and 57.

8. Right to a fair and public hearing by a competent, independent and impartial tribunal in determination of rights and obligations and of any criminal charge against an individual (Universal Declaration of Human Rights, Article 10; International Convention on Elimination of All Forms of Racial Discrimination, Article 5(a); and International Covenant on Civil and Political Rights, Article 14(1).	Article 50 ; Part V, Chapter IV; Part VI, Chapters V and VI; Code of Criminal Procedure, 1973, 55. 303, 304, 310, 327, 461, 479 etc.
9. Right to be presumed innocent until proved guilty; prohibition of retroactive penal laws and of double jeopardy (Universal Declaration of Human Rights, Article 11; and International Covenant of Civil and Political Rights, Articles 14(1) and (2) and 15(1).	Articles 20 and 22; Code of Criminal Procedure, Section 300.
10. Right to certain minimum guarantees in determination of criminal charge against an individual; procedure in case of juvenile persons to be such as takes account of their age and promotes their rehabilitation; right to one's conviction and sentence being reviewed by a higher tribunal. (International Covenant on Civil and Political Rights, Article 14(3), (4) and (5).	Code of Criminal Procedure, 1973; Probation of Offenders Act, 1958.

11.	Protection against arbitrary interference with privacy, family, home or correspondence, and against unlawful attacks on honour and reputation (Universal Declaration of Human Rights, Article 12; International Covenant on Civil and Political Rights, Article 17).	Article 21 (as interpreted in Kharak Singh's case, A.I.R. 1963 S.C. 1295); Indian Penal Code, 1860, Sections 441, 447, 499-503.
12.	Right to freedom of movement and residence within a State; right to leave any country, including one's own, and to return to one's country (Universal Declaration on Human Rights, Article 13; International Covenant on Civil and Political Rights, Article 12).	Article 19(1) (d) and (e) and Article 21 as interpreted in the Passport Case (Satwant Singh. Regional Passport Officer, New Delhi, A.I.R. 1967 SC 1836).
13.	Right to nationality; prohibition against arbitrary deprivation of nationality and right to change it; right of the child to a name and nationality from birth; women to have to same rights as men to acquire, change or retain their nationality, marriage to an alien not to automatically affect nationality of wife (Universal Declaration of Human Rights, Article 15 ; Declaration of the Rights of the Child, principle 3 ; Declaration on Elimination of Discrimination against women, Article 5).	Citizenship Act 1955.

14.	Right to marriage and to find a family; marriage with free and full consent of intending spouses; family to be protected by society and State : equality of rights and responsibilities of spouses as to marriage, during marriage, and at its dissolution; prohibition of child marriage and betrothal of young girls before puberty; specification of a minimum age for marriage, compulsory registration of marriages [Universal Declaration of Human Rights, Article 16, declaration on elimination of discrimination against women, Article 6 (2) and (3) ; International Convention on Elimination of all Forms of Racial Discrimination, Article 5; International Convention on Economic, Social and Cultural Rights, Article 10 (10).]	Hindu Widows' Remarriage Act, 1856; Indian Christian Marriage Act, 1872; Anand Marriage Act, 1909; Parsi Marriage and Divorce Act, 1936; Dissolution of Muslim Marriages Act, 1939 ; Arya Marriage Validation Act, 1937; Special Marriage Act, 1954; Hindu Marriage Act, 1955; Dowry Prohibition Act, 1961; Foreign Marriage Act, 1969; Child Marriage Restraint Act, 1929; Indian Penal Code, Sections 366, 493-498.
15.	Right to own property, and protection from arbitrary deprivation; women to be ensured equal rights with men in civil law and in particular the right to acquire, administer, enjoy, dispose of, and inherit property [Universal Declaration of Human Rights, Article 17, and Declaration on Elimination of Discrimination against Women, Article 6(1) (a)].	Article 19 (1) (f) and 31 (1) Requisitioning and Acquisition of immovable property Act, 1952; Married Women's Property Act, 1874; Married Women's Property (Extension) Act, 1959; and Hindu Succession Act, 1956.

16.	Right to freedom of thought, conscience and religion including freedom to manifest religion in teaching, practice, worship and observance; right of ethnic, religious or linguistic minorities to profess and practice their own religion (Universal Declaration of Human Rights Article 18; and International Covenant on civil and political rights, Articles 18 and 27).	Articles 19, 25, 26, 29 and 30; Indian Penal Code Sections 295-298.
17.	Right to freedom of opinion and expression; right to freedom of peaceful assembly and association; prohibition against compulsion to belong to an association (Universal Declaration of Human Rights, Articles 19 and 20; and International Covenant of Civil and Political Rights, Articles 19 and 21.)	Article 19(1) (a), (b) and (c); the Trade Unions Act, 1926.
18.	Right to take part in government of one's country ; right of equal access to public services; expression of people's will in free, universal and equal sufferage by periodic elections to be the basis of Government; right of women, on equal terms with men, to vote and to stand for elections, to hold public office, and to exercise public functions (Universal Declara-	Preamble, Articles 16, 55, 56, 58, 62, 66, 67, 83, 84, 172, 173, 326; Representation of the people act, 1950 ; Representation of the people act, 1951; Representation of the People (Miscellaneous Provisions) Act, 1956; Presidential and Vice-Presidential Elections Act, 1952 Union Territories (Direct Election to the House of the people) Act,

	tion of Human Rights, Article 21; Convention of Political Rights of Women 1953, Articles I, II and III; Declaration on Elimination of Women, Article-4; International Covenant on Civil and Political Rights, Articles 1 and 25; International Covenant on Economic, Social and Cultural Rights, Article 1).	1965; Parliament (Prevention of Disqualifications) Act, 1959.
19.	Right to social security to realisation of economic, social and cultural rights indispensable to one's dignity and development of personality (Universal Declaration of Human Rights, Article 22; and International Covenant on Economic, Social and Cultural Rights, Article 9),	Preamble.
20.	Right to work, to free choice of employment, to just and favourable conditions of work, and to protection against unemployment; Right to equal remuneration for men and women for work of equal value; Right to just and favourable remuneration ; Right to form and join trade unions for protection of one's interests. [Universal Declaration of Human Rights, Article 23 Convention concerning Equal Remuneration for men and women workers for works of equal value, Article 2; International Covenant on Civil and Political Rights,	Articles 16, 19, 39, 41, 42, 43 and 43A; Work men's Compensation Act, 1923; Trade Unions Act, 1926; Industrial Employment (Standing Orders) Act, 1946 ; Mica Mines Labour Welfare Fund Act, 1946; Coal Mines Labour Welfare Fund Act, 1947; Industrial Disputes Act, 1947; the Factories Act 1948; the Dock Workers (Regulation of employment) Act, 1948; Employment State Insurance Act, 1948; Mines Act 1952 ; the Employees Provident Funds and Miscellaneous Provisions

	Article 22(1) and (2); International Covenant on Economic, Social and Cultural Rights, Articles 7 and 8(1) (a)].	Act, 1952; Apprentices Act, 1961; Motor Transport Workers Act 1961; Iron Ore Mines Labour Welfare Cess Act, 1961; Equal Remuneration Act, 1976. The payment of Wages Act, 1936.
21.	Right to rest and leisure, including limitation of working hours and periodic holidays with pay (Universal Declaration of Human Rights, Article 24; International Covenant on Economic, Social and Cultural Rights, Art. 7).	Article 43, Weekly Holidays Act, 1942; the Coal Mines Labour Welfare Act, 1947; Industrial Employment (Standing Orders) Act, 1946.
22.	Right to an adequate standard of living and right to security in the event of unemployment, sickness, disability, widowhood, old age or other lack of livelihood; Maternity and Child Welfare—Prevention of dismissal of women on account of marriage or maternity leave and necessary social services; Protection of children and young persons from economic and social exploitation; child not to be admitted to employment before an appropriate minimum age and not to be caused or permitted to engage in any occupation or employment interfering with his physical, mental and moral development; Duty of society and public authorities to extend particular care to children without a family and to these without adequate	Articles 24, 39, 41, 42, and 47. Children (Pledging of Labour) Act, 1933, Employment of Children Act, 1938; Maternity Benefit Act, 1941; Employees State Insurance Act, 1948 ; Plantations Labour Act, 1951; Orphanages and other Charitable Homes (Supervision and Control) Act, 1960, Maternity Benefit Act 1961 ; Children Act, 1960 ; Personal Injuries (Compensation Insurance) Act, 1963; the Factories Act, 1948; Workmen's Compensation Act, 1923; Mica Mines Labour Welfare Fund Act, 1946; Coal Mines Labour Welfare Fund Act, 1947, Coal Mines Provident Fund and Miscellaneous Provisions Act, 1948;

	means of support; special treatment, education and care to be given to a physically, mentally or socially handicapped child (Universal Declaration of Human Rights, Article 25; Declaration of the Rights of the child, principles 5, 6 and 9; Declaration on Elimination of Discrimination against women, Article 10; International Covenant on Economic, Social and Cultural Rights, Article 10 and 11(1).	Employment of Children Act, 1938; the Mines Act, 1952; the Apprentices Act, 1961; Dock Workers (Regulation of employment) Act, 1948, Local Authorities Pensions and Gratuities Act, 1919, Employers' Liability Act, 1938.
23.	Right to education — elementary education to be free and compulsory; technical, professional and higher education to be made available on merit; Education for full development of human personality, strengthening of respect for human rights and to further activities of U.N. for maintenance of peace; prior right of parents to choose the kind of education for their children; freedom of individuals and bodies to establish and direct educational institutions subject to certain requirements; Girls and Women to be ensured equal rights with men in education (Universal Declaration of human rights, Article 26; Declaration of the rights of the child, principle 7; Declaration of Elimination of Discrimination against women, Article	Articles 15, 28, 30, 45, 46 and 51; Delhi Primary Education Act, 1960.

	9, International Covenant on Economic, Social and Cultural Rights, Articles 13 and 14.)	
24.	Right to freely participate in the cultural life of the community, to enjoy arts and to share in scientific advancement and its benefits; Right to protection of moral and material interests resulting to an author from his scientific, literary or artistic production; Right of ethnic, religious or linguistic minorities to enjoy their own culture and to use their own language [Universal Declaration of Human Rights, Article 27, International Covenant on Civil and Political Rights, Articles 2 (1) and 27].	Articles 29 and 39; Designs Act, 1911; Copyright Act, 1957; Parents Act, 1970.
25.	Limitations in exercise of rights and freedoms only for securing due recognition and respect for rights and freedoms of others and for morality, public order and general welfare (Universal Declaration of Human Rights, Article 29; International Covenant on Civil and Political Rights, Articles 12, 18, 19, 21 and 22).	Articles 19(2) to (6), 23(2), 25(1), 26(1), 31(2), 31 C, 31 D and 33.

Emergency and its Impact on Human Rights

Constitution of India, Part XVIII (Articles 352-360), provides a separate set of provisions to deal with situations such as a war or external aggression or even internal rebellion, civil war or iike which render it impossible for the normal constitutional machinary to cope with the abnormal situation. During emergency, certain human rights can be derogated in the internal covenant of civil and political rights 1966. During public emergencies which threaten the organised life of the nation (communities), certain human rights can be derogated as a temporary measure till continuance of an exceptional situation of crisis or emergency crisis or threat to the nation may be either actual or imminent and such provisions exist in Article 352 (1) of the Indian Constitution which has been as under :

"Explanation — A Proclamation of Emergency declaring that the security of India or any part of the territory thereof is threatened by war or by external aggression or by armed rebellion may be made before the actual occurrence of war or of any such aggression or rebellion, if the President is satisfied that there is an eminent danger thereof"[16] Article 4 of the International Covenant on civil and political rights says: "Article 4-1. In time of public emergency which threatens the life of the nation and the existence of which is officially proclaimed, the State parties to the present covenant may take measures derogating from their obligations under the present covenant to the extent strictly required by the exigencies of the situation, provided that such measures are not inconsistent with their own obligations under international law and do not involve discrimination solely on the ground of race, colour, sex, language, religion or social origin.

2. No derogation from Articles 6, 7 and 8 (Paragraphs 1 and 2) 11, 15, 16 and 18 may be made under this provision.

Human rights are thus of two categories. One category is called "non-derogable rights" and the other category is called "derogable rights" under the Indian Constitution. Articles 358-359 are provisions derogating from the fundamental rights during the operation of a proclamation of Emergency by the President, under Indian Constitution "armed rebellion" implies something like the offence of waging war against the Government in power or a conspiracy or combination to overthrow lawful government by force" (Section 121 of Indian Penal Code is relevant). The 44th Constitutional Amendment Act 1978 got 352(1) by substituting "armed rebellion" for "internal disturbance". The 42nd Amendment Act 1976 empowers the President to proclaim emergency confined to a particular area only without effecting the rest of India.

Restrictions and Limitations

Under the exercise of the right of "derogation", for preserving the life and existence of the nation-State itself, the State is free from the obligations imposed by the human rights in times of "war and other public emergency. When the violation of human rights are sought to be justified under a limitation clause, the law would be saved only if the terms of the relevant clause such as reasonableness, public interest and the like as satisfied. [Chintaman Rao *vs* State of M.P. (195) SCR 750]. Article 29(s) of the Universal Declaration of Human Rights, Articles 12(3), 14(1), 18(3), 19(3), 21, 22(2) of International Covenants on civil and political rights, and Articles 8(2), 9(2), 10(2), 11(2) of European Convention on Human Rights append specific limitations to each of the human rights, apart from some generic provisions. No human right is absolute and some limitations are needed for the protection of the society and the nation-States (Kochuni *vs* State of Madras A 1960, SC 1960, SC 1080) (1099). Indian Supreme Court in words of Das J. has held that "putting restraint on the freedom of wrong-doing of one person is really securing the liberty of the intended victims. Therefore restraint on liberty should be judged not only subjectively as applied to a few individuals who come within their operations but also objectively as securing the liberty of a greater number of individuals... (Constituting the State" (Gopalan *vs* State of Madras 1950) S.C.R. 88 (292). In the Indian Constitution for human rights the limitation clauses are to be found in clauses (2)-(6) of Article 19, provided the conditions of reasonableness of the restrictions imposed and the grounds specified in the relevant clause are satisfied. (Ram *vs* Union of India) A-1965 SC 1178 (Para 10.13). In Indian Constitution, Articles 31 and 31 C offer complete exceptions to the fundamental rights guaranteed by Part-III of the Constitution and if any law comes within the ambit of above referred articles (Article 31A or 31B or 31C) the law enacted with the safeguard and upheld even though its provisions are unreasonable or arbitrary (State of Tamil Nadu *vs* Abu A 1984 SC 326; Niyami *vs* Union of India, AIR 1990 S.C. 2128 (para 3). It has been held that there cannot be anything as absolute or uncontrolled liberty for that would lead to anarchy and disorder. [Gopalan *vs* State of Madras (1950), SCR 88, Santosh Singh Vs Delhi Administration AIR 1973 SC 1091].

Judicial Activism and Protection

Justice Bhagwati has pointed out that public interest litigation is intended to bring justice within the reach of the poor masses who constitute the low visibility area of humanity. Article 23 of the constitution is clearly designed to protect the individual not only against the State but also against other private citizens. Article 23 strikes at forced labour in whatever form it may manifest itself, because it is violative of human dignity and is contrary to basic human values. (Rolut Vasuvada *vs* General Manager IFFCO AIR 1984 Guj 10—also Asiad Workers Case AIR 1982 SC 1473). Bandhua Mukti Morcha *vs* Union of India is a landmark judgement of the Supreme Court where the bonded labourers have been protected from exploitation. (AIR 1992 SC 802) Regarding Protection of children from exploitation, Supreme Court has observed "Construction work is clearly a hazardous essential that the employment of children under the age of 14 years must be prohibited in every type of construction work. This is a constitutional prohibition which, even if not followed by appropriate legislation, must operate Proprio Viaore" (People's Union for Democratic Rights and Union of India AIR 1982 SC 1473). In Sheela Barse *vs* Secretary, Children and Society, the Supreme Court observed, "Every society must devote full attention to ensure that children are properly cared for and brought up in a proper atmosphere where they could receive adequate training, education, and guidance in order that they may be able to have their rightful place in the society when they grow up. (AIR 1987 SC 656) Supreme Court has also followed the activist approach and provided judgements granting the right to live in healthy environment. Ratlam Municipality *vs* Vardi Chand (AIR 1980 SC 1622) and M.C. Mehta *vs* Union of India (AIR 1987 SC 1087) are landmarks judgements on environment.

Internal Security: Challenges and Issues

In plural, secular and democratic societies violent movements arise out of socio-economic and political discontents. When available political processes are found inadequate to provide outlets for redressal of grievances, when there are credibility gaps in socio-political systems, when population of a particular area feels threatened with identify crisis, certain sections at times resort to violent political movements. When the nation-States use police and security forces to put down politically violent movements, excessive use of force or aberrations in the conduct and behaviour of police officers further alienate the population and the political discontent at times gets identified. Police and PMF have a very limited role to play in combating and containing the criminality of political movements. Terrorism, insurgency and extremism are basically violent political movements born due to the existence of political discontent and which seek redressal through violent means. Unfortunately generally at many occasions political leaders try to put down politically violent movements with use of force through deployment of police and para-military forces. When the State uses police and para-military forces to put down such movements, excessive use of forces alienate the local population and the discontent intensifies. The first requisite therefore is to realise that political ideologies cannot be put down by force and the use of force should be limited to dealing with the criminality endemic in such situations.[17] The problem of human rights in areas torn by intense strife and such manifestations of violence as terrorism and secessionist activities need to be looked at from a different perspective.[18] What is the solution to the internal security challenges when the very life and integrity of the nation are at stake ? When the very existence of a secular plural and democratic society is in real peril, are human rights more important than the preservation of the nation's integrity ? Indeed who lives if the nation withers? Therefore to meet such critical situations, policing is assisted and partly replaced by the para-military forces because in the clash of arms, laws are silent. Nations make the so-called draconian laws to meet such serious situations. Political movements of disturbed areas like Kashmir and north-eastern states cannot be put down only with the use of force and deployment of security forces, because the solutions to such violent political movements lie in the political processes in the ultimate analysis. Internal security operations are often very challenging, complex and difficult because internal security has to be maintained in accordance with the laws of the land and rule of law. During internal security operations carried out by the commandos in Punjab till 31 January 1993, there were 117 encounters, in which 222 terrorists were killed including 56 hardcore ones and 283 weapons were seized.[19] Since 1989 in internal security operations more than 1300 police casualties took place. In Kashmir, Pakistan is waging a proxy war with the help of mercenaries. Insurgents and terrorists commit murders, kidnapping, extortions, rapes and all other types of crime which are ultimately violations of human rights. Internal security forces are performing their duties under tremendous pressure, strains and stresses. They are highly overworked, in most hazardous working environment, without local people's support at times, thousands of miles away from their families. Often in disturbed areas, one would find the local police highly demoralised and often infected with the dissident ideology.[20] "Human Rights", says Claire Palley, "provide criteria for making value judgements—reflect normative judgements as to what is permissible to be done by free and responsible persons, acting either individually or collectively through the Government. Human Rights can be used to evaluate the law of States by deciding whether the standards inherent in such rights are reflected in positive law". "The path of Human Rights", says an author, "does not run smooth and straight. Every day we stumble against the irrational, reason is pushed to one side and rights are trodden underfoot." In Keshvananda Bharati's case, Justice Dwivedi observed : "The Constitution is not intended to be the arena of legal quibbling for men with long purses. It is made for the common people".[21] Speaking in the similar tone Justice Chandrachud noted : "It is really the poor, starved and mindless millions who need the court's protection for securing to themselves the enjoyment of human rights."[22]

"Today we find that in Third World countries there are large number of groups which are being subjected to exploitation, injustice, and even violence. In this climate of conflict and injustice, judges have to play a positive role and they cannot content themselves by invoking the doctrines of self-restraint and passive interpretation. The judges in India have fortunately a most potent judicial power in their hands, namely, the power of judicial review. The judicious and sustained use of its power to further the cause of social justice has come to be regarded by many as not only beneficent but imperative in a developing country where there is large-scale poverty and ignorance. The judiciary has to play a vital and important role not only in preventing the remedying abuse and misuse of power but also in eliminating exploitation and injustice."[23] "It would be no exaggeration to state that human rights would remain safe in a society governed by a written Constitution so long as its judges are strong and independent, do not come into pressures or influence of centres of power and are committed to the cause of human rights. The judiciary has to be ever alert to repel all attacks, gross or subtle, against human rights and they have to guard against the danger of allowing themselves to be persuaded to be attenuate or constrict human rights out of misconceived concern for the State interest or concealed political preference or sometimes ambition or weakness or blandishments or fear of executive reaction. Judicial somnambulance, indifference or timidity can be the source of greater threat to human rights enforcement than the aggression of the violators, for the greatest bulwark against State authoritarianism or arbitrariness would then be gone."[24] "A heavy responsibility immediately falls on the shoulders of the judges in discharging the judicial function particularly in relation to enforcement of human rights. The approach of the judiciary in the interpretation of human rights should be creative and purposive and the judiciary must adopt an activist goal oriented approach and the interpretation of the fundamental rights embodied in the Bill of Rights or in a statutory legislation. The judges must boldly interpret the charter of human rights enshrined in the Constitution ... There is considerable scope for creativity for a judge if only he is dedicated to the cause of human rights and is prepared to advance human rights jurisprudence by a process of judicial interpretation.[25] "The so-called protagonists of human rights are preoccupied only with the superstructure civil and political rights of urban and rural elite to the exclusion of other rights."[26] "The expression 'protective custody', was a euphemism calculated to disguise what was really and in truth nothing short of a blatant violation of personal liberty guaranteed under Article 21, because there was no provisions of law under which a woman could be kept in jail by way of 'protective custody' merely because she was required for the purpose of giving evidence. Taking a bold approach he directed that all women and children who are in the jails in the State of Bihar under protective custody or who are in jail because their presence is required for giving or who are victims of offence should be released and taken forthwith to welfare homes or rescue homes and should be kept there and properly looked after." Justice Bhagwati proceeded to fill up the gap through creative interpretation of Article 21 following upon his own judgement in Maneka Ghandhi's case. He maintained that a procedure which does not make legal services available to an accused person who is too poor to afford a lawyer and who would, therefore, go through the trial without legal assistance cannot be regarded as responsible, fair and just. He held that the right to legal assistance was an essential element of any reasonable, fair and just procedure for a person accused of an offence and it must be held implicit in the guarantee of Article 21. Justice Bhagwati thus spelt out the right to legal aid in a criminal proceeding from the language of Article 21 and held that this, "is a constitutional right of every accused person who is unable to engage a lawyer and secure legal services on account of reasons such as poverty, indigence or incommunicado situation and the State is under a mandate to provide a lawyer to an accused person if the circumstances of the case and the needs of justice so require, provided of course the accused person does not object to the provision of such lawyer." The right to life protected under Article 21 of the Constitution was not confined merely to the right to physical existence but it also included within its broad matrix the right to the use of every faculty or limb through which life is enjoyed as also the right to live with basic human dignity. Using 'creative' approach and 'elaboration of rights strategy in Francis Mullan's case Justice Bhagwati elevated immunity against torture or cruel, inhuman or degrading treatment or punishment to the status of a fundamental right under Article 21, though it was not specifically enumerated as a fundamental right in the Constitution.

— Four or five police lock-ups should be selected in reasonably good localities where only female suspects should be kept and they should be guarded by female constables. Female suspects should not be kept in the same Police lock up in which male suspects are detained;

— Interrogation of women should be carried out only in the presence of women police officers/constables;

- Whenever a person is arrested by the Police without warrant, he must be immediately informed of the grounds of his arrest and in case of every arrest, it must be immediately made known to the arrested person that he is entitled to apply for bail;
- Whenever a person is arrested and taken to the police lock-up the intimation of such arrest must immediately be given to the nearest Legal Aid Committee so that immediate steps can be taken for the purpose of providing legal assistance to the arrested person at the State cost;
- As soon as a person is arrested, the police must immediately obtain from him the name of any relative or friend whom he would like to be informed of his arrest and the police should get in touch with such relative or friend and inform him about the arrest;
- The Magistrate before whom the arrested person is produced should enquire from him whether he has any complaint of torture or maltreatment in police custody and inform him that he has a right under Section 54 of the Code of Criminal Procedure to be medically examined.

Violations of Human Rights

Shri Dharma Vira, Chairman of National Police Commission has observed, "We may modify our laws to safeguard human dignity or talk loudly about such dignity or rights but so long as the police behaviour, in our country, remains as it is today, all such provisions and declarations would prove to be only on paper and not in reality".[27] There is a general feeling of immunity that persists among police offices in India, particularly in the civil police, that they are above law and the system will provide them protection. Modern scientific methods of interrogation like lie detectors, are not available at grass root levels in police and there is constant pressure from superior police officers and politicians to deliver quick results. There are numerous causes and factors responsible for various violations of human rights by the Indian police. Inadequate police training, inadequate supervision by senior officers and corruption in police are some of the main causes of violations of human rights. Lack of adequate recognition of human rights by the police and the police sub-culture of violence also contribute for the violations of human rights by the police. "Clearly the rot in top echelons is responsible for the mess down below. A senior police officer commented that only extra-constitutional methods could restore law and order in Punjab".[28] When police officers violating human rights and even indicated by High Courts for violations of human rights are awarded medals, the message goes round that police could get away with such aberrations. The apathy of the public and insensitivity of the Government have emboldened the guardians of law to go ahead with more daring forms of violations of human rights. A retired police chief says all cases of custodial deaths and police misdeanor are quietly buried after the initial furore is over. The cases are investigated and charges framed in such a manner that there are enough loopholes for the guilty to escape. The political masters are led to believe by the top police leaders that if police are taken to task, it would demoralise them and consequently they would not be able to perform their arduous tasks effectively. The police violations of human rights in India have increased over the last 5 years because of an ineffective criminal justice system. According to Shri N.S. Saksena, the dishonest IPS Officer who cannot control his station house officers, lets this evil degenerate to a point where policemen beat any one who annoys them.[29] Violations of human rights in terms of police excesses in torture and brutality are committed with great frequency and extensively in India where police officers are with sadistic temperament and there is lack of effective supervision by the senior officers. When there is undue delay in bringing the offenders to justice and there is reluctance on the part of the public to come forward as witnesses, police start resorting to rough and ready short-cut methods to justice. In several States of India, the police have merged into a powerful autonomous body with the senior officers having hardly any effective control over the policemen who have close links with politicians and caste lords. "Encounters" and "disappearances" are often reported by human right organisations. The Chief Minister of West Bengal Shri Jyoti Basu, admitted on the floor of the Assembly in June 4, 1992 that 78 prisoners died in police custody between April 1987 and June 1992 in West Bengal. Since independence, a large number of Commissions of Inquiry to probe into the complaints of torture and death in police custody, brutalities committed during police operations, have made various recommendations, but because of the reluctance on the part of the government to implement their recommendations, all reports are gathering dust. Justic V.V. Chandra Chud, Former Chief Justice of India in 1985, has observed, "Police officers, alone, and none else, can give evidence regarding the circumstances in which a person in their custody comes to receive injuries. Bound by the ties of a kind of brotherhood, they often prefer to remain silent to such situations and when they choose to speak, they put their own gloss upon facts and pervert the truth". It is very well established that Indian society tactly expects and approves the use of violence on suspects to get at the truth and provides social sanction to the principle of "an eye for an eye". Many unscrupulous police officers tend to play psychological factors freely in obtaining confessions and work out cases successfully. Overwork and pressure of work also tend to cause violations of human rights in a society where professionalism is at a discount and where politicians want quick results ignoring means. Legal hurdles, like inability to keep a suspect for longer duration are also responsible partly for violations of human rights by the police. Very often policemen find themselves caught in a dilemma when they find that criminals apprehended after great difficulty and risk, are released by Courts on bail. Police brutality and violations of human rights are symptoms of a sick society where criminal justice administration has almost collapsed and political masters demand control of crime and violence. However, violations of human rights by the police are on the increase of late because the senior officers and inquiring officers are reluctant and slow to investigate cases of police excesses because of the illusion that to do so will sap public confidence in the police generally and will demoralise the policemen.

Analysis of Violations

In a significant reflection of the high incidence of human rights violations by security forces, the highest number of cases admitted by the National Human Rights Commission in its very first year are in the category of custodial deaths and other police excesses. For the period from October 1993 to March **1994 a** total of 496 cases were registered. As per record, 174 cases were admitted for further investigation and enquiry. Atleast 34 of these pertain to custodial deaths, 61 cases of police excesses and 10 cases of reported excesses by the Armed Forces.[30] Of the total cases registered the nine defaulting States and one union territory in terms of human rights violations with number of human rights violations are as under:

1. Uttar Pradesh	102	No. of cases
2. Tamil Nadu	61	,,
3. Orissa	51	,,
4. Gujarat	45	,,
5. Madhya Pradesh	43	,,
6. Delhi	36	,,
7. Kerala	25	,,
8. Rajasthan	24	,,
9. Andhra Pradesh	17	,,
10. West Bengal	15	,,

The Human Rights Commission undertook 26 suo moto inquiries including the infamous Bijbehara massacre in Jammu and Kashmir when atleast 60 civilians died in a firing by personnel of the Border Security Force.

Punishment for Human Rights Excesses

Punishment have been meted out to 39 army personnel in the past four years for human rights excesses during operations in Jammu & Kashmir. These include 15 officers, two JCOs, and 22 other ranks. There were 245 cases of human rights violations in the past four years by the BSF in J & K. Of these 134 cases are still being investigated while punishment of varying degree has been meted in 111 cases. During the period 1990-94 there was one case of death of a militant in army custody for which a lieutenant-colonel was charged under Sec. 63 of the Army Act and censured with "displeasure" for not exercising effective control while a captain and second lieutenant "reprimanded" in the same case. Of the 39 army personnel punished, 15 have been charged with rape, molestation and outraging the modesty of women. In one instance, two captains were cashiered and asked to undergo one year rigorous imprisonment for allegedly raping a Canadian woman. Twelve others, in the rank of havildars and sepoys were dismissed with punishment ranging from six months to 12 years rigorous imprisonment. They were charged with the rape of local woman and attempted molestation. In certain cases punishments varying from "reprimand" to a reduction in rank were awarded to certain personnel for failure to exercise proper control of their subordinates resulting in violation of human rights. In one case a lieutenant colonel, a major and a captain, under whose supervision an "anti-national element" sustained injuries in army custody, were censured with severe displeasure. (Anita Katyal, "Army men punished for human rights excesses" *Times of India*, April 11, 1995). During the last four years three officers, one Inspector, 5 Sub-Inspectors, 5 HCs and 4 NKs, 3 LNKs and 46 Cts making it to 64 have been punished for violation of human rights in CRPF. In CRPF the details of violation of human rights from 1991-93 are as under :

Year	*Total No. of cases*	*Allegations found false*	*Allegations confirmed*	*Cases decided*	*Cases pending*
1991	51	26	4	29	22
1992	9	5	4	1	8
1993	1	—	—	—	1

In India as per official figures 69 incidents of custodial deaths were reported in 1990, 59 in 1991 and 69 in 1992 and 68 in 1993. The number of deaths in police custody during 1981-84 in some of the States are as under :

States	*1981*	*1982*	*1983*	*1984*
1. Andhra Pradesh	4	8	7	7
2. Bihar	5	10	NA	7
3. Gujarat	5	3	7	5
4. Haryana	2	NA	4	5
5. Karnataka	3	3	2	NA
6. Kerala	1	2	3	NA
7. Madhya Pradesh	7	9	6	9
8. Maharashtra	23	21	27	26
9. Orissa	2	7	3	2

	States	*1981*	*1982*	*1983*	*1984*
10.	Punjab	2	2	1	2
11.	Rajasthan	7	1	2	12
12.	Tamil Nadu	NA	NA	6	12
13.	Uttar Pradesh	5	10	16	NA
14.	West Bengal	17	13	11	14
15.	Delhi	2	5	2	4

In Rajasthan 12 deaths had taken place in various police stations during the year 1994.[31] In Delhi alone there were nine custodial rapes in 1988, ten in 1989 and four upto 31 March 1990 were noted.[32] A People's Union for Democratic Rights (PUDR) study of 14 cases of custodial rape in Delhi between 1988-90 make it clear that the rapist invariably manages to escape.

National Human Rights Commission of India

Section 3 of the Protection of Human Rights Act 1993 provides for the Constitution of a Commission consisting of :

(a) A Chairperson who has been a Chief Justice of the Supreme Court;

(b) One Member who is, or has been, a Judge of the Supreme Court;

(c) One Member who is, or has been, the Chief Justice of a High Court;

(d) Two Members to be appointed from amongst persons having knowledge of, or practical experience in, matters relating to human rights.

The Chairpersons of the National Commission for Minorities, the National Commission for Scheduled Castes and Scheduled Tribes and the National Commission for Women are deemed to be Members of the Commission for the discharge of the various functions assigned to it, except for the function relating to inquiry into complaints of violation of human rights, viz., that are mentioned in Section 12 (a) (i) and (ii) of the Act.

Functions of the Commission

The functions of the national human rights commission are given below:

(a) inquire, suo motu or on a petition presented to it by a victim or any person on his behalf, into complaint of :

   (i) violation of human rights or abetment thereof or

   (ii) negligence in the prevention of such violation, by a public servant;

(b) intervene in any proceeding involving any allegation of violation of human rights pending before a Court with the approval of such Court;

(c) visit, under intimation to the State Government any jail or any other institution under the control of the State Government, where persons are detained or lodged for purposes of treatment reformation or protection to study the living conditions of the inmates and make recommendations thereon;

(d) review the safeguards provided by or under the Constitution or any law for the time being in force for the protection of human rights and recommend measures for their effective implementation;

(e) review the factors, including acts of terrorism that inhibit the enjoyment of human rights and recommend appropriate remedial measures;

(f) study treaties and other international instruments on human rights and make recommendations for their effective implementation;

(g) undertake and promote research in the field of human rights;

(h) spread human rights literacy among various sections of society and promote awareness of the safeguards available for the protection of these rights through publications, the media, seminars and other available means;

(i) encourage the efforts of non-governmental organisations and institutions working in the field of human rights;

(j) such other functions as it may consider necessary for the promotion of human rights.

Inquiry into complaints: During the relatively brief period covered by this report, the commission had already registered 496 cases. Of these, 174 were admitted for further investigation/ inquiry/report while 274 were dismissed. In respect of 48 cases the Commission disposed of complaint with observations to the effect that remedies were more appropriately available in other fora, and that the complaints should seek such remedies from them. In accordance with its statute and regulations, the grounds for the dismissal of complaints were broadly that :

(i) The complaints did not fall within the purview of the Commission;

(ii) The matter was sub-judice or pending before another Commission;

(iii) The event, which was the object of the complaint had occurred more than one year before the making of the complaint;

(iv) The complaint was vague or frivolous and no specific case had been made out of a human rights violation.

Illustrative cases: Firing by Security Forces in Bijbehara, Jammu & Kashmir.

On 1 November 1993, the Commission, suo motu, took cognizance of press reports about the death of about 60 persons in and around Bijbehara in Jammu & Kashmir as a result of firing by security forces operating in the area and called for reports from the Ministries of Defence and Home Affairs as also the Government of J. & K. While the Ministry of Defence clarified that the army was not involved, the Ministry of Home Affairs sent a report to the Commission on the basis of the Magisterial Inquiry ordered by the State Government into the incident and the Staff Court of Inquiry ordered by BSF authorities. On examination of the report, the Commission felt that perusal of copies of evidence given by six witnesses was necessary and accordingly called for additional material, viz., the evidence given by the witnesses. That evidence having been made available to the Commission and considered by it, together with the report and material provided earlier, the Commission made the following observations recommendations:

(a) The Commission noted that disciplinary proceedings had been initiated under the Border Security Force Act against 14 members of the Force, and further that, on the basis of a Magisterial Inquiry, steps may be initiated to launch prosecutions. The commission expected that the dual proceedings would be pursued their respective logical ends and that it would be kept informed the action taken against those found guilty.

(b) Payment was recommended of interim compensation on a graded scale.

(c) It was recommended that a thorough review should be undertaken by Government of the circumstances and conditions in which Units of the Border Security Force are deployed and expected to operate in situations involving only civilian population.

These were communicated to the Central Government and the Commission has since been informed that the recommendations made by it have been accepted.

Review of Existing Laws, Implementation of Treaties and other International Instruments

Sub-sections (d) and (f) of Section 12 of the Act respectively empower the Commission to review the safeguards provided by or under the Constitution or any law for the time being in force, and study treaties and other international instruments on human rights with a view to making recommendations for their effective implementation. In the short period since its inception, the Commission has directed its attention to starting an in-depth study of the Terrorist and Disruptive Activities (Prevention) Act (TADA), a task in which it has enlisted the assistance of the Law Commission. A second area of study for the Commission relates to the range of issues concerning the rights of the child including the vexed and cruel question of child labour. A third area of study for the Commission relates to legislation affecting the rights of women. The National Commission for Women, which is represented in the National Human Rights Commission through its chairperson, has done considerable work in this area with the help of most eminent committee which it established for this purpose. The National Human Rights Commission intends to remain in close touch with its sister Commission on this matter, with a view to examining the issues on which it can best be of support and encouragement.

Promotion of Human Rights Literacy. The promotion of human rights literacy in a society as complex and textured as ours is a task that is, at once, both daunting and crucially important. It is also a task that calls for great perseverance, for it requires deep and lasting commitment. Indeed, there is no easy way to create a culture of human rights: all sections of society have a role to play, and an ideal to sustain, if the cause of human rights is to take root and flourish against the cruel odds of social injustice and inequality, the problems of poverty and the fanatical destructiveness of terrorism. Soon after its establishment, the Commission decided—as a first series of steps—to concentrate on three key sectors of our society : first, the political parties, for ours is a nation profoundly devoted to multi-party democracy; second, the executive authority at all levels, for ours is a federal structure and third, educationists and those responsible for curricula monitoring, for human rights literacy needs its teachers—and pupils if it is to take deep root in our soil. The Commission accordingly addressed letters to the Presidents of political parties represented in the Lok Sabha, the Rajya Sabha or in the State Legislatures. The Commission observed the political parties, by their behaviour and the ideals that they propagate, can create the most powerful force for the promotion and protection of human rights of all of the citizens of our country. In so far as the educational system is concerned, a number of steps have been taken. Meetings have been initiated with the Department of Education, Ministry of Human Resource Development and the National Council for Educational Research and Training (NCERT), for evolving appropriately graded curricula for various levels of schooling. The Department of Education and the NCERT are in the process of preparing drafts for the imminent consideration of the Commission. At the University level, the Commission has addressed communications to all Vice-Chancellors, proposing four measures:

(i) that the subject of human rights, in all of its dimensions, may find a clear place in the curriculam of the University;

(ii) that research, seminars and publications concerning human rights should be furthered;

(iii) that the Commission would encourage linkages between the academic community and non-governmental organisations so that the best academic minds can bring their talents to bear up on the practical work being done by such groups; and

(iv) that the Commission would welcome continuing contact with the universities in these areas and that it would help, within its means and possibilities.

Other training institutions have also engaged the attention of the Commission. The most notable of these is the Sardar Vallabhabhi Patel National Police Academy in Hyderabad which has included the teaching of human rights in its courses at the instance of the Commission. At the State level, too, there are increasing instances of police training institutes focussing on this key aspect of professional training. Contacts have also been instituted with the armed forces, amongst whom there is a notably heightened appreciation of the necessity and value of imparting training in respect of human rights. Indeed, at the senior-most level of the armed forces, the Commission has recently noted an increasing sensitivity towards, and recognition of, the need to develop a culture of human rights.

A Crime cannot be a Part of Duty[33]

The Constitution expects the bureaucracy, politicians and the judiciary to play their independent roles, says the Allahabad High Court's landmark judgement in the Uttarakhand case, but "politics in India is moving away from health into a diseased state where the contest for power has made those in power lose their perspective." Way back in 1948, the Privy Council had said: "A public servant can only be said to act or to purports to act in the discharge of his official duty, if his act is to lie within the scope of his official duty. Thus, a judge neither acts nor purports to act as a judge in receiving bribe, though the judgement which he delivers may be such an act; nor does a government medical officer act or purports to act as a public servant in picking the pocket of a patient whom he is examining though the examination itself may be such an act. The test may well be whether the public servant if challenged can reasonably claim that what he does, he does so by virtue of his office." If a minister assaults an officer within the secretariat premises, the act is not connected with his official duty and no sanction to prosecute him is needed. Cheating or abetting it is not a public duty. The Court has come down heavily on the aberrations in the administration run by UP Chief Minister Mulayam Singh Yadav and his successor Mayawati. These were the aberrations which had led to the ghastly assault on one of the women protestors, killing of men by trigger-happy police and abduction of others who were on a peaceful march to Delhi to demand a separate Uttarakhand State. One Chief Minister feigned ignorance about the bloody and beastly acts of the police and his successor, who spent a brief stint in office, defended the policemen accused of rape and killings, saying they were merely carrying out their responsibilities. Sanction to prosecute these men in uniform was denied as the accused defended their despicable acts saying these were performed in discharge of their official duties. Justice Ravi S. Dhavan and Justice A.B. Srivastava's 271 page trend setting verdict has the potential of strengthening the cause of human rights and dignity. They have questioned the accused officials' defence that they could not be prosecuted for committing penal offences like murders, rape, molestation, assault, disposing of bodies, abductions and last but not the lease tampering with records to eliminate evidence which could be conclusive. Were these not the crimes against public justice? Is firing at unarmed civil right activists or political dissenters part of the sovereign function of any State? Is burying a body with parents seeking it, part of official duty? It is a settled law that should there be an occasion to seek sanction on a prosecution, the trial court where the chargesheet is filed would decide the issue. Recently, the Supreme Court bench headed by Justice J.S. Verma which is seized of the Hawala scam said so.

Security Forces: Combating Organised Violence

C.R.P.F., B.S.F., I.T.B.P., N.S.G., C.I.S.F., Assam Rifles are some of the security forces engaged in combating organised crime today. Civil Police usually depends on security forces for all law and order duties. Security forces have to combat organised violence whether it is ethnic, communal or terrorist violence. My own experience of last thirty-three years has led me to the firm conviction that security forces, while combating organised violence, must observe human rights mainly for the following reasons:

Firstly, it is a constitutional mandate and every citizen has the fundamental rights under the constitution for a dignified human existence.

Secondly, those who violate human rights are liable to be prosecuted and made to pay compensation to the victims.

Therefore, it is in the interest of the members of the security forces not to violate HR.

Thirdly, security forces no longer get any protection under "sovereign immunity doctrine" because recent Supreme Court in Bilabati Behare *vs* State of Orissa (1993) 2-Sec-513 has held that the principle of sovereign immunity shall be inapplicable in such cases.

Fourthly, security forces can get public cooperation and support for combating organised violence only if they observe human rights and are respected by the public as their saviours against militants.

Fifthly, non-observance of human rights is counter productive and not beneficial in the long run. Violations of human rights by the security forces generally take the following shapes :

(1) Use of third degree methods during interrogation.

(2) Deaths in custody of security forces.

(3) Disappearances and fake encounters by the security forces.

(4) Illegal and unauthorised searches and raids causing inconvenience to the public.

(5) Unauthorised detentions in custody of security forces.

(6) Atrocities against women and children including cases of rapes.

(7) Discrimination against people on grounds of religion, race, caste or sex.

(8) Hand-cuffing of the people.

A number of Supreme Court judgements and human right organisations like Amnesty International and others have brought out such cases of violations of human rights by the security forces. National Human Rights Commission have also thrown light on some cases such as Bijbehara incident of Kashmir.

Sixthly, security forces must atride by the code of conduct laid out by the United Nations. They must perform their limited and well defined role. Security forces should not usurp the role of judiciary at any time and must work within the parameters of code of conduct. The code of conduct for security forces as laid down by UNO is as under:

Articel 1—Law enforcement official shall at all times fulfil the duty imposed upon them by the law, by serving the community and by protecting all persons against illegal acts, consistent with high degree of responsibility required by the profession.

Article 2—In the performance of their duty, law enforcement officials shall respect and protect human dignity and maintain and uphold the human rights of all persons.

Article 3—Law enforcement officers may use force only when strictly necessary and to the extent required for the performance of their duty.

Article 4—Matters of confidential nature in the possession of the law enforcement officers shall be kept confidential, unless the performance of duty or the need of justice strictly require otherwise.

Article 5—No law enforcement officer may inflict, instigate or tolerate any act of torture or other cruel, inhuman or degrading treatment or punishment nor may any law enforcement official invoke superior orders or exceptional circumstances, such as a state of war or a threat to war, a threat to national security, internal political instability or any other public emergency as a justification of torture or other emergency as a justification of turture or other cruel inhuman or degrading treatment or punishment.

Article 6—LEO shall ensure the full protection of the persons in their custody and in particular, shall take immediate action to security medical treatment whenever required.

Article 7—LEO shall not commit any act of corruption. They shall also rigorously oppose and combat all such acts.

Article 8—LEO shall respect the law and the present code. They shall also, to the best of their capability, prevent and rigorously oppose any violations of them.

Seventhly, security forces have to develop "a culture of human rights" where there is respect for liberty, equality and dignity of the individuals.

Eighthly, for combating organised violence, security forces have to be equipped with—

(1) uptodate and correct intelligence.

(2) sophisticate weaponry,

(3) good and modern scientific equipment and infrastructure such as lie detectors,

(4) good training for combating organised violance,

(5) dynamic leadership,

(6) high motivation, and

(7) lastly but not the least public support which cannot be earned unless human rights are protected.

Ninthly—In case security forces fail to observe human rights, it may lead to mal practices, corruption, high-handedness and arrogance in the system which will dilute its combat effectiveness to deal with organised violence. "Listening the call of the conscience" and ethical mode of righteous living is an essential requirement of security forces, State sponsored terrorism by security forces cannot be allowed in a democratic society like India.

Tenthly—"Means are as important as ends" and organised violence has to be controlled by observance of human rights by the security forces.

Today security forces are facing the greatest challenge of organised violence, insurgency, terrorism and low intensity war during the last four decades have caused lot of violations in India. Statistics reveal that more citizens have been killed in terrorist violences in Punjab and Kashmir than army men killed in the three Indo-Pak wars. In the 1947-48 war, between India and Pakistan, the Indian Army lost about 2500 soldiers including about 1000 personnel declared missing in action. Another 3261 soldiers were killed including 359 daclared as missing in action in the highly intensive 1965 war while 1525 army men died in the eastern front during the 1971 war. The total number of Indian soldiers killed in these three wars stands about 7286. In contrast to this between 1981 to April 1993 as many as 21475 citizens including 8126 militants were killed in Punjab alone. In Kashmir between 1988 and 1995 these figures works out to 11656. Thus, violence in the form of terrorism and insurgency in two States alone have taken a toll of 33132, four times more than number of soldiers killed in the three Indo-Pak war. In North Eastern States of India, insurgents in Nagaland, Mizoram, Manipur, Tripura and Assam have also taken a very heavy toll. To combat organised crime, security forces need to be properly trained and equipped and provided effective leadership, motivation and will to fight organised violence. The basic question today is whether security forces which are trained in observing human rights can combat organised violences better than those who are not made aware of the human rights. From the Punjab experience, many people tend to believe that security forces cannot combat organised violence by observing human rights and they have to cut corners of law at various places. I for one do not subscribe to this view. Police and security forces who are deployed to combat organised violences need high standard of discipline and morale, dynamic leadership and co-operation of the people. If security forces violate human rights they will not be able to get volunteer and spontaneous co-operation of the people without whose support organised violence cannot be successfully controlled and contained by the security forces.

Security forces can be divided broadly into two categories: First, category consists of those who observe human rights while combating organised violence and the second category covers those security forces who fail to observe human rights and at times deliberately violate human rights to combat organised violence. My 33 years of experience of operational areas like Mizoram, Manipur, Nagaland and Tripura in various capacities reveal and justify the contention that security forces observing human rights are always better equipped to combat organised violence. As a pragmatic practical person it is felt that police and security forces should observe human rights for their own individual interests and safe career. Political masters at times want policemen and security forces to violate human rights for some temporary gains; but long experience tells us that such temporary gains are counter-productive. The Supreme Court on January 29, 1996 has ordered CBI to prosecute 27 policemen of Punjab who were alleged to have been involved in fake encounters with terrorists in Punjab and Chief Minister Shri Brar has made it clear that his Government will not defend such officers. In such a situation, it is better that security forces combat violence by observing human rights.

Some people make a dividing line between police and security forces and in their opinion civil police is different from security forces which mainly consist of CRPF, BSF, other CPOs and the Army. Statistics prove that security forces generally observe human rights while State police at times violate human rights. During the last two years 52 allegations of excesses and violations of human rights were committed by the para-military personnel according to a statement given in the Lok Sabha by the State Human Minister and there were a total of 351 complaints against troops in Kashmir since 1991 of which 41 soldiers including 15 officers have been punished. Out of 351 complaints only 21 complaints have been found true. According to National Human Rights Commission, between 1990 to 1994, 245 cases have been registered against the BSF and 39 against the army.

National Police Commission in one of its report has observed that police in normal situations are violating human rights by using third degree methods, fake encounters and other illegal acts and they constitute 60 per cent of the total complaints against the police. Between 1st April 1994 to 31st March 1995, there have been 111 cases of custodial deaths, 55 cases of disappearances of people from police custody and 487 cases of other police excessism have been noted. These violations of human rights by the security forces and the police are due to lack of training and awareness about human rights. Insurgency and terrorism cannot survive unless there is popular public support to their cases. Security forces by violating human rights give scope for furtherance of the cause of terrorists and insurgents. Security forces can win the hearts and minds of the people only when they observe human rights. There are numerous examples when security forces have been able to combat organised crime more effectively while observing human rights. Organised violence can be broadly categorised into the following: (i) communal violence, (ii) caste violence, (iii) industrial labour unrest, (iv) ethnic violence, (v) political terrorism, (vi) agrarian rights and violence, (vii) students violence, (viii) election violence, (ix) group violence by dacoits and other armed gangs, (x) police violence and (xi) State violence. If security forces are not observing human rights it results in police violence and State sponsored violence. A democratic society wedded to the rule of law cannot allow State sponsored violence. Police being the agency created and maintained for combating violence and maintaining law and order cannot become law by themselves and they cannot violate human rights. Recent Supreme Court judgements have clearly indicated that police officers must observe human rights and those who violate human rights are bounded to be dealt in accordance with the law of the land and are bound to suffer in the long run. National Human Rights Commission annual report 1993-94 has given many illustrative cases. Firing by security forces in Bijbhera in Jammu & Kashmir has invited condemnation from all and disciplinary proceedings have been initiated under the Border Security Forces Act against 14 members of the force and further on the basis of a magisterial enquiry steps may be initiated to launch prosecution. In Punjab, there have been a number of cases of disappearances of people and it is suspected that these people may have been killed in fake encounters. National Police Commission has asked the concerned authorities to submit report in each case.

Analysing the anatomy of organised police David H. Beyley categorised them into three categories, (a) the violence of remonstrance, (b) the violence of confrontation, and (c) the violence of frustration. For dealing with all these types of violnces, it is necessary that security forces observe human rights. It is a matter of great regret that the Indian Police is having a number of organisational deficiencies and lack of adequate infrastructure for providing proper awareness about the human rights but there is a need for genuine commitment to the human rights values in the police. There is no denial of the fact that Indian police and security forces have lack of adequate infrastructure to combat organised crime. There are hardly a few dozen light detectors with the security forces for interrogation and modern scientific methods of investigation and interrogation are not available to the security forces but this does not justify our failure to observe human rights. If we do some introspection we find that the training in police organisations is defective and does not provide enough focus on human rights. A conviction of commitment for the human rights has to be inculcated in the police and security forces if we have to implement the human rights in its true form and spirit. There is a need for sensitisation of the police and security forces in the ethos and values of human rights. Promotion of human rights literacy and awareness will go a long way in equipping security forces for better combating organised violence. Today the scene is very dismal. There have been 6835 cases of complaints registered against the police and there have been

152 cases of custodial deaths and custodial rapes between the period 1st April 1994 to 31st March 1995. These violations of human rights can be attributed to number of factors but the basic reasons are lack of faith and commitment to the human rights. Short-term successes and quick results demanded by the powers of that be at times encourage corrupt and enthusiastic police officers to violate human rights.

Basic Issues for Discussion

(1) Is it possible for the security forces to operate within the given laws always and under all circumstances and to observe human rights—Yes and No—It becomes difficult in areas like Kashmir and North-Eastern States.

(2) If it is not possible to work within the given laws under all conditions, to what extent, laws can be ignored or disregarded and what consequences? If laws are ignored, it will imply violations of human rights and will invite adverse public criticism.

(3) Do you agree that every disregard of law by the security forces may not violate human rights? Yes and No.

(4) Should we not differentiate between normal policing and policing in terrorist-infested or insurgency infested areas? Yes.

(5) Where disregard of law by the security forces involves violation of human rights, does it produce results? Is it not counter-productive?

(6) Can good results be achieved in insurgency affected areas by working within the bounds of laws? What we can learn from history and past experiences.

(7) Do we need to enquire circumstances and compelling situations when security forces will suffer for observing human rights to the advantage of the terrorists and insurgents.

(8) What are the handicaps and problems in observing human rights by the security forces in Kashmir, North-Eastern States and other places effected by organised violence.

(9) What action-plan can be made for observance of human

rights in combating organised violence?

(10) How can we better equip security forces observing human rights in better combating organised violence—rights.

Above issues need to be discussed at various levels in Central Police Organisations.

Because of the extremely complex and serious ground situations, dilemma and difficulties will continue to be faced in observing human rights by the security personnel deployed in areas where organised violence is being committed by anti-social and anti-national forces. Security forces need effective supervision and good leadership alongwith better equipment and high motivation.

In the present day context, security forces, observing human rights are better equipped to combat organised violence.

(1) If people are providing willing and positive support to the S.P.

(2) If criminal justice system is effective and can deliver justice without fear or favour within a reasonable time frame.

(3) Organised violence is not caused by support from external factors and effective border surveillance is exercised.

(4) Media is free and supportive of psychological operations launched against those who organised violence are responsible for.

(5) If security forces have dynamic leadership and correct positive inner motivation to combat organisation violence.

(6) Political system provides effective support to the security forces.

All security personnel from top to bottom should be given courses in human rights. In operational areas security forces have to earn the cooperation and support of the local people which will come spontaneously if security forces observe human rights. Although security forces are called when the situation reaches a boiling point, restraint, perseverance and self-control become necessary for security forces. Fifty-two allegations of excesses committed by the security forces were received during the last two years and this itself indicates that security forces are observing human rights.

Human Rights Education

Section 12(h) of the Protection of Human Rights Act 1993 (No. 10 of 1994) states the functions of the Commission, which are as under: "Spread human rights literacy among various sections of society and promote awareness of the safeguards available for the protection of these rights through publication, the media, the seminars and other available means". Human rights education is most crucial for the fulfilment of the commitment made in the Indian Constitution but the task is enormously difficult. Some of the basic issues related to human rights education can be as under: (i) What kind of training is required for teachers of human rights? (ii) What sources and texts are to be drawn upon for teaching material? (iii) How human rights education to be imparted and through what training techniques? (iv) What plays, tales, stories and songs are likely to impart education of human rights with the possibility of both emotional response and further thinking? (v) What will constitute the core of its course for various levels of educational classes? (vi) Can NCERT develop model course modules for primary and secondary classes as standards to provide a basis for action by the States? (vii) Can the core book prepared by the UNESCO on human rights be adopted with necessary modification in it to suit Indian situations and conditions? (viii) Can appropriate modules be prepared and introduced in the training programmes of different levels especially in the Police and Security Forces to promote awareness of human rights? The basic question which is often asked is: Will mere human rights education stop or reduce human rights violation? There is an assumption that lack of information on human rights illiteracy is the source of violation of human rights. One of the worst form of violation of human rights in Indian society is because of intolerance.

Complaints Received by the Commission

The National Human Rights Commission has been constantly monitoring violation of human rights and public relations subjects cases taken up by the Supreme Court have also brought a sea-change in the perception regarding violation of human rights. National Human Rights Commission received 496 complaints about violations of Human Rights upto 31st March 1994 out of which 274 were dismissed by the Commission, 48 were disposed of with observations and 174 were admitted. There were 34 complaints of custodial deaths, one custodial rape case, 61 cases of other police excesses, seven rape cases, two dowry death cases, three cases of indignity to women, 10 cases of excesses by Armed Forces and 56 other miscellaneous cases, totally to 174 cases of violations of human rights admitted by the National Human Rights Commissions. Tables 1-2 show statewise position of complaints and cases admitted. During the period 1st April 1994 to 31st March 1995, 6835 complaints were received by the Commission and 152 cases of custodial death/custodial rapes were reported. Out of total 6987 cases registered, 5710 cases were considered by the Commission. Table 3 shows Statewise details of cases registered and considered. Table 4 shows number of cases considered by the Commission giving Statewise details. Table 5 gives Statewise statement of category of cases admitted by the Commission for the period ending 31st March 1995. The Commission registered 5449 cases from 1st April 1995 to 31st October, 1995, out of which 115 cases are yet to be placed before the Commission.

TABLE 1

Position of Complaints Received by the Commission

Name of State / Union Territory	*Admitted*	*Disposed of with observation*	*Dismissed by the Commission*	*Total*
Andhra Pradesh	11	1	5	17
Assam	6	—	5	11
A & N	—	—	2	2
Bihar	17	3	16	36
Delhi	17	3	25	45
Gujarat	1	—	2	3
Haryana	1	—	6	7
Himachal Pradesh	—	—	1	1
J & K	8	—	2	10
Kerala	5	—	20	25
Karnataka	2	—	9	11
Maharashtra	—	1	7	8
Madhya Pradesh	8	10	25	43
Manipur	3	—	—	3
Meghalaya	1	—	1	2
Orissa	13	7	31	51
Punjab	7	1	9	17
Pondicherry	1	1	—	2
Rajasthan	7	5	12	24
Tamil Nadu	18	3	40	61
Uttar Pradesh	40	13	49	102
West Bengal	8	—	7	15
Total	174	48	274	496

Source: National Human Rights Commission—Annual Report 1993-94 (from October 1993 to March 1994).

TABLE 2

Statewise Statement of Category of Case Admitted for Disposal by the Commission.

Name of State/Union Territory	*Custodial Deaths*	*Custodial Rapes*	*Other Police Excesses*	*Rape*	*Dowry Deaths*	*Indignity to women*	*Excesses by Armed Forces*	*Other*	*Total*
Andhra Pradesh	—	—	4	4	—	—	—	3	11
Assam	1	—	1	—	—	—	1	3	6
Bihar	4	—	8	—	—	—	—	5	17
Delhi	7	—	2	1	1	—	—	6	17
Gujarat	—	—	—	—	—	—	—	1	1
Haryana	1	—	—	—	—	—	—	—	1
J & K	1	—	—	—	—	—	6	1	8
Kerala	1	—	1	—	—	—	—	3	5
Karnataka	—	—	2	—	—	—	—	—	2
Madhya Pradesh	1	—	1	—	—	—	—	6	8
Manipur	1	—	—	—	—	—	2	—	3

(Contd.)

Name of State/Union Territory	*Custodial Deaths*	*Custodial Rapes*	*Other Police Excesses*	*Rape*	*Dowry Deaths*	*Indignity to women*	*Excesses by Armed Forces*	*Other*	*Total*
Meghalaya	1	—	—	—	—	—	—	—	1
Orissa	—	—	3	—	1	1	1	7	13
Punjab	—	—	6	1	—	—	—	—	7
Pondicherry	1	—	—	—	—	—	—	—	1
Rajasthan	1	—	4	—	—	—	—	2	7
Tamil Nadu	6	1	7	—	—	—	—	4	18
Uttar Pradesh	8	—	17	1	—	1	—	13	40
West Bengal	—	—	5	—	—	1	—	2	8
	34	1	61	7	2	3	10	56	174

Source: National Human Rights Commission—Annual Report 1993-94 (From October 1993 to March 1994).

TABLE 3

Number of Cases Registered; Considered by the Commission, and Cases Processed but Pending Consideration by the Commission.

Name of the State / Union Territory	*No. of cases Registered*		*Total*	*No. of cases considered*	*No. of cases processed but pending consideration*
	Complaints	*Custodial deaths and Rapes*			
(1)	(2)	(3)	(4)	(5)	(6)
Andhra Pradesh	1637	6	1643	1558	85
Arunachal Pradesh	5	—	5	1	4
Assam	57	18	75	47	28
Bihar	563	3	566	415	151
Goa	6	2	8	7	1
Gujarat	47	—	47	32	15
Haryana	159	2	161	134	27
Himachal Pradesh	26	2	28	25	3
J & K	131	1	132	117	15
Karnataka	82	1	83	79	4
Kerala	103	3	106	105	1
Madhya Pradesh	458	6	464	205	259
Maharashtra	224	2	226	200	26
Manipur	16	3	19	13	6
Meghalaya	6	3	9	9	—
Mizoram	1	—	1	1	—

(*Contd.*)

(1)	(2)	(3)	(4)	(5)	(6)
Nagaland	2	2	4	3	1
Orissa	241	6	247	197	50
Punjab	538	11	549	469	80
Rajasthan	285	10	295	207	88
Sikkim	1	—	1	—	1
Tamil Nadu	644	10	654	599	55
Tripura	6	1	7	5	2
Uttar Pradesh	976	6	982	773	209
West Bengal	138	15	153	109	44
A & N Islands	2	—	2	2	—
Chandigarh	11	—	11	10	1
D & N Haveli	—	—	—	—	—
Daman & Diu	—	—	—	—	—
Delhi	457	39	496	376	120
Lakshadweep	2	—	2	2	—
Pondicherry	11	—	11	10	1
Total	6835	152	6987	5710	1277

Source: National Human Rights Commission—Annual Report 1994-95.

TABLE 4

Number of Cases Considered by the Commission During 1994-95 (Position as on 31.3.95).

Name of the State / Union Territory	*Dismissed in limini*	*Disposed of with directions*	*Taken Cognizance of*		*Total*
			Concluded	*Pending*	
Andhra Pradesh	311	1151	17	79	1558
Arunachal Pradesh	—	—	—	1	1
Assam	8	1	7	31	47
Bihar	244	41	3	127	415
Goa	3	—	2	2	7
Gujarat	23	—	1	8	32
Haryana	73	13	9	39	134
Himachal Pradesh	15	2	1	7	25
J & K	25	8	11	73	117
Karnataka	40	8	6	25	79
Kerala	55	15	6	29	105
Madhya Pradesh	139	22	4	40	205
Maharashtra	120	30	14	36	200
Manipur	1	—	3	9	13
Meghalaya	3	1	1	4	9
Mizoram	—	1	—	—	1
Nagaland	—	—	—	3	3
Orissa	124	19	7	47	197
Punjab	171	22	46	230	469
Rajasthan	119	27	6	55	207
Sikkim	—	—	—	—	—
Tamil Nadu	285	68	52	194	599
Tripura	1	2	—	2	5
Uttar Pradesh	449	101	26	197	773
West Bengal	62	7	5	35	109
A & N Islands	2	—	—	—	2
Chandigarh	6	1	2	1	10
D & N Haveli	—	—	—	—	—
Daman & Diu	—	—	—	—	—
Delhi	199	25	45	107	376
Lakshadweep	—	—	—	2	2
Pondicherry	5	2	2	1	10
Total	2483	1567	276	1384	5710

Source: National Human Rights Commission—Annual Report, 1994-95.

TABLE 5

Category of Cases Admitted by the Commission for Disposal from 1st April 1994 to 31st March 1995.

Name of the State / Union Territory	*Custodial deaths*			*Custodial Rape*	*Disappearance*	*Illegal detention*	*False implication*	*Other Police Excesses*	*Indignity to women*	*Terrorist / Naxalite violation*	*Others*	*Total*
	*PC**	*JC**	*Os**									
(1)	(2)	(3)	(4)	(5)	(6)	(7)	(8)	(9)	(10)	(11)	(12)	(13)
Andhra Pradesh	6	—	—	—	—	11	—	28	2	9	40	96
Arunachal Pradesh	—	—	—	—	—	—	—	1	—	—	—	1
Assam	14	4	—	—	—	2	—	9	1	3	5	38
Bihar	17	—	—	—	2	3	1	47	7	2	51	130
Goa	1	1	—	—	—	—	—	1	—	—	1	4
Gujarat	—	—	—	—	—	1	—	6	—	—	2	9
Haryana	2	—	—	—	1	—	—	23	—	—	22	48
Himachal Pradesh	2	—	—	—	—	—	—	1	—	—	5	8
J & K	—	—	3	—	—	6	6	12	3	8	46	84
Karnataka	1	—	—	—	—	—	—	10	2	1	17	31
Kerala	3	—	—	—	—	—	—	4	1	—	27	35

(Contd.)

(1)	(2)	(3)	(4)	(5)	(6)	(7)	(8)	(9)	(10)	(11)	(12)	(13)
Madhya Pradesh	2	8	1	—	1	—	—	8	2	—	22	44
Maharashtra	2	—	—	—	—	4	2	21	1	—	20	50
Manipur	2	1	—	—	—	—	—	2	1	—	6	12
Meghalaya	3	—	—	—	—	—	—	1	—	—	1	5
Nagaland	1	—	1	—	—	—	—	1	—	—	—	3
Orissa	3	1	1	1	2	1	1	15	6	—	23	54
Punjab	10	2	—	—	44	39	—	85	2	41	53	276
Rajasthan	10	—	—	—	—	1	—	14	6	—	30	61
Tamil Nadu	7	—	2	1	2	37	7	62	12	—	116	246
Tripura	1	—	—	—	—	—	—	—	—	—	1	2
Uttar Pradesh	5	—	—	—	2	5	2	104	19	—	85	223
West Bengal	14	1	—	—	—	3	—	8	2	—	12	40
Chandigarh	—	—	—	—	—	—	—	—	—	—	3	3
Delhi	5	33	—	1	1	1	2	31	2	1	75	152
Lakshadweep	—	—	—	—	—	—	—	1	—	—	1	2
Pondicherry	—	—	—	—	—	—	—	2	—	—	1	3
Total	111	51	9	3	55	114	21	497	69	65	665	1660

PC—Police Custody, JC—Judicial Custody, OS—Others, @ includes third degree method abuse/torture *in the custody of security forces/Assam Rifles/Forest Deptt. *Source:* National Human Rights Commission, Annual Report, 1994-95.

Human Rights and TADA

The Terrorist and Disruptive Activities (Prevention) Act 1985, popularly known by its acronym TADA has stood the scrutiny of Supreme Court in many cases. The Peoples Union for Democratic Rights (PUDR) presents the statistics that of the 52998 persons arrested under TADA between May 1985 and March 1993 only 434 or 0.81 per cent of the total number of those detained, were actually convicted. With 23 of the 24 metropolitan cities declared as "notified areas", nearly 93 per cent of the country was covered under the Act. TADA has been used to fight terrorists of Kashmir and Punjab where the Government is locked in several areas of low intensity conflict against its own citizens who are armed to the teeth with ultra-sophisticated weapons. In several other States TADA has been used to fight the smugglers, drug peddlers, Naxalites (as in Andhra Pradesh) and the underworld operators in Gujarat. Details of TADA of some badly affected areas are as under :

Number of TADA Cases in Badly Affected States.

No. of TADA cases registered in badly affected States	*Regd.*	*Dropped*	*Arrested*	*Convicted*	*Acquitted*	*Discharged*	*In Jail*
Andhra Pradesh	3655	660	7434	44	3254	581	267
Assam	4792		12715		15		706
Gujarat	3154	619	18584	174	5190	11925	252
Haryana	1443	108	1770	192	871	—	145
J & K	14475	425	10987			2024	1720
Maharashtra	733	—	2419	36	330	316	900
Manipur	946	—	1601	1	14	266	196
Punjab	17518	7378	—	—	—	—	—

Few case studies given below will indicate how TADA has been applied to Indian citizens during the last few years :

(1) In 1986-87, a student from Andhra Pradesh protesting a bus fare hike was booked under sections 3, 4 & 5 of

TADA and lanquished in prison for a while year before he was released.

(2) In Andhra Pradesh Dalits asking for title to the land they cultivated were falsely charged and arrested under TADA. Though there was no material evidence against the accused, the designated Court refused to release them until civil rights advocates and PUCL President K.G. Kannabiran filed applications at the Supreme Court, High Court and Designated Court. Even then it was six months before they were released.

(3) In Baroda, a 14-year old mentally retarded boy who was out on the street during a communal riot was rounded up by the police and booked under TADA.

(4) In 1990, 45 striking workers of Universal Luggage in Aurangabad (Maharashtra) were arrested under TADA. One of them, Vishwas Bhagwan Lotange was beaten up for 15 days and died in jail. The doctor's report noted welts and cigarette burns on his body.

(5) Two hundred and forty agitating Bharatiya Kisan Sangh activists were booked under TADA during a *raste roko* agitation.

(6) Muslim women, youth and the aged were picked up under TADA by the Bombay Police following the bomb blasts in March 1993.

(7) In Ahmedabad, in 1991-92, a Muslim women whose husband had only a few hours ago fallen victim of police bullets, was summarily booked under TADA and held for 10 months because she had argued heatedly with the police over their unjust action.

Government of India had decided that the Terrorist and Disruptive Act will expire on 23rd May 1995. The basic issue, however, is that whether the police personnel have been able to understand the dimensions of human rights and how far that have been able to protect it. Many thinkers believe that there has been misuse of TADA over the few years that have passed because of excess politicalisation of Police Forces and neglect of training in Police Organisations.

Punjab Cops': Violating Human Rights

The Supreme Court on 17th April 1995 ordered suspension and prosecution of five members of Punjab Police for cold blooded murder of a suspected terrorist couple on May 17, 1993 in Tijala, a suburb of Calcutta and later disposing of their bodies without knowledge of West Bengal Government. The order was passed by the Court after a CBI report *prima facie* found the five police officers guilty of criminal conspiracy, abduction, murder and destruction of evidence to liquidate the couple. Stating that their "worst apprehensions" about the Punjab Police had "come true" the judges said the killing of the couple in cold blood by men in uniform revealed a state of affairs where human rights had virtually no value for the police who were expected to function as protectors of citizens. According to the CBI report, the police officers were involved in the killing of the deceased Mohd Bashir Ahmed alias Lakshman Singh former constable of Punjab Police who deserted the police and his wife Sakina Begum alias Rani on early hours of May 17, 1993 while they were in sleep and their bodies were dragged into one of the two gypsies in which the killers escaped. A three-Judge bench comprising the Chief Justice Justice, A.K. Ahmedi, Justice K.S. Paripoornan and Justice K. Venkataswami, passed the order on a public interest petition filed by Dr. B.L. Wadehra seeking judicial inquiry into the killing of the couple apparently by members of a Punjab police party from Sangrur. Expressing their "great distress" at the manner in which the incident took place and the "collousness" at which the report of the West Bengal Chief Secretary complaining about the incident to his Punjab counterpart, had been dealt with, the judges said even more distressing was the affidavit of the then Punjab State Under Secretary Karnail Chand Banga who stated on affidavit that the Sangrur Police had no knowledge of the antecedents and whereabouts of the couple.

The latest case is the Supreme Court ruling ordering the suspension of five police officials including a Superintendent of Police and a Deputy Superintendent of Police for the involvement in the killing of a militant couple in Calcutta on May 17, 1993. While directing the prosecution of the five police officials in the Calcutta killing case, the Supreme Court had observed, "Our worst apprehensions have come true. The killing of the couple in the cold blood reveals a state of affairs where human life has virtually no value for the officers who wear uniform and are supposed to be the protectors of life." The Court verdict was a sequel to the CBI enquiry following the protest by the West Bengal Government.[34]

Human Rights Record: An International Perspective

The history of mankind has been firmly associated with the continuous on-going struggle of individuals against injustice, exploitation and discrimination. Human rights remain both a statement of reality and an ever-expanding set of objectives waiting to be actualised and their realisation is possible only through a process of constant struggle. Media plays an important part in bringing out alleged violations of human rights in different countries. Violations of human rights is a global phenomenon. "Racial discrimination and religious bigotry represent a unique and frightening phenomena of human rights violations in U.S.A. In the majority of European countries racialist or Xenophobic sentiments are shared by an increasingly large percentage of population and in a number of European countries immigrants and ethnic minorities are faced with discrimination in access to housing".[35] Charles Humana has made lot of research regarding violation of human rights by fifteen countries of the world. He has given the following human rights rating.

TABLE 1

Assessment of Countries in Questionnaire Form

Country	*Capital*	*Form of Govt.*	*Human Rights rating*	
World average			*(better)* 55	*(worse)*
1. Bangladesh	Dacca	MIL		44
2. China	Beijing	I-P		23
3. India	New Delhi	DEM	60	
4. Indonesia	Jakarta	I-P		30
5. Iraq	Baghdad	MIL		19
6. Japan	Tokyo	DEM	88	

7. Kuwait	Kuwait	I-P		49
8. Libya	Tripoli	I-P		23
9. Pakistan	Islamabad	MIL		40
10. Saudi Arabia	Riyadh	I-P		28
11. Singapore	Singapore	I-P	59	
12. Sri Lanka	Colombo	DEM		52
13. Sweden	Stockholm	DEM	98	
14. UK	London	DEM	94	
15. USA	Washington DC	DEM	90	

* Form of Governments included in the Guide

Abbreviations:		1984 populations
MIL	Military or effective Military Rule	440,000,000 (98)
I-P	One-Party or similar or one Person rule	2,400,000,000(518)
DEM	Multi-party democracy or similar	1,900,000,000 (408)
	Total	4,740,000,000

In fifteen countries India ranks fifth in protecting human rights after the USA, UK, Sweden and Japan. These ratings may not be very scientific but they do provide us a comparative analysis of human rights observance in different countries. In India, our record is quite good between 1993 to March 1994, a total of 496 cases of human rights violations were registered by the National Human Rights Commission and 174 cases were admitted for further investigation and inquiry. The ten defaulting States in human rights violations are as under :

1. Uttar Pradesh	102 cases
2. Tamil Nadu	61 cases
3. Orissa	51 cases
4. Gujarat	45 cases
5. Madhya Pradesh	43 cases
6. Delhi	36 cases
7. Kerala	25 cases

8. Rajasthan 25 cases
9. Andhra Pradesh 17 cases
10. West Bengal 15 cases

Some Recent Trends in Human Rights Movement

1. Police Officers Individual Accountability

In case of Bhim Singh (AIR 1968 SC 945) Supreme Court has held "The two police officers, the one who arrested him and the one who obtained the orders of remand, are but minions in the lower rungs of the ladder. We do not have the slightest doubt that the responsibilities rest elsewhere and with the highest echelons of the precisely where and with whom, on the material now before us" (Bhim Singh *vs.* State of J & K AIR 1986 SC 494). For handcuffing and taking the offender in procession through the streets of a Solapur city. The Bombay High Court held a public servant accountable who happened to be an Inspector of Police (for violating fundamental rights) and "directed him to pay Rs. 10000 as compensation to the aggrieved person". (Ravi Kant Patel *vs.* Director General of Police, Maharashtra 1981 or ZJ 2344-Bombay). The award of compensation was held by the apex Court (State of Maharashtra *vs* Ravi Kant Patel (1991) 2 SCC 373). Karnataka High Court directed a police officer Sub-Insp. Chikkana to pay compensation to a citizen for violation of his fundamental rights (compensation of Rs. 2500 to be personally paid by SI for detaining Govind Raju at the PS when no case was registered against him). (Smt. Susheelamma Vs. State of Karnataka 1991 Cr. IJ 2436 Para 13).

2. The Role of Supreme Court and High Courts

(i) Supreme Court recently directed "the UP Govt. to pay compensation to Rs. 50000 to two brothers, wrongfully confined in a Police Station in Noida for seven days without any criminal case registered against them." A division bench comprising Justice Kuldip Singh and Justice N. Venkatachalliah made it clear that the Govt. can recover the compensation amount from Sub. Insp. S.K. Sharma who has been held responsible for the illegal confinement. (*The Hindustan Times*, 25 January, 1995).

(ii) An amount of Rs. 20000 is fixed as compensation to be paid to him. Rs. 19000 shall be paid by the State of UP and Rs.

1000 shall be recovered out of the salary of Shri Pandey, the Constable. (Ms. Indira Jai singh *vs*. Union of India) of March 1990. Supreme Court held "the whole amount shall be deposited in this Court within three weeks and recover Rs. 10000 from Pandey to meet his share of the liability".

(iii) *Compensation in "appropriate cases"*. Supreme Court held it would award compensation only in "appropriate cases" and not in every case where there is breach of fundamental rights" (M.C. Mehta *vs*. Union of India AIR 1987, SC 1086). In M.C. Mehta *vs* Union of India, Supreme Court has held : "The infringement of fundamental right must be gross and patent and either such infringement should be on a large scale affecting the fundamental rights of a large number of persons or it should appear unjust or unduly harsh or oppressive on account of their poverty or disability or social or economically disadvantaged position to require the person or persons affected by such infringement to initiate and pursue action in the civil courts (M.C. Mehta *vs* Union of India—AIR 1987 SC 1086). The Supreme Court, explaining Article 32 of the Constitution held that "Article 32 which itself is a fundamental right, imposes a constitutional obligation on the court to forge such new tools, which may be necessary for doing complete justice and enforcing the fundamental rights guaranteed in the constitution, which enable the award of monetary compensation in appropriate cases where that is the only mode of redress available". (Smt. Nilabati Behra *vs* The State of Orissa—Supreme Court AIR 1993 SC 1960).

3. **Greater Awareness of Human Rights due to media and role of human right bodies like Amnesty International and other such organisations.**

4. **Proliferation of Human Rights Organisation in India and Abroad.**

(i) During the last two decades Independent Civil Liberties Organisations include The Andhra Pradesh Civil Liberties Committee (APCLC), The Association for the Protection of Democratic Rights (APDR), The Civil Liberties and Human Rights Organisations (CLAHRO) in Manipur, Citizen for Democracy (CFD) Delhi, The Committee for the Protection of Democratic Rights (CPDR), Bombay, The Free Legal Aid Committee (FLAC) in Bihar, The Jammu and Kashmir Peoples Basic Right (Protection) Committee, The Naga People's Movement for Human

Rights (NPMHR), The People's Union for Civil Liberties (PUCL) and the People's Union for Democratic Rights (PUDR). On June 30, 1993 Asia Watch and Psysicians for Human Rights, Denmark (AW-PHR) published a report titled "The Human Rights Crisis in Kashmir: A Pattern of Impunity". The report alleges that "Among the worst violations have been the summary executions of hundreds of detainees in the custody of the security forces in Kashmir."

5. Global Concern for Human Rights

At international forums human rights are discussed in great depth and UN Commission on Human Rights has been playing a very effective role. National Human Rights Commission during the last one year has visited J & K, Punjab, North-East States and many other parts of India to contact people and get first hand information about the violation of human rights. This has also given an impatus to various violations of human rights in different States.

Judgements of the Supreme Court

In Kishore Singh *vs.* State of Rajasthan, AIR 1981 SC 1597 the Supreme Court showed its deep concern regarding the police atrocities in the following words : No police life-style which relies more on fists than on wits, on torture more than on culture can control crime because means boomerang on ends and re-fuel the vice which it seeks to extinguish. Secondly, the State must re-educate the constabulary out of their sadistic arts and inculcate a respect for human person—a process which must begin more by example than by precept if the lower rungs are really to emulate ...... Nothing is more cowardly and unconscionable than a person in police custody being beaten up and nothing inflicts a deeper wound on our Constitutional culture than a State official running berserk regardless of human rights. (AIR 1981 SC 625). The Supreme Court in Prem Shankar *vs.* Delhi Admn. (AIR 1980 SC 1535) Justice Krishna Iyer held that handcuffs should not be used in routine and they were to be only when the person was "desperate", "rowdy" or the one who was involved in non-bailable offence. (AIR 1980 SC 1541) Supreme Court further observed : Handcuffing is *prima facie* inhuman and, therefore, unreasonable, is over harsh and at the first blush, arbitrary. Absent fair procedure and objective monitoring to inflict 'irons' is to resort to zeological strategies repugnant to article 21. Despite the eye opening judgements of the Supreme Court, against handcuffing, the police has been resorting to handcuffing in subsequent cases. (Aeltemesh Rein *vs.* Union of India, AIR 1988 SC 1768 : Harbans Singh *vs.* State of UP—AIR 1991 SC 531, Sunil Gupta *vs.* State of MP—1990 3 SCC 119.) Khatri *vs.* State of Bihar (AIR 1981 SC 928) popularly known as Bhagalpur Blinding Case, at one point of time even shocked the entire nation. This case depicts the extent to which police can go in committing atrocities on persons under its custody. In this case the Supreme Court considered the question of granting compensation to the victims of police atrocities and answered it in affirmative saying that if it were not so, Article 21 of the Constitution would be reduced to a nullity, "a mere rope of sand". Khatri *vs.* State of Bihar, AIR 1981 SC 1068 at 1074) . The three police officials who were involved in the shocking incident of blinding of the undertrials at Bhagalpur were finally convicted for taking the law into their hands. From Rudul Sah *vs.* State of Bihar, (AIR 1983 SC 1086) to PUDR *vs.* State of Bihar (AIR 1987 SC 365) the Supreme Court has brought about revolutionary breakthrough in the "human rights jurisprudence' by evolving the principle that monetary compensation has to be paid to the victim of police atrocities. The Court has ruled that the State must repair the damage done by its officers by paying compensation to the victim and it may have recourse against the guilty officials. Rudul Sah *vs.* State of Bihar (AIR 1987 SC). See also Sebastian M. Hongray *vs.* Union of India AIR 1984 SC 571 and AIR 1984 SC 1026 Bhim Singh *vs.* State of J & K (AIR 1986 SC 494) Nilabati Behera *vs* State of Orissa (1993) 2 SCC 746 is yet another case of custodial death where the deceased was taken in police custody and next day his body was found on railway track with multiple injuries. The principle of "Sovereign immunity" shall be inapplicable in such cases. Having regard to the age and income of the deceased's mother, the State was directed in this case to Rs. 150000 as compensation to the Deceased's mother. The Court held: "The Court is not helpless and the wide powers given to the Supreme Court by Article 32, which itself is a fundamental right, imposes a constitutional obligation on the Court to forge such new tools, which may be necessary for doing complete justice and enforcing the fundamental rights guaranteed in the Constitution, which enable the award of monetary compensation in appropriate cases...... (Nilabari Behera *vs.* State of Orissa 1993 2 SCC 746) to support to the above observation, the Court rightly referred to Article 9(5) of the International Covenant on Civil and Political Rights, 1966 and held that the said provision indicates that an enforceable right to compensation is not alien to the concept of guaranteed rights. In Pratul Kumar Sinha *vs.* State of Bihar (1994 Supp. (3) SCC 100), also R.S. Sodhi *vs.* State of UP 1994 Supp. (1) SCC 142 and 143) Police atrocities lead to the death of three young persons. One of them was bachelor while the other two were married and left behind their young widows. The Court issued directions for the ex-gratia payment of Rs. 25000 to the families of the deceased. The Court further held that if the State Government so desires it would be free to take such action as it considers necessary to recover this amount from the tort feasors. Arvinder Singh Bagga *vs.* State of UP (AIR 1995 SC 117 (1994) 6 SCC 565) is also a case of police atrocities where police officers were guilty of illegal arrest and torture in police station. The Court took serious note of the human rights violation and directed the State to launch prosecution against the police officials concerned and directed to pay compensation of Rs. 10000 to the victim woman and her husband and Rs. 5000 to each of the other victims. The Court further held that upon such payment it will be open to the State to recover personally the amount of compensation from the police officers concerned. For the effective enforcement of fundamental rights enshrined in Articles 21 and 22 of the Constitution of India and for protecting the human rights violation due to police atrocities, the Supreme Court has laid down following requirements:

1. An arrested person being held in custody is entitled, if he so requests to have one friend, relative or other person who is known to him or likely to take an interest in his welfare told as far as is practicable that he has been arrested and where he

is being detained.

2. The police officer shall inform the arrested person when he is brought to the police station of this right.

3. An entry shall be required to be made in the diary as to who was informed of the arrest.

It shall be the duty of the Magistrate, before whom the arrested person is produced, to satisfy himself that these requirements mentioned above have been complied with. (Joginder Kumar *vs*. State of UP 1994 4 SCC 260 at 268).

In Raghubir Singh *vs*. State of Haryana Supreme Court has observed : "We are deeply disturbed by the diabolical recurrence of police torture resulting in a terrible scare in the minds of common citizens ... when the guardians of law become the violators of human rights, (*Ibid*, p. 1120). In Bhim Singh *vs*. State of J & K (AIR 1986 SC 494) the Court awarded Rs. 50000 as compensation to Bhim Singh who had been illegally detained for delivering an inflammatory speech in September, 1985. In Saheli *vs*. Commissioner of Police, (AIR 1990 SC 513) the Supreme Court awarded Rs. 75000 as compensation to Mrs. Kamlesh Kumari whose 9-year old son was beaten to death by the Delhi police officials and directed to recover the amount from the erring police officials. In State of Maharashtra *vs*. Ravikanth (1991) 2 SCC 373, the Supreme Court held that delinquent police officers could not be made personally liable to pay compensation. The Supreme Court in Nilabati's case made observations regarding applicability of doctrine of sovereign immunity in Constitutional remedy and remedy under law of torts as : "Award of compensation in proceeding under Article 32 by this Court by the High Court under Article 226 of the Constitution is a remedy available in public law based on strict liability for contravention of fundamental rights to which the principle of sovereign immunity does not apply, even though it may be available as a defence in private law in an action based on tort. In Saheli, principles of damages under civil law was considered in the writ petition and compensation was allowed by the Supreme Court. Regarding State immunity reference was made to Vidyawati *vs*. State of Rajasthan (AIR 1962 SC 933) and State liability was fixed. No reference was made to later decision of Kasturi Lal's case (Kasturi Lal *vs*. State of UP, AIR 1965 SC 1039). In Nilabati's case

Supreme Court made reference to its earlier decision in Saheli as : "In Saheli *vs.* Commissioner of Police, the State was held liable to pay compensation payable to the mother of the deceased who dies as a result of beating and assault by the police. However, the principle indicated therein was that the State is responsible for tortuous acts of its employees ... In Saheli, no reference has been made to the decision of Kasturi Lal's case wherein sovereign immunity was upheld in the case of vicarious liability of the State for tort of its employees. The decision in Saheli is, therefore, more in accord with the principles indicated in Radul Shah case. (Kasturi Lal *vs.* State of UP. AIR 1965 SC 1967). The doctrine of sovereign immunity is an archaic principle which should not be applicable against the redressal of Human Rights at any forum. These judgements should be taught to all officers of the police and security forces so that they may in their own interest of career, not violate human rights. It is high time that police and security forces recognise and respect the fundamental rights of life, liberty, equality and dignity of an individual since these are now rights "enforceable by courts" in India.

Human Rights During Internal Conflicts

Even in situation of internal disturbances and tensions, every person can and must respect at least the following rules, without discrimination :

1. Every person shall be treated with the respect due to the inherent dignity of the human person. His or her life, moral and physical integrity, and honour shall be respected in all circumstances and regardless of the allegations against him or her. No one shall be arbitrarily deprived of his or her life.
2. Acts which are prohibited in particular are murder, torture and all other cruel, inhuman or degrading treatment or punishment, the taking of hostages, enforced or involuntary disappearance of persons, collective penalties and all acts, methods and practices of terrorism, whether committed by public officials or by any other person.

3. Persons exercising police powers shall, out of respect for human dignity, limit their use of force to the strictly necessary minimum.
4. No one shall be arbitrarily deprived of his or her liberty. Anyone who is arrested, detained, interned or deprived in any other way of freedom of movement shall be informed without delay of the reasons for which such measures have been taken. The authorities responsible for the detention of a person have the duty to inform that person's family of his or her situation. The measures taken against any person shall be reviewed periodically.
5. Any person deprived of his or her liberty shall be treated humanely. He or she shall be afforded proper conditions with regard to hygiene, food, quarters and applicable work. Wounded or sick detainees shall receive the care they require. A person deprived of his or her liberty shall have the possibility of communicating periodically with his or her family.
6. Other restrictions of individual liberty, such as forcible displacement for assigned residence, may be imposed only by decision of a competent authority. Persons affected by such measures shall be treated humanely. No one may be deprived of his or her nationality nor expelled from his or her own country.
7. No one shall be held guilty on account of acts or omissions which did not constitute a criminal offence at the time when they took place.
8. No one shall be sentenced and no penalty carried out without a judgement handed down by an impartial court respecting the fundamental judicial guarantees. In particular, any person charged with an offence :
   (a) shall be presumed innocent until proved guilty according to the law;
   (b) shall be informed of the particulars of the offence alleged against him or her;
   (c) shall be afforded the necessary rights and means of defence;
   (d) shall be tried without undue delay.

A convicted person shall be advised of his or her judicial and other remedies.

9. In as much as retention of the death penalty is considered necessary, it may be pronounced only for the most serious crimes. The death penalty shall not be pronounced on persons who were under the age of eighteen years at the time of the offence, nor carried out on pregnant women or mothers of young children. A condemned person has the right to ask for clemency : he or she must be advised of this right.

   Any summary or arbitrary execution constitutes murder.

10. All wounded and sick persons shall receive care and attention, without discrimination. Medical assistance shall be facilitated. No one shall suffer harassment for the simple fact of having assisted wounded or sick persons.

11. The authorities concerned shall do everything possible to establish the whereabouts of persons reported missing. The authorities shall inform the next of kin on the progress of the investigation and notify them of any result.

12. Children, particularly if deprived of their liberty, shall be accorded the respect due to them on account of their age. They must never be compelled or encouraged to take part in acts of violence.

13. The authorities concerned shall take all necessary measures to ensure that these rules are known and respected by all. They shall include them in the training of those exercising police powers, such as members of the police forces, prison staff and, where applicable, members of the armed forces. The authorities shall prosecute in accordance with national law anyone who violates these rules.

Above instructions and code of conduct apply in situations when police and security forces carry out operations against insurgents, terrorists and organised armed gangs.

Main Recommendations

1. With a view to removing ambiguities and impediments concerning its competence and autonomy, the National

Human Rights Commission had in its report for the period ending 31st March, 1994, made certain recommendations for amendments to the protection of Human Rights Act, 1993. The Commission urges that measures be taken to bring out these amendments.

2. The Commission recommends that in states where the security forces are called upon to assist the civil authorities, local magistrates and/or police officers, should be associated, in particular, with cordon and search operations, in order to allay misgivings regarding the conduct of personnel of the security forces and to prevent misuse of powers.
3. In insurgency affected areas, at the level of the district, the Commission recommends that district magistrates should chair regular meetings involving the security forces and be kept informed of operations by the latter. To the extent possible, leading non-officials, representatives of non-governmental organisations and others should be associated with such meetings.
4. More fundamentally, however, the Commission has considered it its responsibility to recommend in its report on areas facing insurgencies or militancy, that while the restoration of peace may indeed by the *sine qua non* for the full respect of human rights, timely and sagacious political measures that are truly democratic in character are necessary, as in the long run, they have far more lasting and beneficial results than reliance essentially on security forces, however devoted and disciplined they are, or on restrictive laws, however carefully they may be applied. The Commission accordingly recommends that appropriate political measures and initiatives be taken.
5. In almost all parts of the country there is a clear and increasing need to reform the police itself, to retrain and to reorganize it and to restore to it the skills and the integrity that the country so desperately needs if the function of preserving law and order is to be improved. It is for this reason that the Commission recommends that serious action be taken on the Second Report of the

Police Reforms Commission which, in 1979, made a series of proposals that remain highly pertinent today—including those suggesting the insulation of the investigative function of the police from political pressure.

6. The Commission recommends the revision of the Indian Prison Act, 1894, bearing in mind the considerable work already done by various committees and organisations and the work that is currently under way.
7. A high level committee be set up in each State to review the cases of prisoners in order to ensure that they are not detained unlawfully.
8. The Commission has raised the matter of 'lock-ups' and sub-jails with the State Governments and recommends that appropriate corrective actions be taken to improve conditions in 'lock-ups' and sub-jails.
9. The Commission recommends that the Central Government accede to the 1984 Convention against Torture and other forms of Cruel, Inhuman and Degrading Treatment or Punishment.
10. The Commission recommends expeditious and effective implementation of the project prepared by the Government of Uttar Pradesh for the elimination of child labour in the glass industry in Ferozabad.
11. The Commission recommends the adoptation of appropriate legislation on compulsory primary education, matched with the necessary resources required for its purpose. The Commission supports the Government move to amend the child labour (Prohibition and Regulation) Act to make it more efficacious and recommends that early action be taken in this regard.
12. The Commission recommends vigorous implementation of the country's obligations under the Convention on Elimination of All Forms of Discrimination against Women.
13. The Commission has noted that legislation is being contemplated in regard to persons suffering disabilities. Supporting this, it strongly recommends early passage of an appropriate act on behalf of such persons whose rights must be respected and supported.

14. The Commission recommends that timely action be taken on the plans of the University Grants Commission to have support extended to five Universities by April, 1996 and various others by 1997 for the teaching of human rights at the University level.
15. The Commission recommends an improvement in the quality of training of police, military and para-military personnel and taking of special measures in order to ensure respect for the human rights of people particularly in areas of insurgency.
16. The Commission further recommends that where violations of human rights occur as a result of the conduct of armed forces personnel, prompt and effective action be taken under the law to prosecute those accused of wrong doing. This would be in the interests of all concerned—the victim, the armed forces themselves and the country at large.
17 The Commission recommends that 10th December every year be observed as Human Rights Day in all schools, colleges, universities and other educational institutions.
18. The Commission recommends that the Govt. of India takes steps for evolving suitable institutional mechanism in the Union Territories including the National Capital Territory of Delhi so that they can have their own arrangements, functionally analoguous to State Commissions, for the protection of human rights.

Concluding Remarks

Mere talks, seminars, discussions and debates cannot serve a meaningful role unless there is a political will to honestly implement and observe human rights. Remedial measures need to be taken to remedy the malady of delays in the Criminal Proceedings. Experience of the working of our political system holds ample testimony to the fact that at times there is an active involvement of political figures in using the machinery of the police to gag the voice of dissent or opposition to paralyse the system. Passing laws cannot be sufficient unless effective implementation can be enforced of all laws which safeguard human rights of the individuals. Human rights and human survival are inalienably linked. Any democratic society, while countering terrorism, becomes subject to charges of "excesses" and "violations of human rights". Implementation of human rights has come to be acknowledged nationally and internationally as a major concern of many human right organisations. It is necessary that these organisations must handle the tangled web of facts, circumstances, perceptions, compulsions and the situation more realistically and in a more holistic manner. As a watch dog body, the National Human Rights Commission has so far done a very creditable job in not only promoting human rights in the country but also raised the image of the nation in international forums. By enacting, the Protection of Human Rights Act 1993, India has reaffirmed its strong commitment to protect and promote the human rights of its people. The voluntary organisations and the mass media can play more positive roles in promoting human rights. The time has come when the legal and judicial system has to be revamped and reconstructed so that such injustices do not occur and disfigure the fair and otherwise luminous face of our nascent democracy.[36] The talk of human rights would become meaningful only when poor, illiterate and helpless people are provided with free legal service as an unalienable right for fair and just trial. The Supreme Court has emphasised the role of people, voluntary organisations and social action groups in making legal aid meaningful, effective and purpose oriented.[37]

REFERENCES

1. Hersch Lauterpacht, International Law—The collected papers of Hersch Lauterpacht, edited by E. Lauterpacht, Vol. II, Cambridge Mass 1975, p. 74.
2. K. M. Mathur, *Indian Police — Role and Challenges,* p. 87.
3. Dr. Durga Das Basu, *Human Rights in Constitutional Law Practice,* Hell of India, Private Ltd. New Delhi, 1994, p. 5.
4. Justice H.R. Khanna, *Issued Before the Nation,* 1988 B.R. Publishing Corporation, Delhi.

5. Myres S. Mc. Dongal, Harold D. Lasswell and Lung-Chu Chen, *Human Rights and World Public Order,* 1986 pp. 64-65.
6. World Public Information Campaign For Human Rights — Fact Sheet No. 8 at 3 (1995).
7. K. M. Mathur, *Management of Internal Security and Related Issues*, Gyan Publishing House, New Delhi, 1995, p. 182.
8. Nagendra Singh, *India and International Law, IO,* (1969).
9. Report of the Amnesty International, Dec. 23, 1993.
10. Balraj Puri, *Human Rights View from Geneva*, Occasional papers on human rights, February-March 1994.
11. K. Vasak, *A Thirty Year Struggle—the Sustained Efforts to give Force of Law to the Universal Declaration of Human Rights*, UNESCO Courier (Nov. 1977) 29.
12. J.B. Marie, Le Commission des Droits de L 'Homme De I'ONU, Deuxieme Partie (1975).
13. Ahmad Yamini, *Islamic Law and Contemporary Issues*, (Jidda—The Sandi Publishing House, 1988, p. 15).
14. Asmarom Legesse, *Human Rights in African political culture in Kenneth W. Thompson (ed.) The Moral Imperatives of Human Rights : A World Survey,* 1980, pp. 123-24.
15. See F. Capotorti, *Study on the Rights of Persons belonging to Ethnic, Religious and Linguistic Minorities,* E/CN 4/ Sub 2/384/Rev I (1979).
16. Dr. D.D. Basu, *Constitutional Law of India,* 6th Edition, p. 399.
17. Dr. S. Subramanian, Issue of Internal Security, *The Tribune,* Chandigarh 31 May 1994.
18. S. Venugopal Rao, Human Rights and Law Enforcement, *Hindu,* 3 May 1994.
19. Ramesh Vinayak, Police Commando—The Strong Arm of the Law—*India Today,* 31 May, 1994, p. 75.
20. Dr. S. Subramanian, Issue of Internal Security—*The Tribune,* Chandigarh 31 May 1994.

21. P.N. Bhagwati, Presidential address delivered at the XII Annual Conference of the Indian Society of Criminology (1983).

22. Generally speaking, the Constitutional rights in the context of criminal jurisprudence are contained in Articles 20, 21, 22 of the Constitution. Article 20 prohibits ex-post facto operation of law and confers immunity against double jeopardy and protection against self-incrimination. Article 21 provides that no person shall be deprived of his life and liberty except according to procedure established by law. Article 22 provides protection against arrest and detention in certain cases. Clause (1) of that Article provides that no person who is arrested shall be detained in custody without being informed, as soon as may be, of the grounds for such arrest nor shall be denied the right to consult and be defended by a legal practitioner of his choice and Clause (2) enacts that every person who is arrested and detained in custody shall be produced before the nearest Magistrate within a period of 24 hours and no person shall be detained in custody beyond such period without the authority of a Magistrate. Clause (3) contains a safeguard against self-incrimination. Clauses (4) to (7) provide certain safeguards in case of preventive detention which is accepted as a necessary evil.

23. P.N. Bhagwati, *Human Rights in the Criminal Justice System 12 Indian Bar Review,* 1985. Also see Mool Chand Sharma, Judicial Creativity and the Due Process Clause 12, Indian Bar Review, 1985.

24. P.N. Bhagwati, *Domestic Application of Human Rights Norms in Developing Human Rights Jurisprudence* (Fourth Judicial Colloquium on the Domestic Application of International Human Rights, 1991).

25. Supra note—I.

26. P.N. Bhagwati, *Human Rights in the Criminal Justice System* (The Kumarappa Reckless Lecture, 1985).

27. Note recorded by Shri Dharma Vira, *Seminar on the Protection of Human Rights in Criminal Procedure.* Working paper, background papers and proceedings—SVP NPA Hyderabad 1969.

28. Kunwar Sandhu, Policing Punjab, Gill's boys now have to restore the system instead of usurping it, *Indian Express,* 12 Oct. 1993.
29. N.S. Saksena, Hold Chiefs responsible for Police Excesses, *Indian Express,* 6 April 1992.
30. For further details see Geeta Seshu, 'Police, top rights' violator, says panel, *Indian Express,* 8 Dec. 1994.
31. *The Hindu*—29 April, 1995.
32. *Indian Express*—4 March 1992—No Justice for rape victims—Usha Rai.
33. For similar views, Rakesh Bhatnagar, A Crime cannot be a part of duty, *The Times of India*, 20 Feb. 1996.
34. Jittery Punjab COPS want Rao to step in, *Indian Express*, 29 April 1995.
35. K.M. Mathur, *Management of Internal Security and Related Issues*, Gyan Publishing House, New Delhi, 1995, p. 196.
36. For details see National Human Rights Commission, Annual Report, 1994-95.
37. Supreme Court—Hussamara Khatoon *vs*. State of Bihar AIR 1979 SC 1361.

6

Role of Public Participation in Internal Security

In a secular, socialist, democratic Republic like India, role of public participation in various political and social processes is indispensable. To adopt the words of Malcoln Nuggeridge, never was any generation of man intent upon the pursuit of well-being more advantageously place to attain it, who yet, with seeming deliberation, took the opposite course—towards break down instead of stability, towards death, destructions and darkness, instead of life and light. Public participation in democratic system depends on the awareness of the people about their constitutional rights and duties. The greatest task before Indian people today is to acquire a keener sense of national identity and to create a cohesive society having perfect internal security. The nation is at the crossroads and definitive steps by those who can contribute towards healthy changes in the need of the hour[1].

The term participation has its origin from Latin word *Participare* which means "taking part". Encyclopaedia of Psychology describes participation as (i) "taking part or involvement in an activity", and (ii) "greater involvement of persons in policy decision which affect them directly."[1a] Cohen and Uphoff regarded participation as "generally denoting the involvement of a significant number of persons in situations or actions which enhance their well-beings, e.g., their income, security or self-esteem[2]. Public participation is an important political process which can take shape of involvement in terms of (i) planning, (ii) decision-making, (iii) implementation of the decisions, and (iv) evaluation of any activity, system or programme. Participation of people can be in the shape of consultation, cooperation or association. It is, at the outset, doubtful whether a majority of the people can ever actually participate in the internal security management functions accept in a original or symbolic manner. But in a democratic society, public participation is an important criterion of political development. Participation in internal security should not be taken to mean actual participation in the "law adjudicating" and "law enforcing processes which demand whole time commitment. Lucion Pye held that participation may be either democratic or a form of totalitarian mobilisation.[3] Prof. Alex Inkoles has articulated a participant citizen syndrome which consists of five factors. It "includes identification with an allegiance to supre-local and non-parochial public authority; interest in civic affairs; information about political figures; participation in public organisations and adherence to rational organisational rules as a basis of running government affairs".[4] Public participation in internal security management debate is urgently needed to save the country from a state of "functional anarchy". In recent years there has been an increasing recognition of the potential of the public and the possibility of its being fully involved in the field of social defence.[5] What gives real meaning to popular participation is the collective effort by the people concerned to pool their efforts and whatever other resources they decide to pool together, to attain the objectives they set for themselves.[6] Village defence by the community can be ensured by village volunteers who may in rotation, carry out night patrolling of the village. No country can deal with its crime problems through its criminal justice system alone. There must be understanding and active involvement by the public as a whole.[7]

Role of public participation in internal security depends in great measure, upon people's awareness of their fundamental duties and their willingness to participate in nation-building activities. "They will have to actively cooperate with the police and also participate in organised efforts at self-protection with the support of the police. At the same time, community leaders will have to do everything to promote inter-group unity[8]. During riotous situations, police seek public cooperation through peace committees and appoint some citizens as special police officers[9]. In order to maintain internal security in an effective manner voluntary cooperation of the society is most essential.[10] The concept of policing by the community is well known to all Indians from ancient times and there was self-reliance in village defence.[11] In ancient India there were instances where villagers and the head-man laid down their lives while bravely resisting the onslaughts of depredators.[12] Community policing both in rural and urban areas has assured a new significance in developing society like India where insurgency, terrorism and social conflicts have seriously jeopardised the internal security of the society. No police force could function effectively by means of official police men only and it is vital to secure the aid of the village community.[13] More than seventy-two per cent of the population of India resides in villages and village defence parties can be viewed on a nucleus around which the concept of self-policing by the community should be built and developed further.[14] There has been an increasing recognition of the potentials of the citizens participation in the successful implementation of the programmes and social defence aming at the prevention, treatment, reclamation and rehabilitation of social environs.[15]

Internal security of the country in seriously threatened today by communal riots, ethnic conflicts, rural unrest, terrorism, hijacking, organised crime and insurgency in many parts of the country. Terrorism and trans-border crime continue to pose challenges to the internal security of the country. The caste clashes in Belchi, Dharampura, Kanjhawala and Marathwada, still remind us about the atrocities and harassment of Harijans by the upper classes of the society. Persistent large-scale violence, political agitations and violation of human rights have created serious challenges to the internal security of the country. In view of the emergence of low intensity proxy war, the security policies in India cannot afford to make a water-tight distinction between a pure external dimension of security and internal dimension of security.[16]

Public participation in internal security can be broadly in the following ways :

1. Providing young and motivated people for recruitment in police and Central Police Organisations and thus providing the essential base of building internal security organisations.

2. By enacting laws for the security of the nation through its elected representatives in Parliament and State legislatures.

3. Providing people's cooperation and assistance in furnishing required information and intelligence about all covert activities of the criminals, armed gangs of militants and anti-national elements.

4. Providing support and assistance to the police and Central Police Organisations in arresting or suppressing of offenders and criminals who are trying to disturb the internal security of the society.

5. Assisting local police and Central Police Organisations in internal security operations by acting as guides or witnesses.

6. Assisting the criminal justice system in prosecution and conviction of offenders by acting as truthful witnesses.

7. By not associating themselves in violent public protests, agitations, *dharnas* and acting as law-abiding citizens.

8. Assisting State police in community policing during disturbed situations like riots.

9. By voluntary support to the village volunteer force schemes.

10. By collectively exercising community control of the police.

11. By abjuring violence and assisting police in safeguarding public property.

12. By promoting social harmony and spirit of brotherhood and assisting local police in controlling communal riots and other social conflicts.

13. People should carry out their constitutional and legal obligations and fundamental duties as a good and responsible citizen.

14. Need of public participation is the greatest in emergency situations like droughts, floods, requiring peoples involvement on a massive scale.

Constitutional Duties

On 18th December 1975, President gave consent to the Constitution (42nd Amendment) Act 1975 and incorporated the following fundamental duties of Indian citizens in Article 51A :

"It shall be the duty of every citizen of India

(a) to abide by the Constitution and respect its ideals and institutions, the National Flag and the National Anthem.

(b) to cherish and follow the noble ideals which inspired our national struggle for freedom;

(c) to uphold and protect the sovereignty, unity and integrity of India;

(d) to defend the country and render national services when called upon to do so;

(e) to promote harmony and the spirit of common brotherhood amongst all the people of India transcending religious, linguistic and regional or sectional diversities to renounce practices derogatory to the dignity of woman;

(f) to value and preserve the rich heritage of our composite culture;

(g) to protect and improve the natural environment including forests, lakes, rivers and wildlife, and to have compassion for living creatures;

(h) to develop the scientific temper, humanism and the spirit of inquiry and reform;

(i) to safeguard public property and to abjure violence;

(j) to strive towards excellence in all spheres of individual and collective activity, so that the nation constantly rises to higher levels of endeavour and achievement."

Many of the fundamental duties enumerated above are related to the role of citizens in promoting internal and external security of the country.

The citizen's voluntary force, consisting of all honest persons of excellence committee to the welfare of the people, should along with the movement for electoral reforms, take all measures to evolve a dynamic leadership for the country which will either undertake projects independently or influence the rulers and powers that be, towards certain thrust areas to improve the quality of life of the masses and promote national security.

Legal Obligations and Public Aid

Sections 37, 38, 39, 40, 43, 1000, 129 and 154 of Criminal Procedure Code and sections 174, 176, 177, 178, 179, 182, 187, 188, 199, 200, 201, 202 and 203 of the Indian Penal Code mention certain obligations and legal commitment of the people. It is obligatory fcr a citizen to :

(a) give information pertaining to intention and commission of certain offences ;

(b) assist the police and the magistracy when asked to do so in the prevention of certain offences.

An ommission to assist the police or magistrate or to conceal that information which he is bound to give under law are punishable under sections 118, 175 and 302 Indian Penal Code. Though public participation has been sought in several areas of social defence operations, the public participation is at best minimal.[17] The citizens too have their own responsibility towards the police, to report crime and to help the police in solving them, to support the police in maintaining peace and internal security. There is an urgent need for launching of a passive programme of educating the people about their role and obligation. Basically all problems of internal security emanate from the public. Public participation in various political, social and economic movements create problems of law and order and at times violence, communal disharmony is caused by communal bias, prejudice and hostile belief system. All internal security problems arise and are sustained by public participation alone. Police and community both are interdependent because police are a part of the society and not a part from the community. Public must come forward to help the police in securing internal security of the community. Today there is an alienation of the community from the police and public cooperation to police is not forthcoming in required measures.

Role of Voluntary Organizations

In a democratic society, voluntary organizations have a very vital role to play in internal security, nation-building activities and crime prevention. Members of public as representatives of a community can take part in different ways in programmes and activities of crime prevention and control both under governmental or voluntary sectors.[10] In a plural society voluntary organisations have an important role to play. Activities of the voluntary organizations and agencies can be classified into following categories:

1. *Charity* — Giving food, clothing, medicines and also in cash and kind.
2. *Welfare* — Providing facilities for education, health and drinking water.
3. *Relief* — Responding to calls of duty during natural calamities like floods, droughts, earthquakes and man-made calamities like refugee influx.
4. *Rehabilitation* — Continuing and follow up of work.
5. *Services to the society*—Spread of education and social cause.
6. *Development of human beings*—bringing awakening.
7. Political articulation and political parties.
8. Economic activities.
9. Cultural activities.
10. Social and religious activities.

The strategy to involve voluntary agencies presumes the presence of a healthy atmosphere and goodwill between government agencies and voluntary agencies. "Regretably, the current relationship is far from happy. Instead we find mutual suspicion and lack of trust in each other."[19] Voluntary agencies can perform the following roles: (i) to be the eyes and cears of the people at various levels; (ii) to disseminate information and bring awareness about various activities of the criminal justice system; (iii) to actively participate at citizen's committees at various levels to assist the police and other agencies of the government. Public participation through voluntary agencies/ associations can be broadly classified into the following categories :

1. *Social service and cultural associations*— Rotary/ Lions clubs come under this category and these associations

find areas of cooperation among social groups with a view to satisfy secondary needs of the society and help to make life "happy and contented" (Aristotle).

2. *Religious institutions and associations* — Ramakrishna mission– humanitarian service during emergencies.
3. Professional and consultancy associations—medical doctors.
4. Functional Associations—Trade unions—Teachers associations.
5. Frontline Associations—Political orientation—Kisan Sabha.
6. Action groups/protect groups— general political tilt.
7. Citizen groups— citizen councils— can be ethnic groups.
8. Students and young activists.
9. Political parties.
10. Community associations — Agarwal Samaj, Yadav Sabha —Caste groups.

Voluntary organisations have been very useful in promoting communal harmony in any places during communal riots. Role of voluntary agencies in combating natural calamities has been found very vital. According to Rajni Kothari, "The conception of active citizenship in the political process is rich in diversity for protecting minorities from being overtaken by a homogenising and chauvinistic drive in a highly plural society like ours and make development an instrument of liberties and rights of the poor and the minorities and the diverse populations that inhibit this vast continent size, complex society.[20] In Aligarh, Bhiwandi and Indore, enlightened citizens played a very constructive role in maintaining communal harmony in the aftermanth of December, 1992 riots. Rajni Kothari envisages public participation as micro-movements at the grass roots for justice and inquiry regional movements for autonomy and decentralisation and the larger macro-political movementnts for a truly plural national and international order that is based on various diversities and an array of alternative systems of survival and sustenance.[21]

The last three decades have seen an unprecedented growth of voluntary or non-governmental organisations (NGOs) in India.

Mobilisation role of voluntary organisations is generally referred as capacity building, self-reliance, participation and empowerment. The main elements of mobilisation are providing information, education and training. Modern voluntarism is primarily a political process though non-party, non-electoral and non-parliamentary.[21a] Internal management of the voluntary organisations is mostly undefined since most voluntary organisations are one man organisations. The directors managing trustees, coordinators have no fixed terms or even properly articulated constitution. In many voluntary organisations, irregularity or even corruption in the management of funds, juggling of accounts, diversion of funds in the name flexibility, use of organisation's fund, facilities and infra-structure for personal purposes are becoming general practices. The voluntary organisations have to clean their own houses and have to build on their grass-root strength and develop public advocacy through open, formal and collective orientation.

Public Participation in Communal Harmony

The National Integration Council 1968, has called upon all political parties, voluntary organisations, other citizen groups, the press, the leaders of the public opinion, to actively encourage inter-religions and inter-community harmony. It also recommended halt to communal tensions by the following means :

(a) by discouraging communal ill-will and regional animosities and weaning the misguided elements of society from the path of violence;

(b) by active and energetic propagation of the principles, especially of tolerance and harmony for which this nation stands;

(c) by mobilizing constructive forces of society in the cause of national unity and solidarity and giving them leadership encouragement and articulation; and

(d) by devising suitable community activities and programmes for fostering fellow feeling, emphasising the privileges of common citizenship and in general raising the quality of national life.

There is an urgent need for social mobilisation to combat communalism. Karl M. Dontuch formulated the concept of social mobilisation which, according to him, is "the process in which major clusters of old social-economic and psychological commitments are eroded or broken and people become available for new pattern of socialisation and behaviour." Against, this backdrop of social mobilisation one may find a clue to the problem of communalism in India. Raghubar Dayal Commission Report has observed, "As mutual mistrust between the two communities is the root cause of communal disturbances, it will really help people of all communities from a permanent non-official organisation for doing necessary propaganda to allay the mistrust. The formation of a network of local organisations like neighbourhood and *Mohalla* Committees and citizen forums have been found very useful in mobilising public participation in controlling and preventing communal riots in many parts of the country. The National Integration Council at its Srinagar conference in 1959 recommended among other suggestions :

"the constitution of citizen's committees as consultative bodies at the state and district levels to promote and maintain communal harmony, their functions being the holding of advance consultations with leaders of religious groups to ensure peaceful celebrations of festivals and to endeavour to promote joint participation by all communities in the festivals," and,

"the constitution at the national level of a sub-committee of the National Integration Council to review from time to time the communal situation, the progress of implementation of recommendations of the National Integration Council in regard to Communalism and to advise the government."

Justice Ranganath Mishra Commission of inquiry observed that during riots in Delhi the local residents had formed combined groups and they succeeded in resisting riots groups and the commission feels that such combined groups should be encouraged. The combined groups should be totally free from politics and maintain harmony and friendly relations with similar local organisations around.

Sri Jagmohan, former Governor of J & K has observed people in mature societies understand their civic obligations and discharge them willingly. British public, for instance, respects and helps the British police, which in turn, acts as its friend, guide and protector. On the other hand, the people in India, by and large, run away from their obligations to the police. Even when they are a witness to the crime, they would pretend not to have seen it.[21b]

Decline of Voluntarism in Internal Security Duties

In many cases people of questionable integrity join the ranks of voluntary workers or open a variety of social service agencies and organisations just to create personal empires and swindle government money which is obtained through political manipulations and wire-pulling. At times shortage of free time, long distances in big cities, indifference to socio-political problems amongst the people result in decline of voluntarism. Bureaucratic delays and "red tapism" in the concerned government offices kill initiative of social workers and make them futility of their work. Adequate appreciation and recognition of the work of the voluntary institutions had been affected due to their inability to glamourise their endeavour, their failure to sell their achievements and personal acrimonies between different social workers resulting into a demeaning and defaming "smear each other campaign." Presence of large number of dubious voluntary workers has also caused decline in voluntarism in internal security duties.

Role of the Citizens

Citizens have a direct role to play in crazy prevention and criminal justice system as witness. The willingness of people to participate as witnesses in the criminal justice system, alone can help in getting convictions for the culprits. The extent to which a person is willing to speak out and share with the duly constituted authorities in the criminal justice system all the relevant facts within his knowledge, determines his utility as a witness in any criminal proceeding. A healthy police-public relationship is most vital to secure the involvement of numbers of the public as witness to further the cause of law enforcement.[22] Constructive cooperation by the public in general and specific welfare-minded citizens in particular has to be made a permanent part of crime prevention programme so that the harmful or passive attitude of society which assumes that professionals alone can solve the rapidly growing problems as if by a miracles may give way to responsible citizen action.[23] Because no government policy of social control of correction method (in reality defences against crime) has proven very effective in the reduction of crime, the ultimate solution or alleviation of the crime problems must rest in the hands of general citizenry. It is the citizenry that will curb crime, not the police, nor courts and nor the prisons.[24] If crime rates are to be reduced, it is not enough to rely upon the State mechanism alone. People's participation is the hallmark of any successful plan for crime control.[25] For effective control of crime and delinquency and for maintenance of internal security, active participation by the members of the community is more essential. There must be a smooth flow of relationship between a country's criminal justice system and public participation with the aim of establishing sufficient rapport to achieve efficiency in the prevention and treatment of crime and delinquency. Internal security cannot be preserved by the internal security organisations by themselves. "It needs community involvement".[26]

Community Control and Assistance

Community control of police implies not only closeness of the community to the police as their masters but also entails a healthy, positive and appreciative outlook of the community towards the police. On the pattern of Whitley Council of UK and "Community chests" obtaining in USA Community can play an effective role in internal security by establishing "Citizen Councils and Peace Committees" at different levels with adequate representation of various segments of the society. Public participation in the following areas can be very useful with reference to internal security duties:

(1) Providing intelligence to the police;

(2) Maintenance of public order, public peace and protection of public property;

(3) Prevention, detection and investigation of crimes, riots and public disorders;

(4) Providing security to the VVIP & VIPs;
(5) Enforcement of social legislation, local and special laws;
(6) Assistance and support in rescue and relief operations during natural calamities;
(7) Peoples participation in combating organised violent crimes;
(8) Keeping vigilance over anti-national and subversive forces.

The entire rural police system provides a workable basis for the induction of the vital element of public support.[27] Citizens should certainly play a stronger role in influencing police organisational goals, policies and procedures.[28] Community involvement can be sought in traffic safety weeks and crime prevention week celebrations.

Role of Public Participation

The district administration has often drawn upon the services of voluntary agencies, in times of distress in organising relief as well as rehabilitation of the affected population during natural calamifies and disasters.[29] The community leaders, political leaders and service-oriented village olders, representing the community often organise their own rescue and relief operations till the outside help can reach them. During earthquake in Uttar Kashi in 1991, the bulk of the relief work was done by several non-governmental organisations like Doon School Alumni, Dwine Life Society, Degree College Students, several Ashram members of Rishikesh. Even I.A.S. probationers of Lal Bahadur Shastri Academy of Administration Mussorrie volunteers from Kailash Ashram and Shivanand Ashram fanned out in far flung interior villages preparing lists of affected houses and families and issuing signed steps to them. Relief material was delivered at the doorsteps of the victims by the voluntary agencies. In Maharashtra region earthquakes during 1993 there was not dearth of volunteers and dedicated social workers who took the initiative to feed the survivors. It was truly touching site to see children in the age-group 10 to 15 dressed in their scout/guide and NCC uniforms bustling about to help the villagers. The role of many voluntary organisations in rescue and relief operations has been noteworthy. It is necessary to motivate local citizens and voluntary agencies to provide assistance in coping with disaster situations in the following ways[30] :

(i) Donate blood and save a precious life;

(ii) Assist local police and governmental agencies in rescue and relief operations;

(iii) In identifying victims of disasters;

(iv) By distributing relief stores to the needy victims of disasters;

(v) Evacuation of casualties to the hospital;

(vi) Providing required information about area to the government agencies and serving as guides to take others to the various affected sites.

The role of voluntary organisations in various natural calamities is to help people to overcome the difficulties posed by disasters by providing welfare and relief services according to the specific needs of the people; to act as ears and eyes of the people and also act as an intermediary between the victims and the government; to improve and assist in proper distribution of scarce resources and to organise vigilance groups for prevention of misuse of resources. For each type of disaster, requirements of public participation and role of voluntary organisations will differ. Over a period of time, however, the role of community participation has come down in organising relief and increased dependence is visible on government organised activities.[31]

Need for Better Police-Public Relations

"One objective of the police-public relations should be the direct involvement of the people in the prevention and detection of crime and in the maintenance of order".[32] Police and Central Police Organisations cannot control organised violence and internal security problem without the active goodwill and cooperation of the people. Law is not merely book but includes the manner in which it is understood and perceived by the people in general. A healthy police-public relations in a continuing basis is vital to secure the desired measure of public involvement and co-operation in police work to make it meaningful and acceptable to society.[33] Public is not co-operating with the police because of the police unpopularity and corrupt practices. Following principles of law enforcement propounded by Sir Robert Peel of Metropolitan Police need to be reiterated here:

(a) The ability of the police to perform their duties is dependent upon public approval of police existence, actions, behaviour and the ability of the police to secure and maintain public respect;

(b) The police must secure the willing cooperation in voluntary observance of the law to be able to secure and maintain public respect ;

(c) The police at all times should maintain a relationship with the public that gives reality to the historic tradition that the police are the public and that the public are the police; the police are the only members of the public who are paid to give full-time attention to duties which are incumbent on every citizen in the interest of the community welfare. The police-public *Sampark* campaign launched by the Punjab Chief Minister Mr. Beant Singh on August 16, 1993 has gathered momentum with senior police officer holding meetings with *sarpanches* and *panches* to ascertain their difficulties and wherever possible, trying to solve these on the spot. The main aim of the programme is to assess the shortcomings of the law enforcing agencies so that steps can be taken to improve their functioning and to develop a better and healthy rapport with the public. Contact campaign in Punjab has four-point charter: (i) the first is to collect complaints against the police; (ii) to collect information about residual extremism, if any; (iii) police taking developmental projects with the prior approval of the *Panchayats;* and (iv) collecting complaints concerning departments other than the police.[33a]

'Friends of Police' (FoP), a movement born out of a policeman's desire to bridge the gap between the police and the common man, was aimed at sharing the police power and responsibility with the public. Within a few months of its launch in a backward district of Tamil Nadu, it has blossomed into a movement in 'community policing' with more than 1,000 people in the district enrolling themselves as members. The essence of FoP movement was to 'foster and crystalise the hitherto untapped goodwill for the police that exists among the general public. The police in virtually every nation and state were suffering from a highly negative image not only among the public at large, but also in the media as well as in their own ranks and were being isolated from friends and foes alike. With complaints of torture and custodial violence accentuating the negative image, a general atmosphere of lack of mutual trust, respect and confidence prevailed. On the other hand, the police too failed to distinguish between the vast majority of the law-abiding people and the comparatively smaller number of law breakers who had to be dealt with iron hand. Consequently, the force, which existed for the sake of public, was facing lack of cooperation from them. The movement aimed at enabling the public without caste, creed or status considerations, to establish rapport with the police force and promoting crime awareness among the people to prevent crimes.

The Japanese "Koban" concept is a service oriented police system which can be useful in all democratic societies. This system represents community policing at its best. The policeman counsels young couples in material disputes, setless family quarrels and keeps an avuncular eye on young misfits in his beat, besides the normal police duty of directing strangers to their destinations.[34] In India, the intrusion of a policeman in a *Mohalla* is a matter of suspecion and much curosity because he is scorned by the rich and mighty and he does not even have the status of a skilled worker. The concept of community police can be adopted only when he is better educated, better paid, better trained and is given due respect in the society for his service to the society. A programme sponsored by the Rochester Police department known as the Teen and Patrol Programme (TPP) sought to involve youths in maintaining an orderly atmosphere in parks, playgrounds and other recreational areas in the city of Rochester.[35] Such programmes have proved quite useful in acquainting youths with the police role. Those deployed in TPP were paid minimum wage and were allowed to accompany police officers in routine operations in order to gain first hand information of police procedures. In Jersey city, neighbourhood watch idea was first used in USA to build up police-community bonds. This kind of cooperation is to supplement the role of the police, not be a guardian Angels Englehood watch in Jersey city was commended by local residents in the wake of unwarranted attacks by a group of people.[36] Interesting variations of neighbourhood watch have been encouraged by the U.S. department of justice grants in Newark, New Jersey, Houston, Texas and numerous other cities.[37]

In India, an unmeasurable communication gap exists between the internal security agencies and the masses. In order to maintain internal security in an effective manner, voluntary cooperation of the society is most essential.[37a] A few years back Delhi police devised a package of several measures to build empathy with the community and to closely mingle with the community. Some of these measures include the neighbourhood watch scheme, the senior citizen's scheme, the introduction of the Delhi Tourist Police, the de-addiction centres for drug addicts being run in police stations, the opening of juvenile camps, the running of self-defence camps for girls, the introduction of the scheme of relief to victims of crime, the opening of the police on the Delhi Police Day or during crime prevention weeks, the scheme of special police officers etc. All these were specific police-community synthesising measures which had increased police-community interface in Delhi.

War Against Terrorism and Public Support

Public support for the anti-terrorist operations can go a long way in fighting terrorism and insurgency. Public can provide useful information and intelligence to the security forces about the movement and location of militant groups and can act as guides to the security forces in reaching the hideouts of the terrorists and insurgents. Mobilisation of public support in favour of police and law enforcement agencies has to be achieved by intensive psychological propaganda and media publicity.[38] Every effort should be made to identity and isolate the terrorists and insurgents from the general mass of the community and to insulate the community from the emotional appeal of the terrorists. The basic difference between insurgent and terrorist is the level of public support. In insurgency area, insurgents get a higher level of public support for their cause, while in terrorism, the level of public support is much less. An insurgent has the support of a large section of local population while a terrorist need not have such public support.[39] One very important variable of all civil strife is the mass support to the ideology. Cause and methodology of the conflict (both the quantum and quality of mass support have to be taken into account). Important indicators of public support can be as under :

"(i) supporting ideology or cause;
(ii) agreeing with methodology;
(ii) providing money, material, etc;
(iv) vocal and written public support (in media);
(v) Non-violent participation in rallies etc;
(vi) supplying arms, ammunition, explosives etc;
(vii) providing shelter and safe houses for harbouring purpose;
(viii) action support and participation in violent activities".[40]

Three major types of civil strife can be indicated by three curves in the graph.

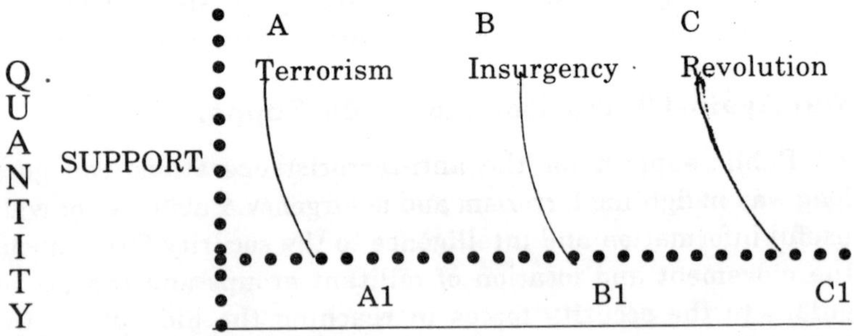

In the given graph curve AAI indicates terrorism which is characterised by very little mass support and the participants are hard core going all the way from an ideology to extreme violence.[41] Curve BB1 shows Guerilla warfare and insurgency who are supported by a very large segment of the population. Curve CC1 describes the stage of revolutions when the number of participants becomes much larger and there is mass uprising.[42] For controlling and combating above mentioned conflicts, the first step has to be erosion of the public support by a combination of initiatives that should include the following :

(1) take care of the underlying socio-economic causes;

(2) restore the people's faith in the just order of the state and the efficiency of its various organs;

(3) educate the public about the misguided nature of the terrorist thinking; and

(4) seek widest possible public cooperation through a consensual approach".[43]

War against terrorism insurgency and other organised crime requires not merely passive acceptance of police activity but active cooperation of the public. No intelligence organisation can be a substitute for the willing information given by the public. Full and complete defeat of terrorism can be ensured only by isolating the terrorists from the people completely. The effective control and containment of terrorism in Punjab can be largely attributed to the active involvement and support of the community in fighting the menace.[43a]

To control the terrorism, a strategy which does not include the winning of confidence of the people as its most important component will never succeed. The ultimate victory will depend on how much intelligence can be gathered about the movements and the plans of the terrorists, and this job can be done mostly by the local police. The confidence of the people, however, cannot be won merely by strong statements. The strategy should be to win both the hearts and minds of the people.[42b]

Public Participation in Internal Security Effort

Conceptually public participation depends upon benefits which one hope to get, the probability that they will actually achieve the benefit and costs (pain) involved to work for the projects. It can be shown in the following formula:

$$P = (B \times Pr) - C$$

where P = Participation which depends upon,

B = Benefits which one hopes to get,

Pr = Probability that they will actually achieve the benefits and,

C = Costs (in terms of pain, efforts) involved to work for the programme.[44]

Basic principles of public participation can be summarised as under :

1. People organise best around the problems they consider most important in assessing needs and in planning initiatives to meet these needs.
2. Local people make rational economic decisions in the context of their own environment and circumstances.
3. Voluntary commitment of labour, time, materials and money to a project is both an evidence of participation and a necessary condition for breaking patterns of development paternalism.
4. Local control over the amount, quality and distribution of benefits increases the chances of the project becoming self-sustainables.

People's cooperation in bringing communal harmony after communal riots and enforcement of curfew, are most essential features of internal security mechanisms. For fighting insurgency, terrorism, communalism, public support to police and security forces is most valuable.

"The worth of a state in the long run" said John Stuart Mill, "is the worth of individuals composing it." It has been noticed that colossal ignorance still prevails in the community about the programmes of social defence. Even enlightened citizens are not fully aware of these programmes.[45] Against the constitutional promise of the government being of the people, the people do not get information about internal security problems easily because of the secretive tendencies. Many matters of public concern which should be matters of public debate are marked confidential and secret. As Upendra Baxi put it : India celebrates the bureaucratic culture of confidentiality and secrecy ; not merely routine and not so routine government papers but also printed reports on matters of common interest are also classified as secret ... In the presence of such a massively growing bureaucratic culture of confidentiality, informed citizen participation in the creation of a just democratic society gets severely retarded.[46] Popular support is essential for public policy to succeed but due to mass illiteracy, poverty, political indifference and collosal ignorance, there is lack of effective public participation. People's apathy or their minimal involvement in the field of social defence, both at the policy formulation and implementation levels has been due to the following main reasons:

(1) There is an in-built public apathy and resistance to crime prevention work and particularly for internal security duties due to unsatisfactory police image;

(2) Not many people are fully conversant with the mechanism and structure of internal security framework and organisations;

(3) The majority of people (including community's opinion leaders and local elites) do not know how best they can involve themselves in internal security duties and social defence programmes;

(4) People in urban areas tend to be highly individualistic and self-centred having no regard for the promotion and preservation of law and order situation in their community;

(5) The urban people are busy with their daily occupations having the tasks of internal security to only those who are officially paid for it;

(6) Voluntarism is declining very fast from urban life and people tend to rely on government agencies;

(7) Political rivalries and group antagonism do not allow citizens to come out voluntarily for promoting law and order when one party is agitating and protesting with certain political objectives in view;

(8) The personnel engaged in internal security duties have not been able to educate people with regard to their role in internal security duties ;

(9) For want of any definite thinking on the need and significance of enlisting public participation in internal security duties, the public is not represented in a formalised way at the national, state, district levels in policy planning for internal security;

(10) Police and other internal security organisations work "in isolation under the guarded cloak of secrecy".[47]

How to Motivate People for Public Participation?

The remedy lies in carrying on an apolitical movement to educate the common man and create awareness about matters which affect internal well-being and national security.[48] Seminars and workshops on police-community relations can be organised by the state police organisations. All India Police-Community Relations Workshops are being regularly arranged in various State capitals of the country. Participation of the people in various internal security efforts depends upon the following factors :

(1) The degree and level of knowledge the people have regarding the programmes and their awareness.

(2) Once the felt needs of the people were identified by themselves with the help of their leaders, people's participation becomes easy.

(3) The people would decide to participate depending on how much it would contribute to the larger interests of the community in their perception. Patriotism, need for their own security and instinct of self-preservation can be motivating factors in enlisting public cooperation for internal security efforts.

(4) People should be made aware of the details of all schemes drawn for communal harmony and people's participation in village defence schemes drawn by the police and security forces. The present "top down" approach should be changed to another approach called "bottom up with support down", where the rural people plan their programmes with the official support.

(5) People can be motivated for internal security duties provided they are infused with a patriotic zeal to defend the unity and integrity of the country. Political awareness and appeal to patriotic sentiments can be useful tools in this respect.

Concluding Remarks

Many voluntary organisations and volunteers find their work in the field of social defence and promotion of law and order quite often frustrating and unrewarding. Public participation issue appears nice on paper or when discussed in seminars and workshops, but when applied to practice, it seems to generate as many problems as it tries to solve.[49] Education of school children in matters of internal security, law enforcement, legal institutions, social control and the police part in them is a very significant aspect of the total community task. Even various sections of the society can be given awareness about the various challenges of internal security through electronic and mass media so that enlightened citizens may provide timely assistance and support to the police in internal security duties. Public participation through voluntary organisations has an important role to play in exposing violations of human rights by the police and security forces and to fight for their protection. The new conceptualisation that is emerging—is around the nation of the rights and liberties of the people, of various sections of the people. Not just political rights in the limited sense of human rights against the state as conceived in the west but rights that obtain from social, ethnic, ecological, gender and ethical mani-springs of a diverse and plural society.[50] It is now opportune time to introduce a nation wide crusade of mass education on internal security by making intensive use of media through the press, radio, and T.V., films etc. and to include internal security as a compulsory subject in the curriculum of all schools and colleges throughout the country.[51] Internal security should be included in core curriculum of various classes so that future citizens are correctly educated about our internal security problems. If Indian nation has to survive as a democratic, secular republic, citizens will have to abandon violence and unconstitutional methods of protest and agitations. "If we wish to maintain democracy not merely in form but also in fact, what we must do ? The first thing, in my judgement, we must do is to hold fast to constitutional methods of achieving our social and economical objectives".[52] Public participation at all levels should be carried out for maintaining internal security of the country. Press, television, radio and audio visual publicity can educate the public about their role in various social defence programmes. In other countries like the Netherland, Sweden and the United Kingdom, campaign to enlighten public opinion by means of exhibitions, articles in the press, films, television and radio broadcasts are being conducted with great success.[53] The amazing thing about India today is that few seem to be bothered about what is likely to take place in the near future despite gathering signs of impending instability.[54] There is a general lack of concern about it in the general masses and even in elite sections of the society. There is an urgent need for people to come forward and dedicate themselves in the nation-building activities which are at once political, moral, social and psychological. There are many patriotic individuals of considerable merit and accumen. This is no time to sit back and watch the apocaltypes. The situation can even now be salvaged and further deterioration prevented. It is important to remember that "liberty lies in the heart of men; when it dies there, no constitution, no law, no court can save it, no constitution no law, no court can even do much to help it. While it lies there, it needs no constitution, no law, no law to save it".[55]

REFERENCES

1. Mukut Sah, Good Governance. The Citizen's Role, *Indian Express*, December 15, 1995.

1a. H.J. Esysenck. *et. al.*, *Encyclopaedia of Psychology*, Vol. 2, London Search Press, 1972.

2. J.M. Cohen and N.T. Uphoff "Participation's place in Rural Development : Seeking clarity through specificity, World Development" Vol. 8 No. 30, 1980, pp. 213-36.

3. Lucian W.W. Pye, *Aspects of Political Development* (Boston; Little, Brown and Co. 1966). p. 45.

4. Alex Inkeles, Participant citizenship in Six Developing Countries, *The American Political Science Review*, 63 (Dec. 1969). p. 1139.

5. Yasuyoshi Shiono, "Use of volunteers in the Non-institutional Treatment of offenders in Japan, *International Review of Criminal Policy*. No. 27, 1969. United Nations, 1970, p. 25.
6. "ACC Task Force on Rural Development", Report of the Third Meeting of the working group on programme harmonisation, Rome, 1978.
7. F. Lovell Bixby, Introduction to Papers presented by the participants of the 25th International Training Course UNAFFI— Resource material series No. 1, p. 39.
8. Report of Fifth National Police Commission, Govt. of India Nov. 1980 Para 41.4, p. 47.
9. Fifth Report of the National Police Commission, Govt. of India, Nov. 1980, Para 41.15, p. 49.
10. Dr. K.M. Mathur, *Internal Security Challenges and Police in a Developing Society*. R.B.S.A. Publishers, Jaipur, 1989, p. 22.
11. For further details see *Kautilya Arthsastra* BK 11 Ch. I Edited by Dr. Shain Sastry.
12. Refer to Dr. A.S. Altekar — State Government in Ancient India — 1955, 2nd Edition, p. 221.
13. Consult Report of the Indian Police Commission 1902-03, p. 36.
14. Report of the National Police Commission (Dharma Vira) Third Report Para 20-17.
15. K.M. Mathur, *Indian Police — Role and Challenges —* Gyan Publishing House, New Delhi, 1994, p. 201.
16. K.M. Mathur, *Indian Police — Role and Challenges —* Gyan Publishing House, New Delhi, 1994, p. 188
17. For similar views see S.P. Srivastava, Public Participation in Social Defence, B.R. Publishing Corporation, Delhi, 1981, p. 74.
18. J. Guha Roy — Role of voluntary agencies in prevention of crime and treatment of offenders — *Indian Journal of Public Administration* July-September 1987, Vol. XXXIII, No. 3, p. 654.
19. Sanjit (Bunker) Roy — Voluntary Agencies in Development — Their Role, Policy and Programmes, *Indian Journal of Public Administration*, July-September, 1987, Vol. XXXIII No. 3, p. 457.

20. Rajni Kothari, Voluntary organisations in a plural society- *The Indian Journal of Public Administration*. July-September, 1987, Vol. XXXIII, No. 3 (3), p. 447.

21. *Ibid.*

22a. Rajni Kothari, (1984), The Non-party Political Process— *Economic and Political Weekly*, Vol. XIX, No. 5. February 4, 1984. Also Harsh Seth — The Non-party Political Process: Uncertain Alternatives (Mimeo) UNRISO Geneva, 1983.

21b. Jagmohan, Don't shoot the cop, he is doing his job, *The Hindustan Times*, New Delhi, 8 May, 1995.

22. Fifth Report of the National Police Commission, Govt. of India, November, 1980, Para 41.2, p. 47.

23. A Gardenwitz, The role of volunteers in work with Juvenile delinquents — *International Review of Criminal Policy* — No. 22, 1964, p. 68.

24. Dac H. Chang, Crimilogy : A cross-cultural perspective, New Delhi, 1976, p. 125.

25. Mahmoodbin Muhammad : Planning and Research for Crime Prevention. Resource Material Series No. 8. UNAFEI, October 1974 No. 1, p. 29.

26. Robert E. Keldgord and Robert Onorries — New Directions in Corrections, Federal Probation, Vol. 36, March 1977, No. 1, p. 2.

27. N.S. Saksena — Public Support in the Investigation of Crime — *Indian Police Journal*, July-September 1975, Vol. XXVII.

28. Louis A Radet, The Police & the Community, Biverly Hills 1973, p. 509.

29. Dr. Indu Prakash, *Disaster Management*, Rashtra Prahari Prakashan, Ghaziabad 1994, p. 278.

30. For further details see— K.M. Mathur, *Management of Internal Security and Related Issue*, Gyan Publishing House, New Delhi, 1995, pp. 163-64.

31. Dr. Indu Prakash — Disaster Management — Rashtra Prahari Prakashan, Ghaziabad 1994, p. 278.

32. Fifth Report of the National Police Commission, Govt. of India, November 1980. Para 41.4, p. 47.

33. Fifth Report of the National Police Commission, Govt. of India, November 1980, Para 41.4, p. 47.

33(a). Sampark Campaign in Punjab, *The Times of India*, 27th August, 1993.

34. Julie Riveire, Community Policing not at all, *Indian Express,* 19 January, 1995.

35. Brown L.P., Evaluation of Police Community Relations Programmes, *Police* 19 (2), p. 29.

36. India Abroad (October 23, 1987).

37. Radelet, Louis A., The Police and the Community, Beverly Hills, Glencol Press, 1973, p. 483.

37(a) K.M. Mathur, *Internal Security Challenges and Police in a Developing Society*, R.B.S.A. Publishers, SMS Highway's, Jaipur 1989, p. 22.

38. K.M. Mathur, *Concerns and Constraints in Administration,* — RBSA Publishers, Jaipur 1991, p. 16.

39. K.M. Mathur, *Police in India — Problems and Perspective,* Gyan Publishing House, New Delhi, 1991, p. 75.

40. Dr. B. Varma — Terrorism — Paper presented at the National Seminar on the problems of Terrorism in Contemporary India, October 8-10, 1988 at Jabalpore.

41. Richard Clutterbuck, Guerillas and Terrorists, Faber London, p. 20 ; Z.K. Zawoony, Infrastructure of terrorist organisations in Lawrence Zelic Freedman and Yonal Alexander (ed.). Perspectives on Terrorism. Hindustan Publishing Corporation, Delhi, 1985.

42. Dr. B. Varma, Insurgency and Counter Insurgency, Uppal Publishing House, New Delhi, 1988, p. 10.

43. R.K. Khandelwal, Combating Terrorism — Political strategies, Intelligence-gathering and police - para- military responses—Paper presented at National Seminar on the problems of Terrorism in contemporary India, October 8-10, 1988 at Jabalpur.

43(a). K.M. Mathur, *Management of Internal Security and Related Issues*, Gyan Publishing House, New Delhi, 1995, p. 45.

43(b). Ved Marwah, The Task in Kashmir — Importance of cohesive team to win people's confidence, *The Indian Express*, 12 May 1994.

44. D.D. Gew and J. Vansant, Beyond the Rhetoric of Rural Development participation : How can it be done, *World Development* Vol. II, 1983.

45. Dr. Sunil Kanta Bhattacharyya — Social Defence — An Indian Perspective, Manas Publications, 1985, p. 190.

46. Upendra Baxi, Democratic Dimensions of the Right to Information (Monograph), Govt. of India, DAVP, New Delhi, 1990 June, pp. 1-2.

47. T. Ananthachari, National Security - Playing of Politics, *The Hindustan Times*, 20 January 1995.

48. For similar views see S.P. Srivastava, *Public Participation in Social Defence*, B.R. Publishing Corporation, Delhi, 1981, pp. 7-8.

49. *Ibid.*, p. 215.

50. Rajni Kothari, Voluntary Organisations in a Plural Society, *Indian Journal of Public Administration,* July-September 1987, Vol. XXXIII No. 3, p. 452.

51. J.S. Saldana, A Plan for national internal security in internal security, some current issues (Ed). H.M. Mathur, 1976, p. 19.

52. B.R. Ambedkar in the Constituent Assembly on 25th Nov. 1949 - See Constituent Assembly Debates, Vol. XI, Delhi Manager of Publications, pp. 972-81.

53. Dr. S.K. Bhattacharyya, *Social Defence—An Indian Perspectives,* Manas Publications Delhi, 1985, p. 191.

54. Rajni Kothari — Crisis in the System — Declining Congress—Moribund Opposition, *Times of India*, 18 June 1994.

55. Justice Hand, *The Spirit of Liberty* 1953, p. 144.

7

Training for Excellence for Internal Security

Introduction—The Concept of Excellence

Excellence means extraordinarily great merit; surpassing others in very good quality ; of great virtue and worth. Excellence stands for blameless conduct, surpassing merit, virtue and honest performance. Excellence refers to very high performance which can become a trial blazer for others. "We seem to easily recognise excellence. Bethoven, Mozart, Shakespeare, Hemingway, and Leonardo da Vinci created it. Gandhi, Socrates, Franklin, Confucius and Einstein had it. John Wooden, the legency UCLA Coach, brought it to the basket-ball floor, Vince Lambardi inspired it on the football field and Jesse Owens showed it at the 1936 summer olympics. Every one recognises that an olympic gold medal and a Nobel Prize reward it".[1] Excellence refers to surpassing or outstanding achievement. Human excellence is achieved by being "the best" at something; by making significant improvements over past performances, by doing something unique and by innovating or inventing. Organisations can facilitate and nurture human excellence by providing a potential site for the flowering of the most forms of human excellence. Organisations can also encourage team efforts to achieve collective levels of excellence that individuals cannot achieve alone. In the business world, products such as Kleenex, Xerox machines and scotch tape have come to refer generically to all similar products, regardless of their manufacturers because of excellence. When we talk of companies that embody excellence, IBM, Hewlett-Packard, General Electric & Sony leap to mind as models of excellence. How have these business organisations provided outstanding products and services to their customer ? Excellence can be easily measured with both objective and subjective yardsticks. The issue here is how the best training can be imparted to Police and Central Police Organisations to create excellence in them for internal security duties. How can we make our training institutions capable of creating excellence in trainees for internal security duties? Generally individuals, not organisations, create excellence. But if good leaders and team captains with excellence can be built up, they can lead their groups along the pathway to excellence, carefully cultivating those who will later assume the control. Japanese police is world famous for its excellence in performance and civility. U.K. Bobby is well known for its cordial police-community relations. In organisations, excellence does not happen miraculously but springs gradually from pacesetting levels of personal effectiveness and efficiency of the members of the organisations over many years. Transforming mediocre organisations into excellent ones, takes a tremendous investment of time and efforts by the great leaders who are culture builders and strategic thinkers. Training and human resource development are two important and useful effective tools for achieving excellence. For organisational excellence, short-term orientation, shallow thinking and quick-fix expectations are three deadly attitudes. For building a culture of excellence, high level of commitments to a common purpose and competence to deliver superior performance and consistency are needed. For sustaining culture of excellence, good selection, high level of motivation, appropriate and ongoing training, commitment to the culture of excellence and retention of committed employees is needed. "Evolution has made man a teaching as well as a learning animal, for dependency and maturity is guided by the nature of that which must be cared for. Generativity, then is primarily the concern for establishing and guiding the next generation ......, the concept of generativity is meant to include productivity and creativity, neither of which, however can replace it as designations of a crisis in development ...... Generativity is itself a driving power in human organisation".[2]

Training for Excellence

In India, Central Reserve Police has earned a name for its mobility, discipline and excellence in dealing with internal security duties. The issue before us is how to organise training for excellence in internal duties in State police forces and other central police organisations. Internal security duties can be categorised into four categories :

1. Duties pertaining to collection of intelligence,
2. Duties pertaining to civil police with relation to internal security.
3. Training for internal security operations.
4. Training for other specialised internal security duties like industrial security and VIP security.

For police and security forces, earmarked for internal security duties, excellence need to be injected through sustained organisational efforts and training. High level of commitment of trainers and trainees, required motivation for trainers and trainees and a supportive organisational culture need to be built up for expecting excellence by the internal security organisations. Training for excellence, for internal security duties would require not only self-sustaining culture of excellence in various police and security forces, but also restricting of our training institutions, and continuous job-oriented training of police and security forces. Well planned, well structured and effectively implemented training will enable them (i) to learn new techniques of internal security operations, (ii) use of new weapons, equipment and tools, (iii) to inculcate new work ethics and commitment to the job, (iv) to orient them to changing socio-economic and political challenges, and (v) to develop a new organisational philosophy of constant endeavour for excellence in their assigned jobs. Quality circles in police and security forces alone will safeguard human rights and bring excellence in their effective, responsive and good quality service to the society.

For creating and maintaining excellence, leadership at the various levels must acquire the following skills :[3]

(i) Creative insight;

(ii) Sensitivity to developing events;

(iii) Vision of a grand future;

(iv) Versatility to deal with complex challenges;

(v) Focus on quality control and excellence;

(vi) Patience to pursue the difficult path of constant commitment to the organisational goals.

Excellence in internal security will require high level of motivation, modernisation and high level of commitments to the organisational goals. Internal security duties are largely undefined and fall under the jurisdiction of state according to the Constitution. Internal security has not been defined in the Constitution of India nor under any law of the country so far.

Characteristics of Excellent Organisations

Organisation excellence, like human excellence may take many forms. There can be six major forms of needed organisational excellence—competitive, renuvenatory, institutionalised, creative, missionary and versatile. In words of Pradip N. Khandwalla: "Competitive excellence is needed to increase the adaptability, market orientation and resourcefulness of third world organisations. Rejuvenatory excellence is needed because of the unhealthy conditions and the need for turn around activity in most large third world organisations. Institutionalised excellence is needed in third world organisations where competitiveness is weak. Creative excellence is needed to spur innovations in the third world societies. Missionary excellence is needed to foster the achievement of vast social and economic missions in the context of the third world backwardness.

Lastly versatile excellence is needed by those organisations that have numerous stakeholders and many goals to pursue. Excellence is powered by strong commitments.[4] CRPF has versatile excellence and can carry out any assigned tasks with excellence. CRPF keeps organisational excellence through mission, vision and core values. Some of the important characteristics of excellent organisations can be as under :

1. A wide spread concern and commitment for excellence among the members to make the organisation successful.

2. A cohesive team and synergistic collective action.
3. Constant and strong emphasis on quality of service to be rendered to the society/nation.
4. Responsive and outstanding leadership with commitment to excellence.
5. Rapid paced problem solving organisation ability with focus on results rather than personal dominance.
6. Free flow of information and communication throughout the organisation.
7. A belief in the capabilities and intensions of all the members of the organisation.
8. Value is placed on diversity and confirmity in thought and style is discouraged"[5].

7-S Model for Excellence

The famous 7-S Model of excellence consists of the following seven variables[6] :

1. *Shared Values.* Shared values or supraordinate goals refer to a set of values and aspirations that go beyond the conventional formal statement of organisational objectives and mission. These fundamental values give rise to a certain spirit among organisational members which is reflected in their values, attitudes, actions and philosophy. No organisation can become a trail blazer, unless properly articulated superordinate goals can provide a strong basis for the survival and growth of the organisation.

2. *Strategy.* Strategy refers to a long-term plan chosen deliberately and consciously after a thorough analysis of the internal and external environment of the organisation. Examples of strategy include cost effectiveness, good quality of service to the clients, technological dominance strategic managerial responses to changing environment.

3. *Structure.* Organisation structure is the basis of the whole organisational structure and performs following major tasks :

(a). It reduces uncertainty or random human behaviour by prescribing roles and the formal relationship among various positions and activities.

(b). It enables the organisation to keep its activities coordinated.

(c). It leads to effective allocation of tasks and establishes communication channels and the role each member is to play.

4. *System.* System is the superstructure consisting of all the rules, regulations and procedures, both formal and informal that complement the organisational structure. Systems reflect the logic and experience of the past meant to enhance organisational effectiveness without the disruptive side effects. The effectiveness of systems depends on the support of top management to the established systems and procedures and on the ability to distill experience and knowledge into procedures.

5. *Style.* Style is more than top management behaviour; it includes the organisational culture which refers to the basic understanding shared by the members of the organisation. It is reflected in the traditions, norms, rituals and working style of the organisation. Clarity of communication, openness, organisational thrust, willingness to delegate decision-making, achievement orientation and encouragement to innovations are some of the elements of style that contribute to the organisational excellence.

6. *Staff.* Staffing refers to selecting people for specific organisational positions and developing in them the competence, capabilities and confidence for effective performance. Excellent organisations manage their human resources in such a way that they are able to generate amongst their employees the belief that they are the real performers.

7. *Skill.* All high performing organisations have distinct capabilities and skills which are constantly sharpened by new bearing and effective utilisation of the distinctive skills.

7-S Frame

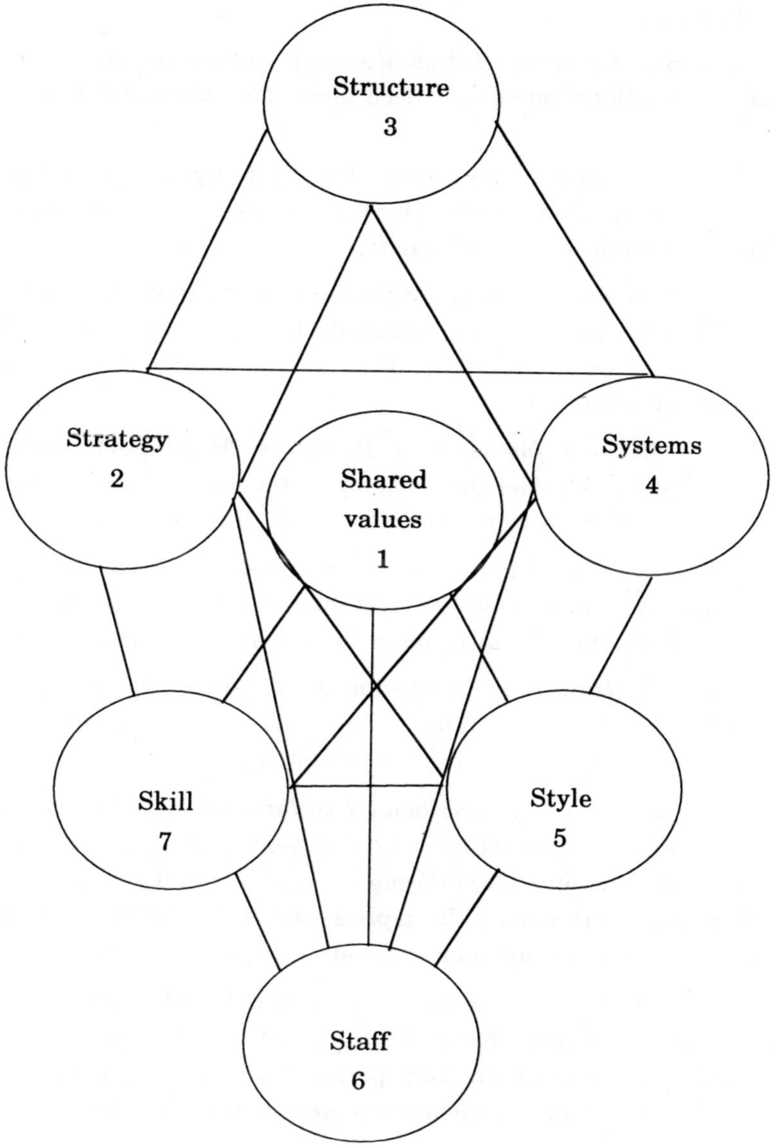
Structure
3
Strategy
2
Shared
values
1
Systems
4
Skill
7
Style
5
Staff
6

Common Dimensions

Some of the common dimensions of excellent organisational culture are as under[7] :

1. *Bias for Action.* Action-orientation is the key ingredient of organisational success. It need inner motivation and urge to act.

2. *Closeness to the client.* The best organisations are responsive to their clients. There is an obsession to serve the client through unparalled quality.

3. *Autonomy.* Excellent organisations give freedom to their employees and foster innovations through informal communications, intense creativity and non-monetary and monetary incentives.

4. *Respect for Human Resource.* High performing organisations consider their employees the most valuable asset. Recognition and reward are linked with achievements.

5. *Coherent Value Systems.* Excellent organisations are driven by coherent value systems and beliefs. Honesty, punctuality and commitment to the job are respected values.

6. *Specialisation.* It means the organisation must stay close to the business it knows best and specialises, constant training and practice bring specialisation.

7. *Planned Organisational Development.* Organisations must utilize organisational development techniques to keep constant focus on high performance, and constant responses to changing environment. It implies proper implementation of personnel policies and human resource development techniques.

8. *Constant good organisational health and a passion for excellence.* There should be high level motivation to the employees for constant high performance and a passion for excellence. Good organisational health will depend on the following factors :

(a) Committed and effective leadership.

(b) A sense of mission.

(c) A sense of organisational pride.

(d) A burning zeal for outstanding achievement.

(e) A clarity of vision about the organisational goals and mission.

(f) Well organised on going training of employees.

In words of Pradip. N. Khandwalla, "Many mechanisms have been identified for the improvement of organisational excellence and the most productive of the keys to organisational excellence are :

(i) Mission, vision of excellence and core values;

(ii) Style of Management;

(iii) Strategic Management;

(v) Structure and system;

(v) Organisational renewal process[8]".

Excellence organisations have to remain dynamic and vibrant to keep excellence over a period of time. Strong commitment at the top, high level of training, sound personnel policies, vision, strategy and conducive organisational culture are some of the important essentials of an excellent organisation. Effective communication system, a sense of organisational identity, adequate motivation to the employee are essential for sustaining excellence in organisations. In police organisations, CRPF has been able to maintain its excellence in internal security duties due to its high level of discipline, spirit of sacrifice and high level of mobility. CRP has maintained excellence through its core values of obedience, loyalty, integrity, conscientiousness, discipline, sincerity and so on.

Concept of Training

Training is a deliberate and planned process of teaching and learning wherein knowledge, skills, techniques, attitudes and experiences are acquired by the trainees with the help and guidance of the trainers in a given learning environment.

Training represents an intervention strategy with *inter alia,* the following overall objects, namely (a) checking and preventing obsolescence at both organisational and individual levels; (b) curing pre-active shortcomings of knowledge and professional skills, techniques and procedures; (c) shaping and making adjustments with fast changing socio-technological, environmental changes and demands; (d) promoting and developing new outlook, and ethnological version of quality, excellence and accomplishment in one's profession; (e) transforming and making a total man with new professional and cultural attribute and vision; (f) providing and opportunities for the fullest development of individuals and the organisation over a period of time.

Training as a System

Central Police Organisations should recognise and restructure their training efforts for the accomplishments of the above mentioned objectives. Training is a continuous process and an organised system of rotational arrangements of inputs, technology, people, material events and processes designed to elicit behavioural outputs which produce further social and economic outputs increasing organisations effectiveness and efficient organisation people. For achieving excellence, training system must provide excellent support. Training as a system has to be geared for excellence and there are many problem areas as shown in the figure.

FIGURE

A System's Approach to Training for Excellence

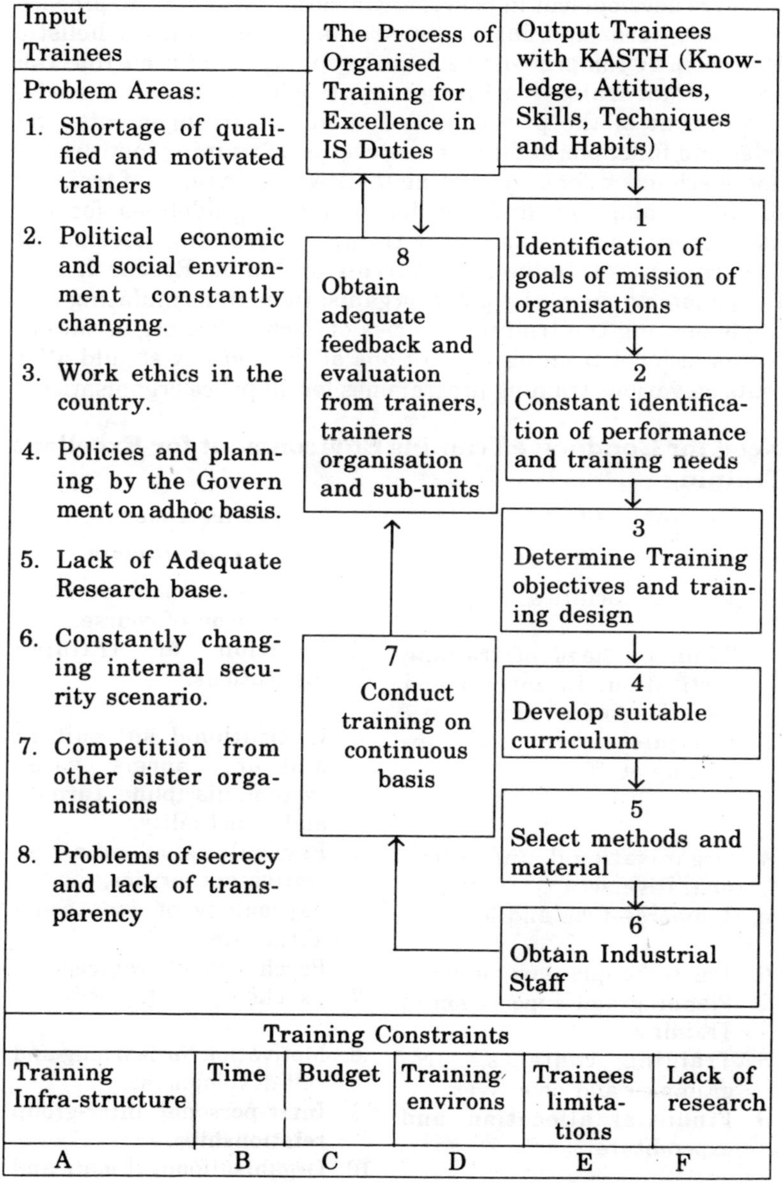

Need for a Training Policy

For achieving excellence through training and human resource development in police, organisations will have to prepare both long-term and short-term training policy with a holistic approach. A comprehensive training policy should outline the scope of "all training acturities, approaches to training needs, assessment of the priorities and financial arrangements, the roles and functions of different categories of training institutions and mechanism for coordinating their work, linkages of training to career planning and development and guidelines for the monitoring and evaluation of training[9]. Training Division of Government of India and Bureau of Police Research and Development can assist police organisations in formulating and implementing the training policies of each police organisation. National level training institutions of the country should allot seats on various training programmes for all police organisations.

Need for Conducive Training Environment for Excellent Training

Environment of training can be divided as under[10] :

Tangible Constituents	*Intangible Constituents*
1. Physical facilities.	1. Time constituent duration and season of course.
2. Trainers, head of training institution, incentives and facilities to trainers.	2. Location of training institutions.
3. Administrative and supporting staff.	3. Institutional sub-culture and org. norms, value system, discipline, turnout and punctuality.
4. Organisational and administrative setup.	4. Psychology of administrative authorities.
5. Trainers—type and level.	5. Psychology of sponsoring authorities.
6. Trg. techniques and methods.	6. Psychology of trainees.
7. Planning and supervision of Training.	7. Psychology of trainers.
8. Training contents, programmes and objectives.	8. Motivation for learning and self-development.
9. Financial allocation and expenditure.	9. Inter-personal, inter-group relationships.
	10. Organisational climate and health.

A review of the training environs of most of the police training institutions reveals that training environment are not very conducive to effective, job-oriented training of police officer. Only lit service is being paid to training and most of the police training institutions continue to be deficient of motivated trainers, required infra-structure. Even basic amenities needed for training institutions are not available in many training institutions. Adequate motivation and incentives are not available to trainers in most of the training institutions.

Training for Excellence

Police forces are not autonomous institutions, free standing and independent but reflect the social setting in which they operate[11]. For achieving excellence for internal security duties, police organisations have to acquire a large number of attributes and objective criteria, a very high quality of management, quality of services to the community and the nation; innovation; value as a long-term investment, financial soundness, ability to attract, develop and keep talented people, community and environmental responsibility and optimum use of organisation assets. Excellence does not happen miraculously but springs from pace setting levels of personal effectiveness and efficiency by great leaders who mastered required skills and passed those skills to the succeeding generation of executives and managers[12]. For high performance organisations six famous tends are as under:

1. Treat employees like a family and as great assets;
2. Maintain strict consistency in high quality performance;
3. Thoroughly plan facilities and equipment;
4. Attract talented people, develop them and provide them with new age skills (a) creative insight, (b) vision, (c) sensitivity, (d) versatility, (c) focus and, (d) patience.
5. Organisational leaders must toil to prepare themselves to go marathon distances, surmounting all the obstacles, with utmost efforts and at times pains to achieve excellence by fine tuning of strategy and culture.
6. Organisations have to build a culture of excellence

through constant training and the highest levels of personal and group motivations, and at the same time keeping organisational leaders away from the three deadly attitudes; (a) short-term orientation, (b) shallow thinking, and (c) quickfix expectations. Patience is very important because impatience runs like a vein through all three of them.

Need for Strategic Thinking

For successful strategic thinking organisational leaders and organisational trainers have to cater for three requirements of successful strategy, i.e., (i) satisfying the needs of the customers and clients ; (ii) keep competitive advantage over other organisational competitors, and (iii) capitalize on organisational strengths remembering that it takes time to develop them. Organisations have to carry out constantly swot analysis; organisations has to carefully list its strengths and weakness; and think of all the opportunities organisation's strength can seize and the threats that could take advantage of the weakness of the organisation.

Problem Areas and Constraints

Etzioni (1964) viewed the effectiveness as the degree of goal achievement. Katz and Khan (1966) considered organisational effectiveness in terms of efficiency and maximisation of returns. Organisational effectiveness in internal security duties depends on available equipment, weaponry and other resources. It is for consideration whether the nation has given its security forces the weapons and tools required for internal security duties. Our training in Counter-Insurgency warfare is recognised worldwide. It is not the lack of knowledge, competence or skills but the lack of the wherewithal and possibly, even more important, the will to use them that must come under scrutiny.[13] For carrying out operations against militants, certain constraints and limitations are realised by the security forces. Over the years internal security problems have increased both in magnitude and complexity unfortunately in our country, while the problems are assuming serious dimensions, neither the political manipulations are showing any signs of abatement nor the infirmities of the police machinery are being attended to with the seriousness and promptitude they deserve.[14] The "resource crunch" has led to many shortages, of new and secure communication equipment, night fighting devices, high fire power, short range weapons and so on in adequate numbers.[15] Most of the current weaponry and munitions are not entirely suitable for insurgency warfare and they need to be augmented by modern crowd control civil action type additions. Police needs for internal security duties water canons, fire fighting equipment with powerful fire extinguishing capacity and non-lethal chemical weapons which can temporarily incapacitate people.

Performance of police and security forces in internal security duties depends upon the policies framed by the government and the decisions / guidelines given to them. According to K.F. Rustamji, some of the main faults in our policies are as under :

"(1) Panicky and thoughtless decisions;

(2) Defective planning of manpower, weapons and tactics without any long-term plans;

(3) Frequent deployment of army over long periods;

(4) Barbarity and banditry by the police forces and reckless searches and insults to citizens;

(5) Improper, use of central forces"[16]

Psychological Theory of Learning

For achieving excellence behaviour contract theory is a modern counselling technique. Learning, the behavioural psychologist believes, is a matter of reinforcing successful behaviour. According to the behavioural scientists suppose you are obese and overweight take a contract with yourself that you will cut out sweet food for a week. This behaviour will be rewarded by a consequent weight reduction. You may give yourself an additional reward for successfully completing your contact may be a trip to a coverted film show. There is a strong possibility that you will continue this sweetless behaviour (denying fees to yourself after the reward).

Behavioural scientists have suggested behavioural theory as a measure of achieving excellence in organisations. The following simple steps are needed in this behavioural contract theory :

1. Identify and define behaviour that is to be changed.
2. Think out a way of measuring that behaviour.
3. Decide on a consequent reward which is greatly desirable.
4. Place consequence on the behaviour.
5. Continue measurement and
6. Give yourself the reward if you reach the desired goal.[17]

With certain modifications this theory of behavioural theory can be usefully applied to Police and Internal Security organisations for achieving excellence. The central idea of the technique is that every human being graves for reward for his behaviour and the more pleasurable the contingency, the better chance for the behaviour to be repeated. This theory of possibility re-inforcement has been developed by the psychologists Premack and re-inforcement principle is generally termed as a Premack principle.

Core Competencies

Core competencies are those capabilities, skills, attitudes, knowledge and technique which are essential keeping in view one's organisational strength, one's work culture and the trends in the macro and micro-environment. Core competencies can be defined as certain basic strengths of the organisation, either in terms of its resources its services, its products or its culture. For internal security duties, the core competencies can be as under :

(i) Capability to analyse and foresee impending internal security challenges with all its dimensions and ramifications;

(ii) Capability to effectively and quick respond to the challenge in a most professional manner within the democratic norms;

(iii) Capability and skills needed to handle political agitations, riots and large scale disturbances with promptness with minimum use of force;

(iv) Competence and preparedness to carry out anti-terrorist or anti-insurgency operations in disturbed areas and to root out the strong holds of the militants ;

(v) Flexibility and verstality in doing various internal security jobs ranging from handling peaceful demonstrations, controlling riots, carrying out operations against terrorism, insurgency and low intensity operations inspired by foreign forces with utmost confidence and success;

(vi) Ability for moving out quickly from one type of deployment to another with minimum response time and capability to provide assistance to local police in various type of internal security duties;

(vii) Having maximum self-restraint and control in spite of all possible provocations and having full regard to human rights and rule of law;

(viii) Having capability to promote people's participation in internal security duties and capability to maintain good and cordial relations with the people, press and public leaders.

Organisational Learning

Do organisations learn? Members of the organisations, we do know learn. The organisation, provides their members the means and also a climate for learning. Such learning by individual members results in growth of the individual for self-advancement. Individual learning need not necessarily lead to organisational learning. Learning assumes two dimensions. First organisational members learn in order to promote their self-development, there is also a collateral learning through the self-same members to promote the interest of the organisation. If the latter takes place then it leads to organisational learning. Members of the organisation particularly at the strategic level at the top should be continuously open to learning. If such learning is internalised and transferred down the line and also formalised in the form of evolution of normatives for changed ways of working, changed styles of acting, generating results and managing functions then the organisation is a learning organisation. In this learning process, the apex management is the change level. So the learning cycle starts at the apex level and has the canscading effect. Organisations learn by taking a hard look at themselves. If products do not move in the market, if certain personnel practices being followed have failed in their impact, certain decisions have become outmoded, some of the approaches have gone wayward, the organisation should sit up and examine as to what is happening and why is it happening. This sensitivity should be demonstrated by the top management by instituting processes whereby appropriate reflections on their past experience are made. Such an introspection would lead to learning. It would be a very difficult exercise this self-mirroring. What generally happens in such exercises is 'group think'. There would appear to be mind guarding tendencies bordering on either of these extremes, viz., illusions of invulnerability 'nothing can go wrong with us' syndrome resulting in 'white washing' or going in the other extreme of 'breast beating and wailing', i.e., pleading helplessness. If these happen then the process of introspection gets stymied and the organisation has ceased to learn.

There are three types of learning—single loop learning, double loop learning and deutro learning. In single loop learning, an error has been detected as a violation of existing norms and the organisation has means of detecting the error and rectifying the same, such that the norms are preserved and only deviations are corrected. In double loop learning, when a deviation in the norm has been detected and examination of why such deviations are taking place is made and if found convincing even the norms are changed to keep in tune with the reality or change in circumstances. Deutro learning by organisation is a kind of learning by organisation to learn how to learn. What most of our organisations need today is this third type of learning — learning how to learn.[18]

Creating Excellence in Organisation

Excellence can be achieved only when following factors contribute to the organisational excellence :

1. Proper recruitment and selection of personnel with right aptitude.

2. Effective job oriented basic training.
3. Training centres providing scientific and well balanced training.

Special techniques for excellence :

1. Individual development in knowledge attitudes—specialised techniques and habits to match the organisational needs.
2. Planned organisational response to the changing tasks in terms of new techniques, new equipment, new methods of work and new work ethics.

Organisational firm commitment to organisational effectiveness :

1. Responsive to changing needs.
2. Fuller all round development of all members.
3. Accountability of members.
4. Respect of human dignity — commitments to Indian Constitution.
5. High commitment to professionalism.

Excellence can be sustained only when organisational climate is conducive for excellence. Excellence in organisational climate can build up following factors :

1. High level of motivation.
2. High level of commitment.
3. Job satisfaction and stress free nature of job.
4. Emphasis on service to the community.
5. Commitment to the following core values for the organisations :
   (a) Loyalty to the Constitution, commitment to the goals of the nation and the concepts of an egalitarian society and the need for national integration;
   (b) Awareness of the problems that arise in the wake of development process, including conflicts, social disorganisation, scarcity and control, regional imbalances, etc. ;

(c) A deep social awareness for comprehending and reacting to complex situations;

(d) Development of analytical and innovative skills since situations will continue to change and no readymade solutions can be prescribed.

(e) A new orientation in dealing with the masses, who come from various strata of society, divided among many contours such as religion, caste, region and income as may lead to the correct response in individual cases.

(f) The need for application of scientific techniques, management concepts and skills and constructive attitudes and values in police work.

6. Need for organisational responsiveness to challenging new situations.

Action Plan for Training in Excellence

For organisational excellence, well-organised institutionalised training becomes an essential input. For inculcating core values of the organisation in all the employees, following action plan for training is suggested.

1. Well planned human resource development and training.
2. The development of proper job standards.
3. Correct identification of training needs and periodical review of training needs.
4. Determining objectives of training with a view to achieve excellence.
5. Developing curriculum and its periodical review with a view to attain excellence.
6. Proper selection of training methods, training techniques and training materials with a view to achieve excellence.
7. Need for quality control of training material and need for periodical revision of training methods and materials.
8. Proper selection and availability of infrastructural resources of commitment to achieve excellence.

9. Need for modification to be instructional sources.
10. Proper conduct of training in an environment conducive to learning.
11. Need for effective regular training and feed back with a view to achieve excellence in training.
12. Need for modern training infrastructure.
13. Need for proper training climate.
14. Need for motivation to the trainees for learning with a view to achieve excellence.

Auditing of Human Resources Development

For achieving excellence, periodical auditing of human resources development is most essential. The HRD audit focusses on (a) how will the plans have been made out suiting to organisational mission and objectives; (b) how will these plans are transilated into action; and (c) how such efforts are viewed by the executives and the employees of the organisation. Auditing will cover the following 12 aspects.[19]

1. *Manpower planning.* For keeping effective link between manpower planning and strategic planning, two issues are analysed: (a) Is the manpower plan worked out in consonance with the organisation's operational effectiveness? and (b) Is the appropriate competencies and expertise inducted in the organisations at the right time at the right places?

2. *Selection and Recruitment.* The process should ensure that people with right attitudes, value system and background are selected for appropriate positions. Recruitment must be broad based, scientific and fair to all but should be able to get individuals with appropriate basic skills, attitude and knowledge.

3. *Induction System.* For moulding the new entrants into a right orientation a very thorough basic induction training is needed. It should be a good mix of outdoor and indoor training supplemented by on the job training under a very good mentor.

4. *Performance Appraisal.* Audit of performance appraisal implied asking following heard questions: (a) Does the system

accurately differentiate levels of performance? (b) Does the appraise understand what is expected from them?

5. *Potential appraisal.* How far appraisal procedure has been effective in identifying development needs of the individuals in guiding career planning, posting and training areas for future development.

6. *Career and Succession Planning.* Job rotation and job enrichment are common methods for preparing employees for succession and future positions. Career planning is essential for each employee.

7. *Rewards and compensation.* Audit must find out the effectiveness and impact of both financial and non-financial rewards in driving performance. Are compensation packages for various risks and inconveniences adequate and fair ?

8. *Employee Morale.* Both group and individual morale of the police personnel need constant monitoring and consideration. Periodical organisational climate surveys should be carried out to assess employee morale.

9. *Organisational Development.* Audit must find out whether organisation development activities and interventions properly in time with the strategic plans and missions of the organisation. How far employees understand organisational development?

10. *Training and Development.* This is most important input in HRD and organisational excellence depends on the quality of training imparted. Training needs of the employees and organisational requirements of performance in terms of technology/tasks/people have to be properly harmonised. Regular periodical inservice training and specialised training to bring excellence in performance is needed.

11. *Participative mechanism.* The audit must include activities carried down to the level of constable to ensure their participation performance and commitment to the organisational goals and mission.

12. *Exit interviews.* Besides a decent farewell and send off to the retiring persons, exit interviews must provide feed back to the organisation for corrective actions and areas which need organisational concern.

A most comprehensive audit of H.R.D. carried out periodically by specialists can help organisations in moving towards achieving excellence.

Need for Structural Reforms

There is a need for a creative overhaul of the administrative system. The need of the hour is decentralisation of power and fixation of responsibilities. People are going to be much more demanding, volatile and at times semi-violent. There is need to adopt modern technology. Our research told us that any intelligent approach to organising had to encompass and treat as interdependent, at least seven variable (i) structure, (ii) strategy, (iii) people, (iv) management style, (v) systems and procedures, (vi) guiding concepts and shared values, i.e. culture, and (vii) the present and hoped for organisational strengths or skills.[20] Innovative training needs of the employees organisations have to be continually responding to change of any sort in their environment. The present environment is fast changing and socio-political scenario is becoming more violent and insecure. For building up excellence in police organisations, certain managerial problems need to be identified. A research survey reveals that in many police organisations following problems are noticed :

"(i) Senior managers lack the right perspective;

(ii) They don't personally identify with what their organisations do;

(iii) They don't take enough interest in their people;

(iv) Top managers and their staff have become isolated in their analytic ivory towers."

It has been noticed that most of the police leaders at the top or near top "need a broad vision, a sense of history and can't cope with the flexibility and lack of structure". Excellence in performance has to do with people being motivated by compelling, simple-even beautiful values. Intrinsic motivation at individual level goes a long way in achieving excellence.

Problems and Challenges

For creating excellence in training for internal security

duties, training institutions face the following main problems:

1. Ironically in regard to both recruitment and training of the subordinate officials, the police organisation has suffered a decline. A recent study has shown that of the 12.38 lakh strong police force in the country, about 45 per cent is untrained.[21] Training as a mechanism of transmission of social goals has serious limitations and inadequacies.

2. A mismatch exists between the premises of training and the reality of training because training has been treated as an Allaudin's lamp to deal with the totality of the personality of an administration. We have faulted in assigning a role to training by confusing it with education.

3. Many trainees feel that very often training in police organisations tend to be theoretical and academic and of no relevance to the professional requirements of the participants. Training cannot be very attractive if the feeling persists in trainees that posting and promotions depend primarily on seniority and the service to which one happens to belong rather than on performance. Trainability is a function of trainees' ability and motivation, but in police trainees, motivation is generally lacking due to various organisational and individual problems.

4. Training is neither a panacea for all ills nor it is a waste of time.[23] Administrative deficienices, role dilemma, systems' defects and resource inadequacy are four maladies which cannot be cured by training alone.[24] Training has many limitations because training cannot compensate for lack of intellectual integrity or the lack of will.

5. Over the last three decades, the number of police training institutions has increase, the infrastructural facilities have improved, the curriculum has been updated and many police officers are attending courses in India and abroad. But there are no signs of improvement in police performance or police behaviour nor is there any improvement in the police image.[25] There are limitations of training and training needs to be made more relevant to the contemporary realities. Trainers have to be trained in the art of teaching and they have to maintain life contracts with the realities. There is need for structural reforms

in police training structures and techniques. Training should be able to provide improvement in police performance. The excellent organisations seem not only to know the value of positive reinforcement but how to manage it as well. CRPF has been able to maintain excellence by a vision of exceptional organisational quality with respect to commitment to its assigned duties, commitment to its core values, a concern for propriety, efficiency and accountability.

Need for Culture-Building

For building an organisational culture, commitment competence and consistency are needed. Police culture is an hidproduct of professional socialisation and a total transformation of police culture is needed. If police organisations want to elevate their professional status in democratic societies. By being humane, committed to the rule of law, having the underlying philosophy of citizen's police, the police organisations can improve their credibility and bring out a total transformation in the police culture through various behavioural modifications and correctional strategies.[26] In order to bring total transformation in police culture, policemen should be encouraged to develop into total human beings aware both intellectually and pragmatically of the changing internal security scenario certain stifling aspects of present police culture have to be removed and replaced by more positive aspects such as greater social intercourse with the community, liberal outlook of life and positive regard for human rights.

Need for Organisational Introspection

John Gardner observed : "Most ailing organisations have developed a functional blindness to their own defects. They are not suffering because they cannot resolve their problems but because they cannot see their problems". For maintaining excellence periodical organisational introspection is needed. Organisations must be capable of noticing the signals of decline, when they need radical surgery for the salvation of the organisation. Organisational leaders must know; what to change and how much ? Organisations which fail to promptly answer this question can never achieve; lasting excellence. All organisations have to face some periods of crisis and turbulance but successful leaders must rely upon all six of the new age skills but particularly upon insight versitility and focus. As Peter Drucker says: "In turbulent times, the fundamentals have to be managed well".[27] Centres for Excellence in various fields of training should be created in police organisations with adequate infrastructure and motivated faculty members.

Concluding Remarks

Excellence and good reputations are built very slowly over many years, on consistency of good quality service to the community, high ethical standards, reliability of conduct and trustworthiness. But reputations built over long years can collapse overnight. Patience enables good leaders to integrate and orchestrate the use of creative insight, sensitivity, vision versatility and focus on change. Impatience invariably leads to poor decisions, compromised competence and focus on short-range results at the expense of long-range ones.[29] For achieving excellence for an organisation, training is only one of the many other essential requisites. Training is only one of the inputs for improving performance and achieving excellence. For State police organisations, achieving excellence is only a goal of endeavour. These organisations at present have very low standards of performance due to various constraints and limitations. Indian police is usually at the receiving end and justice demands that its problems and performance are viewed in the correct context and in the totality of the circumstances prevailing in the country.[30] An essential step in the strategy for making training effective is to strengthen a programme of research and development for training. Revitalisation processes and mechanisms are important for maintaining organisational excellence. Organisational learning, behavioural science, nurturant organisational leaders with high stakes in the organisation and organisational core values, are the principle process and mechanism that are needed to revitalise and nurture organisational excellence. Training is a limited instrument. It is just one piece in the puzzle for improving performance. Other pieces of the puzzle must be secured and put into place. Centres for Excellence in various fields of training should be created in police organisations with adequate infrastructure and motivated faculty member. Training of police officers should aim at improving the performance and developing a total person with new cultural attributes operating in the realm of personality. Character and behaviour and thus serve the people of India ensuring a mutually supportive police-public relationship with a firm commitment to secularism, socialism, democracy, social justice and modernisation.[31]

REFERENCES

1. Craig R. Hickman and Michael A. Silva, *Creating excellence Managing Corporate Culture, Strategy and Change in the New Age,* George Allun & Unwin, London, 1984, p. 21.
2. Erickson, Adult Crisis and Growth : Identity, intimacy and generativity in Facilitating Development. Reading for Trainers, consultants and policymakers (ed.), Rolf P. Pynton and Udai Pareek, New Delhi, Sage Publications, 1992, p. 30.
3. For similar views consult David L. Bradford and Allen R. Cohen, *Managing for Excellence*, Wily Eastern Limited, New Delhi, 1987.
4. Pradip N. Khandwalla, *Organisational Designs for Excellence*, Tata Mc-Graw Hill and Co., New Delhi, Particularly Chapter 3.
5. Craig R. Hickman and Michael A Silva, *Creating Excellence. Managing Corporate Culture, Strategy and Change in the New Age*, George Allun & Unwin, London, 1984, p. 21.
6. Thomas J. Peters and Robert H.Waterman, In Search of Excellence Lessons from Americas Best Run Companies. Harper and Row, New York, 1982. It is generally known as Mckinsey 7-S Frame, p. 9.
7. For similar eight attributes for corporations see Thomas J. Peters and Robert H. Waterman , In Search of Excellence, India Book Distributors, Bombay, 1982, pp. 13-16.
8. Pradip N. Khandwalla, *Organisational Designs for Excellence*; Tata Mc-Graw Hills and Co., New Delhi, Chapter 3.

9. Samuel Paul (1983), *Training for Public Administration and Management in Developing Countries,* Washington, World Bank Staff Working Paper No. 584

10. K.M. Mathur, *Administration of Police Training in India*, Gyan Publishing House, New Delhi, 1987.

11. David H. Bayly, *Police and Society*, Sage Publications, London, 1977, p. 71.

12. Craig R. Hickman and Michail A. Silva, *Creating Excellence—Managing Corporate Culture, Strategy and Change in the New Age*, George Allen and Unwin, London, 1985, p. 23.

13. A.M. Sethna, Lessons from the Chrar Episode, *Indian Express*, Ahmedabad, May 15, 1985, p. 6.

14. Jagmohan, Police—Don't Shoot the Cop. He is doing his job, *The Hindustan Times*, 8 May 1995.

15. Lessons from the Chrar Episode, by A.M. Sethna, *Indian Express*, 15 May 1995.

16. K.F. Rustamji, Police Administration and Insurgency in India, Tour Notes 17.

17. "Sign a contract with yourself" by Sunanda Ghosh, *Indian Express,* 25th April, 1995, Ahmedabad Edition.

18. *Hindu,* 29 April 1995.

19. For similar views see M.S.S. Varadan , Auditing for Human Resource Development, Opportunities, *Hindu*, May 6, 1995.

20. Thomas J. Peters and Robert H. Waterman, *In Search of Excellence. Lessons from America's Best run Companies,* India Book Distributions, Bombay, 1982, p. 9.

21. Jagmohan, Police- Don't Shoot the Cop. He is doing his Job, *The Hindustan Times*, 8 May, 1995.

22. C.P. Bhambhri, Mismaleh between Theory and Practice in Training in Public Administration, *Indian Journal of Police Administration,* July-Sept. 1988, Vol. XXXIV No. 3, p. 481.

23. Lynton and Pareek, *Training for Development,* p. 4.

24. K.M. Mathur, *Administration of Police Training in India*, Gyan Publishing House, New Delhi, 1987, p. 44.

25. P.D. Malaviya, Training of Senior Police Officers—Some Basic Issues—*Indian Journal of Public Administration,* July-September 1988, Vol. XXXVI No. 3, p. 287.

26. K.M. Mathur, *Police in India—Problems and Perspectives,* Gyan Publishing House, New Delhi, 1991, p. 287.

27. Peter Drucker, *Managing in Turbulent Times.*

28. K.M. Mathur, Improving Police Performance Through Training—Search for Thrust Area, *Indian Journal of Criminology,* Vol. 22 (2), July 1994, p. 68.

29. Craig R. Hickman and Micheal A. Silva, *Creating Excellence: Managing Corporate Culture, Strategy and Change in the New Age*, George Allin and Unwin—London, 1984, p. 245.

30. Jagmohan, Police, Don't Shoot the Cop. He is doing his Job, *The Hindustan Times*, 8 May 1995.

31. K.M. Mathur, "Improving Police Performance Through Training : Search for Thrust Areas. *Indian Journal of Criminology,* Vol. 22 (2), July 1994, p. 68.

8

National Security and its Manifold Challenges

While the words "National" and "Security" are both hoary terms, they are often used together very often. The term "Nation" etymologically means a group of people coming from a common stock. But today nation represents vast majority of people in a State brought together by an emotional and political force known as "Nationalism" which is the product of various cultural, religious and psychological factors.[1] When we speak of Indian nation, we mean the Indian people organised in one nation-State and acting spontaneously as a Unit. In India today we face the problem of nation-building by bridging the horizontal and vertical differences created by caste, creed, religion and ethnic groups in order to strengthen the stability of the nation. Security is a concept devoid of operational meaning in the absence of some identification of threat. In all discussions of security, there is an explicit or implicit determination of threat. Security against war, starvation, recession, illegal search and seizure, and inflation— these are threat for the national security.[2] Generally security means preservation of liberty, life, property, honour and culture of individuals and an environment of peace and tranquillity in the society. The general concept of security implies confidence inspired by preventive and protective shields against the disruption or destruction of lives and property and a psychological feeling of protection against crimes and criminals. Security implies survivals and psychological feeling of freedom from any danger. The security of the State and its Government is an important concern of that Government. But who is to decide what "security" means in operational terms ? Security of India comprehends the security of the State, the maintenance of public order and the maintenance of supplies and services essential to the community. The end of the cold war, the continuing globalisation of economy and business and the information revolutions are drastically changing the global security environment. Today we live in a truly multi-centric world in which nations, big and small, need one another's co-operation and help. Environmental degradation, the North-South inequalities, inter-related problems of population, poverty and health, and the over-arching threat of weapons of mass destruction call for integrated and sustained world-wide action.[3] National security basically involves national survival. National security implies not only national survival but the ability of the nation to preserve and protect its chosen way of life and to protect and maintain its vital interests. A threat to national security is any activity, phenomenon, or course of events that poses a danger to either the survival or the existence of the nation of the welfare of the people of a sovereign nation-state. National security can be defined as "the ability of a nation to protect its internal values from external threats"[4]. National security in general terms would include: (i) preserving the territorial integrity of the country against external threat or aggression; (ii) preservation of constitutional and political order (iii) maintenance and development of the economic system; (iv) promotion of national core values; (v) protection of legitimate national interests and internal value; and (vi) preservation and protection of plural multi-religious society. A nation is secure to the extent to which it is not in danger of having to sacrifice core values, if it wishes to avoid war and is able, if challenged, to maintain them by victory in such a war.[5] According to Brown: "A nation has security when it does not have to sacrifice its legitimate interests to avoid war and is able, if challenged, to maintain them by war." Harry S. Truma held that "National security does not depend only of an army, a navy and an airforce...It depends on a sound economy on civil liberties and human freedoms"[6]. Conceptually national security must reflect the threats posted by economic, social and political problems whether threats are manifested due to internal erosion of legitimacy or due to external manipulation of socio-economic or political frustrations by foreign powers.

The United Nations Development Programme Report 1994 focused on people's participation and introduced a newer concept of human security—the security of people in their homes, jobs, communities and the environment. The U.N. report has reminded the socio-economic authorities about urgent nature of correctives that they have to infuse into the society to restore psychological order, mental peace, sociological harmony and a decent order of life and living. These new areas need our attention when we talk of national security. National security challenges can be analysed by a rational process of raising certain basic questions. What are the security objectives and concerns ? What should be the allocation of resources for security as compared to other national needs or how much more is needed for security and defence than for other purposes. What are the missions and tasks to be performed by the armed and security forces of the country inside and outside ? What are the types of weapons and forces required to fulfil these missions ? How capable and prepared are our defence and security forces including the police forces ? What are our economic choices regarding development/ procurement of weapons systems, training of forces, logistics support and management ? What are the basic considerations for the formulation and articulation of national security objectives and defence strategy ? What are the international factors which have direct bearing on the national security ? All the above mentioned issues need indepth study and analysis of our national security strategy and evaluation of emerging threat perceptions to the national security from all possible angles and dimensions. In the present paper, a brief theoretical framework is proposed to be presented to provide an overview of the challenges to the national security.

National Security: Important Considerations

National security is an 'ambiguous symbol', because non-military dimensions of security such as economic vulnerability, ecological scarcity, ethnic/communal fragmentation, protracted social conflict and the inadequacy of social coping mechanisms have received very little attention and all the time externally-oriented political-military dimension received greater attention. The threats posed to the state and regime, territorial integrity, the larger political and socio-economic orders and domestic peace and tranquillity emanating from indigenous sources are often of more immediate concern than those threats emanating from external sources.[7] National security of a country depends on some of the following factors : (i) geographic and geo-strategic conditions including location, extent, physical confirmations, climate, weather of the nation territories and their vulnerability in terms of security and defence, (ii) human and material resources available and their extent of optimum utilization, (iii) industrial, material and economic development of the nation and its potentials for future development in relation to other countries of the world, (vi) political conditions including national policies, political structure, level of national cohesion and level of national consciousness, (v) socio-cultural conditions including level of social cohesion and solidarity, (vi) national power in terms of air power, naval power and military power and their effectiveness and level of national preparedness, (vii) security from all internal and external threats to the vital national values and legitimate national interests, and (viii) maintenance and preservation of political, economic and social structure that the nation has given to its citizens. "When assessing the security concerns of any country, the normal approach is to examine the political and security environment of the region in which it is located, the nature of relations with and its attitudes towards its neighbours and vice versa, the military doctrines, force deployment postures, weapons system capacities of countries in the region and above all, the inter-play of defence and foreign policy objectives of the countries in the area."[8] Defining the national security in terms of physical protection of nation-states from external military threats is not only narrow but also misleading. Dimensions and contents of national security are diverse and complex. Domestic factors such as legitimacy, integration, ideology and policy capacity play equally important roles in shaping the national security postures. National security means the security of a whole socio-political entity of a nation-State and concerns the way of life of a self governing people, including their social, cultural, political and economic models of organisation and their right to develop themselves under their own rule.[9] Security no longer means only military or physical security but it increasingly includes social and economic security of a safe and healthy environment, security of human development through education, adequate nutrition, health care, clothing and shelter, security of employment and guarantee of human rights and fundamental freedoms. A nation, in order to develop or to sustain its economic take-off, needs security, both external and internal. While external security is largely military related, internal security problems arise mostly out of non-military factors, such as economic underdevelopment, political dissidence, often expressed violently, with or without external support, arising out of religious, sectarian, linguistic, tribalistic or other factors.[10] We need to recognise these political realities for what they are and take appropriate steps to counter the challenges to our national interests.[11] Our other security requirements arise out of the fact that we are a large nation rapidly advancing towards a status of a great economic and military power, even if it be merely by virtue of our sheer size because of which it often attracts the not very benign attentions of the existing great powers.[12] The conventional wisdom is that Palmerston enunciated the wise adage : "There are no permanent friends and no permanent enemies ; there are only permanent interests." The geo-strategic security environment of any nation has to be analysed with reference to the existing international security environment at the global level. Subramanyam has observed : "National security does not merely mean safeguarding territorial integrity. It means also ensuring that the country is industrialised rapidly and has a cohesive egalitarian and technological society. Infiltration of foreign nationals from Bangladesh and other neighbouring countries has to be stopped because it poses a threat to the nation's security and integrity.[13] Basic referents to the national security include territorial integrity, sovereignty and lives and culture of the people. National will is an important determinant of national security. Cline argues that national will is the foundation upon which national strategy is formulated and arrived through to success.[14] By defining national will as "the degree of resolve that can be mobilized among the citizens of a nation in support of Govt. decisions about defence and foreign policy", Ray S. Cline identifies as its component parts the effective strength of leadership, relevance of national strategy to national interests in the perception of citizens and the degree of cultural integration. In many parts of the world, where nation-building is in its infancy, regime security and not national security is the dominant game. National security requires the willingness and capability of a nation to secure itself from all unwanted foreign domination and fulfil the following criteria:

(i) The overall national capability to manage the domestic process of economic development and national integration;

(ii) The capacity to resist outside penetration;

(iii) The capability to deter outside states (especially super powers and regional powers) from lending support to its hostile neighbours;

(iv) The capacity to preserve and protect national interests, values and core ideals;

(v) Capability to ensure safety and security of all its citizens from trans border crimes; illicit narcotic trade and terrorism;

(vi) Capacity to protect its citizens from all crimes and attacks and to protect its national property and property of its citizens;

(vii) The capacity to provide psychological assurance of a good quality of life free from all dangers and attacks.

National security encompasses a much wider field than defence. According to Jessica Tuchman Mathews, "Global developments now suggest the need for broadening definition of national security to include resource, international trade, environmental and demographic issues. The green house effect, the depletion of the ozone layer and the rapid extinction of plant and animal species herald unforeseen changes in the global ecosystem with unpredictable consequences. The 1990s will demand a redefinition of what constitutes national security." (*American Review* — Redefining Security, January 1990, p. 3). It includes internal security and also non-military threats to security in such areas as food, energy, technology and economic health of the country.[15] Difference between "national security" and "internal security" under the constitutional framework of India has been explained and interpreted by the Supreme Court of India in the famous judgement in Kartar Singh *vs.* State of

Punjab (1994) (3 SCC — 569). National Security faces serious challenges and threats from globalisation of Indian economy and economic manipulations of multi-national enterprises. The term national security can be defined as immunity (to varying degrees) of a state or nation to all internal and external threats emanating from its own people or from outside its boundaries.[16] National security is as much a psychological concept as it is a physical one. External aggression involving war and border conflicts. Espionage, subversion and other threats operationalized by actual or potential adversaries are the immediate concerns of national security.[17] Security of a nation can be measured by the ability to protect state sovereignty, to preserve territorial integrity and to maintain autonomy. The security of a nation largely depends on internal and external security. The terms internal security and external security have such commonality of characteristics that the threat to one portends threat to the other.

National Security—More Threats from Within

Perhaps the most dangerous threat the nation faces is not so much from its enemies on the borders as from the internal political struggle causing growing violence between ethnic groups, castes and creeds; the political scramble for votes at any cost, and the struggle which makes sworn enemies of those in power and those who wish to wrest this power by all available means fair or foul.[18] The nation is passing through a period of uncertainty and drift which, if not checked, can lead to dangerous consequences, possible chaos, leaving things to the army or the security forces is too often found an easy way out. No one feels ashamed of the implicit failure of the political or the civil authority in tackling a local situation that ought to have been anticipated and handled well in time.[19] An exclusive military strategic approach to the study of national security is not only narrow but also misleading.[20] National security cannot be defined to non-military components such as economic vulnerability, ecological scarcity, ethnic fragmentation and other power commodities alone because quantitative assessment alone is not adequate. Self-reliance is itself considered a valuable component of national defence. The doctrine of self-reliance is a principle with varying degrees of utility depending upon the stage socio-economic and political development of a nation. In a world of mutual interdependence, especially in the economic area, nations today find it difficult to maintain economic, military and political self-reliance and isolation from other countries.

Core Areas of National Security

The core areas of national security are as under :

1. Defence against external aggression by armed forces of the Union with the co-operation of the people.
2. Defence against subversion, espionage and sabotage activities of the hostile powers through intelligence agencies and state police.
3. Defence against internal threats of disintegration and armed rebellion carried out by terrorists/sessionists/naxalites and insurgents carried out through low-intensity operations.
4. Defence against serious public disorders and riots caused by fundamentalists like incident of Ayodhya in 1992.
5. Defence against criminal activities and depradation by anti-social elements, mafia-gangs and organised criminal groups.
6. Defence against man-made and natural calamities and disasters.
7. Security of VVIPs/VIPs and vulnerable sections of the society like women and SC/ST, particularly protection against atrocities.
8. Defence against infiltrators, trans-border criminals, illegal trafficking of narcotics and arms and ammunition.
9. Defence of socio-economic and political structures and systems from outsiders and insiders.
10. Security of national goals, interests and strategies.
11. Security against para-dropping of arms/ammunition and explosives.
12. Security against population explosion, environmental degradation and foreign intelligence agencies.

National security consists of both internal and external security although the divisional is now a misnomer. The integration variable is an important part of national security management in a plural society. In many parts of the world, where nation-building is in its infancy, regime security and not national security, is the dominant game. The issue of emotional integration as a national security concern has not received adequate attention. The fragmentation and deep-rooted communal cleanages do not allow the aggregation of national needs, values or interest because each group in a plural society develops its own collective identity based on communal values. In many cases, communal conflicts blur the demarcation between internal and external threats. Internal security of a nation-state broadly signifies survival and protection of the state from all kinds of internal threats and disturbances. Ranging from espionage, political assassination, hijacking, labour unrest, ethnic conflicts, political terrorism, insurgency, industrial unrest, communal riots, student agitations to various law and order problems, internal security of a nation has multifaceted challenges from its internal sources.

Misconceptions about National Security Doctrines

There are following misconceptions and wrong notions about national security :

1. National security is related exclusively to the defence of territorial integrity and national sovereignty.
2. National security is considered narrowly in terms of a nation being completely occupied and its population being subjugated.
3. Wars will be prolonged and sustained once.
4. Security risks are evaluated in terms of the actual use of force but not in terms of the threat of the use of force or coercion.
5. Nuclear powers are sincere in nuclear non-proliferation treaty and it is a sound proposal for third world.
6. With the break up of the USSR, cold war has come to an end.
7. Economic globalisation will not endanger national security of the developing countries.

Need for a National Security Doctrines for India

An independent nation always and correctly needs to know what its security threats are and where they emanate from ? India must examine its security requirements from all possible perspectives. India must have a clearly enunciated and spelled out security doctrines that take into account all our immediate and long-term threats. Security doctrines should also encompass our economic, political, cultural and religious interests. How do we protect our offshore interests ? What do we do if we were to be denied vital hydrocarbons because of the changed circumstances in the middle-east regions of the world. The national security doctrines must deal with all possibilities and probabilities. It is now universally accepted that disarmament and development are related in a triangular fashion through the concept of security. We must plan for external security, internal security and economic development in a more holistic and integrated manner with a view to counter "destabilisation efforts" of our enemy country particularly hostile neighbours. Security doctrines for India's national security can be as under :

1. National security awareness programme should be launched through media to educate the citizens about national security and need for national integration.
2. Strategic Defence Plans should be prepared by the defence forces to meet all possible contingencies. Threats to a nation can be broadly classified under six categories : (i) Ideological threat, (ii) Conventional nuclear military threat, (iii) Interventionary threat, (iv) Threat of diplomatic containment, (v) Threats arising out of internal instabilities, and (vi) threat of espionage, subversion and religious conflicts.
3. Probability of a nuclear war, though not totally negligible, is relatively low because it will imply all nations committing suicide.
4. India is surrounded by all sides by countries which are relatively more unstable than India. There is consequently the problem of the turbulance around this country spilling over. The present problem of north eastern states is a typical example of spilling over effect of turbulance in Bangladesh.

5. The current international strategic environment and socio-economic and military policies and pacts have to be constantly taken into consideration in preparing our defence strategy. Defence forms the most vital constituent of a nation's security. Defence preparedness of a nation depends on five variables : (i) adequate force levels at a given time, (ii) autonomy of defence production and procurement, (iii) a balance between development and defence of the nation, (iv) morale training and co-ordination in defence forces, and (v) people's voluntary support and backing of the nation for defence. Citizens of the country have a fundamental duty to defend the country and to promote national security. They should not indulge in any type of anti-national activities or activities prejudicial to the unity and integrity of the country. The "anti-national activity" in relation to an individual or association, means any action taken by such individual or association:

"(i) which is intended, or which supports any claim, to bring about, on any ground whatsoever, the cession of a part of the territory of India or the secession of part of the territory of India or which incites any individual or association to bring about such cession or secession;

(ii) which disclaims, questions, threatens, disrupts or is intended to threaten or disrupt the sovereignty and integrity of India or the security of the State or the unity of the nation;

(iii) which is intended, or which is part of a scheme which is intended, to overthrow by force the government as by law established;

(iv) which is intended, or which is part of a scheme which is intended, to create internal disturbance or the disruption of public services;

(v) which is intended, or which is part of a scheme which is intended, to threaten or disrupt harmony between different religious, racial, language or regional groups or castes or communities;

6. Pluralistic and federal states have to be held together by the glue of state power and strong political will to remain united and integrated. Political stability, economic and socio-cultural integration are important factors for the security of a nation. India's security as a nation is inevitably determined by her capacity to overcome ethnic, religion, linguistic and regional differences and capacity to build a strong economic base.
7. The concept of non-alignment should be basic to our national foreign policy. Good diplomacy and cordial foreign relations with all nations should be our constant endeavour.
8. The extended economic zone concept and the growth of extra regional naval presence in the Indian ocean need our serious consideration.
9. National security doctrines are bound to change with the changing international strategic security environment.
10. Besides invasion and territorial occupation, some of the important threats are as under: (a) external support to various secessionist and insurgent movement, (b) intervention in the internal affairs of a nation including manipulation of its economic policies and optimum utilisation of natural resources, (c) transgression in the territorial waters and the extended economic zone, (d) denial and withholding of various resources—such as food, oil, technology, well being of nations, (e) manipulation of neighbours and their policies against the interest of the particular nation, (f) espionage, subversion and carrying out long drawn low-intensity operations and proxy war by infiltration, (g) subverting the loyalties of the people by cultural invasion through media. Constant reappraisal of these threats to the security of the nation needs to be carried out.
11. Internal security good foreign policy, internal diplomacy and strong economic base are essentials for national security.
12. Intelligence about plan, policies and activities of the

foreign powers and intelligence about our own country is a most essential ingredient of national security.

National security needs integrated security doctrines and national consensus on national issues. Effective implementation of the security requirements for a nation require institutional arrangements of security organisations and their constant preparedness. Constant upgradation of skills, techniques and methods for securing national security need adequate funds and a national political will. National Security Council and Joint Intelligence Committee are two essential institutions generally advocated by the security experts. Effective co-ordination between internal security organisation and defence forces on a permanent institutional basis is a national requirement.

In the operationalisation of national security, the following instruments are commonly resorted to in practical politics:

(i) Strategic defence plans and the military measure;

(ii) The police measure;

(iii) The secret service operations;

(iv) Economic measures;

(v) Political measures;

(vi) Socio-psychological operations and throught-control measures;

(vii) diplomatic and international pressures;

(viii) People's voluntary support for national security.

India's national security needs to be analysed in the context of above mentioned doctrines. In the early years of our Republic, Defence Committee of the Cabinet (DCC) presided by the Prime Minister was set up. After the Chinese aggression of 1962, it was converted into the Emergency Committee of the Cabinet. In 1967, with the lifting of national emergency, this committee was merged with the Cabinet Committee for Political Affairs (CCPA). Since the strategic problems of national security are in an area where political, economic, social, psychological and military factors overlap, the notion that national security is the concern of the defence personnel should be given up. National security is too serious a business to be left to generals and politicians alone. Legislative powers for making laws pertaining to national security are with the Parliament under entry I of list I (Union list) The National Security Act No. 65 of 1980 identifies national security to (i) the defence of India, the relation of India with foreign powers or the security of India, or (ii) the security of the state or (iii) the maintenance of supplies and services essential to the community.

Organised Crime is a Serious Threat to National Security

Organised crimes with its international and transnational connection pose a serious threat to the national security of the country. According to Philip Manuel, "Organised crime is made of career criminals of varied backgrounds and criminal specialisations whose only common bond is the attainment of wealth, power and influence by illegal means". Organised crime means the unlawful activities of the members of a highly organised disciplined association engaged in supplying goods and services including but not limited to gambling, prostitution, loan shirking, narcotics, labour racketting and other unlawful activities of members of such organisation. (Section 601 (b) of the Omnibus Crime Control and Safe Street Act 1968 USA).

Important features of organised crime are:

1. It is an urban phenomenon of recent origin.
2. Supplies illegal goods and services.
3. A client public that demands such goods and services.
4. Corrupt public official-dom that protects illegal markets.
5. Subversion of (a) political party, (b) law enforcement machinery, (c) judicial process/Advocate, (d) socio-economic system.
6. General persistance.
7. Political patronage.
8. Police and administrative patronage.
9. Double standards of the society and the people resulting in organised crime.
10. Complex system of network and criminal activity with cut-out system.

"Organised crime is not a pack of ordinary criminals working together. They rely on specialisation division of duty and a well defined hierarchy whereas normal policemen are not adequately equipped to deal with them." [21] However nowadays internal security has become a misnomer because many internal security problems have their external roots and inspiration in foreign countries. Trans-border smuggling, Macro-terrorism, insurgency and many other internal security problems owe their existence to outside influence and foreign inspiration. On December 17, 1995 a huge quantity of arms, ammunition and explosives were para-dropped by an unknown aircraft in the villages of Deradi, Ganodi and Ghatanda of Purulia district of West Bengal. It included 105 AK 47 Rifles, 700 empty magazines of AK 479800 rounds of 7.62 ammunition, seven rocket launchers, 57 anti-tank grenades, 2560 rounds of 9 mm ammunition besides massive quantities of fire arms and explosives in wooden boxes. It has been a major operation having international remifications. How fragile is the country's air space security has been wholly exposed by the aircraft of the Carol Airlines which crossed into Indian territory without being detected.[22] In external terms Pakistan remains a primary source of threat to India's national security. Rising levels of political consciousness, communal and ethnic antagonism and heightened economic expectations can tear apart the fabric of Indian polity. We are now in an era where internal disturbances are triggered from outside. Many a times we are really fighting the external enemy where we are engaged in internal security duties.[23] If the political ethos are infected by the unprincipled search for the power, if the fundamentalism and parochialism are instigated for personal or party gains, if business and administration are permeated with the culture of corruption, if the people are divided on caste and communal lines, if rich are callous in pursuit of consumerism and poor continue to groan under the burden of their poverty, it would be virtually impossible to ensure internal security at reasonable cost and on continuous basis.[24] Nationalisation has long been used as a potential legitimating force in the context of national security. Regime legitimacy is a fundamental requisite for national security. The obvious implication is that government in plural societies should undertake socio-economic and political policies that can enhance their legitimacy and reduce the threat of domestic unrest that might otherwise occur such policies might include programmes to increase employment or improve social services or attempts to establish a popular mandate through elections or appeals to popular symbols. Legal experts are of the view that a State in order to be a person of International law must have four constituents, viz., a permanent population, a defined territory, a government and sovereignty. Internal security threats are nowadays multi-dimensional and emanate from both internal and external sources—subversive espionage, infiltration, sabotage, proxy protracted low-intensity operations, narco-terrorism, trans-border crimes and insurgency are some of the internal security challenges which have their sources of inspiration and active support outside the country. Therefore internal and external security have now overlapping spheres and to talk of mere internal security has no meaning. Infiltration in the east is a serious threat to the internal security of the country. Of late the demography of north-eastern states and West Bengal is under threat due to unauthorised and unabated infiltration of refugees from Bangladesh. The environmental pollution and the distruction of eco-system all over the world have adversely affected the internal security of all nations.

National Security and its Challenges

India's first security concern is to cope with a more complex and competitive international situation.[25] Ensuring the security of India implies, first the creation of favourable conditions which will contribute to its politico-economic and social consolidation and its territorial integrity, secondly the sustaining of these conditions, guaranteeing its existence and its survival and thirdly safeguarding and protecting the freedom of options and choices for India to survive in a volatile international environment as a sovereign secular democratic republic. Buzan concisely describes the challenges to the national security as under :

"Each state exists, in a sense, at the hub of a whole universe of threats. These threats define its insecurity and set the agenda for national security as a policy problem. They do not, unfortunately constitute a clear set of calculable and comparable risks like those faced by players of chees or bridge. Threats to the State come in diverse forms which cannot easily be weighed off against each other, and which are frequently in a state of constant evolution. They vary enormously in range and intensity, pose risks which cannot be assessed accurately, and depend on probabilities which cannot be calculated. Because threats are so ambiguous, and because knowledge of them is limited, national security policy making is a highly imperfect art".[26]

Although the type, source and level of threat are subjectively determined by national security of policy-makers, it is not impossible to elucidate some apparent forms of threat along each security dimension. According to a group of thinkers the eight most important challenges to the national security in the 21st century will be as under :[27]

1. Dangerous technology, nuclear reactors and explosives, molecular biology, chemistry and genetics, mind control.
2. Gradual contamination of the environment, radio-active dubris from peaceful nuclear uses, environment-degrading garbage, noise and overcrowding.
3. Spectacular contamination of the environment, nuclear, bateriological and chemical wars or accidents, artificial moons, weather control.
4. Dangerous internal political issues, computerized records and surveillance, improved techniques for creating or preventing disturbances.
5. Upsetting international consequences, technological obsolescence of unskilled labour, new synthetics like coffee, oil, etc., control and exploitation of the oceans, space, moon.
6. Dangerous personal choices, sex determination, genetic engineering, psychedelic and mood affecting drugs.
7. Bizaree issues, mechanically dependent humans with pacemakers, artificial kidney, external control on what should be a personal of even institutionally private choice.
8. The Cold War has come to an end with the collapse of the former Soviet Union (FSU), but it has unleashed many disruptive forces and deep anxities about the security of the states. Paradoxically the greatest threat which has been articulated today, is the possibility of theft, or leakage, of nuclear weapon material from the FSU due to an erosion of the physical security of nuclear

weapon depots and establishments. On March 13, 1996, Harvard University's Centre for Science and International Affairs has released an authoritative study entitled "Avoiding Nuclear Anarchy (ANA)". The report calls for immediate steps to reverse the broad-based vulnerability of Russia's nuclear custodial system and exhorts the U.S. to secure the cooperation and support of its allies in combating this problem. The finding of ANA is that the following pervasive myths are all dead wrong. These include: (a) building a nuclear weapon is hard to do; (b) fissile materials are too hazardous or too heavy to smuggle; (c) delivery of a nuclear weapon against the U.S. is a challenge; and (d) there is no demand for illicitly acquired nuclear weapons or fissile material. Today all nations including *vs*. are vulnerable to nuclear attack more through a suit-case than a ballistic missile.

Throughout a large number of third world states, the disruptive forces of social change are reducing the social controls exercised by traditional identify groups (ethnic groups, religious groups, tribes and so forth) without the effective substitution of alternative loci of such controls.[28] Joint family system is gradually breaking down under the pressures of urbanisation and industrialisation. Our social life is full of conflicts due to its various pluralistic contradictions. National security of modern nations is threatened by four categories of weapons of mass destruction—Biological, Chemical, Radiological and Nuclear. India has about 5700 kms long coastal line with the Bay of Bengal on its east and Arabian sea on the west and the Indian Ocean in the south. Thus India faces challenges from its coastal line. Recent landings of RDX and other explosives in Maharashtra and Gujarat via sea routes should serve as eye-openers for us. India's national security faces serious internal threats from the following factors :

1. Problems of federalism and Centre-State relations with different political parties at the Centre and in the States.
2. Collapse of criminal justice system and rule of law.
3. Erosion of State authority and State of anomies as happened during Delhi Riots in 1984 and after Ayodhya aftermath in 1992.

4. Collapse of constitutional institutions like Parliament and their subversion by foreign agents and saboteurs.
5. Crisis of the polity due to political horse-trading and nexus between criminals and politicians in power.
6. Social, ethnic, cultural and religious conflicts arising out of plural nature of Indian society.
7. Terrorism and organised violence on a large scale due to easy availability of small arms and hi-tech explosive devices.
8. Corruption at various levels in political, bureaucratic and social institutions.
9. Insurgency and separatist movements under the pretense of right of self-determination.
10. Trans-border smuggling and organised crime by mafia.

The covert actions in the form of terroristic violence, psychological warfare, political warfare and preventive direct action such as support for rival gangs and organisations engaged in sabotage, subversion and assistance to refugees are serious threats to the national security of the liberal states like India. Insufficient economic growth and its imbalanced distribution, regional sectarianism, lack of inner democracy in political system and failure of foreign policy can be real threats to the national security of the country today.[29] India is a plural, federal and secular state. The problems of internal security embrace all aspects of social, economic and political life.[30] Historically national security considerations have shaped the cope, timing and trajectory of economic development policy. The internal military and non-military dimensions of security have to be of great concern. The threats posed to the state and regime, territorial integrity, the larger political and socio-economic order and domestic peace and tranquillity emanating from indigenous sources are often of more immediate concern than those threats emanating from external sources.

According to Ram Jethmalani, "India is in bad shape.........We are immersed in mind-boggling debt, the servicing of which alone eats up three-fourth of our revenue income, leaving precious little for national construction. More than half the population is condemned to appalling poverty, starvation and disease that inevitably go with malnutrition ...... Electoral greed has displaced national good. National solidarity has been broken. Forces within and without threaten our sovereignty and independence.[31] A dangerous religious fundamentalism and its progeny of terrorism are tearing the country apart".[32] The non-military dimensions of security, such as economic vulnerability, ecological scarcity, ethnic/communal fragmentation, protracted social conflicts and the inadequacy of social coping mechanisms have rightly received more attention in recent times.[33] National security, law and order should be kept above party politics. "Recent instances of Govt. of India interfering with the working of intelligence agencies in counter-espionage work, bode ill for the nation. Petty political advantages cannot compensate for the dilution of efforts to safeguard national interest."[34] Lt. Gen. V.P. Malik, while delivering Annual Savarkar Memorial lecture at Pune University on "New Challenges to National Security", warned that "the impact of the Hawala scandal would not only adversely affect our national morale and our international standing but our national security as well". The perils of perpetual adhocism are starkly demonstrated by recent events like Purulia airdrop of arms and ammunition and loss of four frontline IAF fighter aircrafts. In the present confused politico-military milieu, external and internal security have got inextrically fused. India is the only country in the world without a national security mechanism. The present allocation of resources cannot sustain a 35 division army, an 800 combat air-craft airforce and a 100 vessel navy. Restructuring of the armed forces is vital if they have to meet the increasing challenges to national security.

Policy Capacity and Security Performance

Policy capacity comprises threat assessment, decisions, articulation and enforcement of policies and the mobilisation and allocation of resources, as well as planning, formulation and implementation of national security policies. The three prerequisites of the ideal policy capacity are: (1) favourable policy mood; (2) comprehensive and coherent decision-making; and (3) speedy and flexible implementation. Developing countries are seldom able to impose collective costs and enforce obligations on their people by speedy, efficiency and flexible implementation of policies because they are 'weak' or 'soft states'.[35] It is the primarily function of national defence policy to promote national security, a function performed by placing reliance on acquisition of military hardware and building up the defence forces of the country.[36]

Security rests on four important pillars: (1) Combat efficiency of the Defence forces, (2) Morale, motivation and effectiveness of Police and Para-Military Forces, (3) National security threat perceptions and analysis, (4) Effective functioning, formulation and implementation of the national security strategy at various levels and effective co-ordination between various agencies.

The national security has today suffered an erosion both from above and below. Globalisation of the economy, information technology revolution and fundamental restructuring of production, finance and communications has begun to erode national boundaries and undermine State sovereignty, regional, ethnic, communal identities and religious fundamentalism have been debilitating the nations from within. The cold war has given way to wars of identity and civilisational assertion. Old countries like India and Japan whose national characters have been formed by history have their own resilience to survive. India has, during the last decade, become an important transit point, if not a storage centre, for arms, ammunition and explosives, smuggled by international terrorist outfits as is evident from the Purulia arms-drop case and the Delhi arms smuggling case. The following questions come to the mind about Purulia arms-drop:

(1) Why did the Union Home Ministry not act in time on the RAW tip-off about the arms-drop ?

(2) Why was the plane not detained in Madras on December 21, 1995 when the Government was aware that an AN 26 was involved in the arms-drop ?

(3) Why was the plane not cordoned off despite the fact that it was forced to land in Bombay? And how did Kim Davy escape?

Security performance of a nation needs to be evaluated and assessed in the light of the above issues and remedial actions need to be taken for strengthening security.

A sound higher defence organisation and restoration of the elan of the military officer are vital ingredients of national security.[37]

Policy Formulation and Implementation

National Security policies are those policies that governments undertake to protect or extend vital national values against threats from existing or potential adversaries.[38] Vital national values not only include traditional security concerns such as maintenance of national independence and territorial integrity but also matters such as protecting the lives of citizens, improving the material welfare of the population, and guaranteeing political freedom and effective means of political participation. Azar and Moon have suggested "hardware" side and software side of security management. Hardware side includes military and economic capabilities and a policy infrastructure encompassing matters such as strategic doctrine, force structure, intelligence policy and so on.[39] Several authors have advocated economic development and other measures designed to improve living standards as an essential ingredient of national security policy. [40] Software side of national security policy must encompass matters such as an awareness of the political context and policy capacity within which level vital national values are defined and pursued.[42] National policy formulations and implementation need a dedicated band of bureaucrats, defence personnel and National core group management experts. No less a person than the Union Home Secretary Mr. K. Padmanabiah has gone on record to underline that we do not have any "Corporate thinking" in Government's crisis management strategies with different departments and agencies pursuing different goals and working at cross-purposes while tackling the same problem.[42]

Need for Integrated National Security Strategy

National security planning requires institutionalised arrangements for indepth analysis of economic, political, social and international issues and their macro-level complexities. The 19th report of the Estimates Committee of Parliament has revealed that the nation fought four wars and launched a number of low-level military operations without a clearly articulated and integrated defence strategy. According to the classical theory the security potential of a nation combines factors such as geography, population, economic strength and military power which are compounded by political will and people's support. In the opinion of Air Comdr. T. Murugan (Retd) National Security planning has received a stepmotherly treatment in India since independence, the situation reaching its nadir in recent years.[43] National security strategy can be briefly shown in the matrix which is as under :

Matrix for National Security

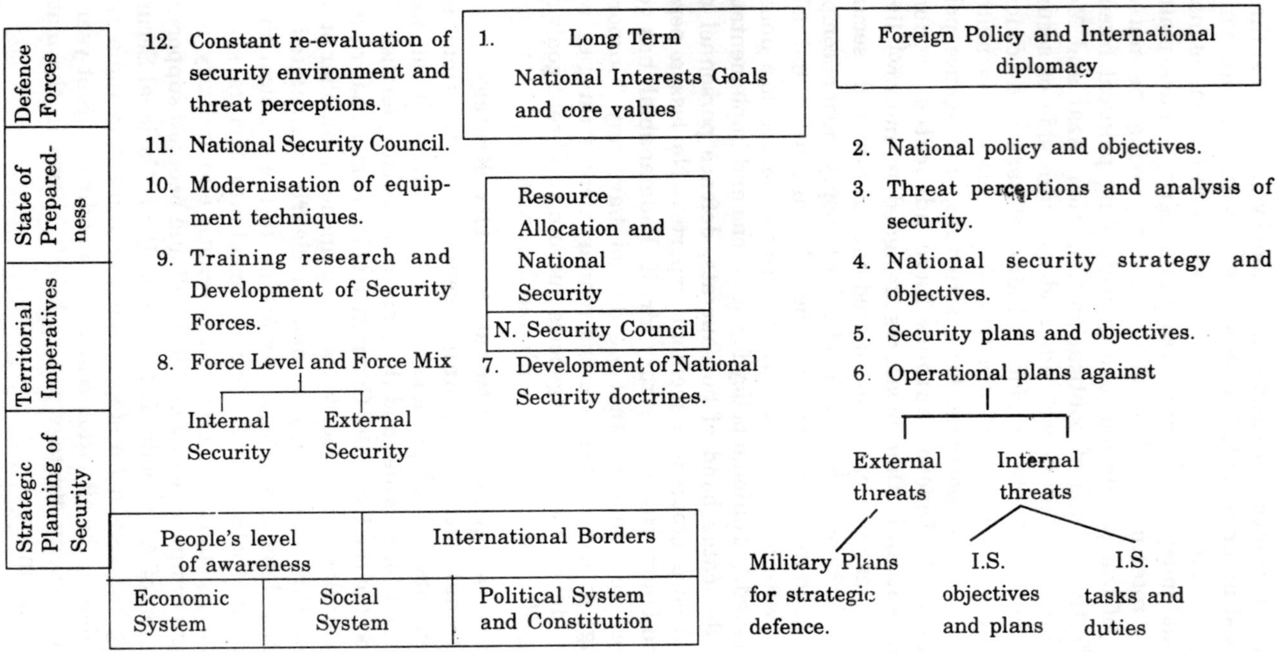

Role of Intelligence

Whatever our conception of national security, intelligence must play a capital role in it.[44] Intelligence and research capabilities in widely diverse fields are critical to providing decision-makers with an accurate portrait of the world. Intelligence refers to the ability to glean valuable insights from open sources; the ability to construct and communicate accurate and balanced assessments; the ability to update information and analysis in accordance with changed or changing circumstances ; the ability to provide time-sensitive data on a timely basis; the ability to integrate diverse types of information from diverse sources into a 'finished' product.[45] In most of the plural societies, the poor quality of automated support, constraints on communication resources, restrictions on personal interaction resulting from political reliability questions, the lack of systematic methods for updating and lack of adequate motivation in the staff all seriously undermine the intelligence efforts. Kautilya's *Arthashastra* is a veritable treasure-house that provides a whole series of national options short of war which can help in subduing an enemy or in winning the strategic national advantage from the national enemies and fifth-columinists. Since the intelligence and police agencies have the mandate to safeguard national security they should be made accountable for protecting sensitive organisations from depradations of foreign intelligence agencies. The "bottom line" is still political and military security but it is a bottom line that recognizes what is above the line too, the substantial interdependence of political, economic, social and military dimensions. Better integration of social, cultural, political and economic factors into national security decision making is realistic and essential. "Without the co-operation of the public, national security cannot be ensured. People's role in detecting illegal aliens, foreign agents, etc., cannot be over-emphasised. Similarly workers in sensitive organisations should be enthused to take positive interest in the security of their installations. [46] The violent incidents in and around Jammu during the last 10 months including over 60 bomb blasts, show how ruthless the Pakistani agents have been in executing their strategy.[47] Terrorism in Jammu and Kashmir is one of the most serious challenges to the national security of the country. Insurgency in north-eastern states including Assam pose another serious challenge to the national security of the country. The abundant availability of sophisticated arms can easily be attributed to across-the-border gun-running. The surplus weapons from the decade-long conflict in Afghanistan are finding their way into this country. Arms are also coming from Pakistan, Bangladesh, Nepal, China and even from across the seas. Pakistan, of course, remains the most common source for procurement of weapons. The All India Arms Market position is reported as under :

All India Arms Market

Centre	*Source*	*Weaponary / seized traded*	*Causes*
Calcutta	Mostly from pilferage from police at Bihar.	Country-made fire-arms, hand-made	Self-protection, gang-rivalry.
Ahemedabad	ISI-trained gun-runners through Kutch/ Banaskanta border, local manufacturing.	Rocket launchers AK-47, AK-56 rifles ; Machine guns Chinese automatic pistols.	To send for Punjab inter-gang rivalry.
Tamil Nadu	LTTE (IPKF)	AK-47, automatic pistols.	For buyers in Bangalore, Kerala, A.P.
Maharashtra	North (country-made) Pakistan-controlled mafia underworld.	AK-47, AK-56 RDX, Czech made 9mm pistols.	Drug-smuggling Gold/Silver smuggling, Punjab terrorism.
Amritsar	Cross-border	Explosive AK-47, AK-56	For militancy in U.P., other areas.

Assam (NE)	Smuggled from China, Thailand (through Myanmar) Bangladesh also (Tripura) storming Police arsenals.	Kalashnikovs Light Machine guns, Chinese M-22 Automatic weapons	Insurgency commercial
Srinagar	Across the border	AK-47, AK-56 Rocket launchers, etc.	Insurgency, for Punjab militancy
Bihar	Punjab ultra	Chinese assault rifle, AK-47	For Dhanbad mafia
U.P.	Nepal border	AK-47, AK-56 grenade, launchers	Heroin trade
Surat	Internal	AK-47, AK-56 crude bombs, gelatine sticks	Self-protection.

Price of AK-47 in different places is as under:

Punjab	Rs. 15,000 (locally made)
	Rs. 40,000 (Chinese French) imported
Ahmedabad	Rs. 1 Lakh (upto)
North-east	Upto Rs. 2 Lakhs.
Surat	Rs. 1.25 to 1.50 Lakhs.
Patna	Rs. 60,000 to 80,000
Bombay	Rs. 1.5 to 2 Lakhs.
Madras	Rs. 25,000 to 50,000
Srinagar	Rs. 27,000

Whether arms are procured by Punjab terrorists or the secessionists of Kashmir valley or the militant outfits of the north-eastern region like ULFA, the Kachin Independence Army, the United National Liberation Front and the People's Army, the weapons find their way into the arms market. For example, most arms in Calcutta come from Bihar. Some of the arms supplied to various Tamil groups in Sri Lanka have been brought back to India and traded in places like Bangalore, parts of Kerala and Andhra Pradesh. The People's War Group, the Naxalite outfit of Andhra Pradesh, is reported to have procured all its arms from the Tamil militants. Kashmir militants are known to have sold arms in U.P. Quite often these transactions in arms are carried out in the spirit of revolutionary brotherhood. On 25 Feb. 1995 atleast 25 security force personnel were killed and several persons were injured when a powerful explosion blasted bogy No. 2137 of the Brahmaputra Mail at Nailang Station, about 270 kms from Guwahati near Diphu. It is suspected that the explosion used in this case was RDX and it was the handiwork of banned NSCN (Muivah) group. Assam and North Eastern States have been suffering from insurgency, narco-terrorism and infiltration from across the borders. Trans-border crimes, insurgency and infiltration are serious challenges to the seven-sister States of India[48].

Tenth Finance Commission Recommendations

The Tenth Finance Commission, headed by Mr. K.C. Pant, has recommended the setting up of a high-power committee to review the entire security scenario both external and internal, of the country. This committee could determine the role, organisation, equipment and finding requirement of various agencies involved in meeting the present and emerging threats to the country's peace and integrity. In its report to the President, which was placed in Parliament recently, the Commission said it had given more than incidental attention to the assessment of defence and security related expenditure, which normally forms part of the mandate of a Finance Commission. There was need for evolving an integrated, cost-effective system of national security. "It is not possible for us to go into the myriad aspects of national security which, to our way of thinking, would also involve the States. We, therefore, recommended that a high powered committee be set up to review the entire security scenario, both external and internal." The Commission took note of the fact that the defence and para-military forces were being repeatedly drawn upon for maintenance of law and order in many States. It recommended that a revised balance be drawn up between the role of the State Police and that of the defence and para-military forces for such duties. "If a holistic view of the internal and external security scenario is taken, it would suggest that the local law and order problems are best left to be dealt with by a strengthened local police force, suitably supplemented by the State's own armed police. It would reduce the strain placed on the resources of the para-military and defence forces."

Espionage Activities of the Foreign Agencies

Espionage activities of the foreign intelligence agencies and subversive activities of explosion are serious threats to national security. According to the latest statistics available till 1994 December out of a total of 247 individuals arrested for spying, 61 were convicted and 73 were yet to face trial. In 1986, six Indians including five Govt. employees were convicted. In Aug. 1994, one person was convicted. Activities of Pakistan ISI and other foreign intelligence agencies pose serious threat to our national security.[49] Media revelations that the ISI of Pakistan had collected vital information of our space programme from the ISRO, have come as a rude shock to many. Subsequent investigations, as reported in the media, reveal that a spy network was in operation in three southern States.

Parliament Questions

Espionage

According to a reply in March 1994, activities have been monitored by the government of India constantly. The government has cleared the prosecution of 33 persons in 14 cases during 1991-93 for their involvement in espionage/leakage of official secrets. The Home Minister Mr. S.B. Chavan said there were four cases involving nine persons, three cases involving 13 persons and seven cases involving 11 persons in 1991, 1992 and 1993 respectively. There was no proposal to amend the 70-year old official secret Act.

(*Times of India,* 18th March 1994, p. 4, New Delhi.)

Since the intelligence and police agencies have the mandate to safeguard national security, they should also be made accountable for protecting sensitive organisations from the depradations of foreign intelligence agencies.[50]

Challenges before the Nation

Thirteen noted economists including Sarva Shri N.K. Chandra, Arun Ghosh, P.C. Joshi, I.S. Gulati, Krishna Raj, N. Krishnaji, K.S. Krishna Swami, C.T. Kurian, Ashok Mitra, Deepak Nayyar, Prabhat Patnaik, K.N. Raj and S.P. Shukla in a joint statement criticised the economic reforms and globalisation. According to them "The strategic and economic interests of the nation must be preserved, otherwise we may end up globalising prices without globalising incomes and ceding spaces of sovereign decision-making without acquiring any significant role in the prevailing global system".[51] The former Governor of the Reserve Bank of India, Mr. I.G. Patel has warned against the blind endorsement of the economic reforms. Economic reforms were susceptible to three dangers—over-simplification, excessive optimism and the neglect of a number of important questions that were beyond the economic policy yet, at the same time, were crucial for growth and eradication of poverty.[52] The politics of minorities has posed a most serious threat to national security of the country. A people, according to Myson Weiner, who do not share what they regard as the central symbols of the society invariably view themselves as a minority.[53] They argue that they are under-represented in India's prestigious civil services, armed forces and large economic concerns owned by government or private companies.[54] Communal riots and communal tensions pose a serious threat to the national security. Communal riots of December 1992 after the demolition of disputed structure at Ayodhya caused serious riots throughout the country and tarnished the secular image of the country. The Ayodhya outrage is "a manifestation of class war, waged upon the constitution and its democratic secular character".

Terrorism and organised crime were the two major threats that needed to be dealt with firmly and immediately. These two problems have become even more dangerous as a trend of mutual co-operation between the two of them is emerging. The recent blasts in Bombay are a testimony to the potential damage the two organisations can unleash.[55]

The economic costs of the continuing confrontation between Pakistan and India are prohibitive, but policy framers in the respective countries seem unable to recognize what is obvious to every one else, that human security is the most important element of national security. The two countries are spending $ 20 billion a year on defence, twice as much as Saudi Arabia, a country 25 times wealthier. Political power not backed by economic strength is unsustainable. The U.S.S.R. collapsed because it could not feed its people; all its tanks, submarine and secret service meant nothing. History of the world has many lessons for us. In 1980, fifteen years ago from now, the ratio of military to social spending was highest in Iraq (eight times), Somalia (five times) and Nicaragua (3.5 times). Yet none could effectively defend its national security when challenge came. On the other hand, Costa Rica abolished its defence forces in 1948, and now spends one-third of its national income on education, nutrition and health. Today it is the only prosperous democracy in a troubled Central America. Both India and Pakistan need to review their defence strategies. Why spend a million dollar a day to contest the frozen heights of Siachen ? Both countries have six times more soldiers than doctors. Both should concentrate their efforts towards economic development and distributive economic justice. Intellectuals, policy planners and enlightened scholars should not be hesitant to challenge increasing defence expenditures which are generally camouflaged under the shroud of national security.[55a]

Management of National Security

Management of national security is a stupendous task. It includes planning, organising, staffing, co-ordinating, directing, monitoring, motivating and administering of various security operations and formulation of short-term and long-term security strategy for the nation. K.M. Panikkar has put it aptly : "The integral relationship between foreign policy and defence is obvious enough and requires no proof to establish it".[56] Kautilya's *Arthsastra is* a seminar work which gives comprehensive account of the techniques of State craft and national security. National security management is a trilogy of foreign policy, defence policy and domestic policy and requires "an understanding and conceptual integration at the formulating and planning level and delicate orchestration at the action level."[57] People's support and co-operation is most important aspect of national security management, mobilisation of support, externally and internally, is an important function of managers of national security. "It is a function of diplomacy to strive to secure allies, weaken adversaries and neutralise unfriendly nations. K.M. Panikkar has observed : "The purpose of foreign policy is primarily to safeguard the independence of the State and the sanction behind is the organised strength of the State. The safety and security of a State and its life as an independent unit are dependent on the capacity of the armed forces to defend it.........it has to be remembered that foreign policy, however wisely conceived and ably followed by, would not be able to achieve any success if it had no adequate military strength to back it. The ultimate and decisive factor in diplomacy is the strength which backs it".[58] India not only possesses strong defence forces but also a large number of Central Police Organisations like CRPF, BSF, CISF, ITBP, CBI, Intelligence Bureau and the like. The personal policies and functional demarcation of duties and responsibilities need constant review and immediate attention of the Central Government. The security environment of the nation needs constant monitoring particularly the developments in Pakistan, Japan, Indonesia, Bangladesh, Myanmar, Saudi Arabia, Iran and China. India's defence expenditure must match well with Pakistan's defence expenditure because our long-term threats are mainly from Pakistan. The comparative defence expenditure (in Billions) for various years are as under :[59]

Year	*India (in Indian Rs.)*	*Pakistan (in Pakistan Rs.)*
1984	66.60	31.79
1985	79.87	34.76
1986	104.77	41.32
1987	119.67	47.01
1988	133.41	51.05
1989	145.00	57.92
1990	157.50	63.59
1991	163.50	70.95
1992	175.00	82.15

In todays context of a new world order following the easing of cold war tension, the diminishing nuclear threat and the emergence of the U.N. peace-keeping and peace-making activities, security cannot be defined in purely political or military terms.[60] Mutual balanced reduction of forces (MBFR) is a rational course and India is in a position to initiate a dialogue on this issue without any risk to its security today. Defence preparedness has two essential components : perceived threats to the country's security and the resources available to meet these threats. To carry out a holistic analysis of national imperatives that flow from the prevailing security environment and the efficacy of the existing systems to formulate and manage the national security strategies, it is time to build up a proper infrastructure and methodology for evolving national security strategies to safeguard India's national interests. Perhaps the most vital element in India's new security environment is America's interest in military co-operation with India.[61] The end of the cold war, disintegration of the USSR, the information revolution of the last decade and the continuing globalisation of business and economy are changing drastically as never before the global security environment. Shri Ved Marwah has analysed the threats to the national security thus: "The rising curve of violence in different parts of the country is creating not only a sense of insecurity among the average citizen but is threatening the very foundations of our society. It is brutalising both the society at large, as well as the instruments of governance; leading to a vicious circle of increased violence. The inequalities of the socio-economic structure and strong regional identities exploited by unscrupulous politicians create potential areas of conflict and national security threat. A society unscrupulous which functions at unequal level in a democracy, duly legalised by the political and the administrative system, is bound to remain in a constant state of ferment. These factors pose a serious challenge to the sagacity of our political system. Unfortunately the political leaders of different parties find it difficult to resist the temptation to manipulate the emotional and commercial sensibilities of the people. Instead of eliminating religious, commercial, regional and linguistic barriers the average politician has been doing all he can to ensure that the disintegration. Indian society operates at various levels of disharmony and so that they can continue their hold on political power. Use of violence for capturing political power negates the very process of democracy, and if allowed to go on unchecked could end up destroying it. The nexus between the politician and the criminal is posing a serious threat to the electoral system. India is becoming increasingly a lawless society where violation of the laws is more profitable and there is not much fear of punishment. The breakdown of the criminal justice system is another important factor responsible for the deteriorating law and order situation. Political instability, erosion of authority of the law and order machinery, rising expectations and economic insecurity are all adding to the feeling of frustration of the people and pose threats to the national security of the country. The unity and integrity of the country can be best preserved by educating our people in the spirit of genuine nationalism, healthy patriotism and international humanism. Proper use of TADA and other national security laws needs to be ensured by the state governments and the active judiciary. As the world shrinks and we talk of a global village, differences all over the world seem to be surfacing with proposals for new kinds of political solutions to dormant problems which are coming to the fore.

Concluding Remarks

India's problem is that it has no organisation to take a holistic overview of its national security, identify vital national interests, examine the options available, and accordingly spell out national strategic objectives and formulate a comprehensive national security plan. Security policy-making institutions are virtually non-existent in India. Shri P.N. Haksar wrote : "I do not recall a single occasion during the last 31 years when problems of our country's security were discussed seriously or in depth".[62] Although national security needs eternal vigilance of the people, there is no need for pessimism due to the following main factors :

1. Mature political wisdom of our people.
2. Our people's faith in electoral processes and their wisdom in exercising their right of voting.
3. Sense of oneness and unity in diversity which assert itself in the face of external threats.
4. Our defence forces, civil and police services and our steel-frame bureaucracy.

5. Ancient culture having resilience and capacity to assimilate new trends and emerging forces.
6. India's foreign policy based on the principles of "Panch Sheel" and coexistence.
7. However there is need for modernisation, expansion and better training of state police, central police organisations and the army, navy and airforce to remain in a state of full alertness to safeguard our national interests both during low intensity operations and proxy wars by foreign nations and also combating internal security challenges.

We must embark upon a permanent defence relationship with the United States. "After all in global real politics, there are no permanent friends or enemies. There are only permanent interests".[63] We must mobilise all our national interest to meet the challenges of national security both outside and within the country. Jawaharlal Nehru in the Constituent Assembly said : "India needs today nothing more than a set of honest men who will have the interest of the country before them ...... it requires men of strong character, men of vision, men who will not sacrifice the interest of the country at large for the sake of small groups and areas and who will rise over the prejudices which are born of these differences".[64] The need of such honest and visionary people is most urgent today for safeguarding and protecting the national security people's role in detecting illegal aliens and foreign agents cannot be over emphasises. All citizens must be enthusiased to take positive interest in the security of the nation because without the active co-operation and support of the public at large, national security cannot be ensured. An apex body or core group like National Security Council needs to be formed at the Central Govt. level with legal and constitutional authority for making the highest level policy decisions on national security, matters. National Security Council should be an institutionalised body which should evolve conceptual plans, initiate co-ordination, issue directives to various security agencies and monitor all security operations with a view to prepare long range strategic security policy for the nation.[65] In USA National Security Council has been created by the United States National Security Act 1947. For National Security Council, there should be a blue-print for staff organisation.[66] There can be no effective security planning at national level unless there is adequate planning within the ministries and services. Responsibility for national security lies with the Centre. If a situation arises in which the country's security is threatened, the President can, under the Constitution, enforce Emergency in a part or the whole of the country. It is also the Centre's responsibility to protect citizens against external aggression and internal disturbances and any State which is not being administered in accordance with the Constitution can be subjected to Central Rule."[67] The Joint Intelligence Committee should play its due role in providing intelligence input on a regular basis. The National Security Council will be a think-tank to advise the Prime Minister and would replicate the functions of the CCPA (Cabinet Committee on Parliamentary Affairs) and also undertake long-term assessments for decisions on matters relating to country's national security. The core of handling national security problem is the display of strong political will supported by professional security-experts. There is a common suggestion by many political thinkers that the nation should be given more details of problems, threats and security assessments and their related matters for public debate so that national awareness can be built up and sustained on vital issues connected with national security.

REFERENCES

1. K.M. Mathur, *Police, Law and Internal Security*, Gyan Publishing House, New Delhi-1994, p. 168.
2. See Richard Ullmani, *Redefining Security—International Security,* Vol. 7 No. I (Summer 1983), p. 133.
3. M. Rasgotra, Security Environment, India's Vital Interest, *The Hindustan Times,* 24 Jan. 1995.
4. Morton Berkowitz and P.G. Bock (eds.), *American National Security; A Reader in Theory and Policy,* (New York, Free Press 1965, p. x).
5. Lippman, *US Foreign Policy : Shield of the Republic,* (Bosten-Little, Brown 1943).
6. Harry S. Truman, State of the Union Address, 6 Jan. 1947.
7. See Mohamed Ayood, Security in the third world : The Worm about to Turn, *International Affairs,* Vol. 60 No. I, (Winter 1983-84), pp. 41-51.

8. Barry Buzan, People, State and Fear : The National Security Problem in the Third World—in National Security in the Third World edited by Edward E. Azar and Moon-Maryland, 1988, pp. 16-17.
9. K. Subrahmanyam, Threats to Security—Internal Ones more Formidable, *The Times of India*, 12 Sept. 1987.
10. Narendra Gupta, India must Rework Its Security Plan, *The Times of India,* 12 Sept. 1995.
11. Mohan Guruswamy, Define, Wanted, a Security Doctrine, *The Hindustan Times*, New Delhi, 18 April 1995.
12. For similar view see B.P. Saha, Infiltration in the East—A Threat to Nation's Security and Integrity, *The Hindu* 2 March 1993.
13. Ray S. Cline, *World Power Trends and the US Foreign Policy for the 1980s*, Boulder-Co : West View 1980, pp. 43-69.
14. K. Subrahmanyam, Planning for Security-Blue-Print for An Apex Body, *The Times of India*, 21 Dec. 1989.
15. K.M. Mathur, *Police, Law and Internal Security*, 1994, p. 164.
16. W. Handrieder and L. Buel, *Worlds and Arms* (Boulders Co. West view 1979), p. 79.
17. Gen. V.N. Sharma, National Security—More threats from within, *The Hindustan Times*, Dec. 18, 1994, p. 13.
18. H.K. Dua, Men who failed, *The Hindustan Times*, 11 Aug. 1992.
19. Edward Azar and Chimg, In-Moon, Third World National Security. Towards a New Conceptual Framework, *International Interactions,* Vol. 11 No. 2, p. 103.
20. K. Padmanabiah, IV Police Memorial Lecture on "Internal Security and Urban Policing" On Oct. 21, 1995, *Indian Express*, Police should gear up to face new challenges, Oct. 22, 1995.
21. S.S. Banyal, Major Security Lapse, *The Hindustan Times*, 24 December 1995.
22. Gen. Shankar Roy Chowdhury, Internal Security has become a misnomer, *The Hindustan Times,* 15 Nov. 1994.
23. Jagmohan, Internal Threats to India's Security, *The Hindustan Times*, 20 Dec. 1991, p. 3.

24. Jag Mohan, Internal Threats to India's Security, *The Hindustan Times*, 20 Dec. 1991, p. 3.
25. Buzan, *People, State and Fear*, pp. 88-89.
26. Herman Kahn, William Brown and Leon Martel, *The Next 200 years,* (See table 17 of the book).
27. R.D. MC Lawrin, Managing National Security. The American Experience and the Lessons for the Third World in Azar and Moon (eds). National Security in the Third World, Centre for International Development and Conflict Management. University of Maryland 1988, p. 263.
28. K.M. Mathur, *Police, Law and Internal Security*, Gyan Publishing House, New Delhi, 1994, p. 171.
29. Alfead Stepan, The New Professionalism of Internal Warfare and Military Role Expansion in Stepan, Authoritarian Brazil, New Haven CT Yali University Press, 1973, p. 51.
30. See Mohammed Ayood, Security in the Third World. The Worm about to Tuen, *International Affairs*, Vol. 60 No. 1, Winter 1983-84, pp. 41-51.
31. Ram Jethmalani, Saving the Country, Wanted a New Party, *Indian Express*, 1 Sept. 1995.
32. See Richard Ullman, Redefining Security, *International Securit,* Vol. 8, No. 1, Summer 1983, pp. 129-153, Robert Jervis-Cooperation under Security Dilimma, *World Politics,* Vol. 30 No. 2, Jan. 1978, pp. 167-214.
33. S. Subramanian, Steps to Safeguard National Interest, *The Hindustan Times,* 10 Jan. 1995.
34. For further discussion see Merilee S. Grindle (ed.), Politics and Policy Implementation in the Third World (Princeton NJ 1980).
35. For significant works from this perspective see-Daird M. Ashire and Richard V. Allen (ed.), *National Security* (New York) 1963 William W. Kanfman (ed.), *Military Power and National Security* (New Jersey NJ 1965), Gordon B. Turner and Richard B. Challener, *National Security in the Nuclear Age,* (London 1960).

36. Lt. Gen. S.K. Sinha (Retd.), On the Ministry's Control—Denigrating the Army, *The Hindustan Times*, New Delhi, Dec. 16, 1995.
37. Concept adopted from Frank N. Trager and Frank L. Simonic, *An Introduction to the Study of National Security,* in Frank N. Trager and Phillips S. Kronenberg (ed.), *National Security and American Society : Theory, Process and Policy,* (Lawrence K.S. University Press of Kainsas 1973), p. 36.
38. Edward E. Azar and Chong-in-Moon, *Reassessing the Third World National Security : Legitimacy, Integration and Policy Capacity,* (Seminar paper presented at CIDCM July 1986).
39. See Robert S Mc Namara, The Essence of Security (New York Harper and Row) 1968. Abdul Monum M.Almashat-National Security in the Third World, (Boulder Co. Westview 1985).
40. Air Comdr J. Murugan (Retd, Needed Indepth Analysis of Security Strategy, *The Hindu*, Dec. 20, 1994, p. 17.
41. Pankaj Vohra, Violent Persuasions-Between Us, *The Hindustan Times*, 3 December 1995.
42. For similar views and ideas see K.M. Mathur, *Management of Internal Security,* Gyan Publishing House, New Delhi, 1995, p. 44.
43. RD Mc Lawring, Managing National Security in (eds.), Azar and Moon, *National Security in the Third World*, Maryland 1988, p. 272.
44. S. Subramanian, Steps to Safeguard National Security, *The Hindustan Times,* 10 Jan. 1995.
45. Hari Om-Jainnu, The ISI Target-*Hindu*, 25 Feb. 1995.
46. For further details see *The Times of India*, Ahmedabad 12 April 1993.
47. Dr. S. Subramanian, Steps to Safeguard National Security, *The Hindustan Times*, 10 Jan. 1995.
48. *Ibid.*
49. *Indian Express,* 26 Feb. 1995, Economists come down hard on reforms, p. 10.

50. *Indian Express,* 26 Feb. 1995, Patel warms against blind acceptance of reforms.
51. Myron Weiner, *The Indian Paradox,* New Delhi, 1989, p. 42.
52. N.J. Akbar, *The Siege Within,* New Delhi, 1985, p. 310.
53. K. Padmanabhiah, IV Police Memorial Lecture on Internal Security and Urban Policing at Vigyan Bhawan, New Delhi on Oct. 21, 1995. See *Indian Express,* 22 Oct. 1995, Police should gear up to face new challenges.
54. K.M. Panikkar, *Problems of Indian Defence,* Bombay 1960, pp. 115-17.
55. Michael Lauw, *National Security : A Modern Approach,* Pretoria SA, 1978, p. 14.
55. (a) For similar views see Mahbub ul Haq., The Sub-continent of sub-Sahara Asia-*The Times of India,* 28 March, 1996.
56. K.M. Panikkar, *Problems of Indian Defence*, Bombay 1969, pp. 115-17.
57. Asian Strategic Review 1991-92 (IDSA) —Also *The Hindustan Times,* 4 July 1993.
58. Lt. Gen. A.M. Vohra (Retd.), Changing Concept of Security, *The Hindustan Times*, 10 July 1993.
59. M. Rasgotra, *Security Environment—India's Vital Interests*.
60. Ved Marwah, In a State of Ferment, *The Hindustan Times,* 4th/15th Aug. 1992.
61. Modhumita Mazumdar, *Patriotism-Myopia is Dangerous, The Hindustan Times,* 31 Dec. 1994.
62. Constituent Assembly Debate, Vol. XI, 1993-94.
63. K.M. Mathur, *Management of Internal Security and Related Issues*, Gyan Publishing House, New Delhi, 1995, p. 43.
64. For further details see K. Subramanyam, Planning for Security. Blue Print for an Apex Body, *The Times of India,* 21 Dec 1989. Also, *The Hindustan Times*, 5 June 1994-NSC likely to be set up soon.
65. K.M. Mathur, *Management of Internal Security and Related Issues*, Gyan Publishing House, New Delhi, 1995. p. 43.

66. For further details see K. Subramanyam, Planning for Security-Blue Print for an Apex Body, *The Times of India*, 21 Dec. 1989. Also, *The Hindustan Times*, 5 June 1994, NSC likely to be set up soon.
67. N.N. Vohra, Home Ministry, A Toothless Mastiff ? *Indian Express,* 21 June 1995.

Appendix A

The Universal Declaration of Human Rights, 1948

PREAMBLE

Whereas recognition of the inherent dignity and of the equal and inalienable rights of all members of the human family is the foundation of freedom, justice and peace in the world,

Whereas disregard and contempt for human rights have resulted in barberous acts which have outraged the conscience of mankind, and the advent of a world in which human beings shall enjoy freedom of speech and belief and freedom from fear and want has been proclaimed as the highest aspiration of the common people,

Whereas it is essential, if man is not to be compelled to have recourse, as last resort, to rebellion against tyranny and oppression, that human rights should be protected by rule of law,

Whereas it is essential to promote the development of friendly relations between nations,

Whereas certain Member-States have not yet granted to women, political rights equal to those granted to men,

(a) Recommends that all Member-States, which have not already done so, adopt measures necessary to fulfil the purposes and aims of the Charter in this respect by granting to women the same political rights as to men,

(b) Invites the Secretary General to communicate this recommendation to the Governments of all Member-States (*Ibid.*, p. 90).

The Economic and Social Council in a resolution adopted on June 21, 1946, stated that :

Pending the adoption of an international bill of rights, the general principle shall be accepted that international treaties involving basic human rights, including to the fullest extent practicable treaties of peace, shall conform to the fundamental standards relative to such rights set forth in the Charter. (Journal of the Economic and Social Council, first year, No 29, p. 521).

Finally the Economic and Social Council decided by a resolution adopted on August 26, 1948 :

To transmit to the General Assembly the Draft International Declaration of Human Rights submitted to the Council by the Commission on Human Rights in the report of its third session (Doc. E/800), together with the remainder of this report and records of the proceedings of the Council at its seventh session on this subject (Doc. E/1046).

Whereas the peoples of the United Nations have in the Charter reaffirmed their faith in fundamental human rights, in the dignity and worth of the human person and in the equal rights of men and women and have determined to promote social progress and better standards of life in larger freedom.

Whereas Member-States have pledged themselves to achieve, in co-operation with the United Nations, the promotion of universal respect for and observance of human rights and fundamental freedoms,

Whereas a common understanding of these rights and freedoms is of the greatest importance for full realisation of this pledge ;

Now, Therefore,

The General Assembly

Proclaims this Universal Declaration of Human Rights as a common standard of achievement for all peoples and all nations, to the end that every individual and every organ of society keeping this declaration constantly in mind, shall strive by teaching and education to promote respect for these rights and freedoms and by progressive measures, national and international, to secure their universal and effective recognition and observance, both among the people of Member-States themselves and among the peoples of territories under their jurisdiction.

Article 1

All human beings are born free and equal in dignity and rights. They are endowed with reason and conscience and should act towards one another in a spirit of brotherhood.

Article 2

Everyone is entitled to all the rights and freedoms set forth in this declaration without distinction of any kind, such as race, colour, sex, language, religion, political or other opinion, national or social origin, property, birth or other status.

Furthermore, no distinction shall be made on the basis of the political, jurisdictional international status of the country or territory to which a person belongs, whether it be independent, trust, on-self-governing or under any other limitation of sovereignty.

Article 3

Everyone has the right to life, liberty and security of person.

Article 4

No one shall be held in slavery or servitude ; slavery and the slave trade shall be prohibited in all their forms.

Article 5

No one shall be subjected to torture or to cruel, inhuman or degrading treatment or punishment.

Article 6

Everyone has the right to recognition everywhere as a person before the law.

Article 7

All are equal before the law and are entitled without any discrimination to equal protection of the law. All are entitled to equal protection against any discrimination in violation of this declaration and against any incitement to such discrimination.

Article 8

Everyone has the right to an effective remedy by the competent national tribunals for acts violating the fundamental rights granted him by constitution or by law.

Article 9

No one shall be subjected to arbitrary arrest, detention or exile.

Article 10

Everyone is entitled in full equality to a fair and public hearing by independent and impartial tribunal, in the determination of his rights and obligations and of any criminal charge against him.

Article 11

1. Everyone charged with a penal offence has the right to be presumed innocent until proved guilty according to law in public trial at which he has had all guarantees necessary for his defence.

2. No one shall be held guilty of any penal offence on account of any act or omission which did not constitute penal offence under national or international law, at the time when it was committed. Nor shall a heavier penalty be imposed than the one that was applicable at the time the penal offence was committed.

Article 12

No one shall be subjected to arbitrary interference with his privacy, family, home or correspondence, nor to attacks upon his honour and reputation. Everyone has the right to the protection of the law against such interference or attacks.

Article 13

1. Everyone has the right to freedom of movement and residence within the borders of each state.

2. Everyone has the right to leave any country, including his own, and to return to his country.

Article 14

1. Everyone has the right to seek and to enjoy in other countries asylum from persecution.

2. This right may not be invoked in the case of prosecutions

genuinely arising from non-political crimes or from acts contrary to the purposes and principles of the United Nations.

Article 15

1. Everyone has the right to a nationality.

2. No one shall be arbitrarily deprived of his nationality nor denied the right to change his nationality.

Article 16

1. Men and women of full age, without any limitation due to race, nationality or religion, have the right to marry and to found a family. They are entitled to equal rights as to marriage, during marriage and at its dissolution.

2. Marriage shall be entered into only with the free and full consent of the intending spouses.

3. The family is the natural and fundamental group unit of society and is entitled to protection by society and the state.

Article 17

1. Everyone has the right to own property alone as well as in association with others.

2. No one shall be arbitrarily deprived of his property.

Article 18

Everyone has the right to freedom of thought, conscience and religion; this right includes the freedom to change his religion or belief, and freedom, either alone or in community with others and a public or private, to manifest his religion or belief in teaching, practice, worship and observance.

Article 19

Everyone has the right to freedom of opinion and expression; this right includes freedom to hold opinions without interference and to seek, receive and impart information and ideas through any media and regardless of frontier.

Article 20

1. Everyone has the right to freedom of peaceful assembly and association.

2. No one may be compelled to belong to an association.

Article 21

1. Everyone has the right to take part in the government of his country, directly or through freely chosen representatives.

2. Everyone has the right of equal access to public service in his country.

3. The will of the people shall be the basis of authority of government; this will shall be expressed in periodic and genuine elections which shall be by universal and equal suffrage and shall be held by secret vote or by equivalent free voting procedures.

Article 22

Everyone, as a member of society, has the right to social security and is entitled to realisation, through national effort and international co-operation and in accordance with the organisation and resources of each state, of the economic, social and cultural rights indispensable for his dignity and the free development of his personality.

Article 23

1. Everyone has the right to work, to free choice of employment, to just and favourable conditions of work and to protection against unemployment.

2. Everyone, without any discrimination, has the right to equal pay for equal work.

3. Everyone who works has the right to just and favourable remuneration, insuring for himself and his family an existence worthy of human dignity, and supplemented, if necessary, by other means of social protection.

4. Everyone has the right to form and to join trade unions for the protection of his interests.

Article 24

Everyone has the right to rest and leisure, including reasonable limitation of working hours and periodic holidays with pay.

Article 25

1. Everyone has the right to a standard of living adequate

for the health and well-being of himself and of his family including food, clothing, housing and medical care and necessary social services, and the right to security in the event of unemployment, sickness, disability, widowhood, old age or other lack of livelihood in circumstances beyond his control.

2. Motherhood and childhood are entitled to special care and assistance. All children, whether born in or out of wedlock, shall enjoy the same social protection.

Article 26

1. Everyone has the right to education. Education shall be free, at least in the elementary and fundamental stages. Elementary education shall be compulsory, technical and professional education shall be made generally available, and higher education shall be equally accessible to all on the basis of merit.

2. Education shall be directed to the full development of human personality and to the strengthening of respect for human rights and fundamental freedoms. It shall promote understanding tolerance and friendship among all nations, racial or religious groups, and shall further the activities of the United Nations for the maintenance of peace.

3. Parents have the prior right to choose the kind of education that shall be given to their children.

Article 27

1. Everyone has the right freely to participate in the cultural life of the community, to enjoy the arts and to share in scientific advancement and its benefits.

2. Everyone has the right to the protection of the moral and material interest resulting from any scientific, literary or artistic production of which he is the author.

Article 28

Everyone is entitled to a social and international order in which the rights and freedoms set forth in this declaration can be fully realised.

Article 29

1. Everyone has duties to the community in which alone

the free and full development of his personality is possible.

2. In the exercise of his rights and freedoms, everyone shall be subject only to such limitations as are determined by law solely for the purpose of securing due recognition and respect for the rights and freedoms of others and of meeting the just requirements of morality, public order and the general welfare in a democratic society.

1. These rights and freedoms may in no case be exercised contrary to the purposes and principles of the United Nations.

Article 30

Nothing in this declaration may be interpreted as implying for any state, group or person any right to engage in any activity or to perform any act aimed at the destruction of any of the rights and freedoms set forth herein.

Appendix B

The Protection of Human Rights Act, 1993

(No. 10 1994)

[*8th January, 1994*]

An Act to provide for the constitution of a National Human Rights Commission, State Human Rights Commissions in States and Human Rights Courts for better protection of human rights and for matters connected therewith or incidental thereto.

Be it enacted by Parliament in the forty-fourth year of the Republic of India as follows :

Chapter I

PRELIMINARY

1. Short title, extent and commencement— (1) This Act may be called the Protection of Human Rights Act, 1993.

(2) It extends to the whole of India :

Provided that it shall apply to the State of Jammu and Kashmir only in so far as it pertains to the matters relatable to any of the entries enumerated in List I or List III in the Seventh Schedule to the Constitution as applicable to that State.

(3) It shall be deemed to have come into force on the 28th day of September, 1993.

2. Definitions— (1) In this Act, unless the context otherwise requires,—

(a) "armed forces" means the naval, military and air forces and includes any other armed forces of the Union;

(b) "Chairperson" means the Chairperson of the Commission or of the State Commission, as the case may be;

(c) "Commission" means the National Human Rights Commission constituted under section 3;

(d) "human rights" means the rights relating to life, liberty, equality and dignity of the individual guaranteed by the Constitution or embodied in the International Convenants and enforceable by courts in India;

(e) "Human Rights Court" means the Human Rights Court specified under section 30;

(f) "International Covenants" means the International Covenant on Civil and Political Rights and the International Covenant on Economic, Social and Cultural Rights adopted by the General Assembly of the United Nations on the 16th December, 1966;

(g) "Member" means a Member of the Commission or of the State Commission, as the case may be, and includes the Chairperson;

(h) "National Commission for Minorities" means the National Commission for Minorities constituted under section 3 of the National Commission for Minorities Act, 1992;

(i) "National Commission for the Scheduled Castes and Scheduled Tribes" means the National Commission for the Scheduled Castes and Scheduled Tribes referred to in Article 338 of the Constitution;

(j) "National Commission for Women" means the National Commission for Women constituted under section 3 of the National Commission for Women Act, 1990;

(k) "notification" means a notification published in the Official Gazette;

(l) "prescribed" means prescribed by rules made under this Act;

(m) "public servant" shall have the meaning assigned to it in section 21 of the Indian Penal Code;

(n) "State Commission" means a State Human Rights Commission constituted under section 21.

(2) Any reference in this Act to a law, which is not in force

in the State of Jammu an all, in relation to that State, be construed as a ref ,rresponding law, if any, in force in that State.

Chaptei -

THE NATIONAL HUMAN RIGHTS COMMISSION

3. Constitution of a National Human Rights Commission— (1) The Central Government shall constitute a body to be known as the National Human Rights Commission to exercise the powers conferred upon, and to perform the functions assigned to, it under this Act.

(2) The Commission shall consist of—

(a) a Chairperson who has been a Chief Justice of the Supreme Cour;

(b) one Member who is, or has been, a Judge of the Supreme Court;

(c) one Member who is, or has been, the Chief Justice of a High Court;

(d) two Members to be appointed from amongst person having knowledge of, or practical experience in, matters relating to human rights.

(3) The Chairpersons of the National Commission for Minorities, the National Commission for the Scheduled Castes and Scheduled Tribes and the National Commission for Women shall be deemed to be Members of the Commission for the discharge of functions specified in clauses (b) to (j) of section 12.

(4) There shall be a Secretary-General who shall be Chief Executive Officer of the Commission and shall exercise such powers and discharge such functions of the Commission as it may delegate to him.

(5) The headquarters of the Commission shall be at Delhi and the Commission may, with the previous approval of the Central Government, establish offices at other places in India.

4. Appointment of Chairperson and other Members— (1) The Chairperson and other Members shall be appointed by the President by warrant under his hand and seal :

Provided that every appointment under this sub-section shall be made after obtaining the recommendations of a Committee consisting of —

(a) the Prime Minister—*Chairperson;*

(b) Speaker of the House of People—*Member*;

(c) Minister in-charge of the Ministry of Home Affairs in the Government of India—*Member;*

(d) Leader of the Opposition in the House of the People—*Member*;

(e) Leader of the Opposition in the Council of States—*Member*;

(f) Deputy Chairman of the Council of States—*Member.*

Provided further that no sitting Judge of the Supreme Court or sitting Chief Justice of a High Court shall be appointed except after consultation with the Chief Justice of India.

(2) No appointment of a Chairperson or a Member shall be invalid merely by reason of any vacancy in the Committee.

5. Removal of a Member of the Commission—(1) Subject to the provisions of sub-section (2), the Chairperson or any other Member of the Commission shall only be removed from his office by order of the President on the ground of proved misbehaviour or incapacity after the Supreme Court, on reference being made to it by the President, has, on inquiry held in accordance with the procedure prescribed in that behalf by the Supreme Court, reported that the Chairperson or such other Member, as the case may be, ought on any such ground to be removed.

(2) Notwithstanding anything in sub-section (1), the President may by order remove from office the Chairperson or any other Member if the Chairperson or such other Member, as the case may be,—

(a) is adjudged an insolvent; or

(b) engages during his term of office in any paid employment outside the duties of his office; or

(c) is unfit to continue in office by reason of infirmity of mind or body ; or

(d) is of unsound mind and stands so declared by a competent cour; or

(e) is convicted and sentenced to imprisonment for an offence which in the opinion of the President involves moral turpitude.

6. Term of office of Members—(1) A person appointed as Chairperson shall hold office for a term of five years from the date on which he enters upon his office or until he attains the age of seventy years, whichever is earlier.

(2) A person appointed as a Member shall hold office for a term of five years from the date on which he enters upon his office and shall be eligible for reappointment for another term of five years.

Provided that no Member shall hold office after he has attainded the age of seventy years.

(3) On ceasing to hold office, a Chairperson or a Member shall be ineligible for further employment under the Government of India or under the Government of any State.

7. Member to act as Chairperson or to discharge his functions in certain circumstances—(1) In the event of the occurrence of any vacancy in the office of the Chairperson by reason of his death, resignation or otherwise, the President may, by notification, authorise one of the Members to act as the Chairperson until the appointment of a new Chairperson to fill such vacancy.

(2) When the Chairperson is unable to discharge his functions owing to absence on leave or otherwise, such one of the Members as the President may, by notification, authorise in this behalf, shall discharge the functions of the Chairperson until the date on which the Chairperson resumes his duties.

8. Terms and Conditions of Service of Members—The salaries and allowances payable to, and other terms and conditions of service of, the Members shall be such as may be prescribed :

Provided that neither the salary and allowances nor the other terms and conditions of service of a Member shall be varied to his disadvantage after his appointment.

9. Vacancies, etc., not to invalidate the proceedings of the Commission— No act or proceedings of the Commission shall be questioned or shall be invalidated merely on the ground of existence of any vacancy or defect in the constitution of the Commission.

10. Procedure to be regulated by the Commission— (1) The Commission shall meet at such time and place as the Chairperson may think fit.

(2) The Commission shall regulate its own procedure.

(3) All orders and decisions of the Commission shall be authenticated by the Secretary-General or any other officer of the Commission duly authorised by the Chairperson in this behalf.

11. Officers and Other Staff of the Commission— (1) The Central Government shall make available to the Commission—

(a) an officer of the rank of Secretary to the Government of India who shall be the Secretary-General of the Commission; and

(b) such police and investigative staff under an officer not below the rank of a Director General of Police and such other officers and staff as may be necessary for the efficient performance of the functions of the Commission.

(2) Subject to such rules as may be made by the Central Government in this behalf, the Commission may appoint such other administrative, technical and scientific staff as it may consider necessary.

(3) The salaries, allowances and conditions of service of the officers and other staff appointed under sub-section (2) shall be such as may be prescribed.

Chapter III

FUNCTIONS AND POWERS OF THE COMMISSION

12. Functions of the Commission— The Commission shall perform all or any of the following functions, namely:

(a) inquire, *suo moto* or on a petition presented to it by a victim or any person on his behalf, into complaint of —

(i) violation of human rights or abetment thereof ; or

(ii) negligence in the prevention of such violation, by a public servant;

(b) intervene in any proceeding involving any allegation of violation of human rights pending before a court with the approval of such court;

(c) visit, under intimation to the State Government, any jail or any other institution under the control of the State Government, where persons are detained or lodged for purposes of treatment, reformation or protection to study the living conditions of the inmates and make recommendations thereon;

(d) review the safeguards provided by or under the Constitution or any law for the time being in force for the protection of human rights and recommend measures for their effective implementation;

(e) review the factors, including acts of terrorism, the inhibit the enjoyment of human rights and recommend appropriate remedial measures;

(f) study treaties and other international instruments on human rights and make recommendations for their effective implementation;

(g) undertake and promote research in the field of human rights;

(h) spread human rights literacy among various sections of society and promote awareness of the safeguards available for the protection of these rights through publications, the media, seminars and other available means;

(i) encourage the efforts of non-governmental organisations and institutions working in the field of human rights;

(j) such other functions as it may consider necessary for the promotion of human rights.

13. Powers relating to inquiries—(1) The Commission shall, while inquiring into complaints under this Act, have all the powers of a civil court trying a suit under the Code of Civil Procedure, 1908, and in particular in respect of the following matters, namely : —

(a) summoning and enforcing the attendance of witnesses and examining them on oath;

(b) discovery and production of any document;

(c) receiving evidence on affidavits;

(d) requisitioning any public record or copy thereof from any court or office;

(e) issuing commissions for the examination of witnesses or documents;

(f) any other matter which may be prescribed.

(2) The Commission shall have power to require any person, subject to any privilege which may be claimed by that person under any law for the time being in force, to furnish information on such points or matters as, in the opinion of the Commission, may be useful for, or relevant to, the subject matter of the inquiry and any person so required shall be deemed to be legally bound to furnish such information within the meaning of section 176 and section 177 of the Indian Penal Code.

(3) The Commission or any other officer, not below the rank of a Gazetted Officer, specially authorised in this behalf by the Commission may enter any building or place where the Commission has reason to believe that any document relating to the subject matter of the inquiry may be found, and may seize any such document or take extracts or copies therefrom subject to the provisions of section 100 of the Code of Criminal Procedure, 1973, in so far as it may be applicable.

(4) The Commission shall be deemed to be a civil court and when any offence as is described in section 175, section 178, section 179, section 180 or section 228 of the Indian Penal Code is committed in the view or presence of the Commission, the Commission may after recording the facts constituting the offence and the statement of the accused as provided for in the Code of Criminal Procedure, 1973, forward the case to a Magistrate having jurisdiction to try the same and the Magistrate to whom any such case is forwarded shall proceed to hear the complaint against the accused as if the case has been forwarded to him under section 346 of the Code of Criminal Procedure, 1973.

(5) Every proceeding before the Commission shall be deemed to be a judicial proceeding within the meaning of sections 193

and 228, and for the purposes of section 196, of the Indian Penal Code, and the Commission shall be deemed to be a civil court for all the purposes of section 195 and Chapter XXVI of the Code of Criminal Procedure, 1973.

14. Investigation— (1) The Commission may, for the purpose of conducting any investigation pertaining to the inquiry, utilise the services of any officer or investigation agency of the Central Government or any State Government with the concurrence of the Central Government or any State Government, as the case may be.

(2) For the purpose of investigating into any matter pertaining to the inquiry, any officer or agency whose services of utilised under sub-section (1) may, subject to the direction and control of the Commission—

(a) summon and enforce the attendance of any person and examine him ;

(b) require the discovery and production of any document; and

(c) requisition any public record or copy thereof from any office.

(3) The officer or agency whose services are utilised under sub-section (1) shall investigate into any matter pertaining to the inquiry and submit a report thereon to the Commission within such period as may be specified by the Commission in this behalf.

(4) The Commission shall satisfy itself about the correctness of the facts stated and the conclusion, if any, arrived at in the report submitted to it under sub-section (4) and for this purpose the Commission may make such inquiry (including the examination of the person or persons who conducted or assisted in the investigation) as it thinks fit.

15. Statement made by persons to the Commission— No statement made by a person in the course of giving evidence before the Commission shall subject him to, or be used against him in, any civil or criminal proceeding except a prosecution for giving false evidence by such statement :

Provided that the statement —

(a) is made in reply to the question which he is required by the Commission to answer; or

(b) is relevant to the subject matter of the inquiry.

16. Persons likely to be prejudicially affected to be heard—If, at any stage of the inquiry, the Commission—

(a) considers it necessary to inquire into the conduct of any person; or

(b) is of the opinion that the reputation of any person is likely to be prejudicially affected by the inquiry,

it shall give to the person a reasonable opportunity of being heard in the inquiry and to produce evidence in his defence :

Provided that nothing in this section shall apply where the credit of a witness is being impeached.

Chapter IV

PROCEDURE

17. Inquiry into complaints— The Commission while inquiring into the complaints of violations of human rights may—

(i) call for information or report from the Central Government or any State Government or any other authority or organisation subordinate there to within such time as may be specified by it :

Provided that —

(a) if the information or report is not received within the time stipulated by the Commission, it may proceed to inquire into the complaint on its own ;

(b) if, on receipt of information or report, the Commission is satisfied either that no further inquiry is required or that the required action has been initiated or taken by the concerned Government or authority, it may not proceed with the complaint and inform the complainant accordingly ;

(ii) without prejudice to anything contained in clause (i), if it considers necessary, having regard to the nature of the complaint, initiate an inquiry.

18. Steps after inquiry— The Commission may take any of the following steps upon the completion of an inquiry held under this Act, namely :

(1) where the inquiry discloses, the commission of violation of human rights or negligence in the prevention of violation of human rights by a public servant, it may recommend to the concerned Government or authority the initiation of proceedings for prosecution or such other action as the Commission may deem fit against the concerned person or persons;

(2) approach the Supreme Court or the High Court concerned for such directions, orders or writs as the Court may deem necessary;

(3) recommend to the concerned Government or authority for the grant of such immediate interim relief to the victim or the members of the family as the Commission may consider necessary;

(4) subject to the provisions of claue (5) provide a copy of the inquire report to the petitioner or his representative;

(5) the Commission shall send a copy of its inquiry report together with its recommendations to the concerned Government or authority and the concerned Government or authority shall, within a period of one month, or such further time as the Commission may allow, forward its comments on the report, including the action taken or proposed to be taken thereon, to the Commission;

(6) the Commission shall publish its inquiry report together with the comments of the concerned Government or authority, if any, and the action taken or proposed to be taken by the concerned Government or authority on the recommendations of the Commission.

19. Procedure with respect to armed forces—(1) Notwithstanding anything contained in this Act, while dealing with complaints of violation of human rights by members of the armed forces, the Commission shall adopt the following procedure, namely :

(a) it may, either on its own motion or on receipt of a petition, seek a report from the Central Government;

(b) after the receipt of the report, it may, either not proceed with the complaint or, as the case may be, make its recommendations to that Government.

(2) The Central Government shall inform the Commission of the action taken on the recommendations within three months or such further time as the Commission may allow.

(3) The Commission shall publish its report together with its recommendations made to the Central Government and the action taken by that Government on such recommendations.

(4) The Commission shall provide a copy of the report published under sub-section(3) to the petitioner or his representative.

20. Annual and special reports of the Commission— (1) The Commission shall submit an annual report to the Central Government and to the State Government concerned and may at any time submit special reports on any matter which, in its opinion, is of such urgency or importance that it should not be deferred till submission of the annual report.

(2) The Central Government and the State Government, as the case may be, shall cause the annual and special reports of the Commission to be laid before each House of Parliament or the State Legislature respectively, as the case may be, along with a memorandum of action taken or proposed to be taken on the recommendations of the Commission and the reasons for non-acceptance of the recommendations, if any.

Chapter V

STATE HUMAN RIGHTS COMMISSIONS

21. Constitution of State Human Rights Commission— (1) A State Government may constitute a body to be known as the .... (name of the State) Human Rights Commission to exercise the powers conferred upon, and to perform the functions assigned to a State Commission under this Chapter.

(2) The State Commission shall consist of:

(a) a Chairperson who has been a Chief Justice of a High Court;

(b) one Member who is, or has been, a Judge of a High Court;

(c) one Member who is, or has been, a district judge in that State;

(d) two members to be appointed from amongst persons having knowledge of, or practical experience in, matters relating to human rights.

(3) There shall be a Secretary who shall be the Chief Executive Officer of the State Commission and shall exercise such powers and discharge such functions of the State Commission as it may delegate to him.

(4) The headquarters of the State Commission shall be at such place as the State Government may, by notification, specify.

(5) A State Commission may inquire into violation of human rights only in respect of matters relatable to any of the entries enumerated in List II and List III in the Seventh Schedule to the Constitution :

Provided that if any such matter is already being inquired into by the Commission or any other Commission duly constituted under any law for the time being in force, the State Commission shall not inquire into the said matter :

Provided further that in relation to the Jammu and Kashmir Human Rights Commission, this sub-section shall have effect as if for the words and figures "List II and List III in the Seventh Schedule to the Constitution", the words and figures "List III in the Seventh Schedule to the Constitution as applicable to the State of Jammu and Kashmir and in respect of matters in relation to which the Legislature of that State has power to make laws" had been substituted.

22. Appointment of Chairperson and other Members of State Commission— (1) The Chairperson and other Members shall be appointed by the Governor by warrant under his hand and seal :

Provided that every appointment under this sub-section shall be made after obtaining the recommendation of a Committee consisting of —

(a) the Chief Minister—*Chairperson*;

(b) Speaker of the Legislative Assembly —*Member*:

(c) Minister in charge of the Department of Home in that State—*Member*;

(d) Leader of the Opposition in the Legislative Assembly—*Member*:

Provided further that where there is a Legislative Council in a State, the Chairman of that Council and the Leader of the Opposition in that Council shall also be members of the Committee:

Provided also that no sitting Judge of a High Court or a sitting district judge shall be appointed except after consultation with the Chief Justice of the High Court of the concerned State.

(2) No appointment of a Chairperson or a Member of the State Commission shall be invalid merely by reason of any vacancy in the Committee.

23. Removal of a Member of the State Commission— (1) Subject to the provisions of sub-section (2), the Chairperson or any other Member of the State Commission shall only be removed from his office by order of the President on the ground of proved misbehaviour or incapacity after the Supreme Court, on a reference being made to it by the President, has on inquiry held in accordance with the procedure prescribed in that behalf by the Supreme Court, reported that the Chairperson or such other Member, as the case may be, ought on any such ground to be removed.

(2) Notwithstanding anything in sub-section (1), the President may by order remove from office the Chairperson or any other Member if the Chairperson or such other Member, as the case may be,—

(a) is adjudged an insolvent; or

(b) engages during his term of office in any paid employment outside the duties of his office; or

(c) is unfit to continue in office by reason of infirmity of mind or body; or

(d) is of unsound mind and stands so declared by a competent court; or

(e) is convicted and sentenced to imprisonment for an offence which in the opinion of the President involves moral turpitude.

24. Term of office of Members of the State Commission— (1) A person appointed as Chairperson shall hold office for a term of five years from the date on which he enters upon his office or until he attains the age of seventy years, whichever is earlier.

(2) A person appointed as a Member shall hold office for a term of five years from the date on which he enters upon his office and shall be eligible for reappointment for another term of five years :

Provided that no Member shall hold office after he has attained the age of seventy years.

(3) On ceasing to hold office, a Chairperson or a Member shall be ineligible for further employment under the Government of a State or under the Government of India.

25. Member to act as Chairperson or to discharge his functions in certain circumstances— (1) In the event of the occurrence of any vacancy in the office of the Chairperson by reason of his death, resignation or otherwise, Governor may, by notification, authorise one of the Members to act as Chairperson until the appointment of a new Chairperson to fill such vacancy.

(2) When the Chairperson is unable to discharge his functions owing absence on leave or otherwise, such one of the Members as the Government may, by notification, authorise in this behalf, shall discharge the functions of the Chairperson until the date on which the Chairperson resumes his duties.

26. Terms and conditions of service of Members of the State Commission— The salaries and allowances payable to, and other terms and conditions of service of, the Members shall be such as may be prescribed by the State Government :

Provided that neither the salary and allowances nor the other terms and conditions of service of a Member shall be varied to his disadvantage after his appointment.

27. Officers and other staff of the State Commission— (1) The State Government shall make available to the Commission—

(a) an officer not below the rank of a Secretary to the State Government who shall be the Secretary of the State Commission; and

(b) such police and investigative staff under an officer not below the rank of an Inspector General of Police and such other officers and staff as may be necessary for the efficient performance of the functions of the State Commission.

(2) Subject to such rules as may be made by the State Government in this behalf, the State Commission may appoint such other administrative, technical and scientific staff as it may consider necessary.

(3) The salaries, allowances and conditions of service of the officers and other staff appointed under sub-section (2) shall be such as may be prescribed by the State Government.

28. Annual and special reports of State Commission— (1) The State Commission shall submit an annual report to the State Government and may at any time submit special reports on any matter which, in its opinion, is of such urgency or importance that it should not be deferred till submission of the annual report.

(2) The State Government shall cause the annual and special reports of the State Commission to be laid before each House of State Legislature where it consists of two Houses, or where such Legislature consists of one House, before that House along with a memorandum of action taken or proposed to be taken on the recommendations of the State Commission and the reasons for non-acceptance of the recommendations, if any.

29. Application of certain provisions relating to National Human Rights Commission to State Commissions—The provisions of sections 9, 10, 12, 13, 14, 15, 16, 17 and 18 shall apply to a State Commission and shall have effect, subject to the following modification, namely:

(a) references to "Commission" shall be construed as reference to "State Commission";

(b) in section 10, in sub-section (3), for the word "Secretary-General", the word "Secretary" shall be substituted;

(c) in section 12, clause (f) shall be omitted;

(d) in section 17, in clause (i), the words "Central Government or any" shall be omitted.

Chapter VI

HUMAN RIGHTS COURTS

30. Human Rights Courts— For the purpose of providing speedy trial of offences arising out of violation of human rights, the State Government may, with the concurrence of the Chief Justice of the High Court, by notification, specify for each district a Court of Session to be a Human Rights Court to try the said offences :

Provided that nothing in this section shall apply if :

(a) a Court of session is already specified as a special court; or

(b) a special court is already constituted.

for such offences under any other law for the time being in force.

31. Special Public Prosecutor —For every Human Rights Court, the State Government shall, by notification, specify a Public Prosecutor or appoint an advocate who has been in practice as an advocate for not less than seven years, as a Special Public Prosecutor for the purpose of conducting cases in that Court.

Chapter VII

FINANCE, ACCOUNTS AND AUDIT

32. Grants by the Central Government—(1) The Central Government shall, after due appropriation made by Parliament by law in this behalf, pay to the Commission by way of grants such sums of money as the Central Government may think fit for being utilised for the purposes of this Act.

(2) The Commission may spend such sums as it thinks fit for performing the functions under this Act, and such sums shall be treated as expenditure payable out of the grants referred to in sub-section (1).

33. Grants by the State Government—(1) The State Government shall, after due appropriation made by Legislature by law in this behalf, pay to the State Commission by way of grants such sums of money as the State Government may think fit for being utilised for the purposes of this Act.

(2) The State Commission may spend such sums as it thinks

fit for performing the functions under Charter V, and such sums shall be treated as expenditure payable out of the grants referred to in sub-section (1).

34. Accounts and audit—(1) The Commission shall maintain proper accounts and other relevant records and prepare an annual statement of accounts in such form as may be prescribed by the Central Government in consultation with the Comptroller and Auditor General of India.

(2) The accounts of the Commission shall be audited by the Comptroller and Auditor-General at such intervals as may be specified by him and any expenditure incurred in connection with such audit shall be payable by the Commission to the Comptroller and Auditor-General.

(3) The Comptroller and Auditor-General and any person appointed by him in connection with the audit of the accounts of the Commission under this Act shall have the same rights and privileges and the authority in connection with such audit as the Comptroller and Auditor-General generally has in connection with the audit of Government accounts and, in particular, shall have the right to demand the production of books, accounts, connected vouchers and other documents and papers and to inspect any of the offices of the Commission.

(4) The accounts of the Commission, as certified by the Comptroller and Auditor-General or any other person appointed by him in this behalf, together with the audit report thereon, shall be forwarded annually to the Central Government by the Commission and the Central Government shall cause the audit report to be laid, as soon as may be after it is received, before each House of Parliament.

35. Accounts and audit of State Commission— (1) The State Commission shall maintain proper accounts and other relevant records and prepare an annual statement of accounts in such form as may be prescribed by the State Government in consultation with the Comptroller and Auditor General of India.

(2) The accounts of the State Commission shall be audited by the Comptroller and Auditor-General at such intervals as may be specified by him and any expenditure incurred in connection with such audit shall be payable by the State

Commission to the Comptroller and Auditor-General.

(3) The Comptroller and Auditor-General and any person appointed by him in connection with the audit of the accounts of the State Commission under this Act shall have the same rights and privileges and the authority in connection with such audit as the Comptroller and Auditor-General generally has in connection with the audit of Government accounts and, in particular, shall have the right to demand the production of books, accounts, connected vouchers and other documents and papers and to inspect any of the offices of the State Commission.

(4) The accounts of the State Commission, as certified by the Comptroller and Auditor-General or any other person appointed by him in this behalf, together with the audit report thereon, shall be forwarded annually to the State Government by the State Commission and the State Government shall cause the audit report to be laid, as soon as may be after it is received before the State Legislature.

Chapter VIII

MISCELLANEOUS

36. Matters not subject to jurisdiction of the Commission—(1) The Commission shall not inquire into any matter which is pending before a State Commission or any other Commission duly constituted under any law for the time being in force.

(2) The Commission or the State Commission shall not inquire into any matter after the expiry of one year from the date on which the act constituting violation of human rights is alleged to have been committed.

37. Constitution of special investigation teams—Notwithstanding anything contained in any other law for the time being in force, where the Government considers, it necessary so to do, it may constitute one or more special investigation teams, consisting of such police officers as it thinks necessary for purposes of investigation and prosecution of offences arising out of violations of human rights.

38. Protection of action taken in good faith—(1) No suit or other legal proceeding shall lie against the Central

Government, State Government, Commission, the State Commission or any Member thereof or any person acting under the direction either of the Central Government, State Government, Commission or the State Commission in respect of anything which is in good faith done or intended to be done in pursuance of this Act or of any rules or any order made thereunder or in respect of the publication by or under the authority of the Central Government, State Government, Commission or the State Commission of any Report, paper or proceedings.

39. Members and officers to be public servants—Every Member of the Commission, State Commission and every officer appointed or authorised by the Commission or the State Commission to exercise functions under this Act shall be deemed to be a public servant within the meaning of section 21 of the Indian Penal Code.

40. Power of Central Government to make rules—(1) The Central Government may, by notification make rules to carry out the provisions of this Act.

(2) In particular and without prejudice to the generality of the foregoing power, such rules may provide for all or any of the following matters, namely:

(a) the salaries and allowances and other terms and conditions of service of the Members under section 8;

(b) the conditions subject to which other administrative, technical and scientific staff may be appointed by the Commission and the salaries and allowances of officers and other staff under subsection (3) of section 11;

(c) any other power of a civil court required to be prescribed under clause (1) of sub-section (1) of section 13;

(d) the form in which the annual statement of accounts is to be prepared by the Commission under sub-section (1) of section 34; and

(e) any other matter which has to be or may be prescribed.

(3) Every rule made under this Act shall be laid, as soon as may be after it is made, before each House of Parliament, while

it is in session, for a total period of thirty days which may be comprised in one session or in two or more successive sessions, and if, before the expiry of the session immediately following the session or the successive sessions aforesaid, both Houses agree that the rule should not be made, the rule shall thereafter have effect only in such modified form or be of no effect, as the case may be; so, however, that any such modification or annulment shall be without prejudice to the validity of anything previously done under that rule.

41. Power of State Government to make rules—(1) The State Government may, by notification make rules to carry out the provisions of this Act.

(2) In particular and without prejudice to the generality of the foregoing power, such rules may provide for all or any of the following matters, namely :

(a) the salaries and allowances and other terms and conditions of service of the Members under section 26;

(b) the conditions subject to which other administrative, technical and scientific staff may be appointed by the Staff Commission and the salaries and allowances of officers and other staff under sub-section (3) of section 27 ;

(c) the form in which the annual statement of accounts is to be prepared under sub-section (1) of section 35.

(3) Every rule made by the State Government under this section shall be laid, as soon as may be after it is made, before each House of the State Legislature where it consists of two Houses, or where such Legislature consists of one House, before that House.

42. Power to remove difficulties.— (1) If any difficulty arises in giving effect to the provisions of this Act, the Central Government may, by order published in the Official Gazette, make such provisions, not inconsistent with the provisions of this Act as appear to it to be necessary or expedient for removing the difficulty :

Provided that no such order, shall be made after the expiry of the period of two years from the date of commencement of this Act.

(2) Every order made under this section shall, as soon as may be after it is made, be laid before each House of Parliament.

43. Repeal and savings—(1) The Protection of Human Rights Ordinance, 1993 is hereby repealed.

(2) Notwithstanding such repeal, anything done or any action taken under the said Ordinance, shall be deemed to have been done or taken under the corresponding provisions of this Act.

Bibliography

Adhikari, Gautam — *Conflict and Civilization*, Vikas Publishing House, New Delhi, 1981.

Agarwal, R.S. — *Human Rights in the Modern World*, New Delhi, Cheetana Publications, 1979.

Aiyar, S.P. — *Mass Violence*, Ajmer. Sachin Publications, 1979.

Ali, Aruna Asaf ; Singh, Darbara — *India's Unity and Security : Challenges*, Patriot Publishers, New Delhi, 1984.

Ali, Asghar — *Communal Riots in Post Independence India*, Bombay; Sangam Books, 1984.

——— *Sufism and Communal Harmony*, Jaipur, Printwell, 1991.

Ali, Asghar ; — *Communalism in India*, Delhi,

Alexander, Y. — *Terrorism Inter disciplinary perspectives*, Mc-Graw Hill Book Company (UK) Ltd., 1977.

——— *International Terrorism: National, Regional and Global Perspective*, Praeger Publishers, New York, 1976.

——— *Terrorism : Theory and Practice*, Westview Press, Boulder, Colorade, New York, 1979.

——— *Terrorism and the Media*, Brassey's (US) Inc. New York and London, 1990

Alper, Geoffrey P. — *Legal Rights of Prisoners*, London: Sage Pub., 1989.

Antony, M.J. — *Women's Rights*, Clarion Books, New Delhi, 1989.

Arora, Ramesh K. — *Training and Administrative Development*, HCM Institute, Jaipur, 1979.

Ashraf, Nehal — *Police and Policing in India*, Commonwealth Publishers, New Delhi, 1992.

Azar-Edward, E. Chung-in Moon — *National Security in the Third World*, University of Maryland, England, 1988.

Bailey, S.H. ; Harris, D.J. — *Civil Liberties, Cases and Materials*, Butterworths (London), 1985.

Barman, N.C. — *Para Military Forces in India*, Gogia Law Publications, Allahabad, 1992.

Ballance, O Edgar — *Terrorism in the 1980s*, Published in Great Britain by Arms & Armour Press, 1989.

Bansal, V.K. — *Right to Life and Personal Liberty in India*, New Delhi, Deep & Deep Pub. 1987.

Banu, Zenab — *Politics of Communalism*, Bombay Popular Prakashan, 1989.

Barrier, N.G. — *Roots of Communal Politics*, Delhi, Arnold, Heinemann, 1976.

Bassiouni, M. Cherif — *International Terrorism & Political Crimes*, Charles C. Thomas Publisher Springfield, 1975.

Batra, T.S. — *Human Rights: A Critique,* New Delhi Metropolitan Book Co. Pvt. Ltd., 1971.

Baxi, Upendra — *The Right to be Human*, New Delhi, Lancer International, 1987.

Beres Louis, Reno — *Terrorism & Global Security, The Nuclear Threat*, Westview Press, Boulder & London, 1987.

Berki, R.N. — *Security and Society : Reflections on Law Order and Politics*, First Ed., London : J.M. Dent & Sons Ltd., 1986.

Bhatnagar, O.P. — *Evaluation Methodology for Training*, Oxford & IBH Pub. Co., Delhi, 1987.

Bharatiya, V.P. — *Religion, State Relationship and Constitutional Rights in India*, Deep and Deep Publications, New Delhi.

Bisno, Herb — *Managing Conflict*, Sage Publications, London.

Biswas, U.N. — *Police Perception of Police Public Relations*, BPR & D, New Delhi, 1986.

Bono, Edward — *Conflict a better way to solve them*, Harrap, London, 1985.

Brass, Paul R. — *Ethnicity and Nationalism*, First Ed., New Delhi, Sage Pub., 1991.

Burnard, Philip — *Interpersonal Skills Training*, Viava Books, New Delhi, 1985.

———— — *Counselling Skills Training*, Viava Books, New Delhi, 1985.

Burton, Antheny — *Urban Terrorism Theory, Practice & Response*, Printed in Great Britain by Western Printing Services Ltd., 1975.

Burton, John — *Deviance Terrorism & War*, Martia Rebertson & Co. Ltd., Oxford, 1979.

Canning, John — *50 True Tales of Terror*, Rupa & Co., London, 1991.

Carlton, David — *International Terrorism & World Security*, Green Helm, London, 1975.

Chakravarti, Uma ; Haksar, Nandita — *The Delhi Riots*, New Delhi, Lancer International, 1987.

Chakravartty, Gargi — *Gandhi, A Challenge to Communalism,* New Delhi, Eastern Book, 1987.

Chand, Attar — *Asian Security : The Great Debate,* Ed., Delhi, Gian Publishing House, 1987.

——— *Defence-Democracy on Terrorism Human Rights and Foreign Policy,* New Delhi, Amar Prakashan, 1991.

——— *Terrorism, Political Violence & Security of Nations,* Gyan Publishing House, Delhi, 1988.

Chander, Shailaja — *Justice V.R. Krishna Iyer on Fundamental Rights and Directive Principles,* Deep & Deep Pub., New Delhi, 1992.

Chandra, Kailash — *Jinnath and the Communal Problem in India, Delhi,* Anmol Publications, 1986.

Chandra, Satish — *International Documents on Human Rights,* New Delhi, Mittal Pub., 1990.

——— *International Terrorism and its Control,* Vehra Publisher & Distributors, Allahabad, 1989.

Chandrashekhar, Bhat — *Ethnicity and Mobility : Emerging Ethnic Identity and Social Mobility among the Waddars of south India,* First Ed. New Delhi, Concept Pub., 1984.

Chajunwa, Emeka — *India-US Security Relations,* Chanakya Publications, New Delhi, 1988.

Chaturvedi, A.N. — *Rights Accused under Indian Constitution,* Deep & Deep Pub. New Delhi, 1984.

Chaturvedi, A.N. *Rights of Accused under Indian Constitution,* New Delhi, Deep & Deep Pub., 1984.

Chawla, Sudershan ; Sardesai, D.R. *Changing Patterns of Security and Stability in Asia*, Allied Publishers New Delhi, 1980.

Chemsky, Meam *The Culture of Terrorism,* Plute Press, London, 1988.

Chibber, Aditya *National Security Doctrine*, Ed., New Delhi, Lancer International Pvt. Ltd., 1990.

Clutterbuck, Richard *Terrorism, Drugs & Crime in Europe after 1992*, Routledge, London, 1990.

——— *Terrorism & Guerrilla Warfare*, Routledge, London & New York, 1990.

——— *Guerrilla & Terrorists*, Faber & Faber Ltd., London, 1977.

Cohen Stephen , Philip *Security of South Asia*, Vistar Pub., New Delhi, 1987.

Combell, Ton *Human Rights from Rhetoric to Reality*, London, Basil Blackwell, 1986.

Crawford, James *The Rights of Peoples*, New York, Oxford University Press, 1988.

——— *The Rights of Peoples*, Clarendon Press, Oxford, 1983.

Crelinsten, Ronald D. *Terrorism & Criminal Justice*, Lexonton Books Toronte, 1976.

Danda, Ajit K. *Ethnicity in India,* First Ed., New Delhi, Inter India Pub., 1991.

Dang, Satyapal *Darshan Singh, Canadian Terrorism in Punjab*, Patriot Publisher, New Delhi, 1987.

Dang, Satyapal — *Genesis of Terrorist : An Analytical Study of Punjab Terrorists*, Patriot Publisher, New Delhi, 1988.

Das, S.T. — *National Security in Perspective*, Gyan Publishing House, Delhi, 1987.

Das, Suranjan — *Communal Riots in Bengal,* Delhi, Oxford University Press, 1991.

Das, Victor — *Jharkhand Castle over the Graves,* New Delhi, Inter-India Pub., 1992.

Das, Veena — *Communities Riots and Survivors in South Asia,* Delhi, Oxford University Press, 1990.

Debson, Christopher — *The Terrorists, Their Weapons, Leaders & Tactics,* (Facts on File Inc, New York, 1982.)

——— *War Without End, The Terrorists: An Intelligence Dessier.,* Marrap London, 1986.

Desai, A.R. — *Violation of Democratic Rights in India*, Vol. I, Popular Prakashan, Bombay, 1986.

Dholakia, S.K. — *Rights of Minority Shareholders,* Bombay, N.M. Tripathi Pvt. Ltd., 1983.

Dixit, Prabha — *Communalism—A Struggle for Power,* New Delhi, Orient Longman Ltd., 1974.

Freedom, Lawrence Zelic — *Perspectives on Terrorism,* Scholarly Resources Inc., Wilmington Dalware, 1983.

Gandhi, A.L. — *Rights to Property : Its Changing Dimensions,* Scientific Publishers, Jodhpur, 1985.

Gangrade, K.D. — *Conflict a better way to solve them,* Harrap, London, 1985.

Gammage, Allien Z. *Police Training in the United States,* Charles C. Thomas Publisher, Illinois.

George, Alexandra *Social Ferment in India,* Orient Longman, Hyderabad, 1986.

Ghosh, S.K. *Encyclopedia of Police in India,* Vol. I, Ashish Publishing House, New Delhi, 1983.

——— *Law Enforcement in Tribal Areas,* Ashish Publishing House, New Delhi, 1987.

——— *Communal Riots in India,* Ashish Publishing House, New Delhi, 1987.

——— *Social Order in India,* Ashish Publishing House, New Delhi, 1990.

——— *Protection of Minorities and Scheduled Caste,* Ashish Pub., House, New Delhi, 1990.

——— *Riots Prevention and Control,* Eastern Law House, Calcutta, 1972.

Giegold, William C. *In Training : A Practical Guide to Management Development,* Lifetime Learning Pub., Belmont, 1983.

Gill, Kulwant & Paras, Diwan *Hindu Women's Right to Property in India,* Deep & Deep Pub., New Delhi, 1986.

Gol-Or Neemi *International Cooperation to Suppress Terrorism,* Creem Nelm Ltd., Kent, 1985.

Gore, M.S. *Gore Committee Report,* MHA (GOI, Delhi).

Goyal, Archana *Terrorism Causes & Consequences,* Published by Institute of Environment, Bikaner, 1990.

Goyal, Rajni *State Civil Service Training in India,* RBSA Publishers, Jaipur, 1988.

Gupta Bharat Bushan — *The Seven Freedoms,* Ashish Publishing House, New Delhi, 1977.

Gupta, Ranjit Singh — *Management of Internal Security,* Lancer Pub., New Delhi, 1994.

Gupta, R.S. Col. — *Management of Internal Security, Freedom From Fear,* Lancer Publishers, New Delhi, 1994.

Gupta, Uma — *Supreme Court and Civil Liberties,* Mittal Pub., New Delhi, 1988.

Haasen, David A. ; Culley, Thomas R. — *The Police Training Officer,* Charles C. Thomas Publisher, Illinois, 1973.

Habbs, Jr. ; Douglas A. — *Mass Political Violence,* USA, Inter Science Publication, 1973.

Hall, Sen — *Counter Terrorist,* Donald I Fine Inc., New York, 1987.

Hanle, Donald J. — *Terrorism the Newest Face of Warfare,* Pergamen Brassey's International Defence Publishers Inc., 1989.

Hasan, Mushirul — *Nationalism and Communal Politics in Indian,* Manohar Pub., New Delhi, 1991.

Hasan, Shariful — *Supreme Court Fundamental Rights and Directive Principles,* Deep & Deep Pub., New Delhi, 1981.

Heesterman, J.C. — *The Inner Conflict of Tradition, Essays in Indian Ritual,* Oxford University Press, Bombay, 1985.

Hingorani, R.C. — *Human Rights in India,* Oxford & IBH Publishing Co., New Delhi, 1985.

Hutnik, Nimmi — *Ethnic Minority Identity : A Social Psychological Perspective,* Oxford University Press, New York, 1991.

Iyer, V.R. Krishna — *Human Rights and the Law,* Vedpal Law House, Indore, 1984.

Iyer, V.R. Krishna — *Human Rights and in-Human Wrongs,* B.R. Publishing Corp., Delhi, 1990.

Jayaramu, P.S. — *India's National Security and Foreign Policy*, ABC Publishing House, Delhi, 1987.

Jegatheesan, P. — *Law and Order in Madras Presidency, (118501880).* B.R. Publishing Corp, Delhi, 1987.

Jha, R.C. — *Police Surveillance and Community Security,* (A Study of Historical and Legal Aspects of Police Surveillance in India), Swan Publishers, Delhi, 1991.

——— *A Citizen's Legal Power and Obligation,* Swan Publishers, New Delhi, 1994.

——— *Fundamental Rights and Doctrine of Sovereign Immunity,* Sheriden Book Co., New Delhi, 1995.

Jinks, Michael — *Training,* Blandford Press, Pole, 1979.

Jones, Ken — *Icebreakers, A Source Book of Games,* Viva Books, New Delhi, 1995.

Joshi, R.P. — *Police Training in Community Relations,* Rawat Publications, Jaipur, 1993.

Kakae, Sudhir — *Conflict and Choice, Indian Youth in a Changing Society,* Somaiya Pub., Bombay, 1970.

Kalaiah, A.B. — *Human Rights in International Law,* Deep & Deep Pub., New Delhi, 1986.

Kapoor, H.L. — *Police, Crime and Security,* Ess Ess Publications, New Delhi, 1992.

Karim, Afsir — *Counter Terrorism,* Lancer International, New Delhi, 1991.

Kashyap, Anirban — *Communalism and Constitution,* Lancers Books, New Delhi, 1990.

Kashyap, Subhash — *Human Rights and the Parliament,* Metropolitan Book Co., New Delhi, 1978.

Kathpalia, P.N. — *National Security Perspectives,* Lancer International, New Delhi, 1986.

Khan, Sultan Akhbar — *Power, Police and Public,* Vishal Publications, 1983.

Kumar, Akhilesh — *Communal Riots in India,* Commonwealth Publishers, New Delhi, 1991.

Kumar, Naresh — *Constitutional Rights of Prisoners: A Study of Judicial Trends,* Mittal Publishers, Delhi, 1986.

Kumar, Ravindra — *Problem of Communalism in India,* Mittal Publications, New Delhi, 1990.

Latif, T.A.A. — *Training for Management,* Sterling Publishers, New Delhi, 1977.

Long, David E — *The Anatomy of Terrorism,* The Free Press, A Division of Macmillan INC, New York, 1990.

Mathew, K.K. — *The Right to Equality and Property under the Indian Constitution,* New Delhi, National, 1980.

Mathur, H.M. — *Issues in Service Training,* IIPA, New Delhi, 1982.

Mathur, K.M. Dr. — *Internal Security Challenges and Police in a Developing Society,* RBSA, Jaipur, 1989.

——— — *Management of Internal Security,* Gyan Publishing House, New Delhi, 1995.

Mathur, K.M. Dr. *Police, Law and Internal Security,* Gyan Publishing House, New Delhi, 1994.

——— *Problems of Police in a Democratic Society,* RBSA Publishers, Jaipur, 1987.

——— *Concern and Constraints in Administration,* RBSA Publishers, Jaipur, 1991.

——— *Police in India—Problems and Perspectives,* Gyan Publishing House, Delhi, 1991.

——— *Commentary on CRPF Act, 1949,* Published by CRPF Directorate General, 1976, Revised edition 1990.

——— *Vikassheel Samaj main Samsamyik Police ki Bhoomika* (Hindi), Gyan Publishing, New Delhi.

——— *Swatantrottar Bharat mein Janta ka Uttardayatwa thatha Police ki Bhoomika,* BRP & D, Published by Manager Govt., Printing Press Faridabad, New Delhi, 1992.

——— *Administration of Police Training in India,* Gyan Publishing House, Delhi, 1987.

——— *National Security and its Multi-fold Challenges*—Paper presented at Internal Security Academy Mount Abu at D.I.G.P. Seminar on National Security.

——— *Indian Police Role and Challenges,* Gyan Publishing House, New Delhi, 1994.

Melman, Yossi *The Master Terrorist the true story behind Abu Midal,* Adama Books, New York, 1986.

Menon, Ramesh; Sheth, Pravin — *Caste and Communal Time-Bomb,* Golwala Publication, Ahmedabad, 1986.

Meron, Theodor — *Human Rights in International Law: Legal and Policy Issues,* Oxford University Press, New York, 1989.

Mishra, B.N. — *International Social Security Systems,* Anmol Publications, New Delhi, 1993.

Misra, S.C. — *A Hand Book on Police Organisation and Administration,* BPR & D, New Delhi.

Misra, Shashi P. — *Fundamental Rights and Supreme Court Reasonableness of Restrictions,* Deep & Deep, New Delhi, 1985.

Morneau, Jr. — *Security Administration : A Quantitative Hand Book,* Ed—Boston: Butterworth Publishers, 1982.

Mrs. Kumar Manju — *Social Equality : The Constitutional Experiment in India,* S. Chand & Co., New Delhi, 1982.

Murray, J.A. Capt. — *Police Officer Trainee,* Arco, New York, 1975.

Nagar, K.S. Sharma G. Lt. Col. — *India's Security Super Power Threat,* Reliance Publishing House, Delhi, 1979.

Nagi, R. — *Big Powers and South-East Asian Security,* Lancer Books, New Delhi, 1986.

Nair, Sreekumaran MP. — *Values in Conflict Gandhism C.V. Constitutionalism,* Lalwani Publishing House, Bombay, 1973.

Nanda, J.D. — *Conflict and Co-Existence in Indian,* Concept Publishing Co., New Delhi, 1991.

Nath, Shaileshwar	*Terrorism in India,* National Publishing House, New Delhi, 1980.
Nath, Trilok	*National Security,* B.R. Publishing Corpn., Delhi, 1986.
———	*The Police Problem,* Vision Books Pvt. Ltd., New Delhi, 1993.
Nayar, V.K. Lt. Genl.	*Threat from within—India's Internal Security Environment,* Lancer Pvt. Ltd, New Delhi, 1992.
Neill, Bard E.O.	*Insurgency & Terrorism,* Brasrey's Inc., 1990.
Netanyahu, Banjamia	*Terrorism How the West can win,* Aven Publishers of Bard, Camolot, Discus & Flare Books, 1986.
Nirmal, Anjali	*Role and Functioning of Central Police Organisations,* Uppal Publishing House, New Delhi, 1992.
N.P.A.	*Police Community Relations,* SVP, NPA, Hyderabad, 1985.
Obminsky, Ernest, Bugrov, Andrei	*International Economic Security : A Major Factor of Peace,* Allied Pub., New Delhi, 1988.
O'Hanlon, Rosalind	*Caste, Conflict and Ideology,* Cambridge University Press, New York, 1985.
Orlick, Terry	*In Pursuit of Excellence,* Leisure Press, Ilinois, 1990.
Pakem, B.	*Nationality Ethnicity and Cultural Identity in North-East India,* Omsons Pub., New Delhi, 1990.
Pandey, Gyanendra	*The Construction of Communalism in Colonial North India,* Oxford University, Press New Delhi, 1990.
Pandey, Jitendra	*Civil Liberty Under Indian*

Constitution, Deep & Deep Publications, New Delhi, 1992.

Pandian, J. — *Caste Nationalism and Ethnicity,* Popular Prakashan, Bombay, 1987.

Parmar, M.S. — *Problems of Police Administration,* Reliance Publishing House, Delhi, 1992.

Parrek, Udai ; Lynton, Rolf P. — *Training for Development,* D.B. Taraperevala & Sons, Bombay, 1973.

P.N., Kathpalia — *National Security Perspectives,* Lancer International, New Delhi, 1986.

Proctor, John H. Thornton W.M. — *Training : A Hand Book for Line Managers,* Taraperevala & Sons, Bombay, 1977.

Rae Leslie — *The Skills of Training : A Guide for Managers,* Grover USA, 1991.

Raghavan, R.K. — *Indian Police Problems, Planning and Perspectives,* Manohar, 1989.

Raj, G. Ramchandra — *Industrial Conflict,* Light & Life Publishers, New Delhi.

Rajgopal, P.R. — *Communal Violence in India,* Uppal Publishing House, New Delhi, 1987.

Rastogi, P.N. — *Ethnic Tension in Indian Society,* Mittal Pub., New Delhi, 1986.

Reiss, Alebert J. — *The Police and Public,* Yale University Press, London, 1971.

Rex, John — *Aspects of Modern Sociology, Social Conflict,* Longman Publishers, London, 1981.

Saha, B.P. — *The Police in Free India : Its Facets and Drawbacks,* Konnark Publishers, Delhi, 1989.

Saha, Giriraj — *Elite Forces in India,* Cosmo Pub., New Delhi, 1994.

Saxena, A.P. — *Training in Government Objectives and Opportunities,* IIPA, New Delhi, 1985.

Saksena, K.P. — *Human Rights Perspective and Challenges,* Lancer Books, New Delhi, 1994.

Saksena, N.S. — *Terrorism History & Facts in the World and in India,* Abhinav Pub., New Delhi, 1985.

——— *Communal Riots in India,* Trishul Publications, Delhi, 1988.

——— *Law and Order in India,* Abhinav Publications, New Delhi, 1987.

Sankhdher, M.M. — *National Unity and Religious Minorities,* Gitanjali Pub. House, New Delhi, 1991.

Sarhadi, Ajit Singh — *India's Security in Resurgeny Asia,* B.R. Chawala, New Delhi, 1979.

Samaha, Joel — *Law and Order in Historical Perspective,* Academic Press, New York, 1974.

Scotti, J. Anthony — *Executive Safety & International Terrorism,* A Guide for Travellers, Prentice Hall Inc. Eaglewood Cliffs, New Jersey, 1986.

Sen, Sanker — *Police Training Problems and Perspectives,* Rawat Pub., Jaipur, 1994.

Sethi, Kiran — *Executive Training in India,* Sterling Publishers, New Delhi, 1979.

Shav, Jennifer — *Ten Years of Terrorism,* Collected Views, Published in Great Britain, 1979 by Royal United Services Institute for Defence Studies, London.

Sharma, K.K. — *Law and Order Administration,* National Book Organisation, New Delhi, 1985.

Sharma, Miriam — *The Politics of Inequality,* Hindustan Publishing Corpn., Delhi, 1978.

Sharma, P.D. — *Police, Internal Security and Developmental Disorder in India,* Uppal Publishing, New Delhi, 1988.

——— *Police and Criminal Justice Administration in India,* Uppal Pub. House, Delhi, 1985.

——— *Police and Political Order in India,* Research Pub., Delhi, 1984.

——— *Police Training in Rajasthan,* 1979.

Shukla, K.S. — *Collective Violence,* IIPA., Delhi, 1988.

——— *Collective Violence Genesis and Response,* IIPA, New Delhi, 1988.

Singh, Jasjit — *Asian Security : Old Paradigms and New Challenges,* Lancer International, New Delhi, 1991.

Singh, Nagendra — *Enforcement of Human Rights in Peace and War and the future of Humanity,* Eastern Law House Pvt. Ltd., Delhi, 1986.

Singh, V.V. — *Communal Violence,* Rawat Publications, Jaipur, 1993.

Singh, Yogendra — India International Centre, Delhi, 1969.

Singhvi, Dr. L.M. — *Rights to Property its Changing Dimensions,* Jodhpur, Scientific Pub., 1985.

Smith, C. Davidson — *Combating Terrorism,* Routledge, London, 1990.

Smith, Maurice Temple — *Verm Breido Apostles into Terrorists Women and the Revolutionary Movement in the Russia of Alexander-II,* Published in Great Britain, 1988.

Spradley, James — *Conformity and Conflict, Readings in Cultural Anthropology,* Boston Little Brown, 1987.

Sterling, Claire — *The Terror Network, The Secret War of International Terrorism,* Weidenfeld & Micolson, London, 1981.

Stehi Michael — *The Politics of Terrorism,* Marcel Dekker, Inc., New York & Basel, 1988.

Stokes, Paul M. — *Total Job Training,* Taraprevala Pub. Bombay, 1976.

Subba, Tanka B. — *Ethnicity State and Development : A Case Study of Gorkhaland Movement in Darjeeling,* Har-Anand Pub., Delhi, 1992.

Subrahmanyam, K. — *Indian Security Perspective,* ABC Publishing House, New Delhi, 1982.

——— — *Grobal Security : Some Issues and Trends,* Lancer International, Delhi, 1987.

Subramanian, S. Dr. — *Human Rights and Police,* Hyderabad, Publishers Association for Advancement of Police and Security Science, 1993.

——— — *Human Rights and Police, Assn. For Adv. of Police,* Hyderabad, 1992.

Sullivan, Noel O. — *Terrorism Ideology & Revolution Great Britain in 1986,* by Wheatahoaf Books Ltd.

Tayler, Maxwell — *The Terrorist,* Brassey's Defence Publishers, New Delhi, 1990.

Teheri, Amir — *Holy Terrors The Inside Story of Islamic Terrorism,* Hutchiuson, London, 1987.

Tilly, A. Louise — *Class Conflict and Collective Action,* Sage Publications, London, 1981.

Tiwari, S.C. — *Terrorism in India,* South Asia Pub., New Delhi, 1990.

Tucker, M.M. — *Combating the Terrorists Democratic Responses to Political Violence,* Facts on File, New York, 1988.

Unnithan, T.K. — *Sociology of Non-Violence and Peace,*

Vasak, Karel — *The International Dimensions of Human Rights,* UNESCO, 1982.

Vas E.A. Lt. Gen. — *The Search for Security : Controlling Conflict and Terrorism,* Natraj Pub., Dehra Dun, 1989.

Vijapur, Abdulrahim P. — *Essays on International Human Rights,* South Asian Pub., New Delhi, 1991.

Warner, Martin — *Terrorism Protest & Power,* Reger Crisp University College, Oxford, 1990.

Weinbery, Leonard B. — *Political Terrorism,* Mc.-Graw Hill Publishing Co., New York, 1989.

White, Jonathan R. — *Terrorism on Introduction,* Breaks/ Celo Publishing Co., Pacific Grove, California, 1991.

——— *International Security,* Vol. I, (IBH), 1986.

——— *International Security,* Vol. II, 1986.

Wilkinsem Paul — *Terrorism and the Liberal State,* The Macmillan Press Ltd., London, 1977.

William, J. Bopp — *Police Community Relationships,* Charles C. Thomas, Illinosis, 1972.

Wright, Sam — *Crowds and Riots,* Sage Pub., London, 1978.

Amnesty International : India, Examination of Second Periodic Report by Human Rights Commission, 1993.

Amnesty International India, Torture, Rape & Death in Custody, Amnesty International Pub., 1992.

Amnesty International India Examination of the Second Period Report by Human Rights Committee, Amnesty International Pub., 1993.

Amnesty International India An Unnatural Fate, Disappearances and impunity in the Indian States of Jammu and Kashmir and Punjab, Amnesty International Pub., 1993.

The Protection of Human Rights Act 1993, New Delhi : Universal Book Traders, 1994.

Index